AF598381

Logic Models of Design

Logic Models of Design

Richard Coyne
Department of Architectural Science
The University of Sydney

Pitman

PITMAN PUBLISHING
128 Long Acre, London WC2E 9AN

First published in Great Britain 1988

British Library Cataloguing in Publication Data
Coyne, Richard
Logic models of design.
1. Data processing. Systems analysis
I. Title
004.2′1

ISBN 0 273 08797 5

Reproduced and printed by photolithography
in Great Britain by Biddles Ltd, Guildford

Cover design by Eitetsu Nozawa

Contents

Acknowledgements

The greater part of this work has been supported by the Australian Research Grants Scheme and a Sydney University Postgraduate Research Studentship.

I would like to acknowledge the assistance of the following research colleagues and visitors to the Design Computing Unit in the Faculty of Architecture at the University of Sydney who have contributed to this work at various stages: David Cornell, Andrew Gollan, Stephen Tolhurst, Andrew Taylor, Bala Balachandran, Harold Borkin, Frank de Bruyn, Catherine Manago, Tuncer Akiner, Safaa Hashim, Conrad Mackenzie, Rivka Oxman, Michael Rosenman, Alicia Rosenthal, Tony Radford and Fay Sudweeks.

I would like to thank Aart Bijl and Bill Mitchell for reviewing the work at various stages and providing support and encouragement; and John Lansdown for consistent and diligent assistance in introducing me to the creative side of computing and critically reviewing my work. I also thank John Gero for his help and guidance and for providing a rich and stimulating environment in which to explore logic models of design.

Chapter 1

Introduction

Designers are well served by computer tools for documentation and visualization. However, there is a suspicion that existing systems do not adequately exploit the potential of computing, nor do they satisfy the ever-increasing expectations of those who use them. In spite of the widespread acknowledgement of *operations research* techniques, computing has relatively little impact on design decision making, particularly in the early stages of design projects.

Improvements are possible on many fronts. There is certainly a need for better human machine interfaces (Figure 1.1) and greater computing power. However, the thrust of this book is that better systems lie in how we use computers as repositories of *knowledge.* Knowledge, of the kind we are interested in here, is that expertise which can be externalized and passed on to others. We need a means of representing knowledge in a computer system that captures design expertise. This is worthwhile at whatever level we wish to use computers—whether we are simply interested in a better paint system that responds to the idiosyncrasies of a designer or whether we are aiming for an automated 'intelligent design assistant'.

The most common form of knowledge used in computers is as procedural algorithms. The problem with this form of knowledge is that it carries with it certain expectations of how it will be used. What we really need is to be able to code knowledge into a computer system in such a way that it is available for consultation in much the same way as one consults a professional designer. By consulting its knowledge base a system should be able to perform a range of tasks from answering simple queries and evaluating design proposals to actually generating proposals and explaining how they were derived. The knowledge should not be encumbered by any particular expectations of how it will be used.

The knowledge in such systems should also be in a form that can be

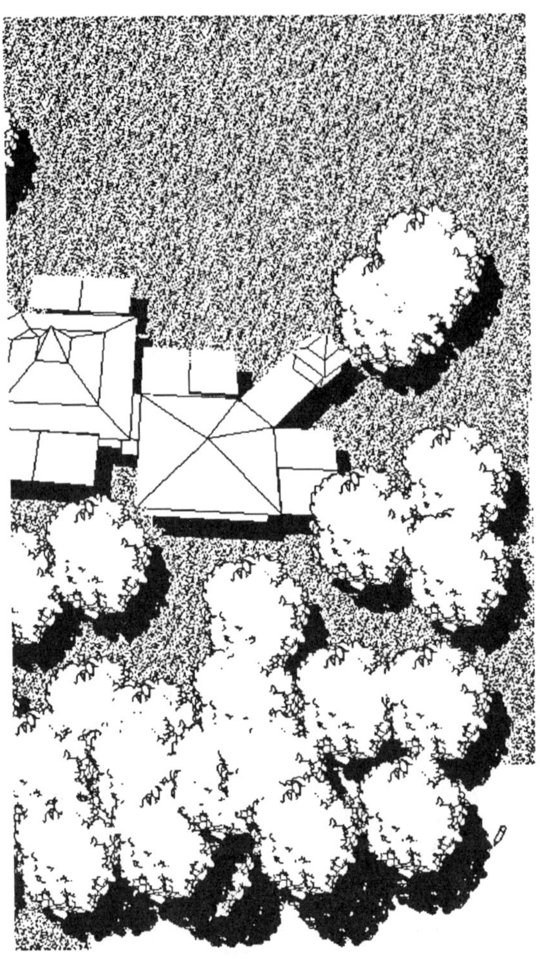

Figure 1.1. There are interesting developments in human-computer interfaces at the level of inexpensive microcomputers, as exemplified by the Apple Macintosh MacPaint interface. However, more needs to be understood about design *knowledge*, and how it can be appropriated in computers, before computer-aided design will have a substantial impact on design decision-making.

understood by humans, so that it is accessible and open to scrutiny. Obviously, the form of knowledge representation we find in books matches these requirements. However, we must also take account of the fact that the knowledge needs to be in a form that can be operated upon by a computer. This is not an easy task. Much design knowledge, even of the kind that can be externalized, would appear to be heuristically based. We are dealing with rules of thumb, uncertainty and informality. In order to create useful computer systems some simple constructions are needed for putting design knowledge together and rendering it operable.

It is difficult to pin down our knowledge in any area of expertise, but it is even more difficult in this area because design is difficult. Without doubt, design carries with it a creative component, an artifact is a contribution to culture, decisions are made in a cultural context—a context that is changing all the time—and design knowledge sometimes appears ethereal. Design is a product of human consciousness. Design is difficult to do, difficult to teach and difficult to construct theories about. Our understanding of design is still only at a rudimentary stage.

This book is one contribution to the better understanding of design so that systems useful to designers can be developed on computers. It explores a particular line of inquiry. This inquiry is pragmatic. It is meant to lead to working systems. In the process certain assumptions and simplifications are made, and we appear to gloss over many of the subtleties and complexities of design processes. There are also other views that are helpful in understanding design that not considered here, simply because they do not present ideas that appear immediately useful in the development of design systems.

It should be noted that throughout this book the emphasis is on *modelling*. The match between the processes described and psychological reality are left to others. The development of theories and models pertinent to *knowledge-based design* will extend well beyond what is described in these pages. It is hoped that this book will stimulate further research in that direction.

What This Book is About

This book contains both a theoretical and a technical exploration into modelling design tasks in logic. The intention is to provide a framework for describing design processes based on logic, achieved primarily by gathering together various strands evident in theories of reasoning, problem solving, design and the technology of knowledge-based systems. This involves demonstrating the applicability of logic programming and knowledge-based techniques to design. The design task by which this is to be demonstrated is *spatial layout*, though the issues reach further than this one application.

There are four basic themes to this book. Each serves to make the difficulties of design tractable in the context of computers. The first is an exploitation of ideas common to logic and language. The second is to exploit a distinction between *knowledge* and *reasoning*. The third is to make use of *hierarchy* in representing design knowledge. The fourth is to exploit the idea of *decomposition*. It is worth briefly directing our attention to each of these ideas in turn.

1 Logic, Language and Design

Design appears to be concerned with the creation of *descriptions* of artifacts. (The translation of these descriptions into artifacts is a separate issue—that of *manufacturing*.) The assumption in this book is that design is accomplished by *reasoning* with *knowledge*. Logic is that system of reasoning concerned with consistency and order—reasoning that follows certain laws. Logic has shortcomings, particularly when applied to human cognition, but because logic is well-understood, and it can be automated, it provides a valuable medium with which to model design processes in computers. Whereas any systems approach to design is essentially 'logical', there are certain ways of talking about design that make the contribution of logic explicit. Design is therefore discussed in this book utilizing the terminology of *axiom, proof* and *inference*, and sample programs are demonstrated employing a form of automated logic called *logic programming*.

Both logic and language are concerned with *interpretation*, but language, more than logic, is concerned with producing things, particularly sentences. It will be argued that the process of generating descriptions can be modelled using logic programming.

2 Knowledge and Reasoning

Knowledge-based systems are computer systems in which an attempt is made to capture and render operable human knowledge about some domain. The goal is to represent knowledge in such a way that it is 'comprehensible' to both human and machine. Working systems that embody knowledge of a particular domain are often termed *expert systems*. Clearly, a knowledge-based system is different to a 'conventional' computer program, as we normally understand it. In conventional programs knowledge about the domain under consideration is bound up in control statements, such as variable declarations, procedure calls, conditionals and loops. If we wish to inspect the knowledge in such a computer program then it is necessary to run it, to understand the language in which the program is written and to disentangle control structures from domain knowledge. Furthermore, the operations of a program are predetermined. The knowledge does *not* exist as a discrete entity that can be processed according to the use the operator of the system wishes to make of it.

The key to knowledge-based systems is in making a distinction between *knowledge* and *reasoning*. Ideally, we should be able to equip a knowledge-based system with a general-purpose reasoning facility, or controller, and then expose it to our *design knowledge*. Of course the knowledge may take many forms.

As we will describe in Chapter 3 it *is* possible to discuss reasoning independently of knowledge. For example, if our knowledge is represented as logical rules then we can apply automated reasoning to process those rules and answer queries. However, it soon becomes apparent that a key part of our knowledge, especially in design, is concerned with *how* we reason with what we know. Controlling knowledge is not just a matter of applying universal principles but involves a kind of *meta*-knowledge that is dependent on the domain. There appear to be *hierarchies* of knowledge and complex interdependencies between types of knowledge other than that suggested by the simple division of knowledge and control. Part of the art of formulating useful and effective knowledge-based design systems is in providing computational structures and systems of organization so that design knowledge of different kinds can be represented and made operable.

3 Hierarchical Abstraction

The automation of certain processes, such as design, can sometimes be made simpler by considering *multiple abstractions* of tasks. The theme developed here is that of abstracting the control of design processes such that knowledge at one level is used for operating on knowledge at another level. Later in this book some uniformities in the way knowledge can be processed at these different levels will be considered. At an intuitive level we can see that it is possible to consider design knowledge in terms of objects, such as walls and spaces, and the configuration of objects. So we may have some knowledge as rules about dining rooms being near kitchens and bathrooms being accessible from bedrooms. It is also possible to consider design knowledge in terms of processes, or sequences of actions—that it is best to position important rooms first, or it is best to decide on the number of occupants before deciding on the number of bedrooms. There may also be knowledge that pertains to the strategies involved in designing something—if there are too many spaces to consider at one time then cluster them into groups and work on each group independently, or get the plan right before considering the elevations then return to the plan taking account of the elevations. We can see that it may be possible to organize some knowledge in terms of a kind of control hierarchy, from knowledge about configuration to knowledge about overall strategies.

There are many other abstraction hierarchies we can exploit in design. For example, we can also take advantage of knowledge pertaining to different views of a design as it is evolving. In the initial stages we may be dealing with amorphous spaces that have no dimensions and whose boundaries are blurred. As the design progresses these spaces become better defined (Figure 1.2). It is as if the designer is progressing through a hierarchy of descriptions in which vague ideas are translated into greater certainty. We may be able to organize knowledge according to the abstraction on which it operates. Designers would

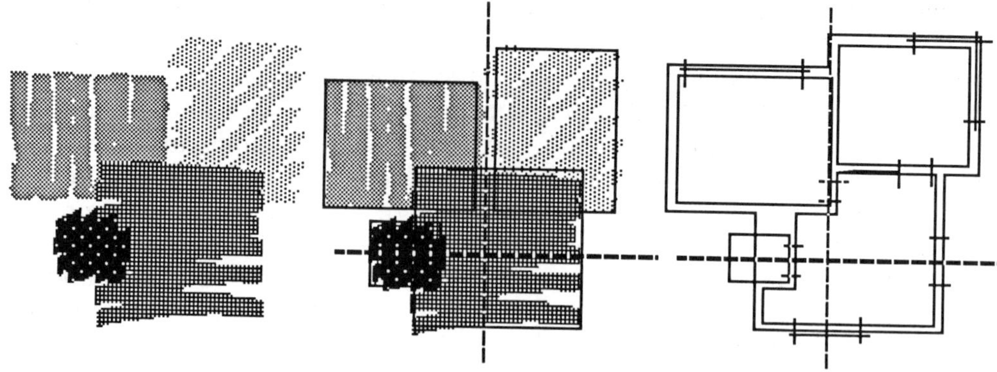

Figure 1.2. Designs sometimes have the appearance of progressing through a hierarchy of descriptions in which vague ideas are translated into greater certainty.

appear to work on different abstractions of their world, sometimes holding multiple views concurrently.

4 Decomposition

One of the keys to making many difficult tasks tractable is *decomposition*—breaking down complex objects into simpler objects and decomposing complex tasks into simple subtasks. The ideas discussed above about organising knowledge according to certain abstraction levels makes use of decomposition. An advantage of considering different *control* abstractions is that, at some level of abstraction, design tasks can be treated as decomposable. For example, in designing a complex artifact, such as a new kind of combustion engine, it is *not* always possible to break the task down into a consideration of independent components, as each component interacts heavily with those around it (Figure 1.3). However, in some cases the problem can be decomposed at another level in some control abstraction. So it may be possible to break the problem down according to strategic steps—look for the most critical component in the design first, consider how the other components relate to it, establish the relationships between the components before specifying their geometry. There are certain implementational advantages if systems (such as design systems) with properties that are difficult to control can be effectively 'tamed' in this way.

Organization of the Book

The book relies substantially on the terminology of logic and language. It is hoped that readers unfamiliar with terms such as 'abduction', 'interpretation', 'semantics' and 'syntax' will soon come to appreciate their descriptive power.

The book relies substantially on predicate calculus and logic as a unifying language for talking about design, and describing some of the complex concepts, particularly control. For those interested enough to experiment, concepts can be explored readily using the logic programming language Prolog.

The development within the book is from theory to application. Chapter 2 provides a summary of various models of design considering views of reasoning derived from the philosophy of science, problem solving, logic and linguistics. This provides a background to the ideas of *abduction*, *problem solving* and the terminology of *generative grammars*. Chapter 3 provides an introduction to *logic programming*. The strengths and shortcomings of logic programming as a means of modelling design are explored.

Chapter 4 introduces the theme of *interpretive knowledge* in design. Logical deduction can be employed to interpret the description of a design in order to discover its performance. Design is seen as involving the creation of artifacts that embody intended meaning. Interpretive knowledge can also be employed in *producing* designs. Although reference is made to this approach,

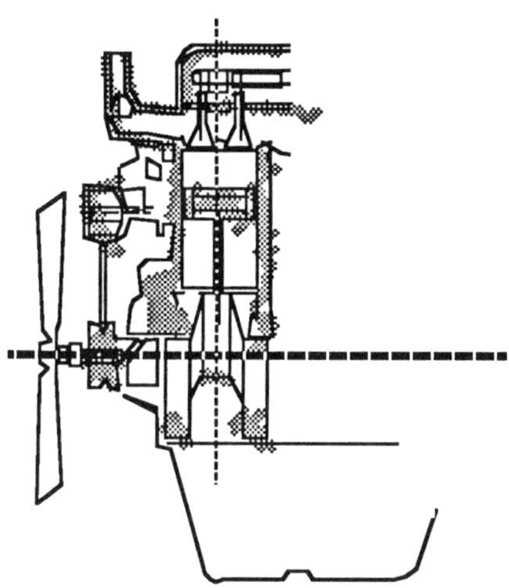

Figure 1.3. Sometimes the interrelationship between design components appears to override any consideration of decompositional structure.

the emphasis is on generative knowledge in the form of grammars. Grammar systems by which design generation can operate are discussed in Chapter 5. The properties of grammars and the means by which they can be controlled are also discussed. Chapter 6 describes examples of grammars applicable to design, and describes how they can be implemented as logic programs. The issue of how grammars are controlled is addressed by the field of *planning*.

In Chapter 7 models of planning are reviewed. In Chapter 8 some of these models are applied to examples from design. In Chapter 9 the organization of a design system is discussed which considers the use of meta-grammars in a hierarchical control regime. The design task considered is that of *spatial layout*: specifically, the generation of floor plan layouts. The details of a working system based on this model of organization are explained in Chapter 10 and samples of output are given. This chapter concludes with a critical discussion of both the implementation and the model. In Chapter 11 the intractable nature of design is discussed, and some tentative insights are offered as to how the model might be extended to account for the exploratory nature of design. The final chapter also provides a summary of where knowledge-based systems are leading.

Chapter 2

Models of Design

Computer-aided design is concerned with using computers to assist in the design process. To this end we are interested in finding appropriate models of design. As a side benefit such models may lead to a better *understanding* of the design process. But our interest in computer-aided design may result in models different from those formulated for other purposes, such as for the study of stylistic change, or for defining the role of artifacts and designers in society. Our interest is therefore essentially pragmatic—from the point of view of what facilitates implementation in a computer system.

The argument will be presented here for a model of design based on an understanding of logic and language, both of which provide vehicles for the representation of design knowledge. Essentially the model adopted is a variation of the *design machine* of Stiny and March (1981), supported by arguments from a different viewpoint than theirs. Another source of the model is provided by researchers into logic and artificial intelligence such as Kowalski (1979) who demonstrate the utility of describing problems in formal logic, particularly when such descriptions are coded into the logic programming language Prolog (Clocksin and Mellish, 1981). A further source is the account of design as *abductive reasoning* by March (1976). In this book it is argued that logic and language represent the basic tools of the computer programmer, but they also provide a medium of expression which is not dissimilar to ways that we are accustomed to thinking about design.

Science, Logic and Language

Various models of design can be placed within the paradigms of science, logic and language. There are several motivations for this. Firstly, the paradigms provide tools which aid in the design process. This is clearly the case in the discipline often referred to as the 'science of architecture' which includes those parts of architecture amenable to scientific analysis, ranging from structural design to business management (Cowan, 1973). Logic provides a facility for reasoning and argument. Language aids in the communication of ideas. Each discipline therefore contributes to the task of design. But more can be claimed of the relationship between these paradigms and design than this. The second motivation places design firmly within the various paradigms. Claim is therefore made for a 'science of design', as in the sense of Simon's (1970) *The Sciences of the Artificial*, or design may be described as a process in logic. Artifacts may also be considered to fall within a system of linguistic signs bringing design within the ambit of semiotics.

The third motivation is to link design to these paradigms in an analogous sense. The methodology here is to slot design within the various paradigms so that the study of design may inherit their descriptive power. This is an expedient for purposes of discussion and understanding, and to aid in computer simulation. In the sense in which models provide analogies we may hold to several models of design. It is often within the nature of our understanding of certain phenomena—at least in science—that conflicting models must be held concurrently to provide adequate descriptions.

It matters little in practical terms for computer-aided design whether design is regarded as falling within a particular paradigm or if the paradigm is employed merely as a descriptive tool. The resolution of the argument will not be entered into here. What is important, however, is the insight into the design process afforded by the various paradigms. The role assumed by the artifact says something about how we formalize the design process. For example, as made evident by Cross et al (1981) and Broadbent (1979), the contribution of a 'scientific view' of design depends, to a large extent, on the particular view of science adopted, and on an understanding of what component within the scientific paradigm constitutes the design. Prior to developing a particular computational design model we will review various models in terms of the role assumed by an artifact within paradigms of science, logic and language.

Artifact as Theorem

In logic one is able to take as a starting point various axioms (also referred to as 'premises') and, by a process of deduction, arrive at a set of theorems. Conversely, one can begin with a set of theorems and proceed to the premises. This constitutes a proof. Logic was the basis of the science of Aristotle and Euclid, and it still forms the basis of mathematics and some philosophy. According to Broadbent (1981) it also constituted a method for some early modern architects such as Wright and Le Corbusier.

It is important to make some distinctions in what we mean by 'logic'. To endorse the role of logic in design is not necessarily to make a commitment to *rationalism.* To say that something is 'logical' is a statement about consistency—that a statement (theorem) is consistent with a set of axioms. It says nothing about the mapping between the axioms and reality (Quine and Ullian, 1970). To describe a design as the product of a logical process is to state that there is some consistency between the design and some set of assumptions, rather than to assert the eternal verity of the assumptions. A logic model of design does not therefore imply a commitment to some supposed *a priori* principles about design.

The second distinction to be made is that the mechanism which drives logic is deduction. Deduction provides a means of establishing the validity of statements, such as mathematical formulae. It can also be a device for discovering new formulae. New statements can be derived from what is known by logical deduction. But the fact that logic serves both as a means of verification and of discovering new truths does not prescribe how mathematicians discover new concepts. Whereas logic may be employed to verify concepts, discovery may take place by various means. Scientific progress would be extremely slow if discovery were based purely on incremental, axiomatic proof procedures.

Thirdly, logic provides the basis of computer systems. The ubiquity of logic in mathematics has been demonstrated by Whitehead and Russell (1910). Logic also constitutes a language by which richer systems can be described, the logical nature of which may be effectively disguised. Any attempt to formalize design is subject to our reliance on logic. Pending the development of a radically new type of computer it is safe to say that that which cannot be formalized in logic cannot be modelled in a computer system. The lesson for computer-aided design here is that logic is the tool we use for formulating artificial systems over which we exercise control, whether we make the logic explicit or not. For our purposes a model of design must therefore take account of logic one way or another. There are various ways in which we can do this. One commonly accepted view of the role of logic is that in which an artifact is considered as a set of theorems. This provides an introduction to a richer model which will be considered in a subsequent section.

In this model of artifact as theorem a design is viewed as a set of statements which are derived from some other statements (axioms). These axioms are assumptions which constitute both the programme (or brief) and also rules or laws about principles of design. The design is described by a theorem which is consistent with these assumptions.

This approach is demonstrated in the so-called *analysis/synthesis model* (Archer, 1969; Maver, 1970). One application, in which the operations of logical deduction are made explicit, is in the constraint satisfaction model (Archer, 1970). The problem starts with the definition of a space of possible designs. All properties required to be present in the final artifact exist to varying degrees in the initial problem state. The design task is concerned with producing a description of an artifact in which certain desired properties are present to as satisfactory or as high a degree as possible. This is accomplished by successively eliminating parts of the space of designs according to various performance criteria. The universe of all possible solutions is successively manipulated until a set of feasible solutions remains. Constraint satisfaction constitutes a set theoretic approach to design, and the process of manipulating sets is essentially deductive.

The idea of constraint satisfaction is not unique to mathematical formulations. Such an approach is also evident in sieve mapping where areas of a building site considered unsuitable for development are progressively marked off as different site factors are considered. The remaining space designates where the proposed facility should be located. Various map overlay techniques employed in land use planning employ a similar approach (McHarg, 1969) (Figure 2.1). Once set boundaries are determined the computation of intersections and unions is essentially deductive.

There is little doubt that deductive processes, in which an artifact constitutes the theorem, are applicable to certain design tasks such as the calculation of the depth of a concrete lintel over an opening in a masonry wall, but there is some question as to its appropriateness as a model of design in general. A critique of the view that form logically follows from analysis (Abbé Laugier's dictum that 'if the question is well posed, the solution will be indicated') has been well aired, notably by Alexander (1964) and Hillier et al (1972). We will return to logic in a later section. In the meantime it is worth considering other ways of looking at the role of the artifact in models based on science.

Artifact as Theory

The empirical view of science is that of starting from observations of the universe then producing theories by a process of *induction*. The theories are able to both explain the phenomena observed and to predict phenomena. Hence, according to this view, Kepler observed and recorded data on the motion of the planets, and this enabled him to produce the theory that planets move in elliptical orbits around the sun.

A model of design based on this approach may state that phenomena in the environment, such as needs, conflicts and patterns of human behaviour are observed and recorded. This constitutes a design programme (or brief). By the process of induction a description of a physical object, such as a building, is derived. The design is the *theory*. There are two arguments put forward against this view.

The first objection is that laws and rules, from which theories are basically

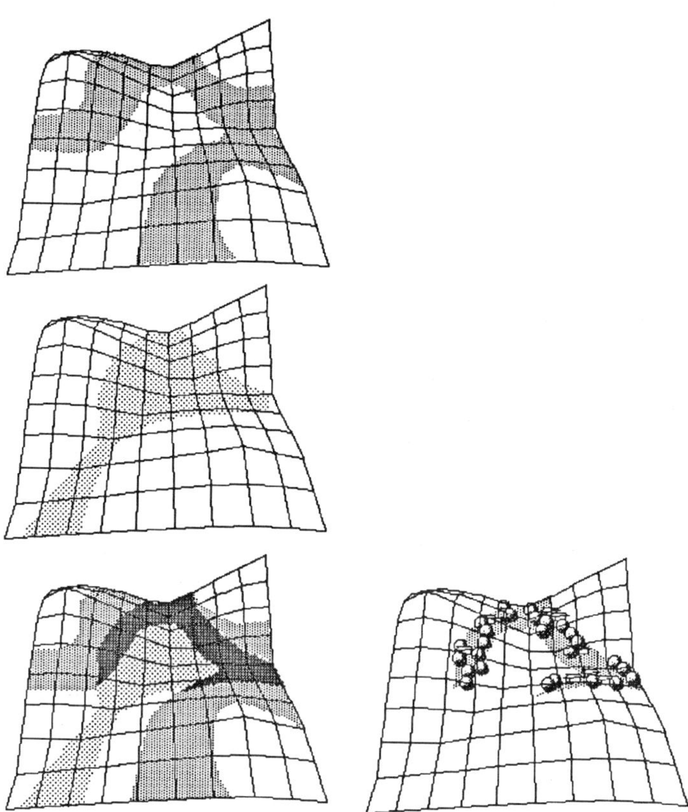

Figure 2.1. The map overlay technique for making land use decisions is essentially a deductive process.

constructed, appear to bear little relation to the description of an artifact. Designers appear to make use of, and be constrained by, rules, but the mapping between a design and a set of rules does not have immediate appeal. However we might permit that theories are the 'edifices' of science, and there may be something to learn from the analogy.

The second objection is that the model of scientific reasoning just presented is often regarded as a poor one. The main advocate of this view has been Popper (1972) who maintains that there is no clear logical link from a set of observations to a theory. If a design is analogous to a theory in science then there is no clear logical jump from a programme for a design to the description of an artifact (Hillier et al, 1972). This interpretation of the process of discovery accounts for some of the difficulty we have in modelling design. There may be something to learn from the Popperian account of scientific progress. Design shares with science the element of discovery which is better accounted for by the view of artifact as *hypothesis*.

Artifact as Hypothesis

Popper (1972) replaces the inductivist view of science with his problem solving schema. Rather than starting from observations, science begins with a problem. A solution is proposed to the problem. This constitutes a hypothesis or conjecture and it is generated by whatever means are available. The generative procedure is not that important, except that the conjecture must contain within it some opportunity for it to be refuted. The conjecture pervades within the scientific community until it can be refuted, as hypotheses can never actually be proved to be valid, only disproved. Theories are therefore on hold until they are found lacking, which creates another problem. A further conjecture is proposed which pervades until it is refuted, and so on. The process is one of trial and error, analogous to natural selection in nature.

According to Popper, this process removes the generation of hypotheses or theories from the realm of rational processes. It all depends on what is made of a hypothesis as to the role of reason. Although one can attain the right frame of mind for having ideas and can abet the process, the process itself is outside logic and cannot be made the subject of logical rules (Medawar, 1967). The success of science therefore appears to depend on "luck, ingenuity, and the purely deductive rules of critical argument" (Popper, 1972, p.53). Whether one is dealing with small problems or major scientific theories, Popper contends that the process is universal. This view of problem solving as comprised of a generate and test cycle has received wide acceptance, and it forms the basis of some automated problem solving systems, though Popper has not been the only source of these ideas.

For the purposes of understanding design we are more interested in accounting for the generative process than Popper. As will be argued in a later section the generator need not be relegated to the realm of intuition, but can be modelled successfully in computer systems. Generation will be considered subsequent to a discussion of an alternative view of progress in science.

Artifact as Paradigm

The idea of paradigm in science was developed by Kuhn (1970). Although he recognized that it is an ambiguous term (which he has since replaced in his writings by 'disciplinary matrix'), it appears to have persisted as a term, albeit an imprecise one, in science. According to its dictionary meaning a paradigm is a pattern or model, in the sense of something that can be copied. So a particular experimental method can be said to be paradigmatic if others in the wider scientific community choose to model their activities on that method. A building can therefore be a paradigm in the sense that its plan form, or some other characteristics, become a model or exemplar for subsequent designs. Such a building may be one which captures the essence of some idea. In this sense a paradigm is a prototype. This fits within Broadbent's (1981) classification of iconic/typologic design.

What is most interesting about this model is what it suggests about the design process. According to Kuhn, the progress of science can be characterized as a process of cycling through various stages. 'Normal science' is a stage during which researchers are uncritical of the paradigm within which they work. Crisis arises when the paradigm proves inadequate in some way. Researchers are eventually pursuaded to transfer allegiance to some new paradigm. They stay with it until a new crisis arrives.

Kuhn's explanation of science incorporates certain psychological interpretations of group behaviour, and does not appear helpful as a model for explaining problem solving at a micro level. To the extent that design is a community activity, however, it may be a useful model. It may therefore be surmized: designers do not operate within a vacuum but adopt and adapt standard solutions and methods practised and taught by the design community; crises arise when the old forms and methods no longer seem to meet the needs and aspirations of the community at large; rival forms eventually become the norm. This approach underlies certain methods in historical criticism in so far as they are concerned with explaining the development of architectural styles and forms. From the point of view of computer-aided design it is more helpful, however, to return to Popper's problem-solving paradigm, which appears to say more about the development of individual designs.

Artifact as Discovery

Search is concerned with exploring a space of potential solutions and partial solutions. The generation and testing of hypotheses can be characterized as a process of search. Simon (1983) describes this process as analogous to exploring a maze. One has some destination in mind. This is a goal. The intersections between passages are solution states and it is necessary to negotiate the passages in some rational way until the goal is reached. Certain techniques in operations research are concerned with search within a numerical domain, but these principles apply also to other forms of symbolic manipulation.

Much of the theoretical impetus for automated problem solving systems has stemmed from the work of Newell and Simon (1972). They describe an automated problem solving system called General Problem Solver (GPS). Simon states that the requirements of such a system are that it must be able to represent the current situation, the desired situation (goals), the differences between the two, and actions that change objects or situations to bring the system closer to the goals. It must also be able to select actions likely to reduce or remove differences. GPS incorporates a table of connections between differences and actions which provides the means of evaluating progress and trying alternative paths. The 'means-ends' mechanism is a way of making the search more efficient. Some such control mechanism is generally required which limits the amount of searching and directs the system's activities in the right direction. The derivation of appropriate search strategies has occupied considerable attention in artificial intelligence research, and Akin (1978, 1979) has observed search strategies at work in the behaviour of designers which parallel the techniques employed in artificial intelligence: such as 'hill climbing', heuristic search and forward processing.

That design generally involves some sort of search process is evident when considering the way in which designers tend to explore possibilites. In a later section we will consider the nature of the operators which transform states of a design. From the model of reasoning presented above it also appears that there is another type of search occurring other than within the space defined by the operators—this is a search for the whole paraphernalia (that is, the goals, the actions and the control strategy) by which those states are generated. This theme, which constitutes a kind of 'meta-search', will be considered in a subsequent section.

As they are dealt with in these models the roles of logic and of discovery appear somewhat unconnected. We will attempt to bring them together by reconsidering the role of logic in design, while the role of search will be pursued further in the context of language.

Artifact as Premise

Previously we have considered an artifact as something which is deducible from a set of statements constituting a design programme and a body of knowledge (rules and procedures) about designs. A further model will be presented here which captures more of the character of the design process.

In this model the description of a design is a set of statements about which one makes logical deductions, and theorems are statements which can be deduced from the design description. This view has been advocated principally by March (1976), calling on the work of the philosopher C.S. Peirce (1839-1914). A simple example serves to illustrate the relationship between premise, theorem and rule. We can consider as a premise the statement that *this is a house*. This constitutes a very simple design description. We may also have a rule that *all houses are buildings*. This constitutes some knowledge about a particular design domain—in a sense it is a *theory* about buildings. From the premise and the rule we can deduce the theorem that therefore *this is a building*. In this case the process of deduction does not produce a design but provides information about the design which is not explicit in the premise. Therefore, deduction serves in the interpretation of designs. The interpretation of a set of logical statements (including premises and rules) is simply that which can be logically inferred from them (Kowalski, 1979). This view provides some insight into the formulation of a computational model.

In a conventional computer-aided design system the description of a design is generally stored in a database as statements about objects, and their attributes and relationships. This may include geometrical information about the locations of objects in space, but it may include any abstraction of designs and processes we may care to make. Computer programs exist by which the performances of artifacts so modelled can be predicted. In the case of a building such programs might compute implicit attributes of the design, such as the winter heat loss or the efficiency of the building's circulation patterns. The artifact description is therefore interpreted by means of programs. The interpretive knowledge of programs can be made explicit as axioms in logic (as in Prolog), but irrespective of the form of the knowledge the process is essentially deductive.

This model says something about the interpretation of designs, but what of the production or generation of designs? Is it possible to take statements about the performance of a design (its interpretations) and arrive at a geometrical description? In order to investigate this it is necessary to discuss the nature of the reasoning process in more detail.

Are there other types of reasoning? Once we venture from the realm of deductive reasoning we are on unsteady ground. Deduction is the basic building block of formal reasoning systems. It is often considered, however, that there are two other modes of reasoning to which humans have recourse: namely *induction* and *abduction*. Reference has already been made to induction. This is the process by which logical rules—such as the rule that *all houses are buildings*—are derived. Induction is an important human reasoning activity by which we generalize rules from our experience of the environment. In science it is regarded as the process by which theories are derived from observations of phenomena. (The strength of Popper's argument against induction essentially relates to how induction is thought to operate rather than how we choose to label it.)

A third mode of reasoning has been proposed, principally by Peirce (Feibleman, 1970). This type of reasoning is sometimes called *abduction*. This is the derivation of statements about the world given logical rules and some logical consequences. In the syllogism illustrated above abduction would be operating if we knew the rule that *all houses are buildings* and the conclusion that *this is a building*, but did not have at our disposal the original statement that *this is a house*. The step by which we might decide that *this is a house* is abductive. That this reasoning step is by no means certain is evident if we consider that it is equally valid to conclude, from the information given, that this might be any other type of building, such as a picture theatre. It is not usually possible to run deductive systems 'backwards' in this fashion, and we generally regard someone's attempt to do so a serious logical error. Nonetheless, Peirce argued that abduction is a valid mode of human reasoning; Eco (1984) sees it operating in Science; Charniak and McDermott (1985) use it to explain the process of medical diagnosis; and March (1976, 1983) sees it as the key reasoning mode operative in the design process. It is a type of reasoning which has been successfully modelled in a formal way.

Modelling abduction presents difficulties. A common approach to modelling this type of reasoning is to attach probability values to various logical statements. This method has been actively pursued in the context of medical knowledge (Shortliffe and Buchanan, 1975). However, further insight is provided into abduction by linguistics. Design shares with language a concern with interpretation and also with generation. We therefore turn to a discussion of language and design.

Artifact as Utterance

Design can conveniently be discussed as operations within a language. According to the view of the semioticist, natural language is just one of many cultural phenomena, from fashion design to architecture, which conforms to a theory of signs called 'semiology'. In natural language, words are pointers (signifiers or symbols) to some idea or thought (signified) (Saussure, 1916). Together, signifiers and the things signified, constitute a sign, and semiotics is concerned with systems of signs. A third component of this model is the actual object, person or event to which the sign refers (the referent). Together, these three components make up the so-called *semiotic triangle* (Ogden and Richards, 1923). When applied to architectural design this model suggests that the physical parts of buildings concerned with form are equated with textual statements, that is, collections of words. The form points to content (meaning).

Whereas the study of such cultural phenomena as literature have been enriched by critical approaches based on semiotics (Hawkes, 1977; Eco, 1984) its application to architecture is at a nascent stage. Though an understanding of the development of architectural styles has been enhanced by a semiotic approach (notably by Jencks [1981]) the application of semiotics to design is not a direct one (Jencks, 1969; Broadbent, 1969). For example, there are two problems which spring to mind. First, the primary purpose of natural language is communication. There can be little debate on this, whereas the extent to which designs, such as buildings, 'communicate', and the importance of this role in our understanding of the *performance* of designs, is the subject of some contention. Second, the question arises as to the relative roles of the players in the semiotic triangle. Broadbent (1977) highlights this in relation to the Parthenon. Architecture is complicated by the observation that any building can, at any time, be signifier, signified or referent. The Parthenon exists on the Acropolis in Athens as an object to which people can make reference (*referent*). It also serves as a *signified* in the form of photographs, diagrams and words. It can also serve as a *signifier* of perfection in architecture or of all that was best in ancient Greek democracy.

In computer-aided design we are interested in manipulating symbolic representations of artifacts. We are therefore primarily interested in the meanings of *statements* about buildings described in computer systems rather than the meanings of the physical artifacts themselves (though it may be possible to infer such meanings from the statements). We therefore employ linguistics as an operational model relevent to the generation of designs rather than for theories of meaning within systems of signs.

Artifact as Instance

There is a variation on the linguistic idea that provides further insight into design. We can extend the links between language and design by considering design as a process that begins with prototypes and progresses to specific designs. Design involves *instantiation*.

One of the concerns of language is in naming things. The original meaning of 'to designate' is to give a name to something. This has the effect of allocating it to a class. To designate this object as a cup is to place it within the class of objects that are cups. To designate someone as a lieutenant is to put that person within the lieutenant class. It can be argued that class divisions are human devices relating to our perceptions of the world and are not inherent in the objects themselves. In contrast, the *holistic* position would be that class distinctions are imaginary lines in a universe that is essentially homogeneous. Certainly, class divisions appear arbitrary at times and may change according to what is convenient to us. Within the context of the western-style kitchen a cup is a vessel with a handle, but we still recognize that there are cups *without* handles, and not all vessels in the kitchen with handles are cups. As with language in general, class distinctions are by social agreement—and complex ones at that.

In design we are accustomed to talking about *types* as well as classes. We can regard a *type* as an abstraction of a class that accounts for the commonality of the members of the class. It is usually a conjunction of features rather than the embodiment of a set of alternatives. Useful types in design are often represented in terms of geometry—as diagrams (although this is by no means the only form that a type can take). Hence, we may consider the cruciform church plan as a type and depict it as two crossed axes of unequal length with perimeter walls of unspecified dimension. At a very simplistic level we could depict the 'catamaran type' of sailing boat as two elongated hulls connected by a rigid frame and a central mast.

It can be argued that designs can not only be *described* by their conformity to type, but also *produced* through them (Moneo, 1978). It is quite usual in design to start with a particular type and to bring 'elements' together to produce an artifact by which the type is exemplified. In other words, design is a process of instantiation—proceeding from a class description to a description of an instance. So, according to this model, in design we select a type and progressively refine it in response to a particular context (Figure 2.2).

This opens up an interesting avenue of exploration, though we will not pursue it in great detail in this book.

Syntactic Systems

It is a feature of our use of natural language that a competent speaker is able to both understand and generate entirely novel utterances, in such a way that other speakers competent in the same language can understand them. The behaviourists' theory of language attempted to describe speech acts in terms of stimulus and response patterns. The contribution of Chomsky in the 1950s and 1960s was to point out the importance of generative grammars, of one type or another, in the operations of natural language (Chomsky, 1957, 1971, 1975; MacIntyre, 1968; Lyons, 1970, 1981). He proposed that language involves a type of 'rule-governed creativity'.

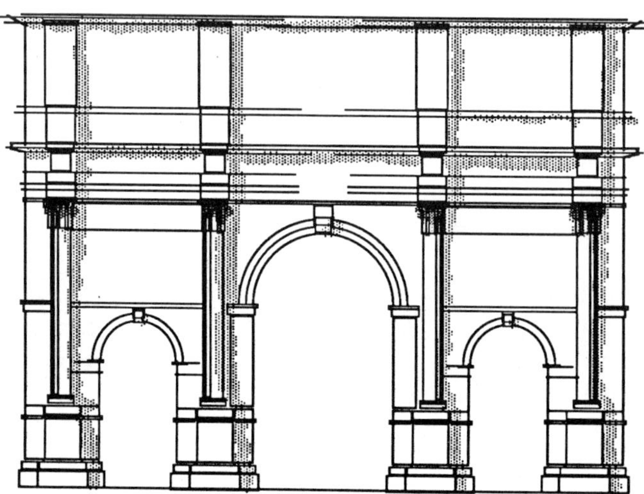

Figure 2.2. A major architectural type that has been subject to significant adaptation and refinement according to changing context.

Chomsky's theories about language have been influential within philosophy, psychology, mathematics, computer science and design theory. Even though there is some controversy within linguistics about Chomsky's notion of the *innateness* of generative grammars, the operational side of his theories has persisted within other disciplines. In generative grammars we have a direct link between a model which says something about creativity and which also provides the basis for describing computational processes.

In computer-aided design we are dealing with representations of objects and ideas in the form of symbols. *Computational theory* is concerned with how strings of symbols are manipulated. According to Church's thesis any computational process can be simulated by a device called a 'Turing machine' (Church, 1936). It matters little for our purposes what a Turing machine is like except that all Turing machines can take as programs a grammar comprised of rewrite rules. A rewrite rule specifies how a string of symbols is to be replaced by another string, for purposes of *parsing* strings of symbols, and for *generating* strings.

It is not necessary to delve into the theory in too much detail here, but it is perhaps worth providing a brief summary of the grammar formalism. More specifically, a grammar system consists of a set of vocabulary elements, a set of rewrite rules, and a start state. A rewrite rule has a left hand side and a right side which contain strings of symbols. When a particular rewrite rule is activated the symbols in the database which match its left side are replaced with those on its right side. A string of symbols in a database is parsed (that is, it is found to constitute a sentence of the language defined by the grammar) if the recursive application of rewrite rules results in the start state. The reverse process of producing sentences given a start state is called 'generation'. The rewrite rules are said to define the *syntax* (that is, the sentence forms) of the language.

In natural language these strings of symbols constitute sentences or utterances in some human language. It is not always convenient to do so, but (according to Church's thesis) any task we may wish a computer-aided design system to perform can be programmed as a set of grammar rules which bring about changes to strings of symbols in a computer database. The application of this principle to design has been explored, and its utility demonstrated, primarily in the realm of architectural geometry, in the theory of *shape grammars* by Stiny (1975, 1980a), Stiny and March (1981) and Mitchell (1983) (Figure 2.3).

Language theory appears to provide a key to modelling the generative process in computer systems. For one thing, all computational processes can be described in these terms. Secondly, there is some link between language and a model of design as discovery, in which the operators of the problem-solving model constitute grammar rules. We have considered the issue of

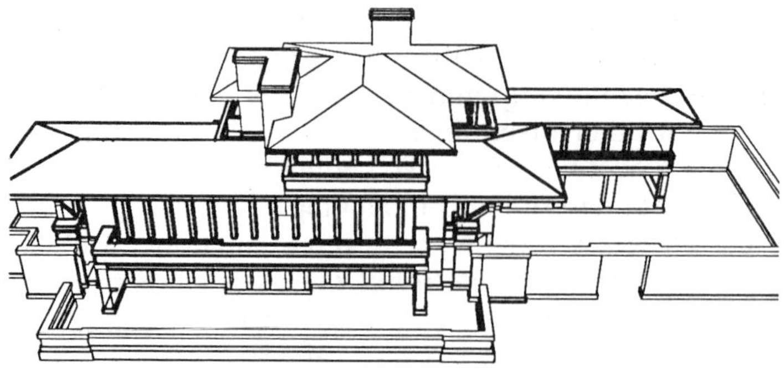

Figure 2.3. Koning and Eizenberg (1981) have demonstrated that it is possible to generate floor plans in the 'style' of Frank Lloyd Wright's prairie houses using shape grammars. (Drawing courtesy of A. Bhahirathan.)

interpretation within logic and the issue of *generation* within linguistics. We now look at how these views can form the basis of a computer-aided design system.

Design Systems

For the purposes of computer-aided design we can consider two types of computational subsystems, those concerned with interpretation and those concerned with the definition of syntax. We may characterize an interpretive system as providing a mapping between some statements about the world, such as a collection of 'facts' in a computer 'database', and the *meaning* of those statements. Taken together, the statements in a database constitute a 'sentence' in some language. The second type of system is concerned with the rules which define the *syntax* of such a language. These are linguistic rewrite rules constituting a grammar. Mappings between sentences and meanings is a concern of semantics. The definition of what constitutes a 'legal' sentence in the language is an issue of syntax.

Even though we may not know about individual designs it is convenient to talk about *spaces* of designs, defined by both the syntactic and the semantic systems. A design space is a set of descriptions of possible designs. There is also a space of possible interpretations which can be mapped onto designs. An interpretation space is a set of statements about designs which belong to some language other than that whose syntax is defined by the system (Mitchell, 1983). An interpretive system therefore establishes which statements about meaning within an interpretation space apply to individual designs described within the design space. It maps an individual design onto a set of interpretations. The reverse process is *abduction*, by which an interpretive system provides a mapping from particular meanings to a space of designs which can be interpreted as embodying those meanings. We should note that abduction typically results in a *space* of designs, rather than an individual design, as particular meanings can generally be mapped onto many designs.

A *syntactic system* also defines a space of possible designs. We would expect a design to constitute a member of the set formed by the intersection between the design space defined by the interpretive system and that defined by the syntactic system. We may therefore characterize a design system as being concerned with the production of designs which belong to the space defined by the rules of syntax, but which also belong to the space defined by the interpretive system, that is, accord with some specified set of meanings.

This can be demonstrated with a simple example. The geometry of a building can be defined by means of a grammar of rewrite rules in the manner of Stiny and Mitchell's (1978) shape grammar system for generating Palladian villa plans. This constitutes a syntactic system. A type of interpretive system with which all architects are familiar is the building code, which provides for the interpretation of a plan as having one of two meanings—compliance or non-compliance. The code also serves to define the space of all conforming designs. (Typically, this space will be bounded, but infinite in extent.) The syntactic system also defines a space of designs. Were we interested in designing a Palladian villa which complies with the code we would want a design which occupies the intersection between these two spaces, defined both syntactically and semantically. This intersection is illustrated in the diagram of the two subsystems shown in Figure 2.4.

We can generalize this process. For the building code we can substitute a complex of interpretive systems concerned with various building performances, and for the Palladian syntax we can substitute the rich and dynamic language systems of the designer. Something of the difficulty of modelling design can be seen when we consider both the complexity of the knowledge within these systems and the computational problems presented by the search for the intersection formed by their design spaces. If this model is to form the basis of a design system then it is necessary to consider not only the production of designs belonging to a particular language but also those designs which exhibit some intended meaning.

How then can we achieve the generation of 'meaningful' designs? We may borrow from the problem-solving paradigm of Newell and Simon (1972). (This is an incomplete model which will be expanded subsequently, but it serves as a useful simplification for our purposes here.) We begin with a set of attributes that the design is to possess (that is, some statement as to the intended meaning—or performance—of the artifact), and an initial state (which may simply be an empty database). This initial state is inconsistent with the interpretive system, which is comprised of knowledge about interpreting designs and the desirable attribute set, and so some syntactic rule is brought

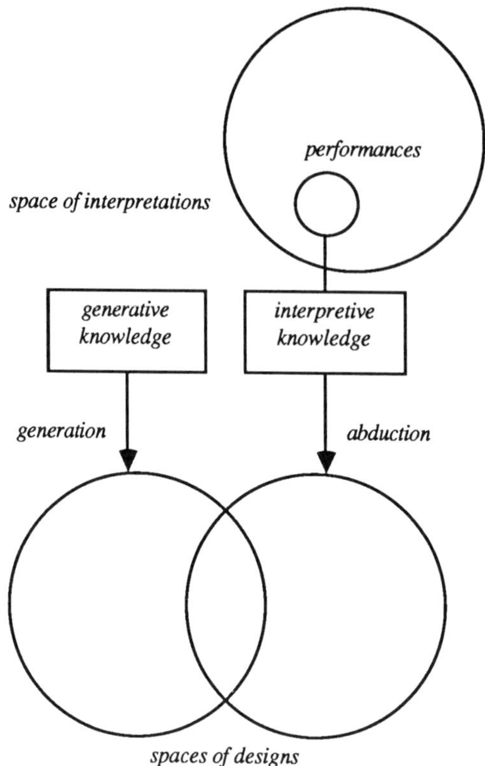

Figure 2.4. A design space as the intersection of spaces defined by syntactic (generative) knowledge and interpretive knowledge.

into play to alter the design description. If the design description is still inconsistent when tested against the interpretive system there are several courses of action open. Either the effect of the rewrite rule can be undone and another rule attempted, or there may be other rules applicable to the current state which may also be attempted. This process constitutes a search through the space of possible designs which conform to the syntax of the grammar, and resembles the search process described above. The process terminates when the design description is consistent with the stated interpretations—the designer's intentions. We might regard this as a default paradigm for a design system to demonstrate that the model will operate at least at a simple level.

At a more conceptual level, however, we can identify the components and processes of a design system. The design task can be characterized as the generation of a description given the syntax of the design language, knowledge about interpretation and some statement of what the artifact is to mean—a set of implicit design attributes. This model also identifies certain 'logical' processes. The processes within an interpretive system include: deduction, by which designs are interpreted; induction, by which interpretive knowledge is derived; and abduction, by which a space of designs conforming to a set of interpretations is delimited. Within a syntactic system the processes are: parsing, by which it is discovered whether or not a design conforms to a language; induction, by which generative knowledge is acquired; and generation, by which a grammar is employed to produce designs. A design system can therefore be formulated which accounts for these various modes of reasoning. We are now in a position to consider some of the advantages afforded by this model.

The Characteristics of Design Systems

This model of a design system affords a convenient way of representing a designer's knowledge, both from the point of view of the designer and from the point of view of computation. Considering artifacts as utterences within a language enables us to formalize certain concepts about design that have had long-standing intuitive appeal. At a simple level, a building can be seen as a composition of vocabulary elements, the arrangement of which is dictated by rules.

The symbol strings which are manipulated by rules of syntax may represent any kind of abstraction we like. For the purposes of architectural design, however, it is sometimes convenient to equate syntax with form. This model is actively pursued by Mitchell (1983) and March and Stiny (1985). Elements within the vocabulary represent geometrical primitives of lines, points and angles which go to make up more complex forms. This enables us to talk about and represent knowledge about form (as grammar rules) independently of knowledge about the interpretation of form (as logical inference rules). We may also suppose, however, that a designer's 'lexicon' could contain elements other than those which are purely geometrical. The advantage of this non-geometrical view of syntax will be explained below.

The linguistic model also provides a direct mapping between design and the ways in which we characterize computation in terms of the computational theory of generative grammars, and in terms of logic. It can be demonstrated that grammar systems and logic systems can each be described in terms of the other (Kowalski, 1979).

A grammar constitutes a problem solving system of the type suggested by Newell and Simon (1972). Rules of grammar constitute operators for transforming solution states, and the discovery of a design meeting a particular interpretation can be modelled as search. In problem solving interpretation is concerned with the evaluation of states.

This model also assists in understanding something of the analysis/synthesis dichotomy (Hillier et al, 1972, Darke, 1979). A large body of architectural knowledge relates to the analysis of designs—testing the performance of designs in some way. This is addressed by the issue of interpretation. An abundance of analytical knowledge does not provide one with the facility for 'synthesizing' designs. More is required. The synthesizing component is replaced by the idea of rules of syntax. Knowledge pertaining to analysis and synthesis is therefore recast in terms of semantics and syntax.

This approach also provides insight into something of the supposed arbitrariness of certain design decisions. We may suppose that there are many design languages. We may model the arbitrariness of certain design behaviour as an adherence to a particular design syntax. March and Stiny (1985) argue that it is possible to account for stylistic differences in terms of grammars. If this is so then arbitrariness is simply a matter of style. The selection of an appropriate language serves to impose constraints to reduce the variety of potential designs—partially serving the purpose of Darke's (1979) 'primary generator'.

It is interesting to consider the transference of syntactic grammars from one domain to another. This may assist in accounting for the idea of analogic design. Experience with building blocks may result in the acquisition of a grammar which later proves applicable to the design of buildings (Stiny, 1980b). The grammar acquired for the purposes of timber furniture design may prove applicable to the realm of masonry building design. A grammar derived from observation of the organization of organisms may also provide the seeds of a language of design as in Broadbent's (1981) characterization of analogic design. This model provides a richer view of analogy than the mere copying of forms from nature. That geometrical grammars can be transformed in some way is demonstrated by Weissman Knight (1986).

The linguistic model helps identify some of the difficulties in modelling design. Within the semantic sphere design is not deductive in character, but can be described in terms of the somewhat elusive and ill-defined process of *abduction*. Design also involves *induction*—the acquisition of knowledge. Presumably designing involves a process of learning (Cross, 1985). These are processes which can be modelled, but with far less assurity than deduction.

The model as presented so far has the advantage that it is simple, but there are two outstanding shortcomings that must be addressed in order to rescue it from the realm of elegant fiction. Firstly, nothing has been said of the practical difficulties brought about by the incumbrance of rich grammars defining large design spaces—the so-called combinatorial problem. In design we are not interested in just any design but a design which meets with a required interpretation. Stiny and Mitchell (1978) have demonstrated that it is possible to formulate rich grammars of rules which capture a particular architectural style, and whose design spaces are quite small (at least small enough for a computer to handle). In this case generate and test provides a good strategy for finding a design which matches with some set of interpretations. Generally, however, generate and test proves unworkable, particularly if we allow for a grammar of 'fine grained' rules, each of which makes small changes to a database. Syntactic systems are characterized by the need to investigate large design spaces. This issue will be addressed in subsequent chapters with reference to *decomposition*. The argument will be presented that this issues can be addressed if we consider that design languages can be modelled as operating on several levels of abstraction.

The second issue is the ill-structured nature of design. Design as problem solving has so far been characterised as well-structured. According to Simon (1973) well-structured problems have the following characteristics: there is a definite criterion for testing solutions and a process for doing so; it is possible to represent various states during the progress of the design; 'legal' moves (grammar rules) can be represented; information that the problem-solver can acquire about the problem can be represented; interactions with the external world can be accurately simulated; all information required is available; and only practicable amounts of computing are required.

Design problems, however, would appear to be categorized more accurately under the heading of 'wicked problems', as defined by Churchman (1967, 1971) and Rittel and Webber (1974). Mitchell (1975) characterizes design problems by observing that a complete and definitive formulation is not obvious in any sense from the design problem, but must be abstracted from an information-rich and often poorly-understood context. The formulation, once achieved, is therefore not rigorous, nor can it be expected to remain stable as the design progresses. There may be conflicts embodied in the formulation which will only come to light during the design process.

There is a view, however, that ill-structuredness itself can be described in terms of problem-solving (Simon, 1973a). The formulation of a design system can be regarded as a design task in itself and one that is undergoing reformulation as the process continues. The rules by which states are changed are themselves in a state of change. The creation and refinement of the design system can therefore be seen as part of the process of design.

This may also apply to the space of interpretations which the artifact is to meet. The set of desirable attributes are as much a product of what is possible as what is desirable. What is possible cannot be known until some kind of exploration has taken place. The control of this exploration represents a further abstraction of the design process, the knowledge for which must be articulated.

This view of design as concerned with multiple abstractions suggests that if design is to be modelled effectively in computer systems there needs to be provision for the representation of knowledge pertaining to different abstractions of both form and process. The question is whether this division provides realistic analogues with the way designers are accustomed to articulating their knowledge.

Conclusion

In this discussion we have reviewed various models of the design process in terms of the way scientific reasoning, logic and language are commonly understood. We have also discussed a model of computer-aided design that is based on drawing a distinction between knowledge pertaining to the interpretation of descriptions of designs in a computer database, and the knowledge about the generation of those descriptions. Both types of knowledge serve to define spaces of designs. The model also applies to the interpretation and generation of descriptions of various abstractions of designs, including design processes. This approach provides certain technical advantages in that it affords a vehicle for making explicit knowledge about decomposition, which renders design tasks tractable. This model therefore provides a structure for representing and organizing knowledge in a computer-aided design system.

The model also serves to identify important areas requiring investigation. These include the definition of languages for the control of generative systems. This is addressed further in subsequent chapters of this book. A further important task concerns modelling the means by which knowledge can be acquired in design systems. In terms of logic this is the process of *induction*. Discovery and learning appear to be key issues in the development of a fully descriptive model of the design process. It is argued that this model holds promise for the representation in computer-aided design systems of knowledge pertaining to these tasks.

The following chapter provides a summary of of some of the important theory about logic and logic programming, and how this can be related to design. This provides a foundation for the rest of the book which focusses on the production of design descriptions by *generation* and how *decomposition* can be exploited in producing designs that match with some intended performance (or set of intended meanings).

Chapter 3

Logic Programming and Design

Reference has already been made to logic as providing a metaphor of design, but in this chapter we will look at logical deduction in a formal and technical sense, such that it is able to serve as a language for representing design knowledge. This will provide a theoretical foundation for the rest of the book. The discussion of logic in this chapter is not intended to present anything novel, and the applications to design will serve only as very simple demonstrations of the utility of logic programming. The design applications will be developed more fully in subsequent chapters.

Logic programming is a system based on a particular form of logic, and with which it is possible to model various aspects of problem solving and design behaviour. It is also amenable to implementation by a computer. It can be argued that logic programming facilitates the simulation of human problem solving behaviour better than procedural computer languages such as FORTRAN, Pascal, BASIC and C, and other high-level languages such as LISP. This is due to both its declarative nature and to its overt use of the operations of pattern matching, inference and search, which map onto commonly understood ways of talking about human problem solving.

Various logic formalisms will be described in this chapter, and the applicability of logic programming to certain key components of design activity will be demonstrated with simple examples. The major benefit of logic programming is the relative ease with which meta-logic systems can be written such that a logic program can reason about, and therefore control, its own reasoning and the reasoning of other systems. This facility appears to reinforce its similarities with ways of understanding human problem solving.

Logic, as a system for representing and manipulating knowledge, possesses certain weaknesses, and methodologies are being developed to handle these. The strength of logic programming, however, rests on its demonstrated utility.

Logic Programming

Logic programming is one particular variant within a family of logic systems, and its syntax is designed such that a logic program is amenable to automation. It is a method of representing knowledge such that statements can be made about a problem which are independent of each other and yet are true and consistent within themselves. From these statements other true statements can then be deduced. These statements constitute an *axiomatic system*. The truth of the statements and the validity of the results does not depend on the procedures by which deductions are made.

This means that logic programs can be understood in two ways: both in terms of the procedures by which they are run and in terms of the truth of the statements of which they are composed. Logic programs can therefore be described as *declarative*. The judicious declaration of beliefs about a problem domain makes it possible to present knowledge *about* a problem as opposed to knowledge of *how* it is to be solved, although a logic program can incorporate both understandings (Genesereth and Ginsberg, 1985). Logic programming therefore provides certain advantages for representing knowledge about design (Swinson, 1982, 1983).

Design and Programming Languages

Programming languages sometimes bear resemblances to certain abstract views of problem domains. For example, something of the character of procedural programming languages is evident in built artifacts, and this can aid in the formulation of programs to represent designs. The repetition of elements in a formal building facade can be modelled by a 'do loop' procedure, variations in modules can be accounted for by 'case' statements and the hierarchical nature of building systems forms an isomorphism with nested function calls (Mitchell et al, 1987).

But mappings can also be established between programming languages and the processes by which certain design tasks are accomplished. So certain features of procedural languages can be mapped onto human approaches to problem solving and design. The 'do loop' suggests the iterative nature of problem solving, and 'if then' constructs can be compared with the concept of choice-points along decision paths. However, these mappings with the design process do not afford the same intuitive appeal—for those unskilled in procedural programming—as those provided by the logic programming formalism.

In design, recognition and recall play an important role. These map onto the central idea in logic programming of symbolic pattern matching. It is possible, for example, to make a statement in a logic language such as: 'the chimney is on the roof'. It is then possible to ask: 'what is on the roof?'. 'What' is a kind of linguistic variable, and the interrogative sentence acts as a *template*. When it is laid over the first statement the variable becomes equated (or *unified*) with 'the chimney'.

Designers deal not only with explicitly stated facts about the world but also with inferences of the type: if an object is *on* another object then that second object must be *under* the first. This type of reasoning is readily simulated in logic programs by means of explicit inference rules. It is also possible for logic programs to 'remember' facts and rules. Knowledge can therefore be *asserted* as part of the program, and it can also be 'forgotten' (*retracted*).

Problem solving generally requires the traversal of various problem states. The idea of being able to move back to earlier states to try alternative paths if the current state proves unsuitable in some way maps onto the control mechanisms built into logic programming languages, such as goal-directed search and automatic backtracking.

Designers are also able to reason about their mental processes. Logic programming facilitates the writing of meta-logic systems that can control automated reasoning processes. This provides a powerful facility for simulating certain aspects of design behaviour.

Before considering the application of logic programming to design in greater detail, the wider family of general logic systems will be discussed.

Formal Logic Systems

Summaries of this field are given by Nilsson (1982), Ballard and Brown (1982), Newton-Smith (1985), and Barr and Feigenbaum (1981). First order predicate calculus is a system of logic that provides a formal language for representing knowledge and making processes of deduction explicit.

Formal logic is essentially concerned with the form or syntax of logical statements, and with the determination of truth by the manipulation of formulae. **Propositional calculus** is the simplest mathematical formalism of logic. Statements (also referred to as axioms, clauses or sentences) consist of propositions and *sentential connectives*. Propositions are simply statements that can be considered as either true or false. Sentential connectives combine propositions. There are various conventions for representing these. Some of the conventions are listed here:

$\wedge$ and
$\vee$ or
$\sim$ not
$\Rightarrow$ implies

$\Leftarrow$ if
$\Leftrightarrow$ if and only if
$\equiv$ equals
(),[] parentheses

The above symbols enable us to construct sentences such as:

$$(X \Rightarrow (Y \wedge Z)) \equiv ((X \Rightarrow Y) \wedge (X \Rightarrow Z)).$$

This statement can be interpreted as: X implies Y and Z is equivalent to the statement that X implies Y and X implies Z, where X, Y and Z are sentential constants for which any logical sentence can be substituted. These constants can be replaced by groups of words which actually carry some meaning, such that the sentence is produced: cloudy skies imply rain and thunder is the same as saying that cloudy skies imply rain and cloudy skies imply thunder. Such tautologies become more useful when they make it possible to deduce new and interesting statements.

There are general rules of inference by which such sentences can be manipulated. These enable new sentences to be deduced from previously given sentences. One such rule of inference that proves useful is:

$$\sim(P \vee Q) \equiv \sim P \wedge \sim Q$$

This equivalence can be established quite readily by means of set theory. If P is used to denote all people who like Gothic architecture and Q is all people who like Classical architecture then Figure 3.1 represents all possible categories of people in relation to P and Q. The intersection of P and Q is all people who like both ($P \wedge Q$). The total space bounded by P and Q is all people who like either

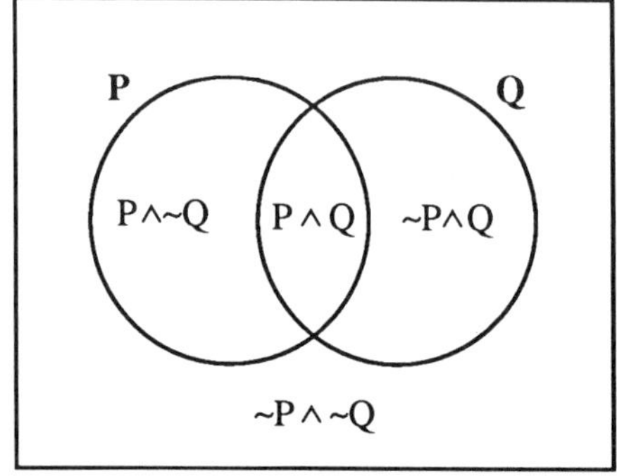

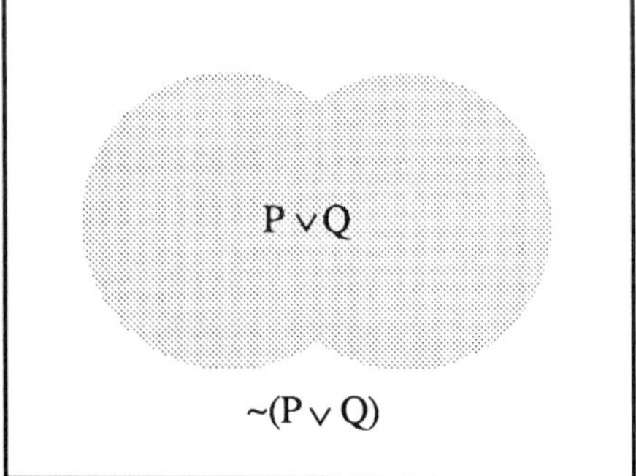

Figure 3.1. Demonstration of the equivalence of $\sim P \wedge \sim Q$ and $\sim(P \vee Q)$.

Gothic architecture or classical architecture ($P \vee Q$). The space outside these two circles is the compliment of $P \vee Q$, which is $\sim(P \vee Q)$. This space can also be defined as the intersection between the complements of P and Q, that is, $\sim P \wedge \sim Q$.

In a similar manner it is possible to establish the equivalence:

$$\sim(P \wedge Q) \equiv \sim P \vee \sim Q.$$

As shown in Figure 3.2 it is also possible to establish a distributive rule:

$$P \vee (Q \wedge R) \equiv (P \vee Q) \wedge (P \vee R).$$

It is also possible to represent logical implication by means of sets. If we are dealing with classes of objects then a statement such as 'all houses are

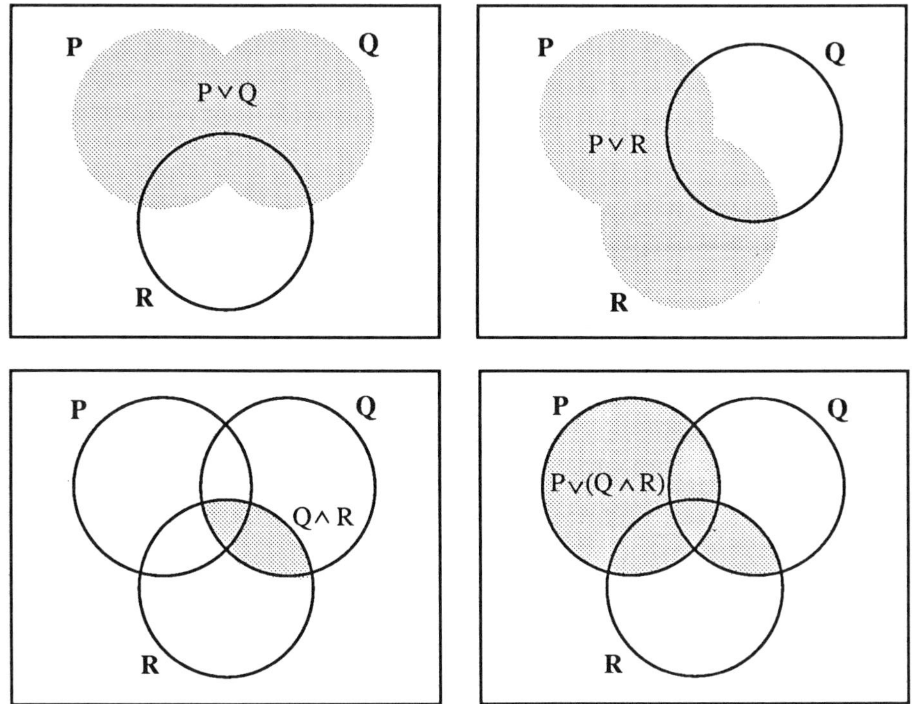

Figure 3.2. Demonstration of the equivalence of $P \vee (Q \wedge R)$ and $(P \vee Q) \wedge (P \vee R)$. The top two diagrams show the combinations $P \vee Q$ and $P \vee R$. The intersection of these spaces is equivalent to the space defined in the diagram at the bottom right.

buildings' is equivalent to saying 'if I have a house then I have a building' or 'x is a house implies x is a building'. If we represent 'x is a house' with P and 'x is a building' with Q then the implication:

$$P \Rightarrow Q$$

can be depicted as in Figure 3.3. We can describe each of the spaces in this diagram in terms of P and Q. The union of these spaces must be equivalent to $P \Rightarrow Q$:

$$(P \wedge Q) \vee (\sim P \wedge Q) \vee (\sim P \wedge \sim Q)$$

By means of inference rules this statement can be reduced to:

$$\sim P \vee Q.$$

This equivalence turns out to be very useful in manipulating statements in logic. However, the most important rule is *modus ponens* which states that if two sentences of the form 'X' and 'X implies Y' are true then it can be inferred that Y is true:

$$(X \wedge (X \Rightarrow Y)) \Rightarrow Y.$$

Of course it is not necessary that propositions only relate to sets. It is also possible to manipulate statements such as 'if you are building a house then consult the building regulations' using propositional calculus.

Predicate calculus is an extension of propositional calculus. With it sentences about objects or sentences which describe relationships between

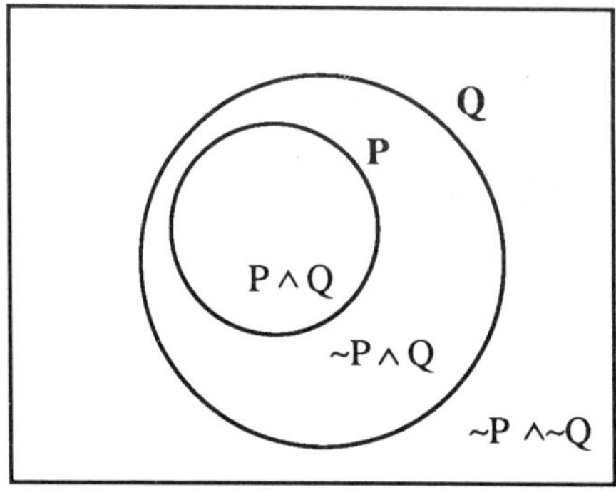

Figure 3.3. Diagram representing the implication $P \Rightarrow Q$.

objects can be constructed and manipulated. It also makes it possible to generalize about objects and relationships by means of variables. Statements about individual objects, or about relationships between objects, can be represented in the general predicate form:

$$X(a_1, a_2, ..., a_i, ..., a_n),$$

where X is the head of a predicate which is a word (or *atom*) that carries some descriptive meaning and a_i is an argument. The entire predicate has a value of either TRUE or FALSE. Examples of predicates and their values are:

LessThan(3, 5)	TRUE
IsRed(FireEngine)	TRUE
Supports(Column, Beam)	TRUE
GreaterThan(3, 5)	FALSE

Arguments can be variables, in which case the TRUE or FALSE values of the predicates will not be known until the variables are instantiated. (The convention here is that arguments beginning with a lower-case character are variables. Arguments beginning with an upper-case characters are constants. The head of a predicate cannot be a variable.) An advantage of using predicates of this form is that they can assume whatever interpretation one wishes to place on them, yet the predicate and its arguments lend themselves to rigorous symbolic manipulation.

A further qualification of logic statements can further enhance their expressive power. This is to make explicit the nature of the variables employed in statements by means of *quantification*. This is a device to handle the expression of such tautologies as: every human has a mother. The logical statement:

$$\text{Human}(x) \Rightarrow \text{Mother}(y)$$

might be interpreted erroneously as: any human has any mother. It needs to be made clear that the statement refers to all humans but only a particular mother for each human. Quantifiers make clear whether statements are universally true for all values of a variable; or whether they are true for a particular instance of a variable. Quantifiers are defined as:

the universal quantifier: $\forall x[p]$,
where p is a statement containing the variable x and is true for all x

the existential quantifier: $\exists x[p]$,
where p is a statement containing the variable x which is true for some instance of x

The above sentence describing the human/mother relationship can therefore be written as:

$$\forall x \exists y[\text{Human}(x) \Rightarrow \text{Mother}(y)]$$

As discussed below it is possible to write logic statements in a form which dispenses with the need to make these distinction about variables.

First order logic introduces functions, or operators, into the formalism. Functions resemble predicates, but they are more powerful in that they are able to return values for variable arguments. This is one of the major operations within logic programming. Values are known as *substitution instances* and the process of discovering substitution instances for two expressions which will make them equivalent is known as *unification*. There is generally no distinction between functions and predicates in logic programming. An example of unification is that in which we determine the values of the variables that will make the following statement true:

$$\text{Object}(\text{Building}(b), \text{NoOfStoreys}(s), \text{Location}(loc), \text{Owner}(\text{Govt})) \equiv$$
$$\text{Object}(\text{Building}(\text{Office}), \text{NoOfStoreys}(6), \text{Location}(\text{City}(\text{Cbd}, \text{South})), q).$$

In order for this expression to be true it is necessary that the following substitution instances be made:

b = Office,
s = 6,
loc= City(Cbd, South),
q = Owner(Govt).

A procedural algorithm for unification was originally described by Robinson (1965) and an algorithm is also described by Nilsson (1982).

Resolution

Resolution is a method by which we may determine that a statement is consistent with and derivable from another set of statements. This will be demonstrated here with a simple example using propositional calculus. Quantification and the use of variables makes the process more complicated but the same general principles apply. The following heuristic knowledge pertains to some characteristics of a building design.

> If there are south-facing windows (A) then this implies that the building will be warm in winter (B).
>
> If the building is warm in winter (B) and there is good summer cooling (C) then this implies that the dwelling will be comfortable (D).

We then assert the following facts:

> south-facing windows (A)
> good summer cooling (C)

The task is to prove that 'the dwelling will be comfortable' (D) is true. These statements can be represented in propositional calculus:

$A \Rightarrow B$
$B \wedge C \Rightarrow D$
A
C

The theorem to be proved is

$D.$

The resolution strategy is to first negate the theorem and then to demonstrate that the system is *inconsistent*. This amounts to a proof by contradiction (*reducto ad absurdam*). This method is *sound*, in that it is impossible to prove a false statement and *complete*, in that any true statement has a proof. A typical inconsistency is that something is both true and *not* true (for example, $D \wedge {\sim}D$). The most general resolution procedure is to use inference rules to convert all statements to 'disjunctive normal' form—that is, statements consisting only of propositions, disjunctions and negations. The above statements then become:

${\sim}A \vee B$
${\sim}B \vee {\sim}C \vee D$
A
C
${\sim}D$

The next step is to bring a resolution rule into play to simplify the statements. One such rule is derived from *modus ponens*:

$$P \wedge (\sim P \vee Q) \Rightarrow Q$$

This enables us to effectively cancel out certain propositions from the above list of statements. The procedure is shown here. Propositions that are eliminated by the resolution rule are shown in italics:

~A ∨ B	***B***			
~B ∨ ~C ∨ D	***~B*** ∨ ~C ∨ D	***~C*** ∨ D	D	*contradiction*
A				
C	C	***C***		
~D	~D	~D	~D	*contradiction*

This method is general and enables us to prove statements of any acceptable form. It is fairly cumbersome, however, and there are many ways in which the resolution rule can be applied. Finding a proof is a matter of search. The process can be made simpler if the form of statements is restricted to implications and single propositions.

This introduces the convention of **Horn clauses**. There is a certain redundancy built into the syntactic conventions of the logic language so far described. There are many ways to express the same set of statements, and it is possible to rewrite any set of statements in logic in a form known as clausal form. This form eliminates the need for the *implies* and the existential and universal quantifiers. The major sentential connectives retained are *and* and *if*. All variables are assumed to be universally quantified. A further refinement on clausal form is the use of *Horn clauses* (named after their most influential exponent). These take the form:

$$B \Leftarrow A_1, \ldots, A_i, \ldots, A_n.$$

The *head* of the clause, B, is true if the *body* of the clause consisting of the terms

$$A_1, \ldots, A_n$$

is true. It can be demonstrated that little is lost of the expressive power of logic with this form and considerable advantages are gained when it comes to automating proof procedures (Kowalski, 1979). It is possible to restate any declaration in standard logic in this form.

Conversion to clausal form involves substitutions based on resolution rules which are employed in theorem proving. (Although these rules are often called *rules of inference* that term can also refer to the Horn clauses themselves.) The following rules are given a full explanation by Nilsson (1982).

$\sim(\sim X)$	$\equiv$	X
$(X \Rightarrow Y)$	$\equiv$	$\sim X \vee Y$

de Morgan's Laws:

$\sim(X \wedge Y)$	$\equiv$	$\sim X \vee \sim Y$
$\sim(X \vee Y)$	$\equiv$	$\sim X \wedge \sim Y$

Distributive Laws:

$X \wedge (Y1 \vee Y2)$	$\equiv$	$(X \wedge Y1) \vee (X \wedge Y2)$
$X \vee (Y1 \wedge Y2)$	$\equiv$	$(X \vee Y1) \wedge (X \vee Y2)$

Commutative Laws:

$X \wedge Y$	$\equiv$	$Y \wedge X$
$X \vee Y$	$\equiv$	$Y \vee X$

Associative Laws:

$(X \wedge Y1) \wedge Y2$	$\equiv$	$X \wedge (Y1 \wedge Y2)$
$(X \vee Y1) \vee Y2$	$\equiv$	$X \vee (Y1 \vee Y2)$

Contrapositive Law:

$X \Rightarrow Y$	$\equiv$	$\sim Y \Rightarrow \sim X$

Quantifier Laws:
(P and Q are statements containing the variable x)

$\sim\exists x P$	$\equiv$	$\forall x[\sim P]$
$\forall x\, P$	$\equiv$	$\exists x\, [\sim P]$
$\forall x\, [P \wedge Q]$	$\equiv$	$\forall x\, P \wedge \forall x\, Q$
$\exists x[P \vee Q]$	$\equiv$	$\exists x\, P \vee \exists x\, Q$

With these rules it is possible to convert a statement in standard form to other forms, including Horn clause form. An example is the statement: an object is above another object if it is on top of the other object or if it is above an object that is above the other object. This can be represented in standard form as:

$$\text{On}(x, y) \vee \exists z[\text{Above}(x, z) \wedge \text{Above}(z, y)] \Rightarrow \text{Above}(x, y).$$

The procedure is based on Robinson's resolution method for proving the consistency of a set of statements, though the purpose is slightly different here. The steps in the conversion are as follows:

1. $\sim(\text{On}(x, y) \vee \exists z[\text{Above}(x, z) \wedge \text{Above}(z, y)]) \vee \text{Above}(x, y)$

2. $(\sim\text{On}(x, y) \wedge \sim \exists z[\text{Above}(x, y) \wedge \text{Above}(z, y)]) \vee \text{Above}(x, y)$

3. $(\text{Above}(x, y) \vee \sim \exists z[\text{Above}(x, z) \wedge \text{Above}(z, y)]) \wedge$
$(\text{Above}(x, y) \vee \sim\text{On}(x, y))$

4. $(\text{Above}(x, y) \vee \forall x[\sim\text{Above}(x, z) \vee \sim\text{Above}(z, y)]) \wedge$
$(\text{Above}(x, y) \vee \sim\text{On}(x, y))$

5. $\forall z[(\text{Above}(x, y) \vee \sim\text{Above}(x, z) \vee \sim\text{Above}(z, y)) \wedge$
$(\text{Above}(x, y) \vee \sim\text{On}(x, y))$

In clausal form all variables are universally quantified, and the formulation of two independent statements implies an *and* condition.

6. $\text{Above}(x, y) \Leftarrow \text{Above}(x, z) \wedge \text{Above}(z, y)$
$\text{Above}(x, y) \Leftarrow \text{On}(x, y)$

This can be readily converted into a Prolog program using the 'Edinburgh syntax' (Clocksin and Mellish, 1981):

above(X, Y) :- *on(X, Y)*.
above(X, Y) :- *above(X, Z), above(Z, Y)*.

In Prolog terminology these statements are called *rules* or *clauses*. The *if* sentential connective (⇐) is represented as ':-', the comma represents *and*, and the full stop (.) defines the end of a clause or fact. The part of the clause to the left of the ':-' symbol is the *head* of the clause and the predicates to the right constitute the *body*. In this system of conventions variables are indicated in upper case.

It has been necessary to swap the order in which the statements are listed for implementational reasons. It is a general rule of Prolog programming (to which there are exceptions) that the stopping condition of a recursive definition precedes the recursive rule. The statements are, none the less, comprehensible in an intuitive manner: an object *X* is above object *Y* if it is on that object *or* *X* is above *Y* if *X* is above another object *Z* which is above *Y*. (In the rest of the book we will use the 'Edinburgh syntax' for representing statements in logic rather than the general form with which we began this chapter.)

Horn clauses lend themselves to automated proof procedures. The theoretical basis of the procedural interpretation of Horn clauses which led to the development of Prolog is attributed to Kowalski (1979), whose textbook on the subject provides a primary reference for the following discussion. The development of Prolog is attributed to Colmerauer and Roussel (Colmerauer et al, 1973).

Prolog

The driving operation in Prolog is *proof* by resolution. A proof in Prolog is achieved by presenting a program, such as the one above, with a goal. The goal is matched against the head of a clause. The body of that clause provides a set of subgoals which must be satisfied. If the procedure is successful and the goals and subgoals can be proved then the program terminates and returns 'yes' to the goal. If the goal contains variables Prolog also returns the substitution instances which make it true.

The clauses defining the *above* relationship can therefore be supplemented by a set of clauses which describe the world in terms of the *on* relationship. The following are unconditional clauses, that is, clauses without a body, or *facts*:

on(house, hill).
on(roof, house).
on(chimney, roof).
on(bridge, hill).
on(car, bridge).

A goal is generally presented to the program in the following form:

?- ***above(chimney, hill).***

In this example the answer will be:

yes.

The goal:

?- ***above(car, house).***

will return the answer:

no.

The goal:

?- ***above(roof, X).***

returns:

$X = house$;
$X = hill$;
no

meaning that the goal is true for X unified with house and hill, but for no other values.

The procedure built into Prolog is a top-down search strategy. Often, there is more than one way in which each goal or subgoal can be satisfied. Prolog keeps a record of paths followed in the search so that it can return to earlier states should it be necessary in the event of the failure of a particular subgoal. It therefore incorporates *automatic backtracking* (Kowalski, 1981a; Sammut and Sammut, 1983). The major texts on Prolog and logic programming are by Clocksin and Mellish (1981), Clark and McCabe (1984), Hogger (1984), Bratko (1986), Sterling and Shapiro (1986), and Amble (1987).

Design

A logic programming language, such as Prolog, facilitates the representation of certain aspects of design knowledge. This will be demonstrated by means of simple examples as well as reference to how the ideas have been developed by others.

Expectations of what computer-aided design systems should be able to do for designers have been discussed by Willey (1976), Berger (1980), Bijl (1984), Lansdown and Maver (1984), and Kalay (1985). There need to be mechanisms for effectively describing designs, and for discovering things about artifacts which are not explicit, such as performances. Mechanisms are required by which knowledge about generating designs can be represented and utilized, and the means of displaying designs and design information are required. There also need to be control regimes for guiding computational processes. These aspects of design knowledge are considered briefly here under the headings of: description; interpretation; generation; display; and control.

Description

In any design system it is necessary to provide a language for describing artifacts and states of artifacts. In procedural programming languages such as FORTRAN or C this involves making decisions about structures for organizing data. A logic programmer (using Prolog) is encumbered by no such considerations as a rich data structure is already determined. It is only necessary for data to conform to the syntax of the predicate calculus. This

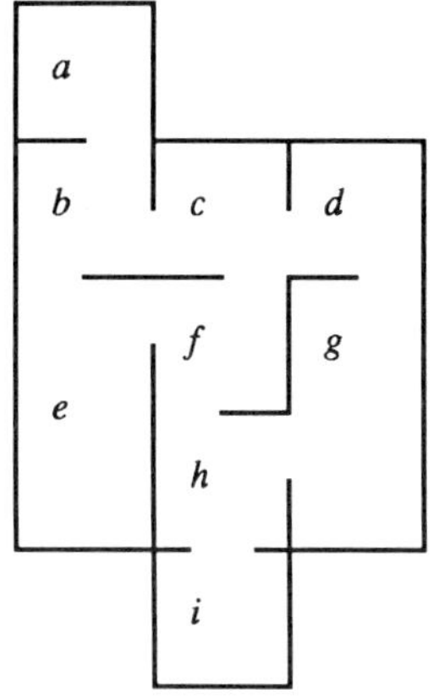

Figure 3.4. A building plan.

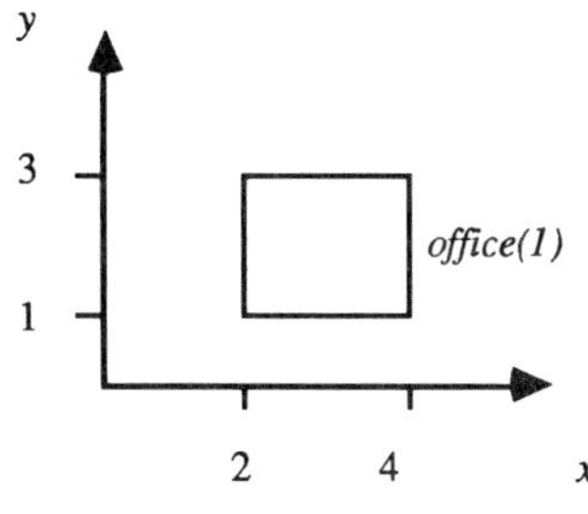

Figure 3.5. The geometrical representation of a room.

permits a higher level view of data to be adopted, such that descriptions in terms of facts about objects, relationships and attributes need only be considered. Facts are therefore primarily collections of *atoms* (or words) and *numbers*.

As demonstrated by the following examples predicate calculus provides a flexible medium with which to describe various attributes of designed objects.

Topological relationships such as the *on* relationship in the program described above can be extended. Circulation within a building, such as that depicted in Figure 3.4, can be described by means of a link relationship. The facts for this view of the world are:

link(a, b).
link(d, g).
link(b, c).
link(g, h).
link(b, e).
link(h, f).
link(c, d).
link(h, i).
link(c, f).
link(f, e).

Geometrical information can also be represented, such as the following fact to describe the room in Figure 3.5:

```
room(office(1), 3, 1, 4, 2).
```

The first argument of the *room* predicate contains the name of the room (as a nested predicate), and the other four arguments give the the common values of the vertices on the north, south, east and west faces respectively. An entire room layout, such as that represented in Figure 3.6 can therefore be described in this way.

Objects can also be described hierarchically as with the simple plan in Figure 3.7. The office is a composite object made up of various components such as columns and walls. Each of these objects is made up of line segments, and these segments are defined by end points, which have coordinate values. A list construct can be employed to depict a list of elements of any length. Each of the following predicates has two arguments. The second argument is a list in each case:

```
composite(office(1), [column(1), column(2), ...,
      wall(1), wall(2), ...]).
object(column(1), [s(1), s(2), s(3), s(4)]).
...
line(s(1), [p(1), p(2)]).
...
point(p(1), [0.00, 0.00]).
point(p(2), [0.00, 0.50]).
...
```

These collections of facts constitute simple logic programs and it is possible to interrogate facts bases, such as the above, by presenting them with goals containing variables. An automated theorem prover, of the type used in Prolog, must unify values which will make the goals true. An example with the office building in Figure 3.6 would be to present the goal:

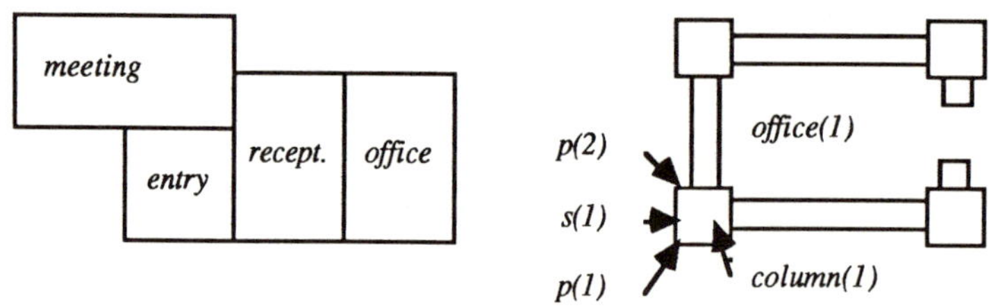

Figure 3.6. A configuration of rooms.

Figure 3.7. A room that can be described hierarchically.

?- *room(X, N, _, _, _), N>4.*

This asks for the room which is north of the line *y=4*. The underscore (_) indicates a variable, the value of which is of no interest. (It is the *anonymous variable.*) The '>' symbol is the normal mathematical inequality operator which tests for 'greater-than'. The answer will be:

X= meeting
N= 5.

This approach uses facts in a manner similar to a relational database system (Kowalski, 1981b; Lloyd, 1983).

With the predicate calculus formalism it is possible to create design descriptions at various levels of abstractions. This redundancy of representation bears some relation to the way designers think about artifacts. So, at one time room relationships may be important but for another purpose geometry may be important.

An ideal medium for representing knowledge about design is one that is capable of enabling any thought to be represented, but which does not anticipate the properties of the things described (Swinson et al, 1983). It should be unconstraining and yet powerful enough to perform operations which are useful to designers. The feasibility of a logic-based modelling environment for design has been explored by Bijl (1985a, 1985b) and Krishnamurti (1985), and a test system (called MoLe) has been implemented in Prolog. Some of these approaches are based on the theory of *frames* (Minsky, 1975), which provides a rich medium for the representation of both *generic* objects and *instances* of objects, and enables the inheritance of properties from one to the other. Frames provide an effective means of representing certain design knowledge, particularly as it relates to 'design prototypes', and can readily be implemented in logic programming (Balachandran, 1988).

Interpretation

Modelling artifacts by means of facts provides a powerful descriptive medium for design, but the strength of logic programming lies in being able to discover facts about the world other than those represented explicitly. The definition of the Above relation is an example of how implicit facts can be derived. In the case of the office building of Figure 3.6 it is possible to formulate a rule for determining certain topological relationships between spaces. For example:

```
direction(X, north, Y) :-
    room(X, _, Sx, _, _), room(Y, Ny, _, _, _), Sx > Ny.
```

states that room *X* is north of room *Y* if the south face of *X* is above the north face of *Y*. Similar rules can be formulated for other directions and also for other topological relationships such as *touching* and *adjacency*. A modelling system for deriving such relationships from geometrical object descriptions has been explored and implemented in Prolog by Akiner (1985a, 1985b).

For the domain about which only linkages between rooms are known (Figure 3.4) Clocksin and Mellish (1981) provide a definition which makes it possible to derive circulation routes through the building:

```
path(X, X, T, T).
path(X, Y, T, L) :-
  (link(X, Z); link(Z, X)), not(member(Z, T)),
    path(Z, Y, [Z|T], L).
```

(The semicolon (;) indicates *or*.) The first argument of *path* is the room from which the journey is to commence, the second argument is the destination. The fourth argument is a list of rooms already visited, and which must not be visited again. The final argument is the list of rooms which constitutes the path. The first clause says that a journey from a room to itself is the same as the list of rooms already visited. The second clause says that there is a path from *X* to *Y* if *X* is linked to another room which has not already been visited and which is connected to the destination by a path. Member is defined here:

```
member(X, [X|_]).
member(X, [_|Y]) :- member(X, Y).
```

It checks whether an object is a member of a list. The [*Z*|*T*] construct indicates that *Z* is to be appended as the first element (head) of a list with *T* constituting the rest of the list (the *tail* of the list). When applied to the facts base for the building of Figure 3.4 the goal:

```
?- path(a, i, [], L).
```

results in the unifications:

```
L = [a, b, c, d, g, h]
L = [a, b, c, f, h]
L = [a, b, e, f, c, d, g, h]
L = [a, b, e, f, h]
```

In a similar way other complex properties of designs can be derived by deductive inference. The derivation of implicit facts is a key operation in design. Computer programs for the evaluation of building performance effectively deduce the properties of objects from explicit information and the knowledge contained within algorithms. The logic programming formalism permits the *explicit* representation as Horn clauses (or deductive inference rules) in logic of the knowledge by which *implicit* facts can be derived. This provides a useful mechanism for the interpretation of design descriptions.

Generation

Inference rules of the type described above can aid in selecting between ranges of candidate attributes for objects, and in this way produce combinations of elements which conform to a set of logical constraints. A simple way to model this is to provide facts representing candidate positions for a set of objects and test the suitability of those positions. An example is the location of three structures on a gridded building site: a house; a garage and a swimming pool. The constraints are:

the garage must be next to the house
the pool may not be next to the garage
the pool must be north of the house and north of the garage
there is a zone on the site that must not be built on

The gridded site is shown in Figure 3.8. The cells suitable as sites for the objects can be represented explicitly as a fact

suitable_cells([*1^1, 1^2, 1^3, 1^4, 2^1, 2^4, 3^1,*
3^2, 3^3, 3^4, 4^1, 4^2, 4^3, 4^4]).

where the special symbol (^) links coordinate pairs. The following program incorporates the constraints in generating site layouts:

```
1 . . . .
2 . . . .
3 . . . .
4 . . . .
  1 2 3 4
```

Figure 3.8. A gridded site.

```
plan(H, G, P) :-
    suitable_cells(L),
    member(H, L), member(G, L), member(P, L),
    next_to(G, H), not(next_to(P, Q)),
    north_of(P, H), north_of(P, G),
    plot([h, p, g], [H, P, G]).
```

The next_to and north_of predicates compare the *X* and *Y* coordinates of the grid cells in much the same way as the office building example of Figure 3.6. The procedure *plot* draws the site with the structures located in position. Results from the program are shown in Figure 3.9.

An examples for generating building layouts in a similar way is provided by Markusz and described by Coelho et al (1980). A simple but powerful logic program determines the location of two rooms relative to one another and establishes the orientations of windows and doors in response to a set of constraints. Markusz also describes a design system which extends this idea and applies it to laying out multi-storey blocks of flats (Markusz, 1982).

Such systems are inefficient for generating layouts unless the search procedure of theorem proving is considerably enhanced by the introduction of sophisticated control knowledge. The utility of logic programs in enabling the representation of this kind of knowledge will be discussed below.

Deductive inference plays an important part in design reasoning but causal relationships of the sort modelled by clauses in logic do not, on their own, provide very powerful devices for generating designs. In the Popperian problem-solving model the transition from problem state to problem state does not necessarily conform to well reasoned steps in logic but rather intuitive jumps. The states so achieved can be evaluated employing all the rigor of logical reasoning and so rejected or accepted, but the operators which bring about those states may not appear to conform so rigorously to the demands of logic.

But 'informality' can be modelled in logic systems to the extent that it can be represented as *re-write* rules (that is, *transformations* or *production rules*). These are rules which make changes to the states of problem domains (in this case facts in logic programs) in some way. Like a Horn clause a transformation rule attempts to match some set of conditions against a set of facts. If successful in this, however, it changes facts in some way to create a new, modified program. (In a purely deductive inference system, new facts are being discovered and effectively added to the store of knowledge.) In a transformation system, facts are being changed into new and different facts. This is how *production systems* are understood and they have provided valuable models for simulating certain aspects of design and other problem solving activity (Gips and Stiny, 1980).

```
4 . . p .                   4 . . . p
3 . . h g                   3 . g h .
2 . . . .                   2 . . . .
1 . . . .                   1 . . . .
  1 2 3 4                     1 2 3 4

G = 4^3                     G = 2^3
P = 3^4;                    P = 4^4;


4 . p . .                   4 . . p .
3 . . h g                   3 . g h .
2 . . . .                   2 . . . .
1 . . . .                   1 . . . .
  1 2 3 4                     1 2 3 4

G = 4^3                     G = 2^3
P = 2^4;                    P = 3^4;

4 p . . .                   4 p . . .
3 . . h g                   3 . g h .
2 . . . .                   2 . . . .
1 . . . .                   1 . . . .
  1 2 3 4                     1 2 3 4

G = 4^3                     G = 2^3
P = 1^4;                    P = 1^4;
                            no
```

Figure 3.9. Output from a Prolog program that plots the position of structures on a site according to rules. The symbols *h, p* and *g* represent a house, a pool and a garage respectively. The output is in response to the goal: ?- ***plan(3^3, G, P)***.

The transformations brought about by such rules are not necessary 'logical' but the rules themselves are subject to processes of logical reasoning. Production systems can therefore be described in the logic programming formalism.

Display

Logic programming languages, such as Prolog, generally contain built-in functions which permit the reading and writing of information to and from display devices. Such functions are given the same status as predicates, and generally return TRUE or FALSE if the operations they are designed to implement can be carried out. Graphics primitives may also be implemented in much the same way as graphics commands in procedural languages. There are therefore *move* and *line* operations which can be incorporated into higher level procedures. For example, a procedure can be devised for drawing a rectangle:

```
draw_rectangle(Xo, Yo, W, H) :-
    X1 is Xo+W, Y1 is Yo+H,
    move(Xo, Yo), line(Xo, Y1),
    line(X1, Y1), line(X1, Yo), line(Xo, Yo).
```

where *Xo* and *Yo* are the coordinates of the origin of the rectangle and *W* and *H* are the width and height respectively. The *is* operator assigns the value achieved by carrying out the arithmetic operations on the right to the variable on the left.

Objects can be described hierarchically, as in Figure 3.7, and they can also be drawn hierarchically:

```
draw_composites(T).
draw_composites([H|T]) :- composite(H, L),
    draw_objects(L), draw_composites(T).

draw_objects([]).
draw_objects([H|T]) :- object(H, L), draw_lines(L),
    draw_objects(T).

draw_lines([]).
draw_lines([H|T]) :-
    line(H, [P1, P2]), point(P1, [X1, Y1]), point(P2, [X2, Y2]),
    move(X1, Y1), line(X2, Y2), draw_lines(T).
```

If the facts associated with Figure 3.3 are incorporated in this program and the following goal is presented:

```
?- draw_composite([office(1)]).
```

then the program will draw *office(1)* by constructing each of its components and subcomponents. Examples of graphics primitives for hierarchical representations in Prolog have also been discussed and implemented by Steel and Szalapaj (1983), and Szalapaj and Bijl (1985).

The formality of logic programs is compromised somewhat by the introduction of function calls to handle communications (Robinson, 1983a). An attempt has been made to fit graphics into the logic of Prolog by F. Pereira

(1982) and Swinson (1983). A line can be defined as a boundary of an infinitely extending half plane (Presque half planes). Graphical objects can therefore be represented as the intersection of various half planes. Mapping the logic of set theory onto that of the predicate calculus is intended to provide a 'declarative graphics' medium.

Control

The control of logic programs involves matching goals against the heads of clauses attempting to satisfy secondary goals and backtracking on the failure of a goal or subgoal. It is possible to produce programs which divert from the normal behaviour pattern of logic programming languages such as Prolog. It may be considered desirable to change certain operational aspects of logic programs, such as: the syntax of Horn clauses; the communications syntax; the order in which goals and subgoals are considered; or the entire control regime of logic programming. Such changes can be achieved by employing the logic programming language as a meta-language for defining other languages.

Logic is such an expressive medium, therefore, that it is possible to employ it to describe its own operation or that of other logics (L.M Pereira, 1982). The activity of defining the implementation of one language in terms of another is called *bootstrapping* when applied to computer languages, but it is a common phenomenon in many formal systems including mathematics. An example of a logic programming routine for 'running' a logic program is:

demonstrate(*true*).
demonstrate((*A*, *B*)) :- *clause*(*A*, *C*),
    demonstrate(*C*), *demonstrate*(*B*).

The Clause predicate is a function for returning both the head of a clause with which it matches and the conjunction of subgoals which make up the body of the matching clause. (This would have to be built into the logic programming language implementation.) The final goal will always be the atom True. This definition states that a set of goals can be demonstrated to be true if the goal is true, or if the first goal matches the head of a clause and the body of the clause can be demonstrated, and the rest of the goals can be demonstrated. When this definition is added to the program that makes use of the *above* relation (on page 40), and the following goal is presented:

?- ***demonstrate***((***above***(***chimney***, ***hill***), ***true***))

the theorem prover returns 'yes', indicating that it is able to demonstrate that the goal is true. This operation is described as *simulation* by Kowalski in that it demonstrates that the goal *could* be satisfied, rather than that it *is* satisfied. Programs tend to be very inefficient if run in this way.

More usefully, it is possible to control the way in which a logic program handles the inability to satisfy a goal. Normally a goal fails when there exists no proof of its truth. It is possible to write a specialized inference system that processes inference rules and prompts for facts as they are required rather than failing directly. Inference rules can be written as facts in order to achieve this :

```
rule([price_is_right, cash_available], buy_property).
rule([good_security, low_interest], cash_available).
```

If the propositions in the list in the first argument of the rule are true then the consequent (second argument) is true. A simple interpreter can be expressed in logic:

```
inference(C) :- rule(A, C), check(A).
inference(C) :- prompt(C).

check([]).
check([H|T]) :- inference(H), check(T).

prompt(Q) :- write(Q), write('? '), read(yes).
```

This states that the proposition *C* can be *inferred* true if there is a *rule* with *C* as its consequent and the antecedents of the rule can be *checked.* If there is no rule with *C* as its consequent then prompt for verification. A list is *checked* if it is empty or if the first element of the list can be *inferred* true and the rest of the list can be *checked.* The prompt for a proposition is successful if it can be written out followed by a question mark and the response is the atom *yes*. The predicates *write* and *read* are 'built-in' logic functions. The goal:

?- ***inference(buy_property).***

therefore results in the following dialogue, where the operator response is in bold type:

price_is_right? ***yes.***
good_security? ***yes.***
low_interest? ***yes.***
yes.

The program requires further enhancements to handle the *no* response more elegantly. Rules can also contain variables, but further mechanisms are needed to handle prompts for values. It is also possible to introduce various control devices for directing attention down the inference tree, such as changing the order in which propositions are handled in the Check definition. These and other issues have been further explored by Clark and McCabe (1982), Hammond (1982), Hammond and Sergot (1983), Mizoguchi (1983), and Rosenman and Gero (1985) in the context of working expert systems in Prolog.

As well as inference systems it is possible to implement controllers for generative production systems for transforming the state of a 'facts base'. A simple example is a set of transformation rules defined as follows:

rule(1, fact(a) → fact(d)).
rule(2, fact(b) → fact(e)).
rule(3, fact(c) → fact(f)).

Each rule has an identification number, a left side containing the fact that is to be changed and a right side containing the new fact that is to be asserted. A facts base can be defined as:

fact(a).
fact(b).
fact(c).

A logical representation of the control strategy is:

implement(X) :- *rule(X, A → B), A, retract(A), assert(B).*

This states that rule X can be implemented if its left side matches the facts base, and it is *retracted* and if the right side of the rule is *asserted*. The goal:

?- ***implement(1), implement(2),***
implement(3), listing(fact).

therefore produces the following:

fact(d)
fact(e)
fact(f)
yes.

The *listing* predicate is a built-in function for displaying all the clauses headed by a predicate whose name is contained in its argument. It is also possible to employ inference in matching the left side of a transformation rule (sometimes known as a *re-write* or *production* rule). For example, the following production rules may be added to the program:

rule(4, fact(g) → fact(i)).
rule(5, fact(h) → fact(j)).

As *fact(g)* and *fact(h)* do not exist in the facts base a match is not strictly possible. But if there are logical rules by which these facts can be inferred from existing facts then the transformation rules can be implemented. It may be the case, for example, that *fact(g)* is true if *fact(a)* exists but *fact(b)* is not true, and *fact(h)* is true if *fact(c)* or *fact(d)* exist:

fact(g) :- *fact(a), not(fact(b)).*
fact(h) :- *fact(c); fact(d).*

With a slightly more complicated control mechanism than that described above, it is possible to devise a controller which implements transformation rules according to what can be inferred about the facts base as well as what is explicitly within it. *Fact(g)* and *fact(h)* are inferred facts and are asserted *en passant* to form part of the facts base.

We should note that the use of *retract* and *assert* procedures effectively disables our logic programming language as a strict theorem proving system. In order to reason effectively about a facts base that is undergoing change in this way it would be necessary to maintain some kind of record of which facts are true and in which state. This can be cumbersome and is not always necessary if the limitations of *retract* and *assert* are taken into account in the design and use of logic programs.

In any production system it is generally necessary to make choices between transformation rules that are competing to be implemented at any state. Exhaustive search of all solution paths can result in inefficiencies. Control rules can be formulated in logic for selecting between competing transformation rules. In order to be effective in this some method of evaluating partial states is generally required. Generally, the final state must exhibit certain properties. These properties constitute goals. Transformation rules which produce sets of facts more nearly resembling the goal state are therefore to be preferred in such a strategy.

A second set of methods for selecting between competing production rules is to simulate the search procedure without actually making any changes to the facts base. This may mean exploring the search space at a level of abstraction where the costs of decisions are not as great as at the 'ground' level. It also makes possible the incorporation of meta-rules for guiding search. This is the role of planning systems which are often discussed in the context of selecting and ordering actions for robots. Planning is generally applicable to the control of any production system and therefore of design systems which adopt this model. Kowalski (1979) has also demonstrated how the behaviour of planning systems can be modelled in logic.

Many different approaches to problem solving can therefore be modelled in logic programming. Kowalski argues that the Horn clause inference of logic programming subsumes many of the alternative models of problem solving developed in artificial intelligence. These include production systems, semantic networks, frames and procedures. Other logical devices could also be simulated in logic programming such as truth tables for reasoning, though this has not yet been explored fully.

The ability of a system to define its own operations and those of 'lower order' languages is a powerful device. This and the ability of logic programs to change their own structure by the retraction and assertion of clauses are important mechanisms for representing and implementing design knowledge.

Inadequacies of Formal Logic as a Means of Representing Design Knowledge

Logic shares with all formal systems the paradox that it is both insufficiently rigorous to simulate all of the reasoning of which humans are readily capable, and too rigorous to model the informality of human reasoning. Gödel (1931, 1962) has proved the inherent failings of formal systems: failings which human intelligence seems able to transcend. It is also well known that human reasoning rarely conforms to the strict rules of logic. Some of the shortcomings of formal logic—which it shares with any other known system of formal representation—are considered here along with various attempts to create 'enhanced logics'. The problems are brought into the foreground when the formulation in logic is made explicit.

Provability

Gödel's theorem states that for any formal but incomplete system there are always statements which can be made which are consistent with the axioms of the system, and are therefore true, but which cannot be proved by that system.

It can be demonstrated that it is impossible to completely formalize the notion of provability. This can be demonstrated by taking the *demonstrate* procedure described above and employing it to attempt the paradoxical task of demonstrating its own denial. This is accomplished by setting up the clause:

d **:-** *not*(*demonstrate*((*d, true*))).

This states that D is true if it is not possible to demonstrate that D is true, and is equivalent to the paradoxical natural language sentence:

This sentence is unprovable.

The *demonstrate* clauses which correctly represent the provability relation are restated here:

demonstrate(*true*).
demonstrate((*A*, *B*)) **:-** *clause*(*A*, *C*),
demonstrate(*C*), *demonstrate*(*B*).

(In order for this statement to accurately represent the Demonstrate relationship it is necessary to introduce further clauses which embody the assumption that both the *not* and the *clause* statements are able to be demonstrated.) The clause with head *d* is true but unprovable as any attempt to run it will show. The goal:

?- ***d*.**

returns no answer, as does:

?- ***not*(*d*).**

The failure of the system to return a verdict is due to an infinite series of recursive calls, but its failure is due to the impossibility of the proof rather than any quirks in the procedural implementation of the proof language. Further discussion of the incompleteness proof is given by Kowalski (1979).

These problems are *not* encountered if the constraints of *first order logic* are adhered to. First order logic is a logical system in which statements can be made about concepts in the world, other than about the system itself. This disallows the use of such functions as those provided by the *clause* predicate of the Demonstrate rule, and the use of *assert* and *retract* as described above. Logical proof can only be assured when a logical system is constrained in this way. As the restrictions on first order logic are relaxed a system becomes harder to understand, and paradoxes such as that described above become more abundant. Mathematical logic is not immune from paradox (DeLong, 1971), neither is the system under which human reasoning operates (Bronowski, 1966; Tarski, 1969).

The shortcomings of formal systems have sometimes been cited by others to support the view that computers will never be able to accomplish anything remotely resembling human intelligence. One criticism points to the paradoxes that arise from this ability to make statements in logic about logic. The ability of a language to be employed in describing not only parts of the world but also parts of the language itself contributes to the richness of language and logic. But, according to Bronowski, this is the cause of its failing as a means of modelling human reasoning.

> ... the brain as a machine is certainly not the kind of machine that we understand now. It is not a logical machine, because no logical machine can reach out of the difficulties and paradoxes created by self-reference. The logic of the mind differs from formal logic in its ability to overcome and indeed exploit the ambivalences of self-reference, so that they become the instruments of imagination ... All that we can say, and all that I can assert, is that we cannot now conceive any kind of law or machine which could formalize the total modes of human reasoning (Bronowski 1966, p. 45-47).

By 'machine' is meant any formal system. This constitutes one of the philosophical objections to attempts to model human reasoning (see also Weizenbaum, 1976; Dreyfus and Dreyfus, 1984, 1986). Some of these arguments are given informal but thorough treatment in a popular book by Hofstadter (1982).

Closed World Assumption

When a theorem prover is unable to find a fact in its facts base it assumes that it is untrue. This is only possible because of the *closed world assumption*: everything about the world that is relevant to the problem is known by the system.

This can be demonstrated with a simple example. It is true that an object is clear (that is, it has a clear top surface) if there is nothing on top of it. This can be represented as:

clear(*X*) :- *not*(*on*(_, *X*)).

In order to be sure that the top of *X* is clear it is necessary to assume that all the information about what is on what is contained in the program, whereas in the *above* relation described earlier, which deals in truth only, insufficient information will merely indicate that the goal is unprovable. Logic programming languages such as Prolog are therefore geared to discovering truth but is less capable of proving negation.

This is a problem in expert systems, which attempt to model problem solving by inference in real (and therefore open) worlds. Attachments can, however, be made to an open world by the introduction of prompts which are activated when a fact cannot be found, as shown in the control example given above. The assumption is that the being with whom the system is communicating is in touch with the real world and has access to the relevant knowledge.

The problem of negation is discussed by Clark (1978), Reiter (1978) and Lloyd (1984), and the issue is summarized by Kowalski (1979). Aida et al (1983) discuss an extension to Prolog to handle negative knowledge, though the theory for handling this is not clearly established.

Monotonicity Assumption

The logic programming formalism embodies purely deductive reasoning. The addition of new clauses has no effect on goals already satisfied. A new clause cannot be accepted if it contradicts what is already known by violating the consistency of the axiomatic system. This is the *monotonicity assumption.* This assumption has come under question as being inadequate for human reasoning processes where contradiction is handled more creatively than with pure logical deduction.

Logic programs can be considered as undergoing changes in state as a proof procedure is under way. Contradictions arise when goals fail. But in a large scale design system it might be expected that the proof procedure is used not only to answer queries but to assimilate new facts. So contradiction can arise in various ways. A contradiction may be a violation of an integrity constraint or an exception to a general rule. In human reasoning, when a contradiction arises, consistency can be restored by rejecting or modifying any assumption which contributes to the derivation of the contradiction (Kowalski, 1979). If the goal causes a conflict it can be rejected. This is the usual mode of operation for logic programs. But there are other possibilities. Other assumptions or beliefs in the form of facts or inference rules may have to be modified.

Contradiction and its reconciliation are often the main driving force behind changes in knowledge, as in the Popperian model of science. Kowalski (1979) states that even the laws of mathematics and logic are subject to critical assessment and change.

Commitment to beliefs may vary. Some beliefs contribute to the derivation of useful consequences more frequently than others. It is more usual, therefore, to abandon beliefs that lead most frequently to contradictions. In the longer term, if the assessed utility of beliefs change it may be necessary to backtrack and reinstate a previously abandoned belief.

A simple example of the way in which a logic system might be modified is in the case of a rule which states: if a building contains a theatre then it is a public building. If a fact is presented to such a system, which cites a particular residence *x* as containing a theatre, then preference is likely to be given for the evidence that such a building exists, and the contradiction will be resolved by modification to the rule such that it states the particular instance as an exception: if a building contains a theatre then it is a public building (unless it is residence *x*).

Another manifestation of this problem can be demonstrated in the area of making decisions about sub-floor construction in a building. There might a statement that if we are to build on sand then this implies that we should use slab on ground construction. Another rule might state that if we require flexible servicing then we should use strip footings and piers. We also assume that slab on ground and strip footings and piers are mutually exclusive. We cannot have both. If we discover that we are in fact building on sand then it is quite reasonable to conclude that we should use slab on ground construction. However, if we then add that we also require flexible servicing we face a contradiction that was not evident in the original statements. The 'theorem proving approach' would be to maintain simply that we cannot have flexible servicing. In a non-monotonic system we reason about which of the statements should be negated to resolve the conflict, possibly deferring a decision until further facts are presented to the system. Several contradictory statements can therefore be held concurrently pending some resolution of the contradiction.

How *non-monotonicity* might operate in design has been summarized informally by Lansdown (1985). A designer tends to tolerate temporary 'inconsistencies' in logic. Designers do not immediately seek to remedy inconsistencies in incomplete proposals. They commonly make assumptions about the artifact which are not borne out by current reality. For example, a few sketchy lines might indicate a proposal assumed to be feasible before it is properly resolved. Consideration of one part of a proposal might be deferred while attention is concentrated on another part. The designer temporarily believes that the deferred elements are already designed.

Attempts to formalize a theory of non-monotonicity have been made by Doyle (1981a, 1981b), Moore (1985) and de Kleer (1986). Some of the ideas have been implemented as *assumption-based truth maintenance systems* (ATMS). The field does not yet enjoy the substantial theoretical base of *monotonic* logic.

Fuzziness and Uncertainty

In logic the assumption is made that an entity it is dealing with is distinct from all other entities. However, objects appear not to be as discrete as the manipulation of objects in logic statements would suggest. The boundaries between objects and concepts are generally blurred. This issue has received attention from Stiny (1982) and Sowa (1984). The problem also applies to the issue of describing categories of objects.

Logic systems, as described here, normally deal in binary truth values. A proposition is either true or false, or its value is unknown. Humans are adept at dealing with much more complex value systems. An example is the proposition that a building is *tall*. Buildings which can be described as tall form a set, but it is one in which objects appear to enjoy unequal membership. There is no particular height at which a building fails to be small or medium in height and can be classified as tall. In *fuzzy set* theory the concept of tall is expressed by a membership function representing the degree to which a building of a particular height can be considered to have that attribute. Fuzzy logic is therefore an attempt to formalize a certain aspect of human reasoning about graded set membership (Zadeh, 1965). The complexity of the calculus of fuzzy sets appears to have hindered its application so far, though it has been discussed in relation to architectural design by Oguntade and Gero (1981).

The issue of *uncertainty* is concerned with measures of belief attached to logical propositions and how these should be taken into account when inferring other propositions. Human reasoning appears to take some account of the strength of evidence in propositions and inference rules when deducing other propositions (Quinlan, 1983).

This involves formalizing a logic system in which clauses have three components. As well as the head and body of Horn clauses there is also a certainty measure, which states the degree to which the head of the clause can be expected to be true given that the conjunction of goals in the body is true. The issue of uncertainty has been discussed in the context of logic programming by Clark and McCabe (1982) and has been discussed extensively in the context of expert systems.

Problems lie in the assumptions necessary in order to apply Bayesian probability theory (Pednault et al., 1981; Konolige, 1982). One problem is the observation that humans do not appear to reason strictly in accordance with probability theory (Lansdown, 1983; Quinlan, 1982a). Workable systems have, however, been developed which demonstrate the utility of this approach in modelling expert behaviour, notably in the MYCIN (Shortliffe and Buchanan, 1975) and Prospector (Duda et al, 1976) expert systems. This approach is also discussed in the next chapter.

Efficiency and Readability

The search and backtracking strategy of the logic programming proof procedure is one that sacrifices efficiency for generality. Control structures can, however be written as logic programs. These incorporate control knowledge specific to the particular problem domain and thus enhance efficiency. The behaviour of a particular logic program can be simulated more efficiently in a procedural program, but with a loss of the benefits of the declarative language.

Certain implementations of Prolog allow functions to be defined in a procedural language and then 'called' by Prolog programs. There is some justification for this where it makes little sense to model purely procedural operations in a logic language which is encumbered by the overheads of unification and backtracking, which are unused. An example would be the drawing of a circle.

Whereas logic programs are intended to provide a declarative medium, the logic programmer is still encumbered by considerations of the procedures by which the logic program will be processed. The question also arises as to the degree to which people readily comprehend statements in logic (either of the standard or Horn clause form), and the value of logic as a means of articulating human knowledge. The shortcomings of the logic programming tool (Prolog) are well understood by those who advocate its use (Clocksin and Mellish, 1981; Kurokawa, 1982). It is regarded by some as an interim language which may eventually be replaced by something better.

Implementations of Prolog are under development which reason in a parallel rather than a serial manner (Hogger, 1982), and machines are being developed which specialize in inference and symbolic manipulation (Fuchi, 1983). Such developments will inevitably enhance the computational efficiency of logic programming.

Summary

Logic programming is a powerful tool for modelling design knowledge. This has been demonstrated in the areas of description, inference, generation and control, although rather less so in the area of display. The tool serves as a useful exploratory device.

The insights which logic programming brings to bear on design are, firstly, that design knowledge can be made explicit in a way not possible in purely procedural languages. This is due to the declarative nature of formal logic. Second, is the way in which logic programming facilitates the definition of one language in another language in order to make knowledge about control explicit. The ability of programs to 'direct themselves' and alter their own structure is a powerful device which comes near to what is understood to be an important property of intelligent behaviour. The implications of this need to be explored in the development of systems which will be of assistance to designers.

Chapter 4

Interpretive Knowledge in Design

In this chapter the role of interpretive knowledge in computer-aided design will be discussed. The argument is presented that interpretive knowledge can be employed not only to derive new facts about a design but also to *produce* new design descriptions. That is, interpretive knowledge can be employed to reason from a set of performance requirements, or intended meanings, to a description of a design that meets those performances.

In this discussion we shall pursue the linguistic metaphor described in Chapter 2. Formally, a system can be characterized as a language if it consists of a set of indivisible elements (an alphabet of symbols), a vocabulary made up of groupings of elements (a lexicon), a set of operations (or a calculus) by which these elements can be manipulated (such as set union and difference), and a grammar. The grammar defines a legal syntax. In natural language systems, the 'output' is primarily an ordered list of vocabulary elements or symbols constituting an utterance. In design the product is generally the description of an artifact.

In order to understand an artifact, such as a building, it is desirable to talk about attributes not immediately evident from its description. Implicit in a linguistic model is the notion of *semantics* (the study of meaning).

The *interpretation* of designs concerns the discovery of meaning. Interpretation is a key task of the recipient of an utterance, and in design it is the primary task of any one (or any system) that is engaged in the process of *evaluation*. We will follow the argument that the derivation of meaning can be modelled as *deductive inference*, and that knowledge about discovering meaning can be formalized as deductive inference rules. *Producing* designs through interpretive knowledge will be demonstrated in terms of plausible reasoning, although reference will also be made to goal decomposition, constraint processing and non-monotonic reasoning.

Semantics

In language, the study of meaning is concerned with the relationship between signs, symbols and the entities to which they refer. In logic it concerns the principles that determine the truth values of statements in axiomatic systems. It is worthwhile considering the role of interpretation in language and logic in order to discuss the place of semantics in design.

Semantics in Language

It is paradoxical that the meaning of the concept of *meaning* in natural language should be so imprecisely understood. Ogden and Richards (1923) in *The Meaning of Meaning* cite no fewer than sixteen favoured definitions of meaning. The role of meaning which they proposed is still widely held today and serves as a reasonable working model of the role of language. Their model is summarized here.

Words and groupings of words constitute symbols. When used appropriately they become signs which refer to ideas or objects. The hearer is involved in *interpretation* which concerns establishing references from the incoming signs. The hearer has caught the speaker's meaning when there is a correspondence between that to which the speaker makes reference and that which the signs suggest to the hearer. Factors which impinge on this transaction are those that constitute the 'sign situation': that is, those past and present experiences which determine psychological reactions to signs. Words have evocative as well as symbolic functions, but there is no *inherent* connection between words and the things to which they refer. The study of linguistics therefore steers away from a concern with the meaning of words to the study of the *interpretation* of signs.

In this discussion it is helpful to consider the *sign situation* as *knowledge*. Interpretive knowledge provides the mapping between signs and their interpretations, that is the ideas and objects to which the signs refer.

Semantics in Logic

There are two ways in which semantics may be discussed in the context of symbolic logic. One is to consider the symbols of predicate calculus and their role as signs. These signs refer to ideas and objects in the same sense as words in natural language. This is a valid but low level view of the semantic content of a logic statement, as it involves relatively simple mappings with natural language.

In the second sense, according to Kowalski (1979), any meaning that might be associated with a logical statement is relative to the collection of statements of the logic system (in terms of knowledge-based systems these statements are the facts and knowledge). The interpretation of a set of logical statements is therefore that which can be logically inferred from them. Kowalski argues that all talk of meaning can be re-expressed in terms of logical implication. Therefore, for our purposes, it is helpful to consider the meaning of a set of statements as that which is *not* stated explicitly but which can be inferred from them.

Although it is a gross simplification of what actually appears to happen, the same view can be taken of a set of linguistic 'statements'. The process by which signs, made up of complexes of symbols, are decoded to give meaning can be modelled as deductive inference. Inference provides a mechanism for interpretation.

Semantics in Design

An artifact can be described by a set of statements (or axioms) in logic, specifically as facts. A description on its own is insufficient for the interpretation of new facts. But, when combined with other statements, generally regarded as constituting interpretive design knowledge, the derivation of meanings is possible. (*Interpretive design knowledge* is used here in roughly the same sense as the term *theoretical context* proposed by Stiny and March [1981]: that which determines the fit between designs and environments and embraces knowledge such as principles of engineering science and production technology.) From the paradigm of language, the interpretation of a design is similar to the problem of interpreting an utterance in natural language. The mapping is provided by interpretive knowledge.

Both understandings (from linguistics and logic) lead to the view that design descriptions and theoretical knowledge combine to provide a logical system which enables the derivation of meaning. Specifically, facts about the design and interpretive knowledge modelled as *rules of deductive inference* constitute a system which facilitates the derivation of meaning.

An artifact possesses attributes other than those sets of symbols which constitute its description. These attributes can be termed *derived*, or *implicit* attributes, and a set of such attributes constitutes the semantic content of the description. In building design these attributes are often to do with *performance*. Typically, in a computer-aided design system the building will be described in terms of geometry and materials. Attributes, such as how many people can occupy the building, whether the building conforms to the building regulations and how much energy it will consume, are generally regarded as performances that must be derived, perhaps by programs, logical rules or some other mechanism of interpretation.

Logic programming provides the advantage that all the knowledge which contributes to the interpretation of a design is made explicit, and the mechanisms that drive the automated inference do so independently of the considerations of the particular interpretation problem. It is therefore theoretically possible to devise logic programs that can be understood relatively easily by humans. (In a procedural program it is necessary to appreciate the patterns of behaviour the program invokes inside the computer in order to understand it.)

There are certain implications of this view of design interpretation that it is helpful to clarify before proceeding.

(i) Explicit Description Hierarchies

A fact derived from a set of logic statements often provides an opportunity for the derivation of further facts. This suggests that there are *hierarchies* of description, in that certain descriptions can be deduced from others. This hierarchy can be derived through the application of interpretive knowledge or it can be represented explicitly.

There are many ways in which description hierarchies can be manifest explicitly in computer-aided design systems. The description of the office in the previous chapter shown in Figure 3.4 is an example of the explicit representation of a description hierarchy. The room is described in terms of the elements of which it is composed, elements are described in terms of line segments, and line segments are described in terms of points. There are other useful systems of description. We can exploit the relationship between *generic* objects and *instances* of objects. So Office(1) is an instance of an office, which is a type of room, and a room is a type of spatial object. In the frames formalism (Minsky, 1975) we can exploit the idea of inheritance between generic objects and instances of objects to describe designs. Examples of knowledge-based design systems that make extensive use of frames include PRIDE (Mittal et al, 1986), a system for the design of paper transport mechanisms in photocopiers, and OPTIMA, a system for the design of structural frames (Balachandran, 1988). The different methods of representing designs and design knowledge is an interesting and valuable area of study.

A complete survey of these methods is beyond the scope of this book. In talking about interpretation in design we are primarily interested in *implicit* description hierarchies.

(ii) Implicit Description Hierarchies

We can describe designs in terms of facts from which other facts about the design can be derived, given the appropriate interpretive knowledge. The facts from which all others can be derived may be termed basic facts, primitive facts or *canonical descriptions* (Bobrow and Collins, 1975). So we may describe a design geometrically in terms of points and lines. This constitutes the canonical description from which spatial attributes can be inferred, such as areas and volumes, and spatial relationships can be inferred, such as adjacencies. If there is information about materials then it is possible to derive other properties such as performances.

It is important to note that commerce through this hierarchy of description essentially occurs in one direction. It is possible to derive spatial relationships from geometry (in terms of the spatial locations of points and lines), but it is not generally possible to infer geometry from spatial relationships. For example, there are many geometries by which two rooms can be adjacent.

(iii) Redundancy in Descriptions

A design description may contain canonical information about a design and also facts that can be derived from that information. It is reasonable that a design description contain redundant information. As new information is derived it may be added to the design description. So a design description may contain information about the geometry of objects and it may also contain information about spatial relationships and performances. If the description is undergoing change, as in a computer-aided design and drafting system, or if the description is being produced through some generative process, then redundancy carries with it the problem of maintaining consistency.

(iv) Semantic Content

In the view presented in this chapter there are no attributes of a design that are *inherently* semantic. The semantic content of a design description is simply that which is *not* represented explicitly, but which can be inferred from the description and interpretive knowledge. Whereas there are hierarchies of description, and certain facts can be derived from other facts, it is confusing to regard certain attributes, such as relationships and performances, as semantic. If these attributes are *explicit* then they are part of the design description. If they are *implicit* then they represent semantic content.

(v) The Meaning of Artifacts

In this discussion we have been dealing essentially with descriptions of designs in computer systems, and the interpretation of these descriptions. In computer-aided design we are concerned with the production and interpretation of statements about artifacts. In this context the linguistic metaphor can be defended quite readily. We are simply dealing with strings of *words* about designs. Linguistics is concerned with the syntax of such strings and with their interpretation.

However, the idea of an *artifact* as *text* or *utterance* presents a more distant analogy with language. Here we are not dealing with descriptions of a design but with the actual artifact itself. In the case of a building design certain elements (such as windows, doors and columns) constitute a vocabulary, and the design is a configuration of vocabulary elements. This is analogous to the way in which configurations of words constitute sentences in natural language. In this use of the linguistic metaphor the issue of what constitutes an interpretation is less clear. Whereas there are intuitive links between these two uses of the linguistic metaphor we will not pursue the matter here. In this book we are concerned simply with the interpretation of descriptions of artifacts, not with the 'meanings' of the artifacts themselves.

(vi) Complexity in Interpretation

Throughout this book we will make the assumption that interpretation can be handled readily by means of deductive inference. There is very little utility in applying this view to natural language in general. Interpretation has to contend with ambiguity. Attempting to understand a sentence may involve choosing between rival hypotheses. Interpretation is also thought to involve parsing, the domain of generative knowledge. In this chapter we have chosen to view interpretation as a relatively simple process divorced from the knowledge by which designs are produced. This is a very simple model, but one which can be demonstrated to have considerable utility in design.

With these assumptions in mind we are now in a position to investigate the application of design interpretation. This will be demonstrated with an example.

Interpretive Systems

The interpretation of designs is achieved by means of a type of knowledge, and the process of interpretation can be modelled as *deductive inference.* This knowledge can therefore be regarded as inferential knowledge. It can be embedded within procedural programs or expressed in a form that makes the mappings between description and interpretation explicit. A useful and intuitively appealing method of representing interpretive knowledge is as rules of the form:

if $a_1, ..., a_n$ **then** $b_1, ..., b_n$.

This is saying that if a design possesses attributes

$a_1, ..., a_n$, (the antecedents)

then infer that attributes

$b_1, ..., b_n$ (the consequents)

are also true. The if-then construct is the same as the *implies* of standard logic. It can therefore be reformulated as a set of Horn clauses employing the *if* connective. The knowledge by which a design is interpreted may consist of many such rules.

Computer systems can be created which facilitate the representation of inferential knowledge in this form and make it amenable to automation. Automated inference systems are often called *expert systems* as their behaviour and performance represent attempts to mimic that of the reasoning expert. Because of the shortcomings of formal logic as a means of modelling human intelligence, the reasoning systems developed often incorporate 'enhanced logics' notably the incorporation of 'uncertain inference'. Introductions to this field are provided by Feigenbaum (1979), Bramer (1979), Quinlan (1980), Michie (1982), Buchanan (1982), Hayes-Roth et al (1983), Nau (1983), Hayes-Roth (1984), and Sriram (1985).

Workable systems can be devised which operate on the basis of formal reasoning, however. This is particularly so in the case of interpreting the properties and performances of buildings where the theory by which interpretations can be made is well understood. This is the case in the current approach of evaluating the compliance of buildings with building codes and regulations. The clauses of the building code (assuming they are consistent) and the description of the building can be modelled as a logical system, the meanings of which are those collections of statements which confirm the building's compliance.

A Building Code Example

Figure 4.1 shows an example of a clause from a provisional code known as the *Model Cluster Code* (Cluster Titles Committee, 1979) which is intended for evaluating certain types of residential development but also leaves some scope for the initiative of the designer. It tends therefore to be orientated towards performance rather than prescription, and offers explanations rather than merely constraints. It can be seen that such a clause lends itself to the *if-then* construct of the inference rule described above:

if sufficient winter sunshine is received in dwelling **and**

there is adequate summer shading to dwelling, **and**
no structure unduly restricts sunlight to private open space
then there is compliance with general requirements regarding sunlight.

Statements such as this can be represented in an *inference network* where the consequents of one rule may become the antecedents of another. The components of the rule can generally be referred to as *propositions*. The inference network for a section of the code is given in Figure 4.2.

The meanings of the logic system of which these statements are a part are therefore those statements which can be inferred from such a system. The hierarchical nature of the system is immediately apparent from the diagram. As they are proved, the propositions in the lower part of the network become statements by which higher levels of description can be inferred.

For any system the issue arises as to how selective the process of interpretation should be. For a realistic set of inference rules the number of facts that can be derived is likely to be very large. There will therefore be

---

3.7.2 SUNLIGHT

PRINCIPAL OBJECTIVES

Buildings should be sited to ensure that unobstructed sunlight is received on a reasonable portion of the allotment, or the face of the building, throughout the year.

GENERAL REQUIREMENTS TO SATISFY OBJECTIVES

The proposed layout of lots and the location and form of dwelling units should be such that:

- sufficient winter sunshine is received in each dwelling;
- there is adequate shading to protect the dwelling from excessive summer sun, particularly from north-west to west;
- no structure unduly restricts sunshine available to an adjoining dwelling.

Figure 4.1. A section of the *Model Cluster Code* (1979) which pertains to sunlight requirements.

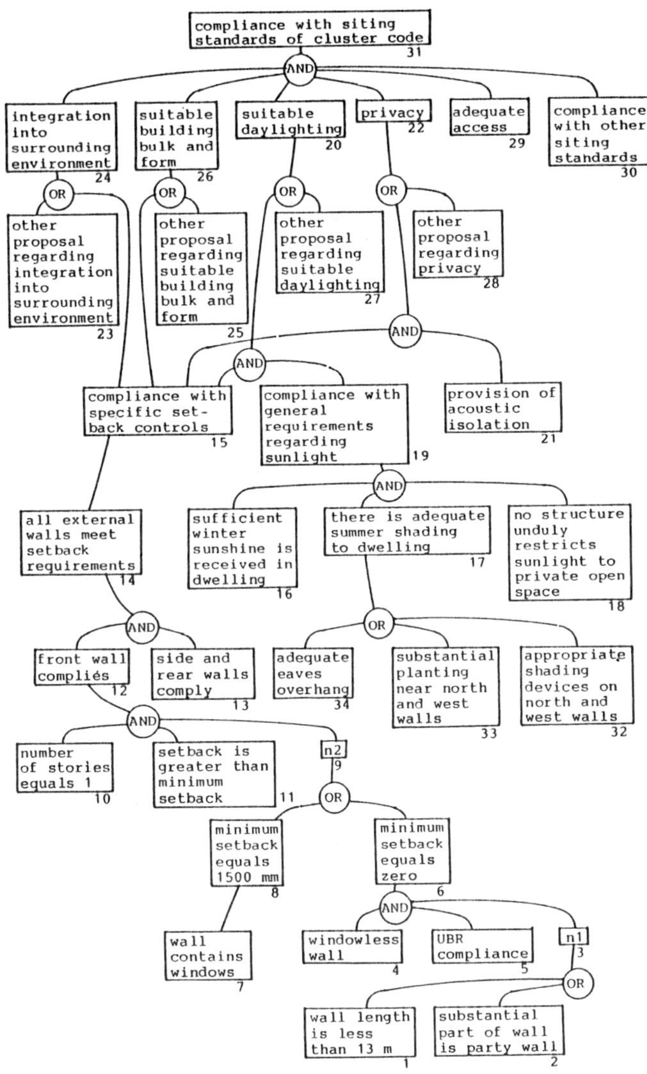

Figure 4.2. Rules from part of the *Model Cluster Code* represented as an inference network.

more work involved in asking of a design: 'What attributes can be inferred from its syntactic description?'; than asking: 'Does the design have this particular set of characteristics?'. The former suggests a data-driven approach. From a design description an attempt is made to infer as much as the rules will allow. The latter is a goal-directed approach which begins with the attributes constituting an interpretation and tries to discover if the artifact possesses those attributes. In this example a goal-directed approach has been adopted.

The partial logic system is of value even when there are no statements constituting a building description. The 'leaf nodes' of the tree of Figure 4.2 correspond to requests for facts about the building, and so can be handled interactively by means of prompts as described in the next section. These nodes can also be regarded as entry points to other logical subsystems which interpret computer databases, or other building code systems, as at node 5. When incorporated into a general purpose inference system a dialogue such as that illustrated in Figure 4.3 is produced. The derived facts constitute the meaning, or interpretation, of the total system.

Such systems are therefore generally intended to be consultative, and ideal systems would communicate by means of natural language (Rich, 1984). Communication also concerns the issue of deciding at which level of description the consultation should take place. If the system is to communicate with a novice, who knows little of the domain of expertise represented by the system, then there may be justification in making the leaf nodes the propositions at which questions are asked.

For experts, questions about propositions higher up in the network may obviate unnecessary search. A sample 'session' with the system is presented in Figure 4.4 where the response 'how' provides an instruction to the inference system that it is to proceed to a lower level of inquiry. A simple explanation facility is also provided by the use of 'why' which retraces the lines of reasoning so far employed in order to offer an explanation of the reasons for a particular question being asked. Systems have been implemented which explore various approaches to these and other communication issues (Hayes-Roth et al, 1983).

This example serves as a simple demonstration of interpretation in a design system. (Clearly, a working system would need to make greater use of variables than demonstrated here.) Interpretation can be seen as a precursor to evaluation in design. The performance of a particular design can be compared with some ideal performance and the design deemed to be satisfactory or unsatisfactory in some way.

Abductive Reasoning Systems

In interpretation we begin with a description of a design and attempt to infer properties of the design other than those explicitly stated. As this knowledge can be obtained readily it is tantalizing to speculate on whether the knowledge for producing interpretations of design descriptions can be used for producing design descriptions from performances. Can interpretive knowledge be employed to produce designs? In Chapter 2 we referred to this process as *abduction*.

As stated above, a rule of deductive inference can be of the form: **if** A **then**

```
>> prove: compliance with siting standards of cluster code.

Enter value of number_of_storeys ... 1.
wall contains windows? (yes or no) ... no.
windowless wall (yes or no) ... yes.
Enter value of wall_length ... 9.
ubr compliance? (yes or no) ... yes.
Enter value of setback ... 1200.
side and rear walls comply? (yes or no) ... yes.
sufficient winter sunshine is received in dwelling? (yes or no) ... yes.
adequate eaves overhang? (yes or no) ... no.
substantial planting near north and west walls? (yes or no) ... yes.
no structure unduly restricts sunlight to private open spaces? (yes or no) ... yes.
provision of acoustic isolation? (yes or no) ... yes.
adequate access? (yes or no) ... yes.
compliance with other siting standards? (yes or no) ... yes.
compliance with siting standards of cluster code
*TRUE*

>> status facts.

The following facts are true ...

    compliance with siting standards of cluster code
    compliance with other siting standards
    adequate access
    privacy
    provision of acoustic isolation
    suitable daylighting
    compliance with general requirements regarding sunlight
    no structure unduly restricts sunlight to private open space
    there is adequate summer shading to dwelling
    substantial planting near north and west walls
    sufficient winter sunshine is received in dwelling
    suitable building bulk and form
    integration into surrounding environment
    compliance with specific setback controls
    all external walls meet setback requirements
    side and rear walls comply
    front wall complies
    setback > min_setback
    min_setback equals 0
    ubr compliance
    wall_length < 13
    windowless wall
    number_of_storeys = 1

The following facts are not true ...

    adequate eaves overhang
    wall contains windows

>> status values.

The following assignments have been made ...
    setback is 1200
    min_setback is 0
    wall_length is 9
    number_of_storeys is 1
```

Figure 4.3. A 'dialogue' with an inference system.

```
>> prove: compliance with general requirements regarding sunlight.

sufficient winter sunshine is received in dwelling? (yes, no, how or why) ... yes.
there is adequate summer shading to dwelling? (yes, no, how or why) ... why.

    ie. why do you want to know about -
        there is adequate summer shading to dwelling?

BECAUSE

compliance with general requirements regarding sunlight - is proved by ...

    sufficient winter sunshine is received in dwelling
    there is adequate summer shading to dwelling
    no structure unduly restricts sunlight to private open space

there is adequate summer shading to dwelling? (yes, no, how or why) ... how.

    ie. How do I prove -
        there is adequate summer shading to dwelling?

there is adequate summer shading to dwelling - is proved by ...
    adequate eaves overhang
    OR
    substantial planting near north and west walls
    OR
    appropriate shading devices on north and west walls

adequate eaves overhang (yes, no, how or why)? ... yes.

there is adequate summer shading to dwelling
*TRUE*

no structure unduly restricts sunlight to private open space? (yes, no, how or why) ...
no.

compliance with general requirements regarding sunlight
not true
```

Figure 4.4. A 'dialogue' with an inference system incorporating an explanation facility.

B. If A is known to be true then, according to the rule of *modus ponens*, B can be inferred true. However, the converse *cannot* be said with any certainty: given B infer A. Abductive inference is concerned with how these 'reverse' inferences can be made (Charniak and McDermott, 1985).

Abduction is often discussed in terms of goal decomposition. The desired performance constitutes a goal, and there are various subgoals that need to be satisfied in order for that goal to be met. There are further subgoals beneath these subgoals. So we may have the goal that a designed object, such as a table, is to be suitable as a work bench. This goal can be broken down into the subgoals that it must be stable, support a heavy load, and be portable. These subgoals can be broken down further. Eventually, certain subgoals resemble decisions about the design, that is, they resemble design descriptions. Goal decomposition was explored by Alexander (1964).

In essence this approach makes use of interpretive rules. The rule:

if stable, supports a heavy load and portable
then suitable as a work bench

has effectively been 'reversed' to *prescribe* the attributes of a workbench. There are several important qualifications to be made to this use of interpretive knowledge.

At some level goal decomposition generally involves the consideration of disjunctions of subgoals—the consideration of alternatives. For example, there may be several alternative subgoals that satisfy the requirements for withstanding heavy loads, and several subgoals that achieve portability. Some of these alternative subgoals may be incompatible, such as a subgoal that the table be made of masonry and a subgoal that it is able to be carried by two people. Subgoals interact with each other. So the subgoal of supporting a heavy load will affect the material from which the bench is made and this should *not* be considered independently of the portability of the table.

A further issue is that the 'reversal' of interpretive knowledge assumes that we are dealing with a *closed world*, that is, that the subgoals are the only ways in which the goal can be satisfied. The rule given above does not state that the *only* requirements of a work bench are that it is stable, supports a heavy load and is portable. However, when we use this knowledge to *produce* a design description we effectively assume that this is the only way that it can be accomplished. In the case of building regulations this is a reasonable assumption, but in other applications this assumption tends to limit design possibilities.

A further problem is that there are typically many ways that a design can satisfy a particular goal. This can be readily demonstrated with a simple rule pertaining to the geometry of two rooms A and B positioned according to an x-y coordinate system:

if the y value of the south face of A is greater than the y value of the north face of B
then room A is north of room B.

Whereas a single interpretation can be derived from a geometrical description of A and B, we can see quite readily that reversing the process, knowing that A is north of B, produces an infinite number of geometrical configurations of A and B. With some reflection it will be apparent that this is a commonly occurring property of interpretive rules used abductively.

Bearing in mind these limitations there is still considerable value in reasoning with interpretive knowledge to produce design descriptions. There are several different approaches to abductive reasoning. The simplest is to formulate our knowledge so that there is a direct mapping between performances and descriptions, in other words the design task is reduced to the *interpretation of a design specification.* So we may say that if the table is to be portable then adopt frame type X. The selection of the materials that ensures that it is able to withstand heavy loads is considered as an independent subproblem within the constraints of the frame type already selected. The knowledge is formulated so that there are no conflicts between subgoals and between decisions—that is, the problem is *decomposable.* This approach has been adopted in the RETWALL expert system for designing earth retaining walls (Hutchinson, 1985; Rosenman et al, 1987) (Figure 4.5).

A further approach is to reason with performance requirements as constraints. The process is essentially one of *constraint propagation.* If we take the simple site layout example of the previous chapter (Figure 3.9) we see that there are various constraints that the design must satisfy: in terms of the orientation of the three structures relative to one another. The approach discussed in Chapter 3 was to generate different configurations of structures and then evaluate them for compliance with the constraints. In *constraint propagation* we selectively combine constraints to produce new constraints and defer a decision about the location of the structures until the last possible

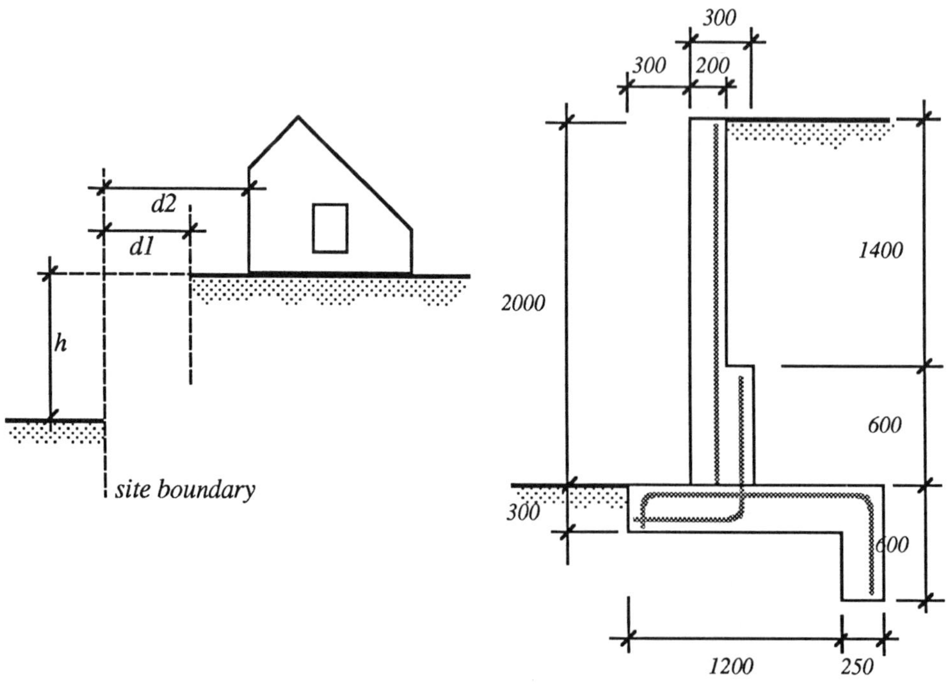

Figure 4.5. RETWALL (Hutchinson, 1986) is an experimental expert system that reasons about site requirements to produce a detailed description of an appropriate retaining wall.

moment. In the example of the work bench given above we might reason about the various subgoals and determine that being able to support a heavy load and being portable may produce a new constraint that the design cannot be of masonry. Constraint propagation is discussed by Stefik (1981a) in the context of planning chemical experiments. This approach requires that knowledge about combining constraints is made explicit.

A further approach to abduction is to make use of assumption-based reasoning (reasoning non-monotonically). This is demonstrated by Dietterich and Ullman (1987). Their approach is to reason from performances to design descriptions and to keep track of which facts are produced by which rules. This assists in reasoning about conflicts as they occur during the design process.

One of the most straightforward approaches to abduction is to reason using plausible inference. This is effective where the design description consists of a small number of independent decisions, and it is possible to attach certainty factors to rules mapping performances to design descriptions. This will be described in the following section.

A Sub-Floor Design Example

Here we consider how degrees of certainty can be incorporated into the abductive reasoning process. Each abductive inference rule has a *certainty factor* associated with it. It is possible to employ this type of reasoning to model aspects of human reasoning (notably diagnosis) and it can be applied to certain types of design problems. This will be demonstrated with a simple system implemented in Prolog.

The rules of the system incorporate parameters which quantify the level of certainty, on a scale of 0 to 1, which can be attached to the antecedent of the abductive rule leading to its consequent. Propositions relate to both the conditions of a building site and requirements of the design specifications. There are two propositions which constitute competing hypotheses: ‘slab on ground’ and ‘strip footings and piers’ (Figure 4.6). The selection of either of these sub-floor structures constitutes a simple design decision (a description of the design). The abductive rules are as follows:

if non-cohesive soil **then** slab on ground (0.8);
if flat site **then** slab on ground (0.6);
if impervious floor finish required **then** slab on ground (0.4);
if floor heating required **then** slab on ground (0.9);
if undulating site **then** strip footings and piers (0.7);
if flexible servicing required **then** strip footings and piers (0.8);

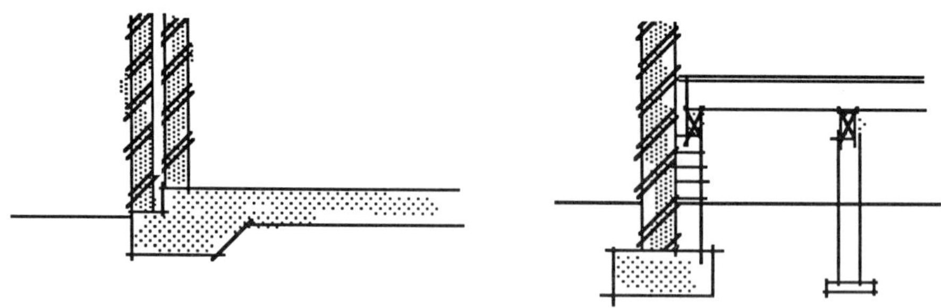

Figure 4.6. Two types of domestic subfloor construction: concrete slab on ground and strip footings and piers.

if timber floor finish required **then** strip footings and piers (0.9);
if cohesive soil **then** strip footings and piers (0.8).

The network resulting from these rules is illustrated in Figure 4.7. Theories of evidential reasoning can be incorporated to model how each proposition contributes to the plausibility of each hypothesis. Measures of belief can also be assigned to the evidential propositions themselves. The simple formula for deriving plausibility measures for the hypotheses is based on that for calculating the increased probability of an event given another event:

$$MB_3 = MB_1 + MB_2(1 - MB_1).$$

where MB_3 is the new measure of belief in a proposition (hypothesis) with an initial value of MB_1, which results after new evidence which has a belief measure of MB_2 is taken into account.

The contribution of each item of new evidence can be added incrementally provided the contributing propositions are independent of one another. For example, it is *not* possible to employ this formula to increase the measure of belief in the first hypothesis by adding evidence that the soil contains sand, as this is a common feature of non-cohesive soil which is already a contributing proposition.

A dialogue with a simple Prolog-based evidential reasoning system is given in Figure 4.8. The design decision is made on the basis of the strength of the competing 'scores'.

This example is based on the formula employed in the MYCIN medical diagnosis system (Shortliffe and Buchanan, 1975; Buchanan and Shortliffe,

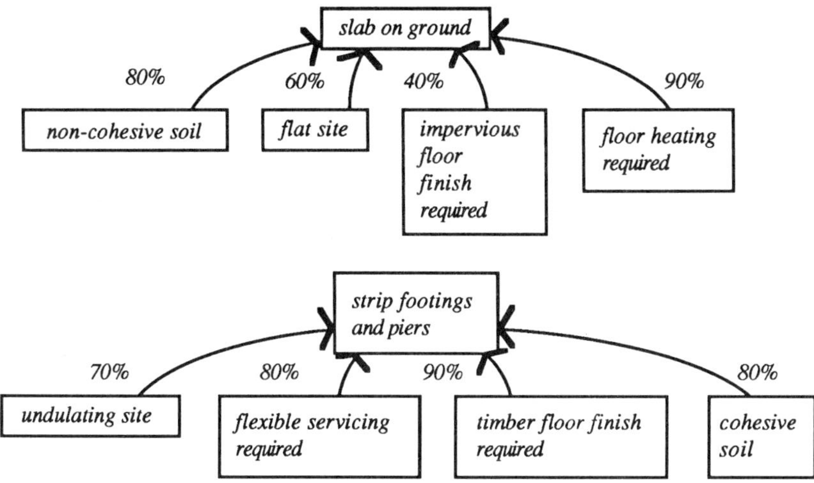

Figure 4.7. Abductive inference network showing the contribution of various evidential propositions (design requirements) to two competing hypotheses (design decisions) about subfloor construction.

1984). The propositions within MYCIN form extensive networks. So considerable complexity is introduced by the necessity to propagate the effects of belief measures through a network of related propositions. MYCIN also incorporates measures of *disbelief*. So it is possible to express the extent to which it is believed that certain evidence points to a hypothesis being untrue.

There are several other approaches to the propagation of plausibility through inference networks, notably in the Prospector system which is intended for computing the likelihood of discovering minerals at particular geological sites (Duda et al, 1976; Gaschnig, 1982). It takes the Bayesian notion of *prior probabilities* into account. The applicability of this and other approaches to making decisions in connection with buildings have been discussed in outline by Lansdown (1982), and a critical review of some of the underlying assumptions of inference systems is provided by Quinlan (1982a, 1983). An example of an alternative approach to uncertain inference is provided by Garvey et al (1981).

Programs exist which incorporate automatic inference mechanisms, to which any appropriate knowledge can be added to create customized inference systems. These are summarized by Hayes-Roth (1984) and their applicability to the construction industry has been reviewed by Allwood and Stewart (1984).

Abductive reasoning, of the type suggested by the systems described above, is relatively simple where a small number of choices are to be made and where

```
?- begin.

Enter percentage weighting for the following ...

impervious floor finish required? ... 20.
(tally for slab on ground - 8%)
(tally for strip footings and piers - 0%)

flexible floor servicing required? ...  50.
(tally for slab on ground - 8%)
(tally for strip footings and piers - 40%)

flat site? ... 90.
(tally for slab on ground - 58%)
(tally for strip footings and piers - 40%)

undulating site? ... 30.
(tally for slab on ground - 58%)
(tally for strip footings and piers - 53%)

timber floor finish required? ...  20.
(tally for slab on ground - 58%)
(tally for strip footings and piers - 62%)

non-cohesive soil? ... 95.
(tally for slab on ground - 90%)
(tally for strip footings and piers - 62%)

cohesive soil? ...  0.
(tally for slab on ground - 90%)
(tally for strip footings and piers - 62%)

floor heating required? ... 80.
(tally for slab on ground - 98%)
(tally for strip footings and piers - 62%)
```

Figure 4.8. Interaction with an evidential reasoning system.

the ranges of options are small. When there are many decisions (which is generally the case) then the interactions between decisions can cause conflicts. Such conflicts generally require the incorporation of further, specialized knowledge concerning its resolution.

Summary

The following argument is a summary of the way in which meaning has been considered when applied to the design of artifacts.

1. The meaning of a sign comprising a string of symbols in natural language is that set of objects or ideas to which it refers.
2. The meaning of a logic system is that set of new statements which can be

derived from it.

3. The relevant linguistic signs plus the knowledge by which they are interpreted can be modelled as a logic system.
4. In design, too, *interpretation* can be modelled as the derivation of new statements in a logic system where the design is represented as a set of facts and the interpretive knowledge is represented as inference rules in logic.
5. Once derived, new statements can lead to the derivation of further statements.
6. There are therefore hierarchies of description in that certain descriptions must be deduced before others, and certain descriptions imply others.

The utility of automated inference systems which interpret descriptions of artifacts has been demonstrated with simple examples. The question arises as to whether design specifications can be similarly interpreted to produce designs. This appears to be the case where simple, non-conflicting design decisions are to be made, and can be modelled as reasoning under uncertainty.

It is contended in this book that the generation of designs requires further knowledge than that which facilitates interpretation. In language part of that knowledge is afforded by a grammar. The study of grammars of design is therefore the next step in understanding the production of design descriptions which conform to an intended interpretation.

Chapter 5

Grammar Systems

This chapter presents a formal discussion of grammars. We consider some of the properties of grammars which will prove valuable in relation to design knowledge. Design applications will be discussed in Chapter 6.

Certain knowledge about design can be formulated as rules of deductive inference. Such rules enable descriptions of artifacts to be interpreted in order to derive their meanings. We have also discussed how this knowledge can be applied to sets of facts representing design specifications in order to derive design descriptions: that is, to *produce* designs. Interpretive knowledge alone appears insufficient as a means of producing designs. Knowledge for producing designs can also be modelled with production systems, which are also a powerful way of representing grammars. In this sense it is helpful to talk of *grammars of design.*

In this chapter grammars as rule sets in production systems are discussed. Production systems can be formulated to display certain characteristics which are important in facilitating design generation. The argument will be presented that a crucial component of a production system is the *control.* Various control devices can be formulated which are themselves modelled on production systems. This introduces the possibility of grammars (*meta-grammars*) which embody rules about the manipulation of grammars.

Grammars

The principles by which vocabulary elements can be put together at the syntactic level to form artifacts constitute a grammar. Inherent in a grammar is a set of mappings between vocabulary elements such that certain groupings of elements can be transformed into other groupings.

The formulation of phrase structure grammars by Chomsky (1957) is based on transformation rules which make explicit the mappings between vocabulary elements. (In Chomskyan linguistics the term 'transformation rule' is often employed to describe a particular type of transformation not considered a part of the grammar. Here it will be used in the general sense as a rule which can be employed to change the state of something.) Like the rules of deductive inference described above, each grammar rule has an antecedent part and a consequent part (or a 'left hand side' and a 'right hand side'). If the vocabulary elements in the antecedent part of the rule are present then they are replaced by the vocabulary elements in the consequent part of the rule.

Rules of grammar in natural language can be employed to *parse* sentences, that is, decompose them into specialized vocabulary elements (called 'syntactic categories' or 'non-terminal elements'), to see whether the sentences conform to the rules of the language.

In natural language the non-terminal symbols can be described as: sentence (*S*), noun phrase (*NP*), verb phrase (*VP*), verb (*V*), noun (*N*), and determiner (*DET*); and the terminals are words in the language. Examples of transformation rules are:

S	→	*NP VP*
VP	→	*V NP*
NP	→	*DET N*
V	→	*eats*
N	→	*boy*
N	→	*apple*
DET	→	*the*

With these transformation rules it is possible to parse a sentence such as: 'the boy eats the apple'. This is shown by the following parse tree which demonstrates that the string of words conforms to the syntax of the language:

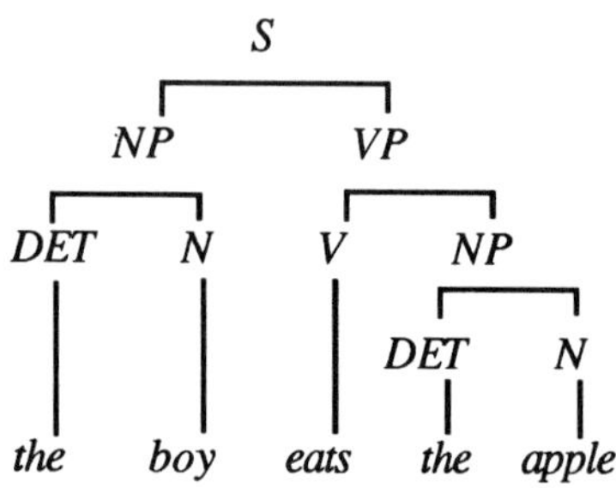

Symbols are replaced by other symbols according to the rules of the grammar. If this process produces the final symbol *S* then the parse has been successful. From this diagram it can be seen that the rules can also be employed to generate sentences. Starting with the symbol S, rules can be applied to produce syntactically correct word sequences.

In the area of automated text generation and natural language understanding, techniques based on approaches other than the use of phrase structure grammars are actively pursued. These are summarized by Winograd (1983). Even though Chomskyan phrase structure grammars are no longer favoured as a relevant paradigm for natural language they assist in understanding computer languages, and they provide a useful model for design generation.

A major part of the linguistic model of design is an attempt to describe design processes in terms of grammars. The grammar rules are applied to bring about changes from some initial representation of a design (the 'initial state'). Intermediate stages in the process may exhibit characteristics which bear no resemblance to the end state. The transformation rules of a grammar operate in a different manner to deductive inference rules. Whereas the successive application of deductive rules builds up a more comprehensive description of the design, under a grammar a design tends to undergo developmental or evolutionary changes.

Because linguistic grammars can be modelled as production systems, it is necessary to consider the formalism of production systems in detail.

Production Systems

The production system formalism is a way of organizing a computational system into particular functional components. The theory is attributed to the work of Post (1943). Davis and King (1977) and Gips and Stiny (1980) provide summaries of the underlying structure common to most production system formalisms. These can be described in various ways, but generally as consisting of three basic components:

1. the domain on which the system is to work
2. production rules for transforming the domain from one state into another (also referred to as transformation rules)
3. a control strategy

The *domain* of operation is that which undergoes transition as a series of states. This domain can also be described as a 'global database'. The global database is generally represented with some uniform structure, such as an ordered list, an array, a network or a set. The elements which make up the global database are literals of some kind. In a language system these are generally the elements of the vocabulary or the syntactic categories. In a logic programming environment these could be facts. The task of a production system is to transform the global database from some initial state to an end state, and there may be any number of intermediate steps along the way.

The application of the *production rules* transforms one state into another. In a language system these rules constitute the grammar. The set of all possible states generated by a set of production rules is termed a *space of states*. This can be represented as a connected graph where nodes are states and directed arcs are the rules which produce them.

Control is concerned with four issues: the first three are to do with implementing rules; the third concerns selecting rules. The implementation of rules concerns matching and execution (or *firing*). A matching mechanism may search for a one-to-one mapping between literals in the conditions part of a production rule and the global database. However, more complicated mechanisms may be involved, for example, where the conditions in the production rule must be *inferred* from the global database. In this case the attributes to which the production rule is to respond are not represented explicitly in the form of literals. This would suggest the need for a body of interpretive knowledge by which these mappings (deductions) could be made.

Control is also concerned with the mechanism by which production rules are executed. In a production system it is expected that production rules are represented in a uniform way and that there is a mechanism appropriate to the execution of all rules. If there is a match between the conditions part of the production rule and the current state then those matching elements are deleted from the global database and those in the consequent part of the rule substituted.

The consequent part of the rule may also consist of a set of actions performing complex operations on the global database. This would require a set of procedures for carrying out actions, in the same way that the conditions may require a special body of knowledge for matching. There may, of course, be more than one type of production rule. That is, there may be classes of productions in the system with each class requiring different matching and execution mechanisms.

The third control issue is concerned with the use of variables. The left side of a production rule may contain variables. So there may be several ways in which a rule can match the global database. The search for possible instantiations of those variables is a control issue.

The fourth control issue concerns the selection of rules and appropriate instantiations. Given any state of the global database there will be several rules applicable for transforming that state, and several sets of instantiations that can be made to variables in the rule. Typically, there will be many choices, and hence many paths through the space of states, and it will be necessary to adopt some strategy for choosing which rules and which instantiations to execute in order to achieve an end state. There are different ways in which a general control regime can operate in order to do this. It can be designed to: produce an arbitrary end state; exhaustively produce all possible end states; or produce an end state (or states) with particular attributes (that is, it can be goal directed).

An example of the first type of control mechanism is one that always selects the first rule applicable from an ordered list of rules. This is equivalent to tracing down the left hand path of a state space graph in a 'depth-first' manner until an end state is reached, at which point the process terminates. A controller for generating all end states may adopt an exhaustive search and backtrack strategy. This is where paths are explored until an end state is achieved. The controller then backtracks to the last state where there was a choice of rules (or instantiations), selects another rule (or set of instantiations) and then proceeds to find another end state. This continues until all possible states have been encountered. Goal directed control generally involves the evaluation of states in some way. It, too, may involve exhaustive search and backtracking but states are evaluated against some set of criteria, and this directs the search. The similarity between these various control regimes and those of logic programming suggest that production systems can be readily modelled in logic.

General search strategies are impractical in production systems which are intended to model problem solving or design in realistic domains. In typical design formulations the number of states to be negotiated is too large to be computationally feasible. The nature of a production system controller therefore assumes great significance in obviating the problem of combinatorial explosion.

This representation of production systems forms the basis of many automated problem solving methods (Newell and Simon, 1972, Nilsson, 1982). Various proof procedures in formal logic can be modelled as production systems. In Robinson's (1965) resolution method the logical statements are the global database and the general rules of inference and the resolution rule (as outlined in Chapter 3) are the production rules.

Conversely, production systems can be devised as logic programs. As described in Chapter 3, production rules can be represented as facts. Facts in the global database can be tagged according to the states in which they are true, and a control structure which manipulates facts according to the production rules can be written as logical rules. Alternatively, the control rules can assert and retract fact in the global database. There is therefore an interesting symmetry to be exploited in the relationship between logic programming and production systems.

Characteristics of Grammars

A production system begins with a global database in some initial state. This is then operated upon by the production rules according to a control regime.

Terminal states are those in which no rules are applicable. Production systems display different characteristics depending on the characteristics of: their rule sets; their starting conditions (the initial state); and their control regime.

There are two categories of characteristics that are important in design systems. The first can be observed by inspecting the structure of individual rules, and relates to their dependence on context. The second concerns the behavioural characteristics of sets of rules and their initial state, and has a bearing on the ease with which they can be controlled.

Context Sensitive Grammars

Grammars which cause designs to pass through a series of states are generally of the sort that are dependent on context. A rule is fired if certain facts are present in the current state of the design. Some of these facts are changed. Those facts which are contextual do not undergo transformation under that rule. So, whether or not a fact is changed may be dependent on the presence of other facts. Production systems which involve some complexity are generally of this type.

Chomsky (1963) defines a hierarchy of language classes according to the form of the grammar rules. The four types of grammars are numbered 0 to 3, proceeding from the most general class to the most restrictive. The order also indicates an increase in computational difficulty.

A *type 3 grammar* (regular grammar) is the most restrictive form of grammar. Rules must take the form:

$X \rightarrow aY$ or

$X \rightarrow a$,

where X and Y are non-terminal symbols, and a is a single terminal. Non-terminals are taken one at a time by such rules and transformed into another non-terminal plus a terminal, or a non-terminal on its own. No account is taken of the context of the symbol on the left side of the rule.

A *type 2 grammar* is also one in which the context is ignored. The only restriction of the rules is that the left side must be a single non-terminal:

$X \rightarrow aY$,

$X \rightarrow Y$ or

$X \rightarrow a$,

where Y and a are arbitrary sets of non-terminal and terminal symbols respectively.

A *type 1 grammar* can take the context of a symbol into consideration. It is of the general form:

$uXv \rightarrow uYv$,

where X is a single non-terminal symbol; u and v are arbitrary strings of symbols and Y is a string of symbols comprised of either terminals or non-terminals. This can be interpreted as: X may be transformed to Y in the context of u and v. The context is unchanged. These grammars are also called *context sensitive* grammars.

A *type 0 grammar* is the most general form. Any string of symbols is transformed into any other string:

$X \rightarrow Y.$

These grammar types assist in categorizing different languages. Computer programming languages, for example, are generally of type 2. The type of grammar has a bearing on the ease with which parsing procedures can be conducted. It is generally recognized that natural language grammars are context sensitive, though the example above assumes a type 2 grammar for ease of demonstrating the parsing mechanism.

In design the most general form of grammar is probably applicable. It is apparent that even though certain symbols may constitute the context for one rule they may also be transformed by other rules for which other symbols constitute the context. So parts of the context may or may not undergo change in a production system. The distinction between terminal and non-terminal symbols is not necessarily applicable to grammars of design either. In any event the status of a symbol is dependent entirely on the rule which happens to be active at a given moment. It will be assumed that the distinctions between contextual and other types of symbols is an arbitrary one from the point of view of setting up control regimes.

'Well-behaved' and 'Poorly-behaved' Systems

Search spaces display different characteristics depending on the characteristics of the production rules and initial conditions. Two types of rule sets are characterized here: 'well behaved' and 'poorly behaved' rule sets. 'Well behaved' rule sets display the desirable properties that they are *commutative* or *decomposable* or both. These will be considered first.

For *commutative* rules sets, at any state where there are several rules applicable any one of these rules can be selected and executed. The system will always reach the same terminal state even though rules are selected arbitrarily. This does not mean that all states will necessarily be encountered by arbitrary rule selection. Nor does it imply that the terminal state will be reached with equal efficiency along all paths. Neither is it necessary that each path encounters *all* production rules.

If a system can be identified as commutative then that affords certain advantages. There is only one terminal state and, if the goal of the system is to reach this state, then it means an irrevocable control regime can be employed. Backtracking is unnecessary. An example of a set of rules which operates on character strings in a commutative fashion is given as follows:

$$a \rightarrow c\,d \quad (1)$$
$$b \rightarrow e\,f \quad (2)$$
$$c \rightarrow g\,h \quad (3)$$
$$d \rightarrow i\,j \quad (4)$$

A rule can be executed if the symbols on its left hand side can be matched against the global database. (For simplicity, the example here is of context *independent* rules.) When the rule is executed it results in the symbol on the left being deleted from the database and the symbols on the right substituted. Each rule is numbered. If the initial state consists of the symbols: *a, b* then the system is commutative. The states and the rules which produce them are depicted in Figure 5.1. The terminal state consists of the symbol string:

g h i j e f.

Certain rule sets have the advantage of being *decomposable*. This is where states can be divided into substates which are operated on independently. The

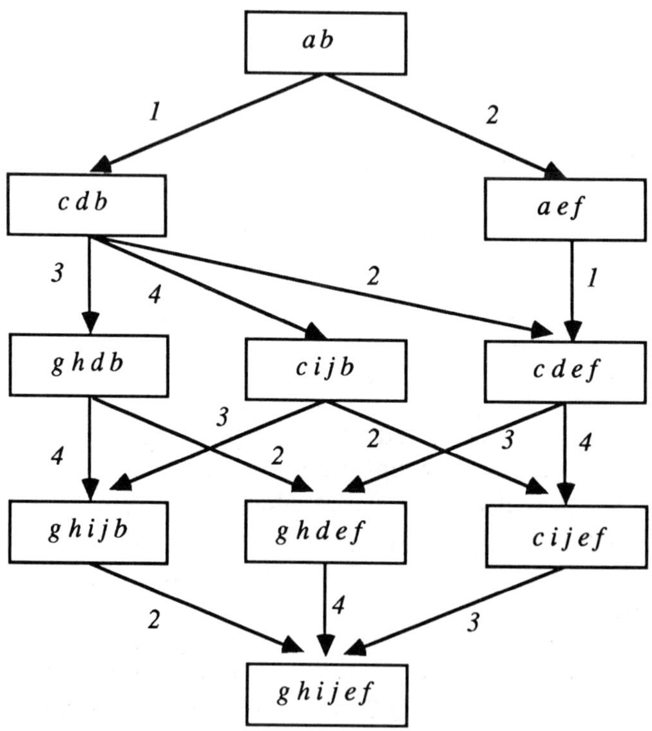

Figure 5.1. Search space for a commutative system.

terminal states so produced need then only be combined. Certain rule sets display both characteristics, and some interesting symmetries between commutative and decomposable systems are discussed by Nilsson (1982). The rule system described above is also decomposable. This is illustrated in Figure 5.2. The vertical bars indicate how states can be decomposed and operated on independently. The terminal state consists of the concatenation of the three states at the branch ends indicated (*). (This type of system has the advantage that not only is rule order unimportant in the achievement of the terminal state, but the rules can also be processed using a control regime which makes use of parallel processing.)

Examples of rule sets exhibiting these characteristics are evident in design. At certain stages in the design process the rules that operate on partial design states can be applied independently of one another. In the design of a single storey house, for example, it can generally be assumed that rules operating on the living room which locate a fireplace have little or no effect on the rules operating on bedrooms which locate wardrobes. The rule set is, to some extent, decomposable at this stage. The order in which certain rules are implemented may not matter either. So, such a system is also commutative. Attempts to formalize architectural design principles often result in the explication of rule sets of this type, as exemplified in Alexander's *A Pattern Language* (Alexander, 1977; Alexander et al, 1968; Alexander and Poyner, 1970). Because rule sets of this type are relatively easy to control, they can be described as 'well behaved' rule sets.

A simple rule set which is 'poorly behaved', that is, neither decomposable nor commutative, is illustrated below:

$$a \rightarrow b \qquad (1)$$
$$a \rightarrow c \qquad (2)$$

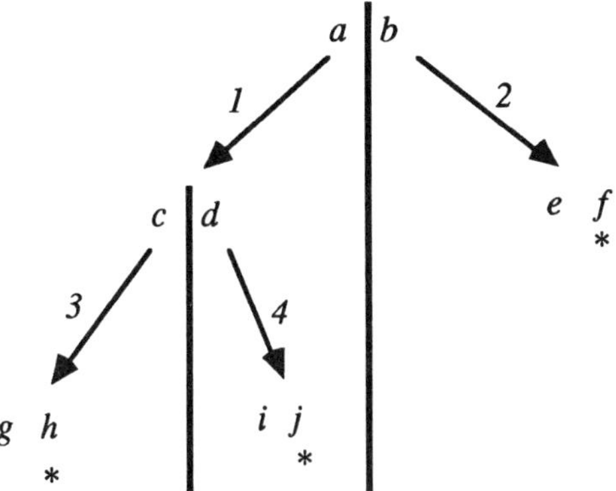

Figure 5.2. A decomposable system.

$$b \rightarrow d \quad (3)$$
$$b \rightarrow e \quad (4)$$

where the initial state is the single symbol:

a.

The search space for this system is shown in Figure 5.3. The application of any rule commits the system to a path which does not converge with any other path, and there is more than one terminal state. The rules exhibit a high degree of *interdependence*.

Design is often concerned with rule sets which have a high degree of interdependence. Rules which govern the placement of spaces in buildings are typically like this. Rules about objects competing for placement tend to produce different results depending on order because a commitment to the location of one object obviates that location as a possible site for another object. The problem of laying out a building could therefore be partitioned into several subproblems: those concerned with interacting rule sets which locate important spaces; and those concerned with decomposable and commutative rule sets about details such as fireplaces and wardrobes. This is, of course, a simplification, but it is the sort of assumption that designers are prepared to make during the development of a design. The most difficult types of problems in design tend to require a grammar which is highly interactive. The shape grammar rules of Stiny and Gips (1978) are mostly of this type.

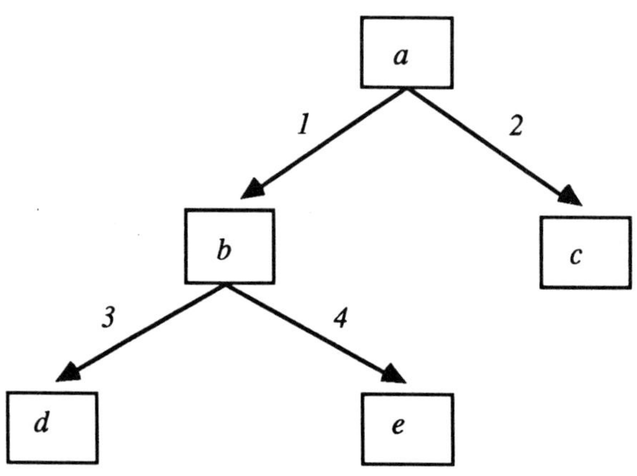

Figure 5.3. Search space for a 'poorly behaved' rule set.

Control

It can be shown that any production system can be reformulated as a commutative system. There is normally no advantage in such a reformulation except in providing a structure which will accommodate explicit control knowledge if it is available. One way of accomplishing this for the search space of Figure 5.3 is to devise the following control regime:

1. match the left side of the first rule with the global database
2. retain the element which has been matched
3. add the right side of the rule to the global database
4. join the element added to the element just matched with an arrow symbol
5. label the arrow with the name of the rule
6. cycle through this procedure for all the rules until none are applicable

This procedure produces the search space illustrated in Figure 5.4. This formulation introduces a complexity of representation to the global database, but the process of selecting between rules is simplified as any ordering of rules produces the one terminal state which is simply the search graph of Figure 5.3. By introducing the following rule it is possible to make explicit the knowledge by which a goal state is matched:

$$goal(X)\,X \;\rightarrow\; found \qquad (5)$$

The rule states that if there is a literal of the form, $goal(X)$, in the global database, where X is a variable, and X also exists as a symbol in the database then add the word Found to the database. This word is a flag which signals that the goal has been satisfied. The initial state of this system therefore contains a statement about how to find a goal state. The search space for this system, using the same control regime outlined above, is illustrated in Figure 5.5. There are therefore two goal states. These are states containing the word Found. What is achieved is simply a way of structuring the problem such that knowledge about control can be made explicit. It follows that if knowledge about efficient search is available then this can be made explicit as rules in the same way.

It can also be demonstrated that this production system is decomposable. The decomposition graph is represented in Figure 5.6. As for Figure 5.2, the end states indicated (*) need to be combined to form the terminal state, which is the entire search space for the original formulation. The advantage of this reformulation is that the task of generating the entire search space has been decomposed into independent subtasks. The rules operate on different components of the partial search trees contained within each state. Provided the necessary preconditions exist for the implementation of a rule it can

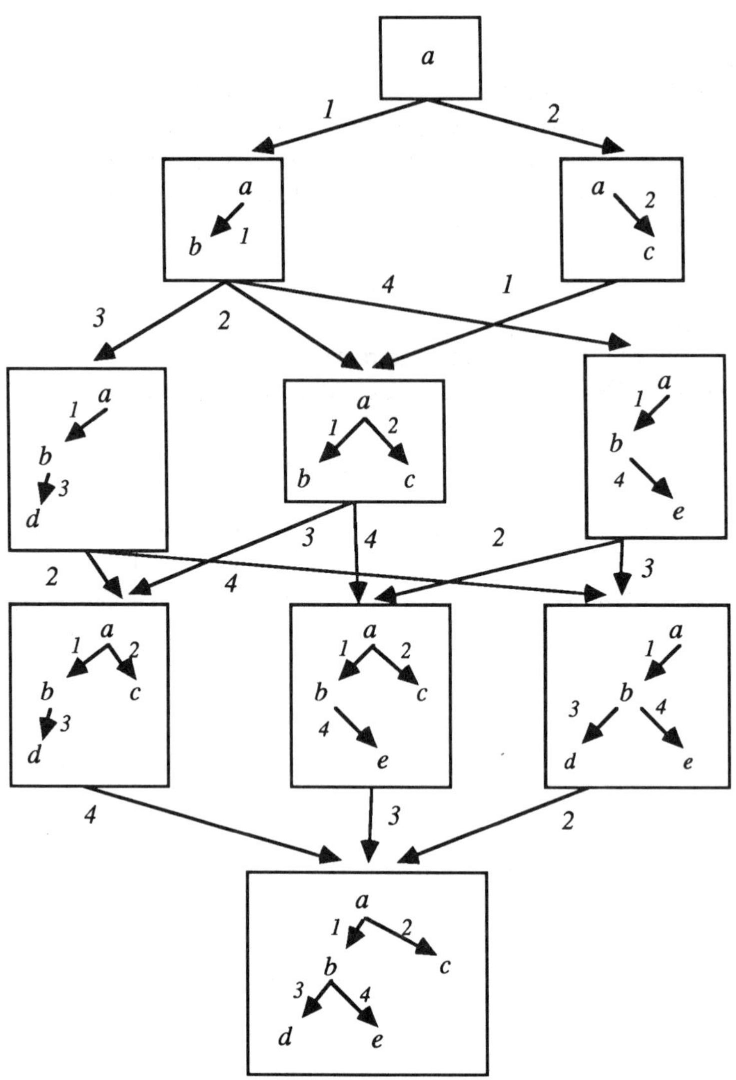

Figure 5.4. Search space for Figure 5.3 as a commutative system.

operate independently of the others with no consideration as to order. This means that a non-decomposable, 'poorly behaved' production system can be 'tamed' such that it can be decomposed into independent subtasks. The implications of this will be discussed in subsequent chapters.

This technique of describing the development of the search space of a production system as states in a meta-system, has been exploited in various

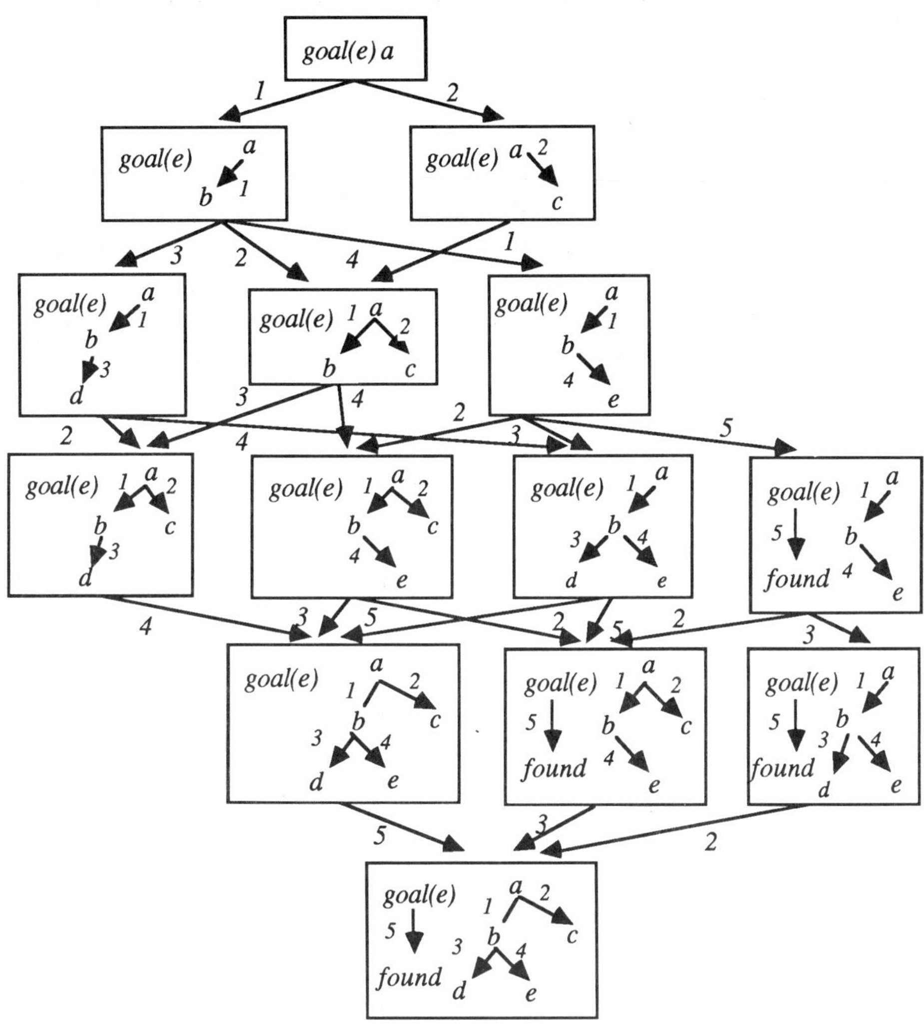

Figure 5.5. The search space of Figure 5.4 incorporating rule 5.

problem solving computer programs—notably, in the NOAH planning system (Sacerdoti, 1977). Instead of representing states as partially formed search trees, however, the approach is to represent the global database as a network of production rules called a *procedural network*. The nodes of the network are the *names* of the production rules. Nodes are connected in such a way that the system begins with little commitment to order, and the final state is one in which the ordering of the rules is resolved. The operations which transform the procedural network are the rules themselves and a type of rule called the 'critic'.

Scheduling

If a system is 'poorly behaved' then the ordering of rules is determined by their interactions. If a system is 'well behaved' then the control issue shifts to that of finding a path which is, in some sense, optimal. The scheduling system for the HEARSAY speech understanding system appears to work on this assumption (Hayes-Roth and Lesser, 1977). Production system control is provided by types of meta-rules (Davis, 1977) called *scheduling rules* which

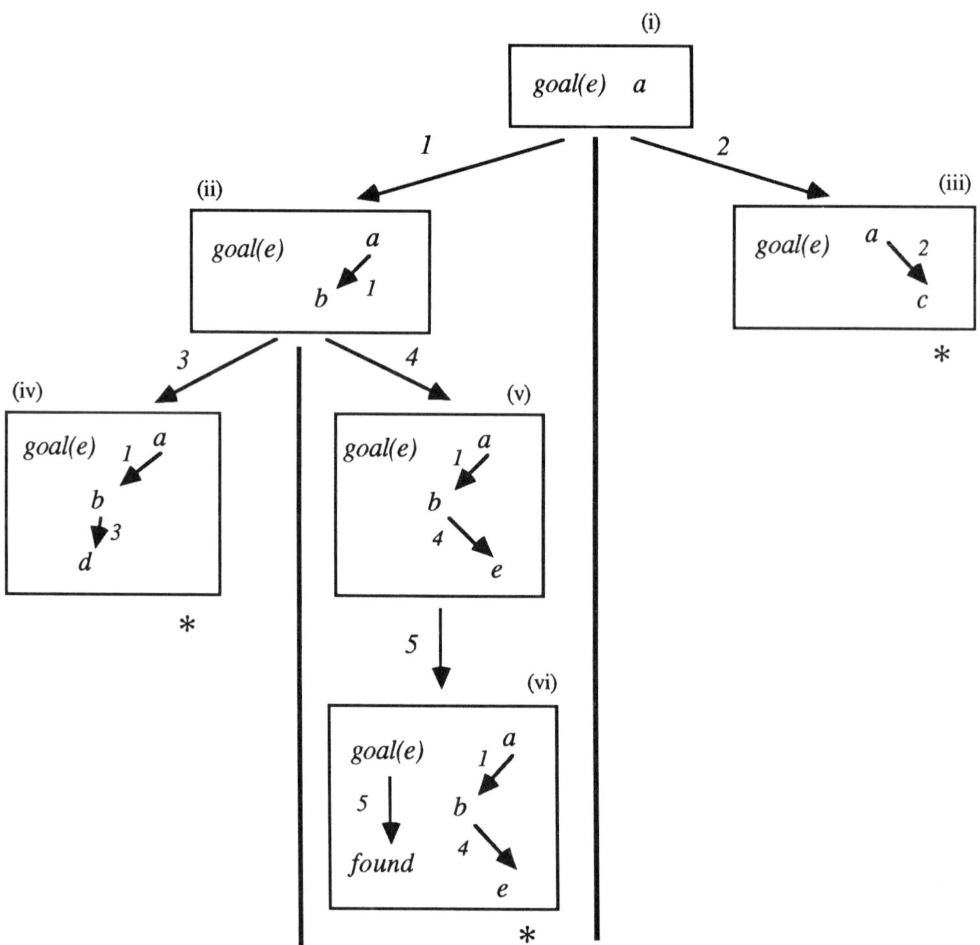

Figure 5.6. The production system of Figure 5.5 as a decomposable system.

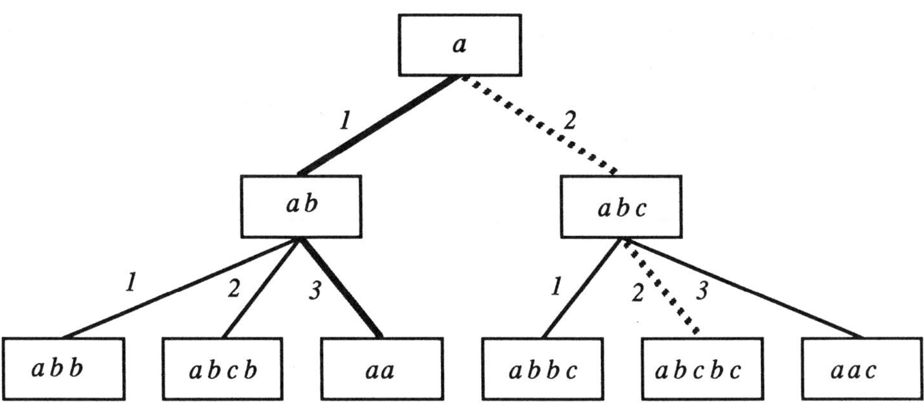

Figure 5.7. Search graph showing alternative paths generated by scheduling rules *s.1* (bold lines) and *s.2* (dotted lines).

select between competing rules. (The arrangement of applicable rules is therefore the schedule.) The information available to the system is that found by *triggering* each of the competing rules to see what changes these make to the global database. *Scheduling rules* check which rule seems to create the most desirable changes and that rule is then executed. This process is repeated for each state. This has been demonstrated to be a useful basis for simulating cognitive activities, such as errand planning (Hayes-Roth and Hayes-Roth, 1979; Hayes-Roth, 1985).

The use of a scheduler can be demonstrated simply by considering a production system which contains the following three rules:

$$a \rightarrow ab \quad (1)$$
$$a \rightarrow abc \quad (2)$$
$$b \rightarrow a \quad (3)$$

The first few branches of the (infinite) search graph are shown in Figure 5.7. Scheduling rules are meta-rules which decide between possible rules at each state. Two such meta-rules might be:

s.1 select the rule which produces the smallest state
s.2 select the rule which produces the largest state

If *s.1* is operating then the search procedure will follow the path indicated with bold arcs in Figure 5.7. If *s.2* is operating then the dotted path will be followed. These scheduling rules are entirely arbitrary in this context, but similar strategies are often followed in general problem solving when there appear to be no better guides. *S.1* bears some intuitive similarity to the strategy of *consolidation*, whereas *s.2* is similar to *diversifying*. Scheduling generally takes advantage of such heuristics.

One way of tackling the problem of determining rule order in a 'poorly behaved' system is therefore to formulate it as a commutative/decomposable system which is controlled by a scheduler. A scheduler is a type of production system which has as its global database the rules of the system that it is controlling.

Summary

Important knowledge about the generation of designs can be formalized as grammars. Grammars can exhibit certain valuable properties depending on the characteristics of their rule sets. A particularly important property is that of commutativity, where the same end state is reached irrespective of the order in which rules are implemented. Another important property is decomposability, where a global database can be decomposed such that the manipulation of its components are treated as independent subtasks. In so far as they can be modelled as production systems, design tasks do not generally exhibit these favourable properties.

Any production system can be reformulated to exhibit these properties however. In some cases it may be advantageous to do this. This argument is important to the developments in the rest of this book and so it will be summarized here.

1. Grammars of design generally display properties which can be characterized as 'poorly behaved'. Rules interact, and the order in which they are implemented has a critical bearing on the outcome of the production system.
2. Any production system can be reformulated as a 'well behaved' (or commutative/decomposable) production system by formulating it so that various states of the *search tree* produced by the successive implementation of the rules are themselves represented as states in a production system.
3. The rules which manipulate this production system will be the rules themselves, and there will be one end state which consists of a complete search tree.
4. There will be many paths but only one end state. This formulation provides the opportunity for knowledge about 'pruning' search trees to be made explicit and operable as production rules (assuming the knowledge is available).

5. This knowledge constitutes a grammar which can be said to operate in a 'language of search trees'.
6. As all paths in this production system lead to the end state one of the tasks of a control regime is to find the most 'efficient' path to the end state.
7. The knowledge by which selections can be made (between rules competing to manipulate search trees) can also be represented as production rules. One model for this is of *scheduling* which can embody rules for making selections on the basis of the size of the search trees produced by each competing rule. The choice of heuristics is not critical as they affect the efficiency with which the system produces a result rather than the nature of the result.
8. This model incorporates a hierarchical view of control. It provides a structure for organizing knowledge about control such that it can be made explicit as production rules.
9. Production systems which are controlled by production systems can be devised in logic programming languages. Logic programming can be used for representing knowledge for reasoning about and controlling other reasoning systems.
10. This model suggests that there are meta-grammars which treat rules of object grammars as if they were components of a vocabulary.

Subsequent chapters will demonstrate that this model facilitates the complex mappings by which designs are generated to conform to particular performances or intended meanings. It also provides a general model for exploring various facets of design activity.

The control of production systems is addressed by the field of *planning* which concerns the selection and ordering of production rules prior to their actual implementation. Planning systems and the knowledge which they afford to this model will be reviewed in Chapter 7. The applicability of planning models to design will be discussed in Chapter 8, and subsequently incorporated into the model developed above.

Prior to that discussion it is appropriate to investigate examples of simple grammars applicable to design.

Chapter 6

Design Grammars

As discussed in the previous chapter grammars can operate on character strings. Like alphabetical strings, descriptions of design can be represented as composed of symbols. Design grammars can therefore comply with the production system formalism.

The grammars explored in the previous chapter are a type a *set grammar:* that is, they are concerned with the manipulation of sets of discrete elements. The applicability of such grammars to design can be demonstrated by considering the various elements of the language of which the grammar is a part: the method of design representation; the knowledge by which inferences can be made; and the control regime. Examples of design grammars which have been implemented in Prolog are given to show something of the scope of design languages. The chapter concludes by introducing *planning,* which is concerned with the selection and ordering of grammar rules in order to produce designs which exhibit intended attributes.

Set Grammars

That grammars expressed as production rules can facilitate the generation of designs has been demonstrated by Stiny and Gips (1978), and the technique has been subsequently employed to produce line drawings resembling building plans, notably those of Palladio (Stiny and Mitchell, 1978) and Frank Lloyd Wright (Koning and Eizenberg, 1981). The term *shape grammar* is employed to describe a particular type of algorithm for performing arithmetic operations on geometric entities called *shapes*. These algorithms are formalized as production systems. The general form of a rule is:

$$A \rightarrow B.$$

Such a rule can be applied to a shape C when there is a transformation T which makes A a subshape of C. When the rule is implemented A is replaced by the subshape B transformed by the matching transformation T.

As described by Stiny and Gips, shape grammars are defined for shapes made up of lines and points. As these are insufficient to facilitate the mappings suggested by the above algorithm in the most general case, labels are incorporated into the formalism. Labels are given a geometrical status by being attached to points, so they can be treated as components of shapes. Labels can also serve as descriptors of shapes. *Parametric grammars* are a variation of shape grammars by which it is possible to perform operations on classes of shapes.

The convention adopted for describing shapes (suitable for computer manipulation) is to represent them as sets of *maximal lines*. A shape is described with the smallest number of lines possible (Krishnamurti, 1980; 1981; Earl, 1985, 1987). As a new subshape is added to a composition the representation must be reformulated in order to retain the maximal line representation.

A shape can be decomposed into subshapes in which ever way required. Spatial ambiguities are allowed, and subshapes can be recombined and decomposed in different ways. Consequently, the implementation of shape grammars on a computer is a matter of some complexity. A shape *editor* for simple shapes has been implemented in Prolog by Krishnamurti and Giraud (1984).

The shape grammar formalism appears to accord with the way a designer exploits the ambiguity of line drawings. Lines such as those which represent axes of symmetry, circulation and construction lines typically change their meaning to become building elements, such as walls, as the design progresses. New forms emerge out of existing forms. In shape grammars a shape can be interpreted in which ever way is appropriate for a particular rule of grammar. It is possible to devise a shape grammar which produces sets of lines which can be interpreted as the plan of a *char-bagh* garden (Stiny and Mitchell, 1980). There may be no representation stored in the system which says which lines are paths and which are walls. However, the shape configuration is able to be so interpreted by a human being.

In the grammar for generating gardens a final design in the language is defined as one in which the shape has no labels. In the case of grammars for generating Frank Lloyd Wright houses (Koning and Eizenberg, 1981) labels also form part of the final design description. These labels describe the functions of certain components of the shapes, such as room types.

A conceptually simpler form of shape grammars is that of *set grammars*. These are grammars which manipulate compositions made up of elements. The distinction of *set* from *shape* grammars is made by Stiny (1980b, 1982).

Under a set grammar designs are made up of discrete elements which retain their integrity as they are operated upon by a grammar. Their disadvantage is that the composition of elements cannot be as readily decomposed and recombined to create emergent forms, as under a shape grammar, but there are certain implementational advantages. Set grammars are more amenable to representation within a computer and conform more readily to the production system formalism as described in the previous chapter.

Set grammars also appear to conform to the way the designer's world is often perceived: as composed of hierarchically describable objects. Complex descriptions of objects can be manipulated more readily than under a shape grammar.

Representing Design Languages

The grammar systems described here are of the set grammar type. They do not necessarily conform to the shape grammar formalism of lines and labelled points, but make use of the predicate calculus as a rich medium for design representation.

In accordance with the production system formalism described in the previous chapter, languages of design require a method by which designs can be represented (the 'global database'), rules by which properties which are not explicitly represented can be inferred, rules of grammar (production or transformation rules) and a system of control.

Design Representation

The domain upon which a grammar has effect is a description of the design. With logic programming any attributes of objects or of relationships between objects can be represented as facts. In a geometrical representation, designs can be described in terms of points, which indicate the ends of lines. Line segments make up surfaces which form recognizable objects. These objects combine to form other objects.

A simple example of two objects which can be described as sets of connected points is shown in Figure 6.1. These are represented by the following facts in predicate calculus:

obj(a, [1^3, 3^1, 1^1]).
obj(b, [4^5, 2^3, 2^5]).

The first argument in each case is the name by which the object is identified,

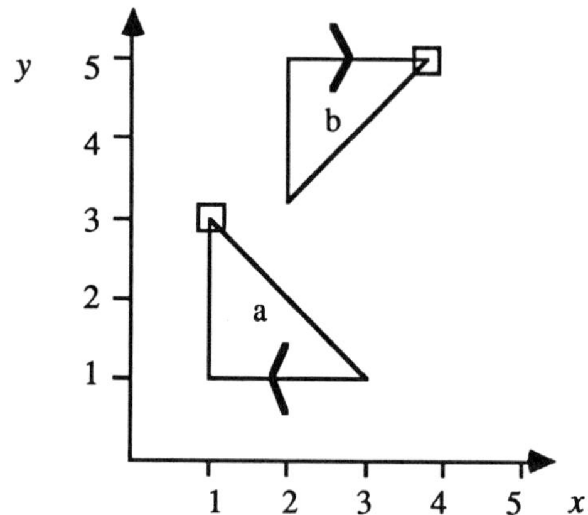

Figure 6.1. Two triangles represented as Prolog facts. The arrows indicate the order in which the vertices are listed, and the small rectangles indicate the first vertices in the respective lists.

the second argument is a list of points (*x* and *y* coordinate pairs). Facts of this type lend themselves to hierarchical representations. Other complex objects could be described as made up of these primitive objects as shown in Chapter 3.

Rules of Deductive Inference

As suggested in Chapter 3 the matching of production rules with a global database can require rules of deductive inference. An example of a type of rule appropriate to a geometrical domain is given here.

The knowledge by which implicit facts can be derived from a design description can be represented as interpretive rules of the form described in Chapter 4. As the derivation of geometrical properties generally involves large numbers of variables and complex subgoals, the logic rule form is a clearer mode for expressing this knowledge. (Such rules can also be expressed in the *if-then* form, however.)

An example of a useful item of geometrical knowledge is that for inferring whether two line segments are collinear and intersecting—that is, that they overlap. This is given by the following set of logic statements:

overlap([*A*^*B*, *C*^*B*], [*E*^*B*, *G*^*B*]) :- *rel*(*A*, *C*, *E*, *G*).
overlap([*A*^*B*, *C*^*B*], [*G*^*B*, *E*^*B*]) :- *rel*(*A*, *C*, *E*, *G*).
overlap([*B*^*A*, *B*^*C*], [*B*^*E*, *B*^*G*]) :- *rel*(*A*, *C*, *E*, *G*).
overlap([*B*^*A*, *B*^*C*], [*B*^*G*, *B*^*E*]) :- *rel*(*A*, *C*, *E*, *G*).

```
rel(A, C, E, G) :- E >= A, E < C, G > A.
rel(A, C, E, G) :- G > A, G =< C, E < G.
rel(A, C, E, G) :- E =< A, G >= C.
```

The Overlap predicate has two arguments. Each argument contains a list containing the end points of the two lines being tested. The three conditions under which two lines overlap are given in Figure 6.2. Further rules for testing the geometrical properties of more complex objects are given by Akiner (1985a) and a systematic approach to general geometric reasoning using logic programming is presented by Arbab and Wing (1985). Rules such as these are valuable for inferring properties and conditions which are implicit in a geometrical description. The knowledge by which other interpreted properties of design descriptions are deduced can also be represented in this way.

Grammars

The model of a grammar rule presented so far is of a production rule (or transformation rule) with a left side and a right side. The facts on the left side of the rule facilitate matching with the current design description. When the rule is implemented those facts are deleted, and those on the right are asserted. There may, however be *contextual* facts which are to be inferred from the description and therefore cannot be deleted. These are essentially conditions under which a match can be made. It can be made explicit that these are *conditional* facts by structuring a grammar rule as follows:

$$N{:}\ A\ C \rightarrow B$$

where N is the name of the rule, A is the list of antecedents (those facts which are to be deleted), C is a list of conditions which must be satisfied but

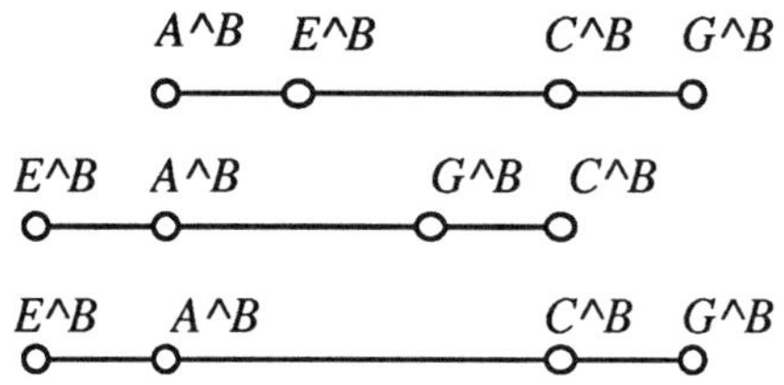

A^B E^B C^B G^B

E^B A^B G^B C^B

E^B A^B C^B G^B

Figure 6.2. The three conditions under which a line with end points *A^B* and *C^B* overlaps a line *E^B* and *G^B*.

which are not explicit in the design description, and *B* is a list of new facts that are to be asserted. This structure allows explicit and implicit facts about design descriptions to be incorporated into rules. As illustrated below, there are also other forms that the grammar may take.

Control

For non-geometrical object descriptions the control for a production system described in Chapter 3 is sufficient. Control for rules involving the transformation of geometrical attributes must incorporate a mechanism for determining transformations.

Such a mechanism is illustrated by considering the facts which describe the two objects in Figure 6.1. These objects are isomorphic but one is a rotation and translation of the other. It could be said that there is a match between the objects if there is a geometrical transformation which maps one object onto the other:

```
match(A, B, T) :- obj(A, L1), obj(B, L2), map(L1, L2, T).
```

The third argument of the *match* predicate is the transformation. So two shapes match if they map onto each other by transformation *T*. The definition of *map* is given below.

```
map([], [], _).
map([X1^Y1|A], [X2^Y2|B], rot_translation(R, Tx, Ty)) :-
    rotx(R, X1, X2, Y2, Tx),
    roty(R, Y1, X2, Y2, Ty),
    map(A, B, rot_translation(R, Tx, Ty)).
```

The third argument of the *match* predicate is the transformation, described as a rotation and a translation (called 'rot_translation'). The first argument of *rot_translation* is the rotation in degrees, the other two arguments are the translation in the *x* and *y* axes respectively. The *rotx* and *roty* predicates are true by the following rules:

```
rotx(0,    X1, X2, _, T)  :- T is X1-X2.
rotx(90,   X1, _, Y2, T)  :- T is X1-Y2.
rotx(180,  X1, X2, _, T)  :- T is X1+X2.
rotx(270,  X1, _, Y2, T)  :- T is X1+Y2.
```

```
roty(0,     Y1, _, Y2, T)   :- T is Y1-Y2.
roty(90,    Y1, X2, _, T)   :- T is Y1+X2.
roty(180,   Y1, _, Y2, T)   :- T is Y1+Y2.
roty(270,   Y1, X2, _, T)   :- T is Y1-X2.
```

The goal:

?- ***match(triangle(a), triangle(b), T).***

produces:

T = rot_translation(270, 6, –1)

which determines that object *triangle(b)*, when rotated by 270 degrees and translated by 6 and –1 along the *x* and *y* axes respectively, provides a one-to-one mapping with shape *triangle(a)*. As defined above rotations are constrained to matchings between orthogonally similar objects. Scaling, reflection and other transformations are not taken into account. (This would make the control considerably more complicated.) The goal can also be given:

?- ***match(triangle(b), X, T).***

This is asking: with what does shape *triangle(b)* match and under what transformation? The goal is satisfied by:

X = triangle(a)
T = rot_translation(90, 1, 6)

and

X = triangle(b)
T = rot_translation(0, 0, 0)

This states that object *triangle(b)* matches *triangle(a)* under a certain transformation and it maps onto itself. (It is a simple matter to provide some sort of check so that the final, redundant match is not made).

The matching process involves comparing the lists of points of which the objects are comprised under the same rotations and translations. If there are many objects then the process becomes computationally expensive.

Based on the transformation rule schema given above a rule for transforming a triangle into a square can be represented:

rule(1, triangle(a), [] → [square(a)]).

The predicate *rule* has five arguments: the rule name, a list of objects to be matched; a list of conditions (in this case empty); the *implies* symbol; and a list of objects to replace those matched.This is represented graphically in Figure 6.3. Assuming we have defined the shape *square*(*a*), and by

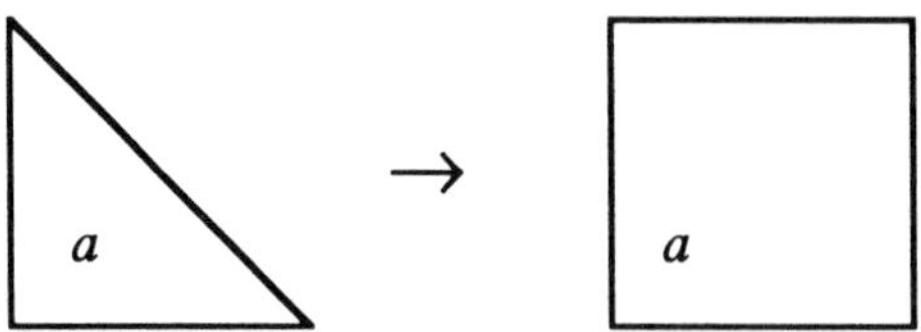

Figure 6.3. A rule for transforming a triangle into a square.

employing the knowledge contained in the logic program above, a control mechanism can be devised which results in the replacement of *triangle*(*a*) with *square*(*a*) according to the rule:

fire(*N*) :- *rule*(*N*, *A*, *B* → *C*),
    match(*A*, *D*, *T*), *test_conditions*(*B*), *copy*(*C*, *T*), *delete*(*D*).

This rule is analogous to that discussed in Chapter 3 for production systems in general, except that the predicates *match* and *copy* take account of transformations. There is no need to elaborate on the *copy* and *test_conditions* predicates here. The definition of *copy* is similar to the *match* predicate.

With this control logic we should be able to prove a goal, such as:

?- *fire*(*1*).

and in the process implement the changes due to *rule*(*1*) to the facts base describing the design. It is a simple matter to devise other mechanisms whereby we could ensure the exhaustive generation of all designs belonging to the space defined by the grammar, or to permit some kind of user interaction.

The components of a simple grammar system for manipulating geometrical descriptions of designs are provided by the above method of representing: geometrical entities; rules of deductive inference and rules of grammar; and the matching mechanism. This approach has been employed in some of the implementations described below.

Examples of Design Grammars

Design grammars can be formulated in many ways to produce different sorts of designs. Five experimental grammars are described here. The order suggests a progression from those involving the simplest to the most complicated grammar.

A Network Grammar

This example is of a non-geometrical grammar for operating on networks. A directed network can be represented with facts such as the following:

node(*start*, [], [*a*, *b*]).
node(*a*, [*start*], [*c*]).
node(*b*, [*start*], [*c*, *d*]).
node(*c*, [*a*, *b*], [*end*]).
node(*d*, [*b*], [*end*]).
node(*end*, [*c*, *d*], []).

Each fact contains three arguments. The first argument is the name of a node, the second argument is the nodes with which it is connected in the direction of *start* (the *parent* nodes) and the third argument is a list of nodes with which it is connected in the direction of *end* (the *child* nodes). This network is displayed here:

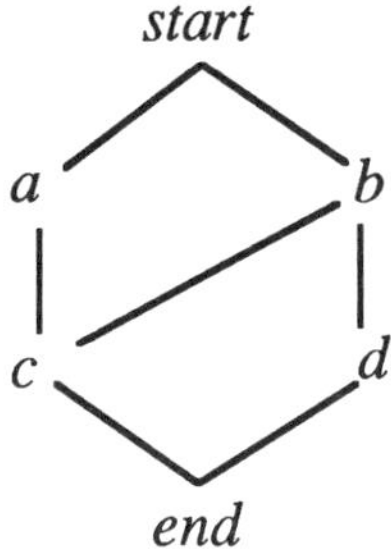

Because this domain is concerned with non-geometrical relationships, rules can be of the simple production system type. An example of a rule is one that states that a node *a* is to be replaced by two nodes *e* and *f* in 'parallel'. This is depicted graphically as:

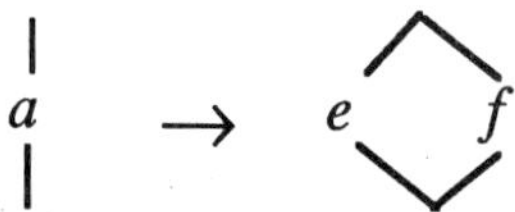

This transformation produces a revised set of facts resulting in the network:

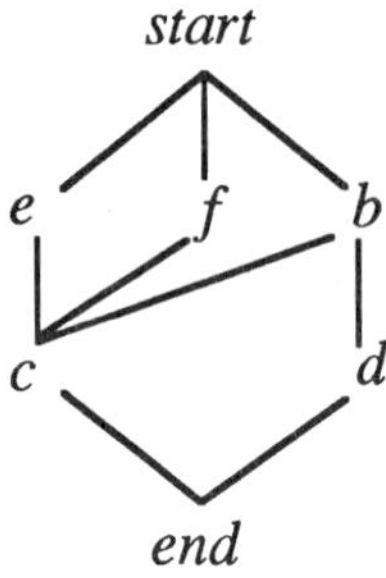

Transformations could be made on the basis of other patterns. A network grammar is of value when considering rules for manipulating sequences of actions, as in planning (which will be addressed in subsequent chapters).

A Blocks Grammar

A simple grammar concerning the placement of rectangular elements is shown in Figure 6.4. Rule 1 matches an initial condition where there is merely a point labelled *i*, and results in a rectangle with a corner labelled *p*. Rule 5 displaces an element to one side. Rule 6 removes the labelled point *p*. (The labelled points assist in avoiding ambiguities in matching objects.) This results in a terminating condition where no other rules can be applied. In order to avoid the possibility of two elements partially overlapping, the left side of the rules 2, 3, 4 and 5 contain the condition that no line segment exists where there is a dotted line. This condition can be tested by means of the inference rule described earlier. The grammar rules are shown here graphically, though they are represented in terms of points, as described above, in logic program form.

Figure 6.5 illustrates a part of the tree of designs and partial designs generated by the rules of Figure 6.4. Not every rule is a candidate for implementation at each node in the tree. For example, certain rules cannot be implemented if they would result in the partial overlapping of elements. The computer output from an interactive program which incorporates this grammar is shown in Figure 6.6.

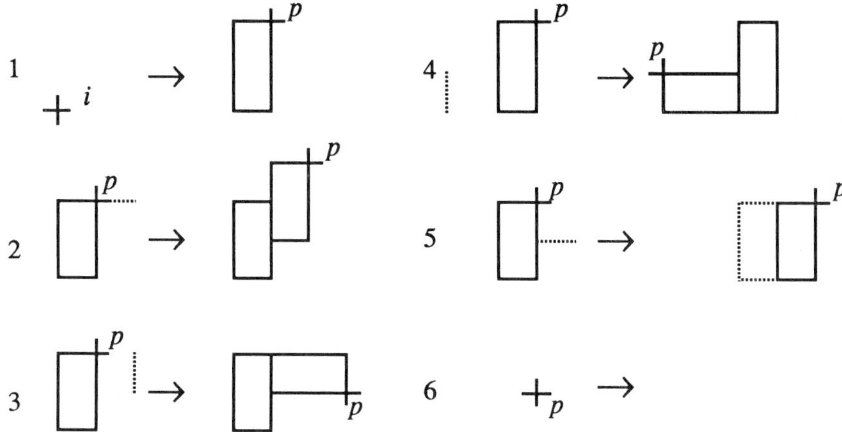

Figure 6.4. Rules of a grammar about the placement of non-overlapping rectangular blocks. The points *i* and *p* are labelled points. The dotted lines are segments which must not overlap existing lines.

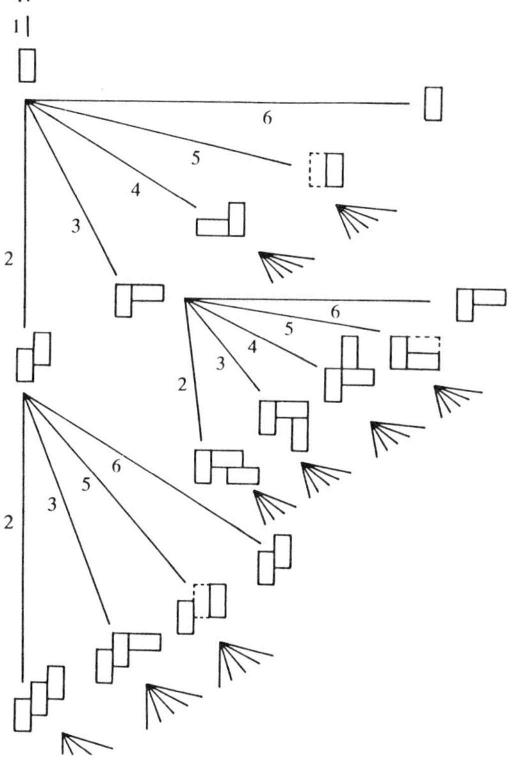

Figure 6.5. Part of the tree of designs and partial designs generated by the rules of Figure 6.4.

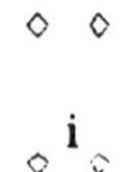

Rule 1: approved match? yes.

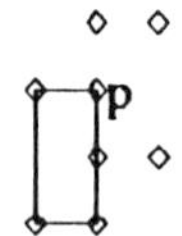

Rule 2: approved match? yes.

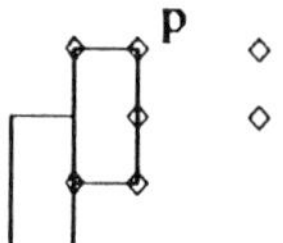

Rule 3: approved match? yes.

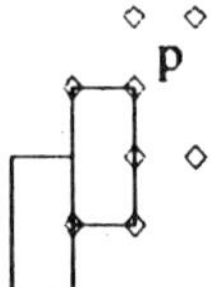

Rule 2: approved match? no.

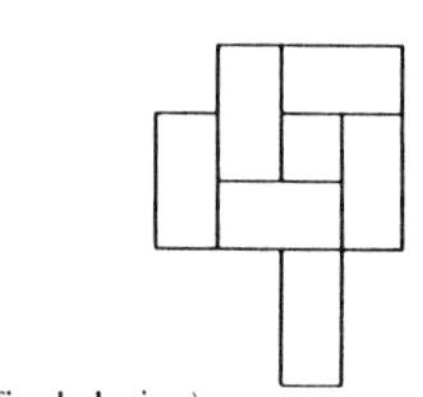

(final design)

Figure 6.6. Graphical output showing the automatic generation of designs where the option of accepting or rejecting the changes proposed by a rule are displayed on a computer screen. The design begins from the initial condition (the labelled point *i*). Rule 1 is applied. The corner points of the shape matched and the corners of the new shape to be added are indicated with diamonds. If the response is 'yes' then the rule is implemented and the next applicable rule (rule 2) is called. The first rule that finds a match in the design description is called each time. In response to 'no' the program calls the next available rule. The final design shown here results from the rule sequence: 1, 2, 3, 3, 3, 4, 6.

A Grammar of Point and Line Sets

The design grammar in Figure 6.7 is also concerned with labelled points and lines. In this case the lines produce shapes resembling simple building components. The first seven rules establish a grid of points labelled *d*, which are the locations of columns, and points *u* which form a secondary grid of mid points between columns. Rule 8 establishes the locations of mid-points which are on the perimeter of the building grid, and changes their labels from *u* to *w*.

Rules 9 to 12 alter the labels at certain points to indicate the positioning of a front entrance, a rear entrance, north windows and east windows. Rules 13 to 16 assert line segments into the design description to represent stylized building elements, such as a column, a wall panel, a front entrance, a semi-opaque wall element (window), and a rear entrance. Rules 18 to 25 simply delete labels. Rules 3, 8, 11 and 12 contain geometrical conditions which have to be met and are inferred from the design description by means of inference rules.

Figure 6.8 illustrates the designs generated by this grammar. Unlike the previous example the number of designs is finite.

Figure 6.9 shows again how a control system can be devised which invokes the rules automatically, but which provides prompts so that a designer can intervene and cause the system to take a different path. In this case Rule 1 is followed by the implementation of rule 2, three times, then rules 4 to 7, to produce the grid. Rule 8 labels the external grid lines *w*. After the firing of rules 9 to 12 the positions of the front entrance, the rear entrance and the windows are fixed. Rules 13 to 17 draw the elements to produce a labelled plan. These are subsequently removed (not shown).

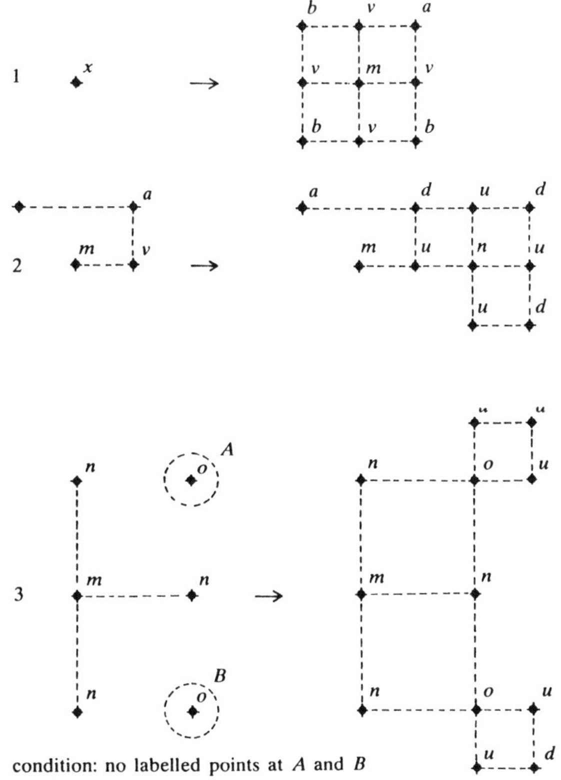

Figure 6.7. Grammar for the generation of the plan of a simple building form.

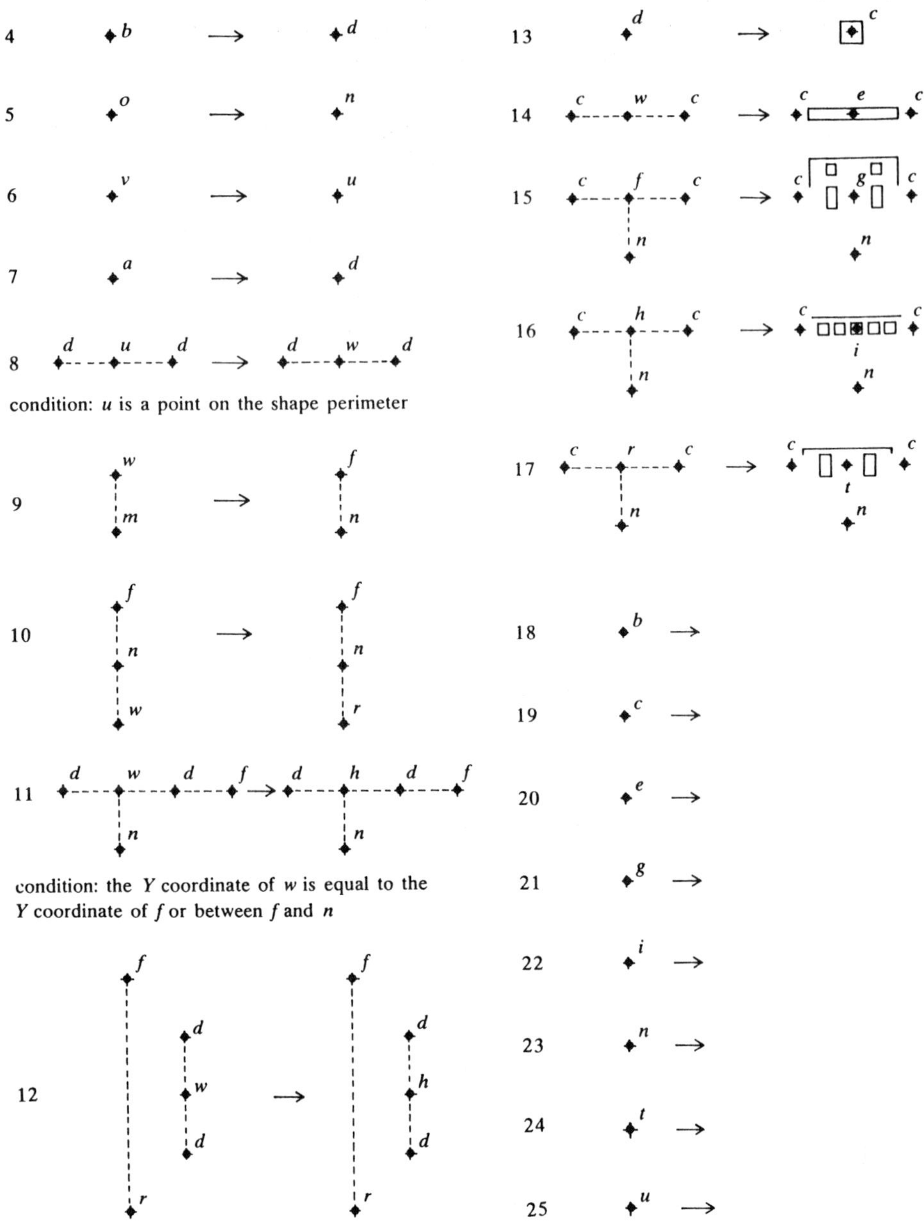

condition: the *X* coordinate of *w* is greater than the *X* coordinate of *f*

Figure 6.7. (continued).

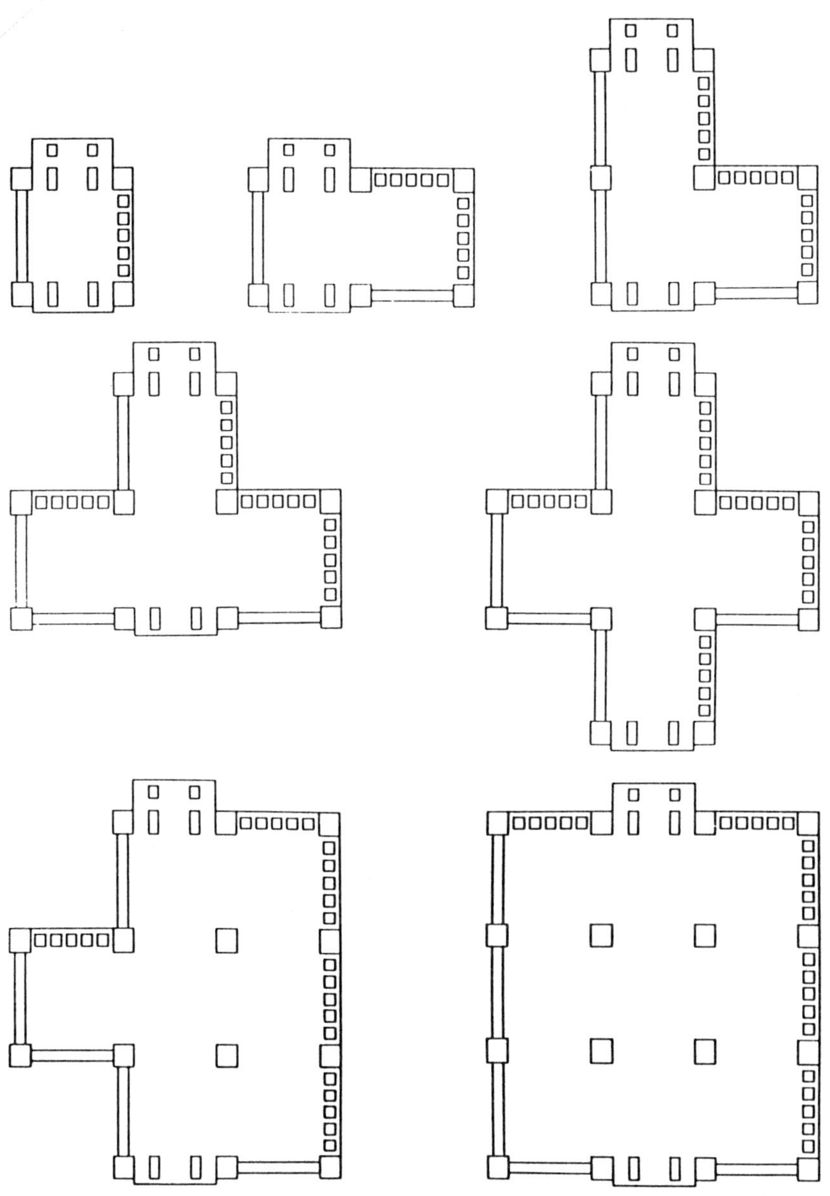

Figure 6.8. Graphic output showing designs generated by the invocation of rules from the grammar of Figure 6.7.

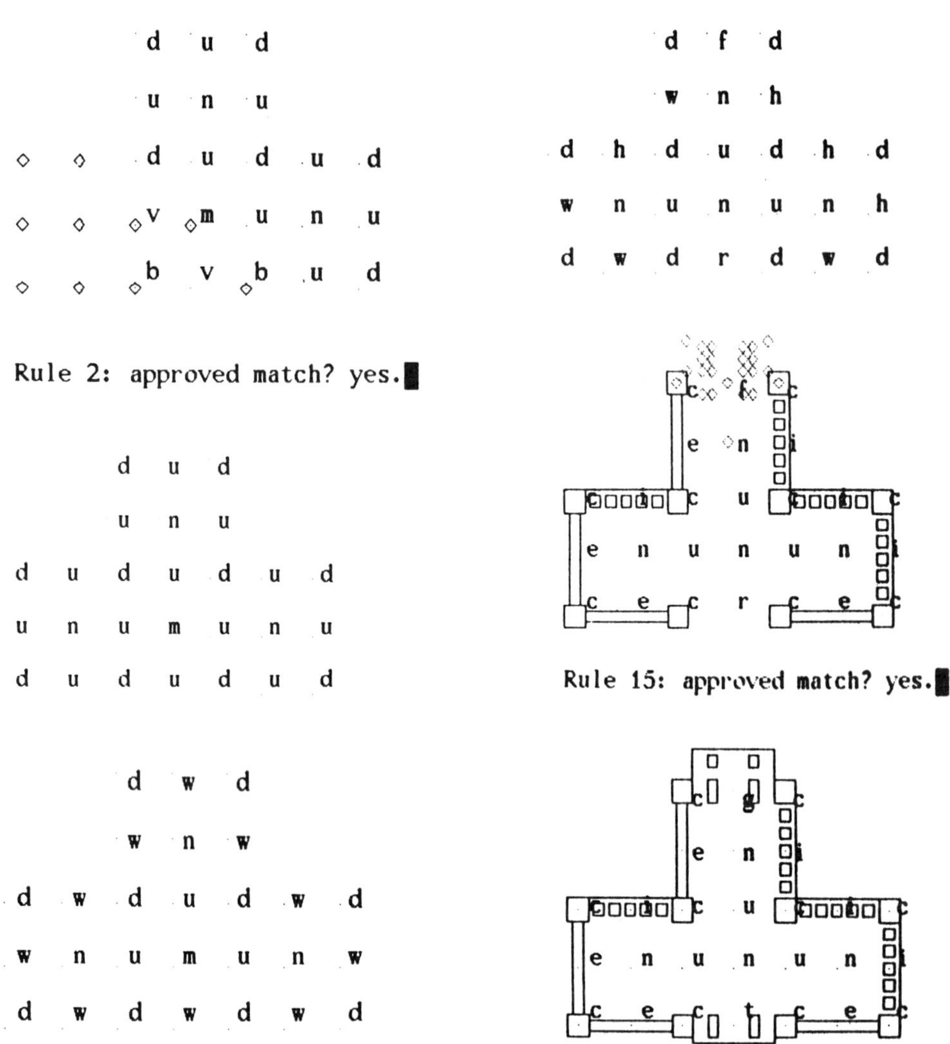

Figure 6.9. Graphic output showing the progress of a design generated by the selective invocation of rules from the grammar of Figure 6.7.

A Grammar of Objects

Figure 6.10 illustrates a set of design rules for generating simple building forms from wall elements and columns. The elements form rooms, each of which has a name and an orientation. A dot indicates the top of a room. The design space is depicted in Figure 6.11 as a tree, with the root node as the

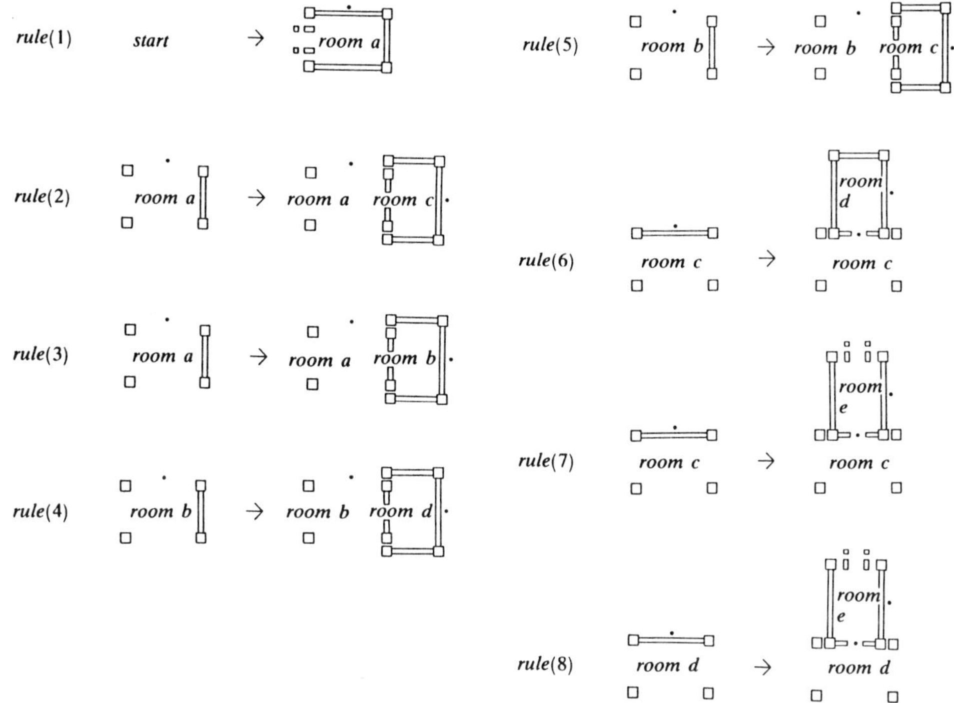

Figure 6.10. Design grammar for a building made up of columns and wall elements.

initial state (the fact *start*), and the ends of the branches as various end states, where no further rules can be applied. As in the examples above the application of certain rules precludes the achievement of certain states. So the end states are all different. The design space for this set of rules is atypical of most design domains, in that it is finite and it is small enough to be represented on one page.

One of the rules, rule 2, is depicted in program form in Figure 6.12. In this grammar only facts about objects are to be matched, and there are no conditions. The rule has a name, a list of preconditions and a list of consequents. Those facts which are not to be deleted appear on both sides of the rule (for example, *room_a(1)*). The objects to which the facts refer are described hierarchically, as shown above.

The rule is also shown diagrammatically in Figure 6.13. A room is defined by four columns. For this rule to be fired, it is necessary that a pattern be found in the current design state which matches the description of *room_a(1)* and *short_wall(2)*. These objects are deleted from the state

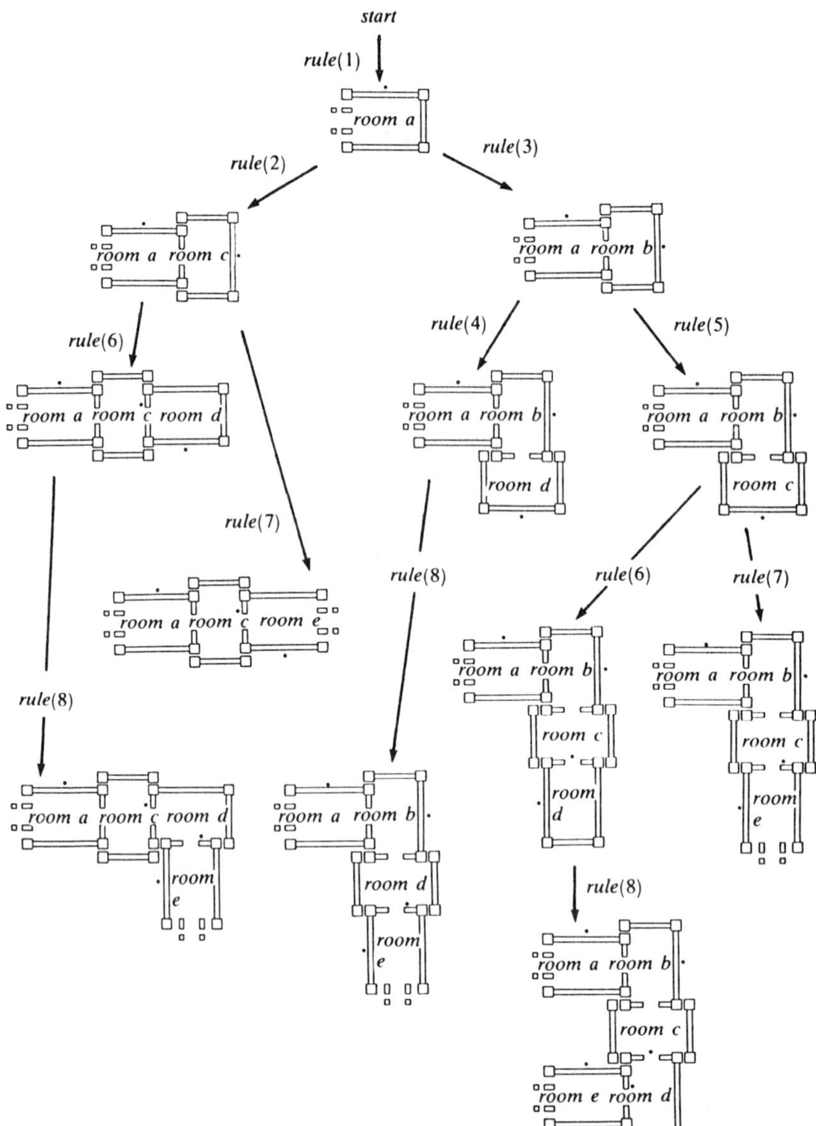

Figure 6.11. State space for the grammar of Figure 6.10.

```
rule(2) #     [room_a(1),
               short_wall(2)]
              >>
              [room_a(1),
               room_c(2),
               short_wall(4),
               short_wall(5),
               long_wall(5),
               open_wall(2)].
```

Figure 6.12. *Rule*(2) of the grammar in Figure 6.10 in program form.

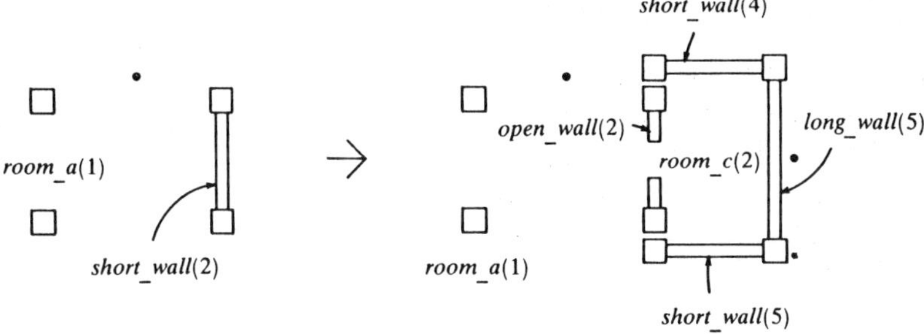

Figure 6.13. A graphical representation of *rule(2)*.

description and replaced with the objects *room_a(1)*, again, *room_c(2)*, *short_wall(4)*, *short_wall(5)*, *long_wall(5)* and *open_wall(2)*. The arguments denote different instances of the same object.

Room_a(1) is a composite object made up of *column(1)*, *column(2)*, *column(3)* and *column(4)*. These objects consist of line segments, which are defined by points expressed in homogeneous coordinate notation:

*composite(room_*a(*1*), [*column(1)*, *column*(2),
    column(3), *column*(4)]).
object(column(1), [*s(1)*, *s*(2), *s(3)*, *s*(4)]).
...
line(s(1), [*p(1)*, *p*(2)]).
...
point(p(1), [*260, 200, 1*]).
point(p(2), [*260, 280, 1*]).
...

It is possible to construct different rules from such object descriptions. A composite object in a rule matches the current design description if there exists a composite object described in the facts base which has the same predicate name, though different instance number, and both are made up of similar objects. The geometrical transformation which enables the object described in the rule to be mapped onto the object in the state description is calculated from the points defining the ends of line segments.

This grammar is employed as an example to explain the application of planning to design in Chapter 8.

A Grammar of Rectangular Dissections

There are many ways of formulating object level grammars. Another type of rule altogether is that which takes dimensionless spaces as vocabulary elements and operates on these. This is an attempt to capture something of the 'fluidity' of spatial representation during the design process, and it is the grammar followed in the example in Chapters 9 and 10.

The grammar proposed is similar to the set of rules described by Mitchell et al (1976) for generating 'rectangular dissections'. Other rules for the same purpose are proposed by Earl (1977) and Flemming (1978), as discussed by Steadman (1983). The study of rectangular dissections is ostensibly concerned with enumerating the different ways in which a rectangle can be divided up into sub-rectangles, but it can also be applied to the generation of building layouts (Bloch, 1979). Dimensioning is of only secondary importance in this context. (Dimensioning can be considered separately, and there are numerical techniques for handling this problem [Balachandran and Gero, 1986]).

Rules by which dissections can be generated are considered here as a means of generating spatial layouts. These are shown schematically in Figure 6.14. Rule *a* adds a rectangle by appending it to the right side of an existing composition. Rule *b* appends a rectangle to the top of the configuration. Rules *c* and *d* operate by extending certain of the rectangles at the edge of the configuration and adding a new rectangle in the space thus formed. Other rules can also be created for adding rectangles in different ways.

The idea is to begin with a single rectangle (a room or space) which then undergoes successive transformations resulting in a complex composition of rectangles. It should be noted that after the operation of each rule the composition retains its overall rectangular shape (as well as being composed only of rectangles). States in the development of a simple rectangular configuration are illustrated in Figure 6.15. The success of the grammar for generating building layouts relies on the following set of assumptions:

1. there is a small set of rules with which it is possible to generate every possible arrangement of rectangular dissections;
2. any geometrically orthogonal arrangement of rectangular spaces can be derived by first creating a rectangular dissection (allowing for the deletion of spaces); and
3. the generation of rectangular dissections is best accomplished if every intermediate state in the generation process is also a rectangular dissection.

The validity of these assumptions is not of concern here. It is also assumed that any deficiencies in the rules proposed can be overcome by the provision of more rules of the same type, or the refinement of the rules. The effectiveness

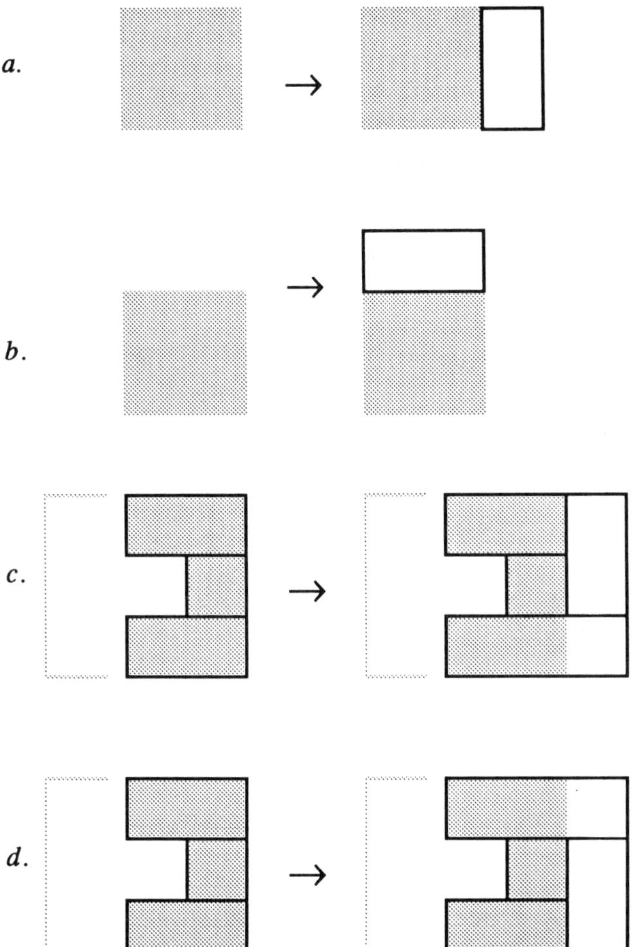

Figure 6.14. A grammar for generating rectangular dissections.

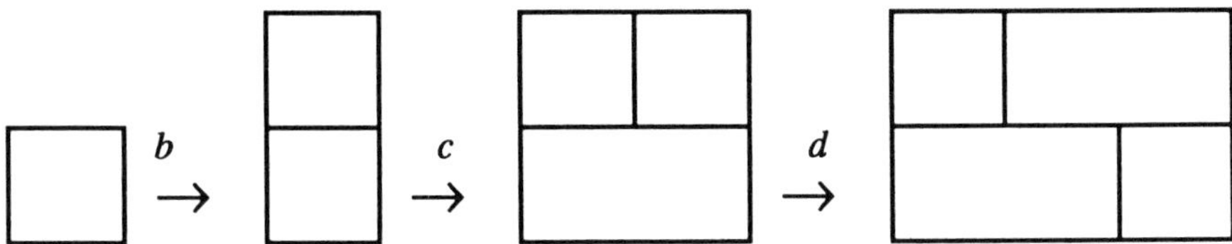

Figure 6.15. States in the development of a rectangular configuration achieved by executing the rule sequence: *b, c, d*, from Figure 6.14.

of the general idea is therefore not dependent on the sophistication of the proposed grammar.

This language is fairly rich and can be employed to generate simple building layouts. (That there is an infinite number of possible layouts can be proved by considering the repeated application of rule *a*.) There are other rules relating to this domain which can be added. These are illustrated in Figure 6.16 and are concerned with the locations of windows, the locations of openings between rooms, and the deletion of spaces.

This grammar requires more complex geometrical operations than the other grammars discussed above. It has therefore been partially implemented in the procedural programming language C, although the facts base is maintained in Prolog, and it is controlled by a Prolog system. This grammar will be discussed further in Chapter 9.

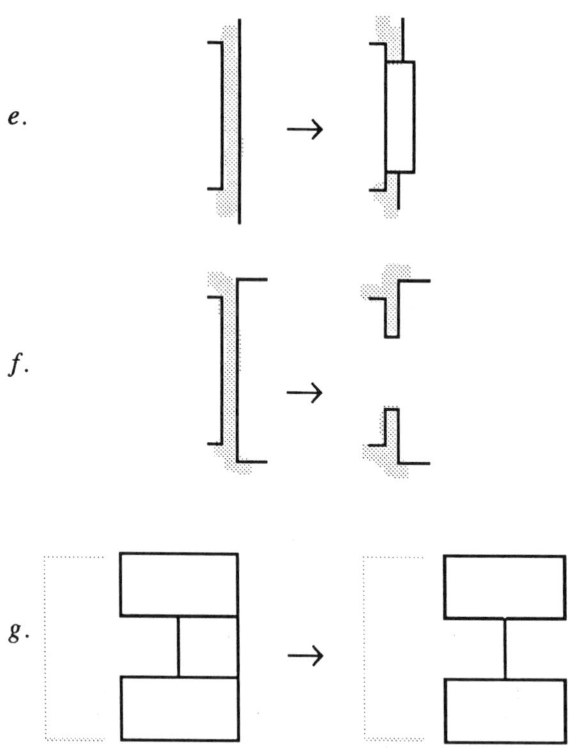

Figure 6.16. Examples of rules for positioning windows (*e*), positioning doors (*f*) and deleting spaces (*g*).

The Role of Planning

In terms of the discussion in the previous chapter, the grammars described above are generally of the type that are 'poorly behaved'. The rules interact with one another to the extent that the implementation of a particular rule might preclude another rule from being fired. There are, typically, several rules applicable at any one state of the design and the selection of the appropriate rule is critical to the outcome. This is a common feature of production systems.

Many automated systems are modelled as production systems. These include systems such as those for game-playing, working out mathematical proofs, and computing robot movements (Latombe, 1983; Christiansen, 1985; Tate, 1985). Production systems provide the basis of general models of problem-solving (Newell and Simon, 1972). The properties of production systems, and the various methods of controlling them have a bearing on the design process. This is where *planning* has a role to play.

Planning can be defined, in the most general sense, as the selection and ordering of rules in a production system to achieve some objective, prior to actually executing the rules. The usual domain in which this is discussed is the field of robotics. An industrial robot is a type of production system. It has a repertoire of actions (rules) with which it can transform some part of the world in order to achieve some desired outcome. A simple control mechanism for a robot might be to attempt a sequence of actions. If an undesirable state is created then it undoes what has just been done and tries some other actions. It would seem important to generate the correct sequence of actions before permitting the robot free rein, as inappropriate actions could be expensive to rectify.

This simple approach to generating states by applying rules in some order then backtracking when an undesirable state is reached is part of a general model of problem-solving and is sometimes called *exhaustive search*, as it involves the systematic investigation of possible states (perhaps *all* the states), until a solution is reached. Planning is concerned with minimizing the amount of searching and backtracking so that desired states can be achieved economically. Planning is therefore not only relevant to robotics but any process modelled on production systems. Planning has therefore been applied to controlling how a system directs attention in analysing a visual image (Ballard and Brown, 1982), working out the steps in chemical experiments (Stefik, 1981a) and modelling how humans go about planning a day's errands (Hayes-Roth and Hayes-Roth, 1979)—to mention but a few applications.

In design, the planning problem can be translated as the selection and ordering of design grammar rules in order to achieve some objective, prior to actually employing those rules to generate the design. The knowledge which permits this is planning knowledge, or alternatively it can be seen as a type of control knowledge, which directs the process of generating designs from a grammar.

Summary

Grammars of design based on the Chomskyan phrase structure model can be created. This model maps onto the production system model of problem-solving described in the previous chapter. The type of grammar with which natural language is concerned, and which has been adopted here, is that of grammars which operate on discrete objects and sets of objects.

Various grammars have been illustrated in this chapter including those concerned with the manipulation of: sets of nodes in a network; sets of lines and points; sets of objects which are described hierarchically; and sets of dimensionless spaces.

The grammars of objects described hierarchically will serve to illustrate some of the features of planning in Chapter 8, and the grammar for producing rectangular dissections will form the basis of the worked example in Chapters 9 and 10. The network grammar provides the basis of a meta-grammar or control grammar. As described here, grammars tend to produce very large numbers of states. There are many sentences in natural language which are syntactically correct (that is, they accord with rules of grammar), but which are meaningless. The task in design is to produce 'meaningful' designs. This issue is partially addressed by planning, which will be the subject of the next chapter.

Chapter 7

Planning Systems

As discussed in the previous chapter design descriptions can be produced by the use of generative grammars. Controlling the generative process so that designs are produced which exhibit some intended performance poses considerable challenge. There would appear to be two broad categories of control regime we can impose on a production system. One is to bring knowledge pertaining to the selection of rules to bear during the execution of the system. This is particularly difficult if the production system is not decomposable. The second is to reason about production rules 'independently' of their execution—that is, to select and order production rules prior to implementing them. We will explore the latter approach in this chapter in the context of planning systems.

We begin by considering how production rules can also be regarded as *actions*. Then we discuss the way in which the idea of abstraction may be exploited in control. The issue of conflict is addressed prior to a review of different planning systems.

Design Actions

The production rules, or grammar rules, by which design states are transformed may also be regarded as design *actions*. For example states may consist of geometrical representations of the object being designed, in the form of lines and labels. The precondition part of the rule will therefore consist of a set of lines and labels to be matched in the current state. If that configuration of lines and labels is present then they are deleted and replaced with the graphical symbols represented in the consequent of the rule. The rules need have no identity other than that represented by the transformations. Each rule could therefore be identified arbitrarily (for example, by a numbering system).

A design grammar may be formulated, however, such that the transformations are related to higher-level actions. The lines and labels may actually describe objects which are to be manipulated in some way. The labels by which the rules are identified are therefore descriptive. Examples of such actions in the design of a building are: place room *a* next to room *b*; place room *a* over room *b*; place object *c* within room *a*; increase width of room *a* to width of room *b*. The preconditions and consequents of these actions incorporate the low-level expression of how these transformations are to be achieved.

Abstraction Levels

Before pursuing the role of planning with actions it is helpful to consider the role of abstractions. It is important to distinguish between three kinds of abstraction hierarchy, each of which can be exploited to some degree in formalizing knowledge about control. These are abstractions of design *descriptions*, abstractions of design *actions* and abstractions of *control*.

(i) Design Description Abstractions

There are obvious economies in carrying out design activity at appropriate levels of abstraction. For example, it is less expensive to design buildings by manipulating walls and spaces, on paper, than it is to design with bricks and concrete on site. It is also generally less expensive to operate on highly abstract descriptions of objects as facts in a computer system than it is to operate on complicated graphical representations. There may be several levels of abstraction that can be considered. In terms of production systems, there are advantages in choosing a system of describing designs and partial designs so that the cost of searching the space of possible states is low. We may explore the space of designs and partial designs by considering only certain attributes of the elements being arranged.

There are at least two kinds of description abstraction that we may consider. Firstly, there is a hierarchy of generality. So we may describe a design in terms of line drawings in which much of the geometry of the design is made explicit. Then there are sketches that are less precise, showing the relationships between elements, their shapes and relative sizes. A further level of abstraction may be portrayed as 'bubble diagrams' which show relationships and relative sizes only. In each case the design is represented at a different level of generality. The 'bubble diagram' is the most general representation.

A further system of description hierarchy is to consider levels of decomposition. So we can describe a design in terms of pylons and spanning members (in the case of a bridge). But the pylons can perhaps be further described in terms of base, shaft and brackets.

We can exploit the idea of different description abstractions in design systems by searching a design space at one level of abstraction then subsequently progressing through more complex abstractions. So we may design with 'bubble diagrams' first, then proceed through to sketches and then to precise line drawings. Or we may design a bridge in terms of pylons and spanning members, then resolve the design by considering the components of each of those elements. We may use the product of the process at one abstraction level to 'guide' the process at another level of abstraction.

(ii) Action Abstractions

As well as abstractions of design description we may consider different abstractions of design *actions*. Again, these can be categorised in terms of generality (or class) and decomposition. Different levels of generality might include actions such as *locate a next to b, locate a touching b,* and *position a east of b*. We may proceed from general statements about the placement of elements to more specific actions. A further system of abstraction might include actions such as *locate, fix in place,* and *bolt*. The abstraction levels proceed from general actions concerned with how elements go together to specific actions about types of fixing.

We may also look at levels of abstraction in terms of the decomposition of actions. So we may have the action that *a* is to be bolted to *b*. This action can be 'expanded' to the actions *put a on b, place a hole in each so that they are aligned,* and *place a bolt in the hole*. Certain design actions can be broken down into other actions, the cumulative effect of which is to achieve the major action.

Again, we can exploit the idea of different action abstractions in a design system by searching a design space by considering actions at one level of abstraction then subsequently progressing through more complex abstractions. We may use the product of the process at one abstraction level to 'guide' the process at another level of abstraction.

(iii) Control Abstractions

That we can have different abstractions of design actions suggests that actions can be treated in much the same way that we treat descriptions of designs. As with design elements, actions can be organized to reflect hierarchies of generality and decomposition. In principle, it is possible to consider the issue of control as simply another abstraction of the design process. Design actions can be treated as objects, and relational statements about actions can be treated as facts. Control knowledge is therefore that which defines spaces of possible action sequences. We may further suppose that there is knowledge pertaining to the *interpretation* of action sequences and knowledge for *generating* action sequences. More generally, we can say that design knowledge can relate to both *form* and *process*. There is knowledge pertaining to the interpretation and generation of *form* in design, and there is knowledge pertaining to the interpretation and generation of *process*. There may also be other abstractions of the design process above this. The exploitation of this idea will be discussed more fully in Chapter 9.

Design Goals

Implicit in the idea of planning is the satisfaction of goals. Goals are certain attributes we require to be exhibited by the final design. Design goals (intended attributes or performances) can be described in different ways. A goal can be expressed in terms of:

1. a certain set of vocabulary elements that are to be present in the final artifact, such as room types or structural elements in a building
2. relationships between elements (for example, that certain rooms are to be adjacent to one another in a building)
3. the attributes of particular elements, such as the requirement that a particular room is square in plan, or that the design as a whole, and not just the individual vocabulary elements, possesses particular attributes
4. constraints, such as minimum floor areas or maximum cost

Goals may be expressed as high-level requirements that need translating into system goals, for example, that the building is to comply with the building regulations or the building is to be of a particular type. Generally, therefore, goals are not expressed in terms of the vocabulary elements on which the grammar operates, but must be inferred in some way from the complex set of relationships within the whole artifact. Attributes can also be expressed in 'fuzzy' terms, such as the requirement that the building be small, or compact, or big. Another issue is that there are often different degrees of commitment to goals. Some cannot be readily satisfied and so are abandoned. In some cases the design process itself suggests which goals are achievable, and a goal set evolves as the design progresses. Some of these issues will be reviewed in Chapter 11.

Apart from these various ways of expressing goals their satisfaction is also complicated by the fact that goals generally conflict or interact with one another in some way. This manifests itself in two ways. Either (i) it proves impossible to achieve a design given a particular goal set, or (ii) during the design process it is found that certain requirements are set up which conflict, but the conflict can be resolved. In the process of searching for a satisfactory sequence of rules it may be discovered that the conditions required to bring about the solution of one goal conflict with the conditions required to bring about the solution to another goal. The task is then to find a means of satisfying the first goal which does not produce a conflict with the means available for satisfying the second goal.

How goals are achieved can depend on the ordering of actions. That the order in which actions are implemented matters can be demonstrated by considering the procedure of stacking three objects on top of each other in a particular order. These objects could be considered as modular components in some very simple building system: a sleeping module (*a*); a living module (*b*); and a service module (*c*). There is only one action, 'place *X* on *Y*', where *X* and *Y* are variables that can be either of the three objects *a*, *b* or *c*.

As there is only enough room for one object on any other object, and an object can only be moved if there is nothing on top of it, the preconditions of the action are that both objects *X* and *Y* are clear on top and that *X* is on something. The consequent of the action is that *X* is still clear, but *Y* is no longer clear, and object *X* is now on top of *Y* and whatever *X* was on is now clear. If the goals are that *a* is to be on top of *b* and *b* is to be on top of *c*, it appears that the order in which an attempt is made to satisfy the goals matters. The initial state is shown in Figure 7.1 as the three objects sitting on a surface (the ground). If we start with the action, place *a* on *b*, it seems that it is not possible to achieve the second goal without undoing the action just performed. Starting with the second goal, however, placing *b* on *c* permits the first goal to be satisfied by the action, place *a* on *b*. There could be a situation, however, in which simply reversing the goals does not work. This is shown in Figure 7.2 where *c* is already on *a* in the initial state. In this case the paths starting with either goal reach a state at which it is not possible to proceed without undoing some action already performed. Yet there must be a simple way to satisfy both goals without performing redundant actions. In planning strategies, therefore, it is generally *not* possible simply to partition goals into independent subproblems.

Because of the general nature of the conflicting goals problem and the simplicity of a blocks world, such as that described above, in modelling it, it is often used as the 'bench test' for planning systems. It does not directly address the complexity of the issues raised above in the representation of design goals, but it serves to demonstrate the general utility of different planning methods in satisfying multiple goals. This example will be employed to introduce some of the approaches to planning demonstrated by different systems.

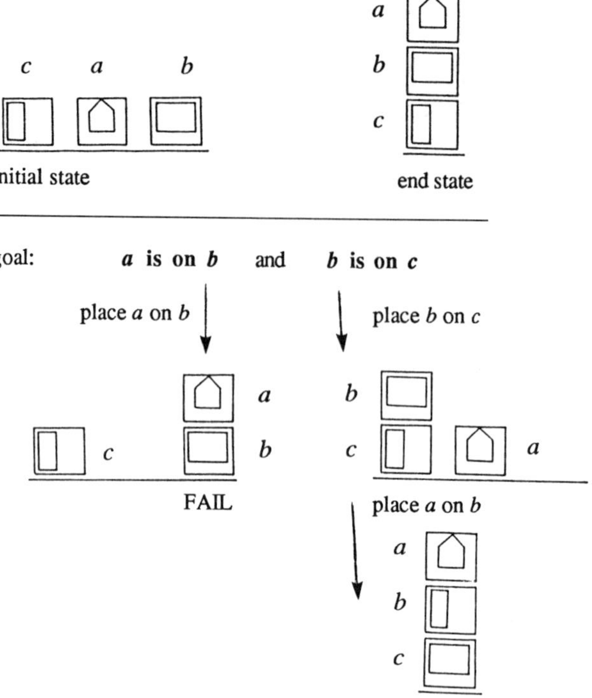

Figure 7.1. Two paths in which an attempt is made to proceed from an initial state to a known end state. The first path starts by attempting to satisfy the first goal. The second path starts from the second goal. The first attempt fails as it is necessary to undo what has already been accomplished in order to satisfy the second goal.

Planning Models

Here some of the major automated planning systems that have been developed to date are considered. Although these systems were not developed as architectural design tools, the generality of the planning issue makes them suitable to design problems as readily as any other sort of problem solving. Akin (1978, 1984) has discussed the parallels between the behaviour of designers and automated problem-solving methods. A formal discussion of some aspects of the following models is provided by Nilsson (1982), with the exception of scheduling and meta-planning systems.

There are two important categories into which planning systems can be divided: those systems which primarily address the issue of goal conflict and those which are more concerned with generalizing the control structure. These concerns overlap, but this serves as a useful general categorization.

Planning systems can, themselves, be described as production systems.

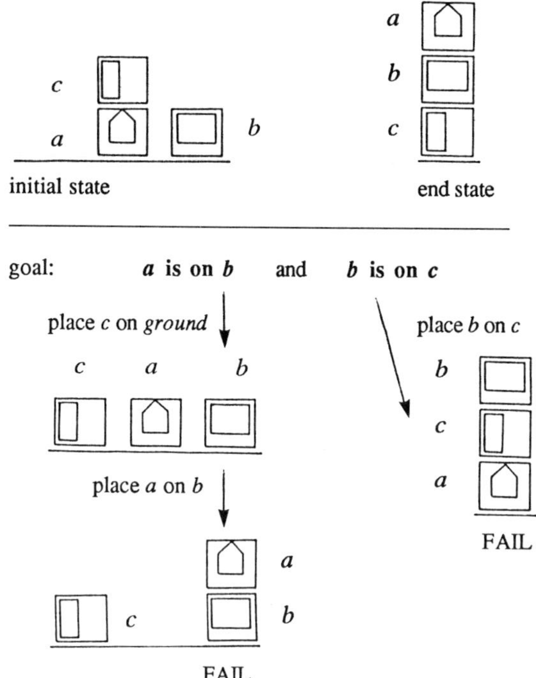

Figure 7.2. Two paths in which an attempt is made to achieve a given end state. Both result in failure.

Where appropriate, the various systems are discussed here in terms of their components: state description (global database); context; planning operators (the production rules of the system); and control. Context refers to that information which is exploited by the system but which does not undergo change. It could therefore also be regarded as part of the global database.

Planning Models for the Efficient Handling of Goal Conflicts

Forward Search

The design action can be represented in the predicate calculus as: **puton**(*X*, *Y*). Its preconditions are: *clear*(*X*); *clear*(*Y*); and *on*(*X*, *Z*). The consequents are: *clear*(*X*); *clear*(*Z*); and *on*(*X*, *Y*). The initial state is represented as: *on*(*c*, *a*), *on*(*b*, *ground*), *clear*(c), *clear*(*b*). The forward search approach is to apply the action to the current state by finding a suitable match for the precondition facts and their variables. These facts are then deleted from the current state and replaced by the consequents. The action is then applied repeatedly until a state which matches the goals is achieved. If a dead-end is encountered, defined as a state in which it is not possible to proceed without undoing an action already performed, then the procedure is to backtrack. The state to which a transformation is applied is therefore simply a list of facts in predicate calculus. The search procedure is shown in Figure 7.3, but states are shown graphically, rather than as lists of facts, for clarity.

This approach provides the advantage that it is a relatively simple matter to evaluate states against any goal set. Provided the knowledge is made available by which the necessary inferences can be made, it is possible, for example, to match the goal: the structure is to contain three storeys with the service module (*c*) at ground level. This is much more difficult with the backward search approach described below. The disadvantage of forward search is that, for realistic problems, it can lead to a combinatorial explosion. Too many states are generated than can be evaluated in a reasonable time. Other approaches have been adopted, therefore, in an attempt to contain the cumbersome nature of the search procedure.

In summary, the forward searching planner can be implemented as a production system with the following characteristics.

STATE DESCRIPTION. A state consists of two components: a *stack* (or ordered list) of actions already attempted and a description of the state of the world resulting from those actions. The *world state* (that is, the state of the blocks world) contains an unordered set of elements. In the example above this includes facts such as: *clear*(*a*) and *on*(*a, b*). The initial state of the planning system corresponds to the initial state of the world, and an empty stack of actions. This is depicted graphically as the state at the top of the network in Figure 7.3. The end state is the goal state plus the stack of actions which produced it.

CONTEXT. In this formulation the context is a set of goals against which the current state is to be evaluated, for example, the goals:

on(*a, b*) and *on*(*b, c*).

PLANNING OPERATORS. The Fikes and Nilsson (1971) formulation of planning operators incorporates three lists of literals or facts. These are: a precondition list; a delete list; and an add list. The operators are represented in the following table. In this example the precondition and delete list for each operator are identical.

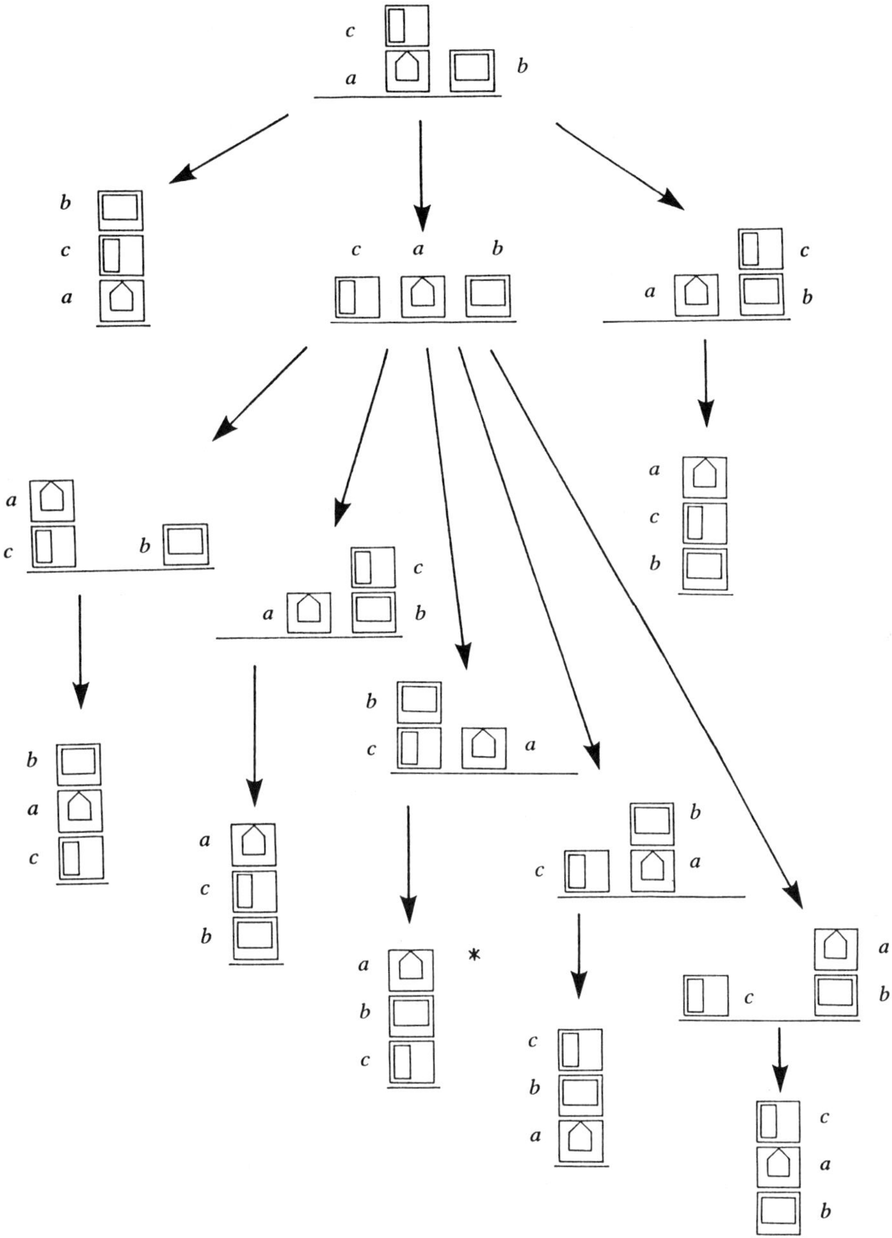

Figure 7.3. Forward search graph for achieving the goal: *on*(*a*, *b*) and *on*(*b*, *c*). The goal state is indicated with *.

action	precondition/delete list	add list
puton(*X*, *Y*)	*clear*(*X*)	*on*(*X*, *Y*)
	clear(*Y*)	*clear*(*X*)
	on(*X*, *Z*)	*clear*(*Z*)

CONTROL. The control mechanism can be described informally as follows.

Consider each planning operator in turn. Search the current state description for a match with the facts in the preconditions part of the operator. If there is a match instantiate the values of the variables with those facts in the state description with which the match is made. Transform the current state by deleting the facts contained in the delete list of the operator and substitute those in the add list. Place the action on the action stack. Evaluate the current state by comparing it with the goal set (in the context). If the current state corresponds with the goal state then terminate, if not then attempt to transform that state in the same way. If no operators are able to be applied without performing redundant actions (that is, repeating a state that has already existed) then backtrack to another rule. This procedure constitutes an exhaustive search through a space of possible states.

Backward Search

Backward search is essentially a reversal of the forward search model, and is described by Nilsson (1982). A system based on this approach is more efficient than forward search provided knowledge which enables it to fail and backtrack when it reaches an impossible state is made available. Such a system is described here.

STATE DESCRIPTION. States consist of unordered sets of facts, as above, and a stack of actions. In this case the initial state consists of facts representing the desired attributes of the final state in the world, and the end state is achieved when the current state matches the *initial* state of the world.

CONTEXT. The context is therefore the initial world state, which constitutes a set of goals for this system. Some knowledge about *impossible* states is also added. This can be represented explicitly as the following impossible conjunctions:

on(*X*, *Y*) and *on*(*Y*, *X*)
on(*X*, *Y*) and *on*(*X*, *Z*) and *not*(*Y* = *Z*)
on(*X*, *Y*) and *X* = *Y*
clear(*X*) and *on*(*Y*, *X*)

PLANNING OPERATORS. The operators are the reverse of those described above, that is, it is necessary to match the facts from the *add* list with the current state. These are deleted and replaced with the *precondition/delete* list of facts.

CONTROL. The procedure is to match the facts in the *add* list of each rule against the facts in the current state. When a match is found, that action is placed on the action stack and all applicable facts related to the world state are deleted. These are replaced with the facts in the *precondition/delete* list of the operator. The tasks of evaluation and backtracking are as discussed in the previous system. The difference is that failure conditions are more difficult to detect. In general, failed states are those in which there is some impossible conjunction of facts as defined above. With knowledge about impossible states it is relatively straight-forward to *prune* those branches of the search tree that lead to failed states. As Nilsson argues, the search tree has more branches than the forward search approach but as the branches are pruned early less search is necessary. The approach is therefore more efficient than forward search. A successful path through the search tree is shown in Figure 7.4. Unsuccessful

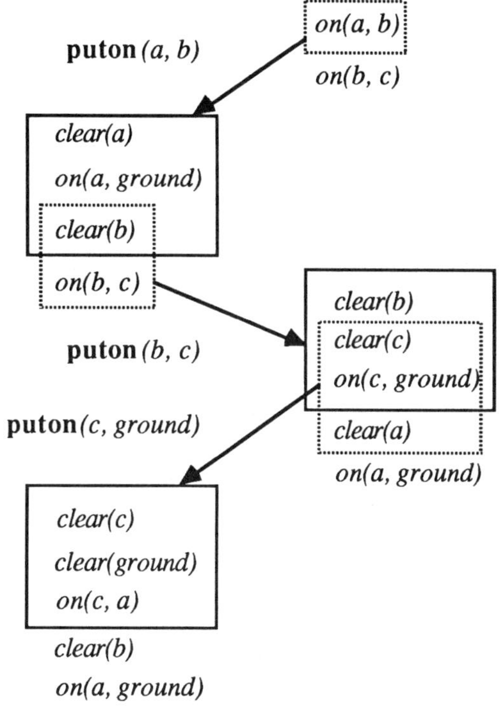

Figure 7.4. The path leading to the satisfaction of the goals *on*(*a*, *b*) and *on*(*b*, *c*) in a backward search graph. Facts which match the add list of an action are enclosed in a box composed of dotted lines. Preconditions are delineated with solid boxes.

paths are omitted for clarity, as are the action stacks.

Instead of stating explicitly those conjunctions of facts which are impossible, they can be deduced from the operators themselves. This requires a mechanism for deducing contradictions within states, and rules of deduction by which these can be determined. This approach introduces efficiencies by introducing more complexity into the control component of the planning system.

Chaining Subgoals

In some cases the search process can be constrained by employing the goals as a starting point and working backwards to see how they can be best achieved. This is behind the planning system by Fikes and Nilsson (1971) called STRIPS. The problem is formulated so that the major component of state descriptions is a stack of goals, the members of which are added and removed one by one according to the conditions which exist in the current description of the world.

That is how the system is implemented, but it can also be described conceptually as operating by matching the first goal against the consequent of an action. This is the same as asking: what action is necessary in order to achieve this goal? The preconditions of this action are then inspected. These preconditions become subgoals, and the system attempts to find what actions are necessary to achieve them. This process of chaining through the actions continues until a set of preconditions is found which match as the initial state of the world. When that state has been reached, the actions which have just been investigated are implemented in order to transform the state of the world.

The second goal is now investigated. If it cannot be satisfied, either by the current state or by some non-redundant action, then the system backtracks to an earlier state and attempts to resatisfy the first goal in an alternative way. This is indicated in Figures 7.5 and 7.6, where the flow of attention from subgoal to subgoal is shown by means of arrows. The letter *T* indicates that a subgoal is true because it matches the current state description. The '*' symbol in Figure 7.5 indicates the subgoal to which the system backtracks in order to produce the graph of Figure 7.6. The sequence of actions is: **puton**(*c, ground*), **puton**(*b, c*) and **puton**(*a, b*).

This approach therefore still involves searching and backtracking. It has the disadvantage that, if the goals are not represented in terms of the consequents of rules it is necessary to furnish the knowledge by which the link can be made.

The STRIPS approach is also amenable to the introduction of certain efficiencies which are discussed below. An early problem solving system was developed by Newell and Simon (1972), called GPS (an acronym for General Problem Solver). Where there are a large number of possible actions by

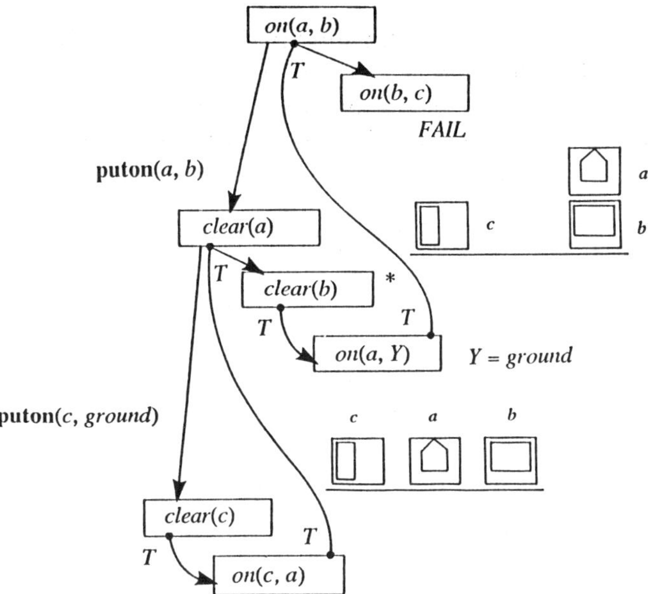

Figure 7.5. Backward search graph to satisfy the goal: *on*(*a*, *b*) and *on*(*b*, *c*), resulting in failure.

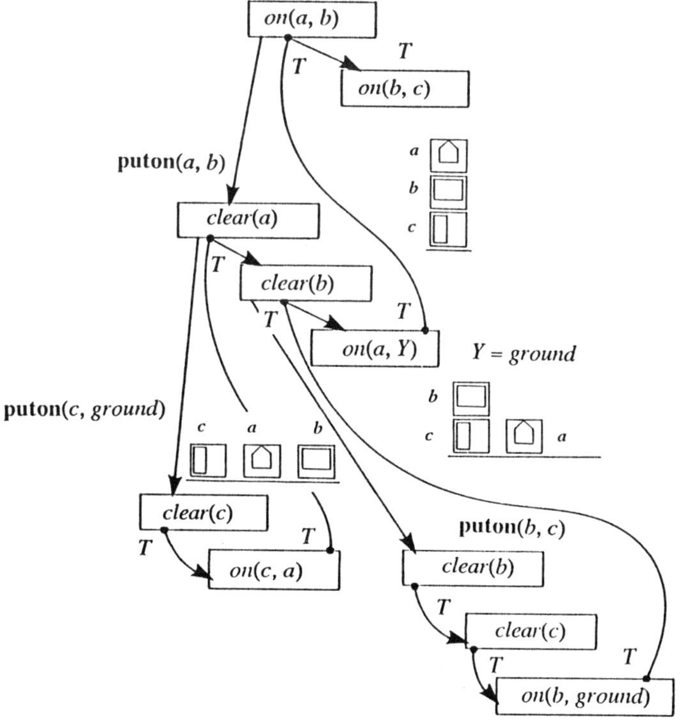

Figure 7.6. Continuation of the search graph of Figure 7.5.

which goals can be achieved, GPS reduces the amount of search by the use of *means-end-analysis*. It identifies appropriate actions by calculating the difference between the current world state and the goals, and selecting an action relevant to reducing the difference. This requires the formulation of a *difference table*, in which actions are ordered according to their ability to reduce certain differences. The search process for an appropriate chain of actions therefore becomes more efficient. The cost is that the difference table has to be given to the system explicitly.

Here the *implementation* of the STRIPS planning system is described. The major component of state descriptions is a stack of goals, the members of which are added and removed one by one according to certain conditions existing in other parts of the state description.

STATE DESCRIPTION. States have three components: an unordered set of facts describing the state of the world brought about by certain actions (*s.1*); a stack of goals and actions (*s.2*); and a stack of actions (*s.3*) which bring about the state in *s.1*. The goals of *s.2* are the facts from the precondition lists of certain actions. For example, in order to achieve the goal *on*(*a, b*) it is necessary to implement the action, **puton**(*a, b*). The preconditions of this action are *clear*(*a*), *clear*(*b*) and *on*(*a*, *Y*). These preconditions can also be seen as plan goals (or subgoals), each of which can be achieved (if they are not already part of the initial world state) by other actions with certain preconditions.

In the initial state of the planner, *s.1* contains facts describing the initial world state, *s.2* contains the goals, and *s.3* is empty. The means by which the end state is evaluated is simply that the goal stack (*s.2*) is empty.

CONTEXT. The context for this interpretation of the STRIPS system consists of the actions outlined as planning operators in the above models, including their *precondition*, *delete* and *add* lists.

PLANNING OPERATORS. Operators are concerned with building up and reducing the goal stack in order to ensure that all goals and subgoals are satisfied. These operators can be described informally as *if-then* rules as follows:

1. **if** the top fact in *s.2* is an action whose preconditions match the facts in *s.1*
   then use it to change *s.1* (that is, delete facts in the *delete* list and substitute those in the *add* list) **and**
   delete the action from *s.2* **and**
   add the action to *s.3*

2. **if** the top fact in *s.2* is a fact describing the state of the world **and** it is true in *s.1*
then delete it from *s.2*

3. **if** the top fact in *s.2* is a fact describing the state of the world **and** it is not true in *s.1*
then find an action with that fact in its *add* list
add that action to the top of the stack in *s.2* **and**
add the preconditions of that action to the top of the stack in *s.2*

CONTROL. The control strategy is the search and backtrack approach already described. Figure 7.7 shows the states in the satisfaction of the goals *on*(*c, b*) and *on*(*a, c*). Only states leading to the satisfaction of the goals are shown here, along with the planning operators which bring about state changes. The action stack (*s.3*) is omitted for simplicity. The STRIPS formulation has actually been simplified. It is possible in the system described here for certain actions to undo goals which have already been solved. STRIPS utilizes the simple expedient of listing goal conjunctions explicitly in the goal stack to ensure that no goal has been violated by the satisfaction of another. This approach is further discussed by Nilsson (1982).

Logic and Theorem Proving Systems

As discussed in Chapter 3 formal logic is concerned with exploring the consistency of sets of statements and determining truth values by the manipulation of those statements. In planning systems based on logic the planning problem is represented as a set of clauses in symbolic logic. Provided the clauses are formulated appropriately, the problem remains to prove the consistency of the statements using any of the various theorem-proving methods available. This offers the advantage that the formulation of the problem is independent of the mechanism used to prove it. Various formulations have been devised, including that by Green (1969) and one by Kowalski (1979). The latter approach is particularly suited to being solved by the logic programming language Prolog.

The following description is of a planning system suitable for implementation in Prolog.

STATE DESCRIPTION. In this formulation states are described by facts and are labelled according to the states in which they are true. So the fact *on*(*a, b*) is true in the state produced by the sequence of actions: **puton**(*c, ground*), **puton**(*a, b*). This can be represented with the predicate:

WORLD STATE	GOAL STACK

s.1	*s.2*
clear(b)	*on(c, b)*
clear(c)	*on(a, c)*
on(c, a)	
on(a, ground)	
on(b, ground)	

(3) ↓

s.1	*s.2*
clear(b)	*clear(c)*
clear(c)	*clear(b)*
on(c, a)	*on(c, a)*
on(a, ground)	**puton**(*c, b*)
on(b, ground)	*on(c, b)*
	on(a, c)

(2) ↓

s.1	*s.2*
clear(b)	**puton**(*c, b*)
clear(c)	*on(c, b)*
on(c, a)	*on(a, c)*
on(a, ground)	
on(b, ground)	

(1) ↓

s.1	*s.2*
on(a, ground)	*on(c, b)*
on(b, ground)	*on(a, c)*
on(c, b)	
clear(c)	
clear(a)	

(2) ↓

s.1	*s.2*
on(a, ground)	*on(a, c)*
on(b, ground)	
on(c, b)	
clear(c)	
clear(a)	

Figure 7.7. State changes in a planning system to satisfy the goals *on(c, b)* and *on(a, c)*. The numbers of the operators which produce the transformations are shown in brackets.

(3) ↓

s.1	*s.2*
on(*a*, *ground*)	*clear*(*a*)
on(*b*, *ground*)	*clear*(*c*)
on(*c*, *b*)	*on*(*a*, *ground*)
clear(*c*)	**puton**(*a*, *c*)
clear(*a*)	*on*(*a*, *c*)

(1) ↓

s.1	*s.2*
on(*a*, *ground*)	**puton**(*a*, *c*)
on(*b*, *ground*)	*on*(*a*, *c*)
on(*c*, *b*)	
clear(*c*)	
clear(*a*)	

(1) ↓

s.1	*s.2*
on(*b*, *ground*)	*on*(*a*, *c*)
on(*c*, *b*)	
clear(*a*)	
on(*a*, *c*)	
clear(*ground*)	

(2) ↓

s.1	*s.2*
on(*b*, *ground*)	*NIL*
on(*c*, *b*)	
clear(*a*)	
on(*a*, *c*)	
clear(*ground*)	

Figure 7.7. (continued).

fact(*on*(*a*, *b*), [**puton**(*a*, *b*), **puton**(*c*, *ground*), *start*]).

The first argument is the literal that is true, and the second argument is a list of actions by which that state is produced. The list is read from the right hand side and begins with the initial state, indicated with *start*.

CONTEXT. In this formulation certain statements about conditions which hold in the initial world state are given as the context. The initial state of the world is:

fact(*on*(*c, a*), [*start*]).
fact(*on*(*a, ground*), [*start*]).
fact(*on*(*b, ground*), [*start*]).
fact(*clear*(c), [*start*]).
fact(*clear*(*b*), [*start*]).

The ground is always clear. This can be represented as an explicit statement:

clear(*ground*).

PLANNING OPERATORS. The planning operators are the actions that transform states, and their precondition, delete and add lists. The general form is:

action(*Name, Preconditions, DeleteList, AddList*).

We can define one operator:

```
action(puton(X, Y),
       [clear(X), clear(Y), on(X, Z)],
       [clear(X), clear(Y), on(X, Z)],
       [on(X, Y), clear(X), clear(Z)]).
```

CONTROL. The control of this system can be made explicit with logical clauses. We need to establish whether or not any fact is true in a particular state. There are four conditions under which a fact can be said to hold true in a given state.

- A fact *holds* **if** it is a fact that is true independently of any state—for example, that the ground is clear.
- A fact *holds* **if** there is some explicit statement in the facts base that the fact is true in that state—for example, that *on*(*c, a*) is true in the initial state.
- A fact *holds* **if** the fact is a consequent of the last action which contributed to that state.
- A fact *holds* **if** it *held* prior to the last action contributing to the current state and is not in the delete list of the last action.

This can be re-stated more formally as:

```
holds(A, _) :- A.
holds(A, B) :- fact(A, B).
holds(A, [B | _]) :- action(B, _, _, C), member(A, C).
```

holds(*A*, [*B*|*C*]) :- *holds*(*A*, *C*),
        action(*B*, _, *D*, _), *not*(*member*(*A*, *D*)).

(The definition of *member* is given on page 46.) We also need to establish whether or not a state is a *possible* state—that is, whether or not actions can logically follow from one another to produce a valid state.

- A state is *possible* **if** it is the initial state.
- A state is *possible* **if** the sequence of actions which produced the last state is *possible* and the last action is consistent with the previous sequence of actions.

This can be re-stated:

possible([*start*]).
possible([*A*|*B*]) :- *possible*(*B*), *consistent*(*A*, *B*).

This definition requires that we are able to ascertain whether or not an action is consistent with the actions that have gone before it.

- An action is *consistent* with a list of actions **if** the action exists and the preconditions of that action *all hold* in the state produced by the list of actions.

consistent(*A*, *B*) :- *action*(*A*, *C*, _, _), *all_hold*(*C*, *B*).

We also require a definition about whether or not a list of facts holds.

- A single fact *holds* in a certain state **if** it *holds* in that state.
- A list of facts *holds* in a certain state **if** the first fact *holds* in that state and the rest of the facts *all hold*.

This can be re-stated:

all_hold([], _).
all_hold([*A*|*B*], *C*) :- *holds*(*A*, *C*), *all_hold*(*B*, *C*).

Armed with this control knowledge it is possible to derive valid states and establish whether or not a fact is true in any given state. Not only will the system establish the truth of a goal statement but also indicate the state in which it is true—that is, the sequence of actions which produces that state. The goal:

?- ***holds*(*on*(*a*, *b*), *X*), *holds*(*on*(*b*, *c*), *X*), *possible*(*X*).**

therefore produces the plan:

$X =$ [**puton**(a, b), **puton**(b, c), **puton**(c, *ground*), *start*]

The disadvantage of this formulation is that generalized theorem provers are very inefficient when it becomes necessary to prove the consistency of large numbers of clauses. The advantage of systems like STRIPS is that certain control strategies appropriate to the domain of planning are built-in. This considerably enhances their efficiency.

Reordering Subgoals

In the above examples, goal conflict is primarily handled by firstly detecting conflicts and then backtracking to earlier states to produce alternative, conflict-free solutions. This entails the inefficient operation of undoing work that has already been performed. An early system which demonstrated the usefulness of reordering goals was the HACKER system developed by Sussman (1975). A more sophisticated approach is exhibited in the INTERPLAN system (Tate, 1975) and the WARPLAN system developed by Warren (Warren, 1974; Coelho et al, 1980), which is similar to the system developed by Waldinger (1977). WARPLAN is similar in principle to the STRIPS system, but is structured to handle the problem of interacting subgoals more efficiently. It has also been formulated as a theorem-proving system in Prolog. It is therefore a system in which the knowledge which pertains specifically to planning problems has been embedded in the logical formulation.

HACKER is primarily a 'learning system' but it also addresses the issue of goal conflicts. It formulates plans which may be defective and then uses various *debugging* procedures to correct them. For the above problem the strategy is to reorder the initial goals. If the ordering means that the first goal is violated by the second then it attempts to solve the second before the first. This approach works in some cases, as in the problem in Figure 7.1, but is not general enough to handle the situation of Figure 7.2.

WARPLAN and INTERPLAN, on the other hand, are able to reorder goals at various levels in the plan. The basic idea is that a plan is constructed by attempting to solve each goal in order, checking that each goal does not interfere with the solution for the previous goal. When the solution to a goal violates a previous goal, that solution is ignored and the goal is moved back to an earlier place in the plan where its solution will not cause any violations.

The basic principles behind these systems are demonstrated by the following formulation.

STATE DESCRIPTION. This system introduces various structures in the form of markers into the goal stack (*s.2*). These include the bracketing together of goals, labels indicating protected goals, and a marker to indicate the site in the goal stack where certain activities are to take place. The initial state of the goal stack *s.2* is therefore:

$$\begin{array}{l}\overline{}\\ \left[\begin{array}{l} on(a,b) \\ on(b,c) \end{array}\right.\end{array}$$

where the horizontal line is the marker and the two goals are bracketed together. The end state is achieved when the marker is at the bottom of the goal stack. The maintenance of the action stack in *s.3* will not be considered here.

CONTEXT. As for STRIPS, the context is the execution operators (actions) and their precondition, delete and add lists.

PLANNING OPERATORS. The planning operators are similar to those for STRIPS, the main difference being that additions to the goal stack do not take place at the top of the stack but at the site just below the marker. There are also rules about the addition and deletion of labels.

1. **if** the fact directly below the marker in *s.2* is an action whose preconditions match the facts in *s.1*
   then use it to change *s.1* (that is, delete facts in the *delete* list **and** substitute those in the *add* list) **and**
   move marker down one line

2. **if** the fact directly below the marker in *s.2* is a fact describing the state of the world **and**
   it is true in *s.1*
   then move the marker down one line.

3. **if** the fact directly below the marker is a fact describing the state of the world **and**
   it is not true in *s.1*
   then find an action with that fact in its *add* list **and**
   add that action above the fact **and**
   add the preconditions of that action above it in the stack **and**
   bracket them together

4. **if** the marker bisects a bracket,
   then place a pointer (*) on the bracketed facts which lie above the marker

5. **if** there is a goal in the stack labelled (*); and
the bracket in which the labelled goal occurs is not bisected by the marker
then delete the label

CONTROL. The procedure is to cycle through the planning operators as they are applicable. The complication in this system is with the detection and remedy of a goal violation. The development of the goal stack is shown in Figure 7.8. Applicable planning operators which produce those states are also

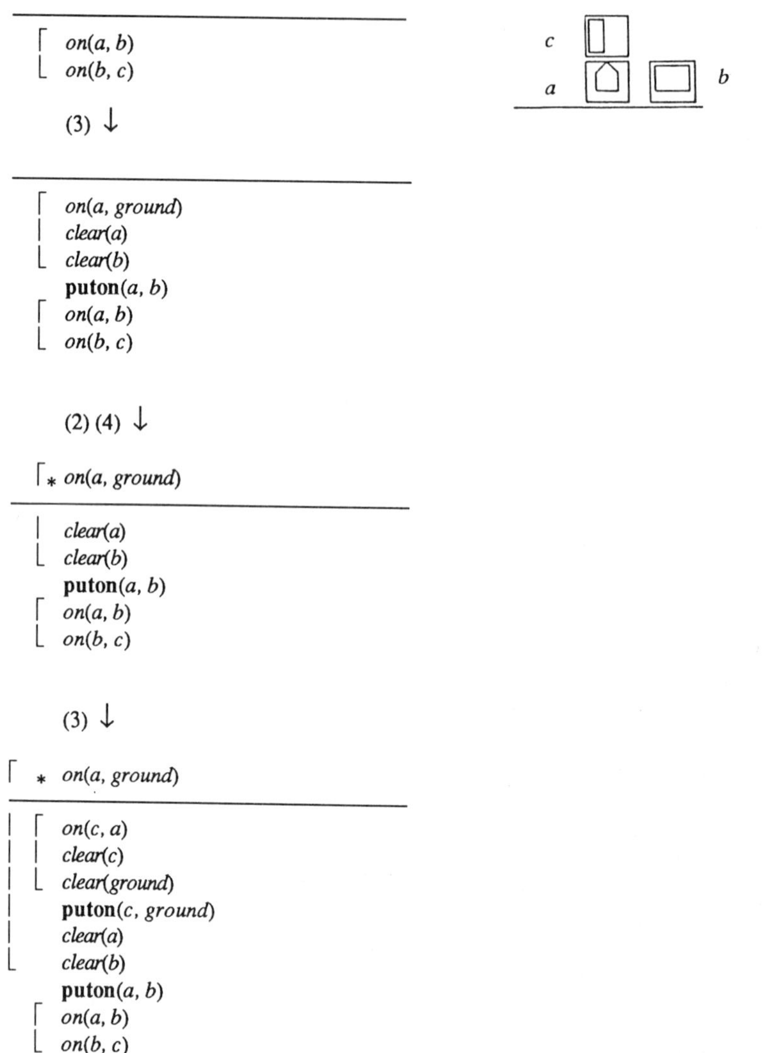

Figure 7.8. Development of the goal stack in the system that reorders subgoals in the event of conflict.

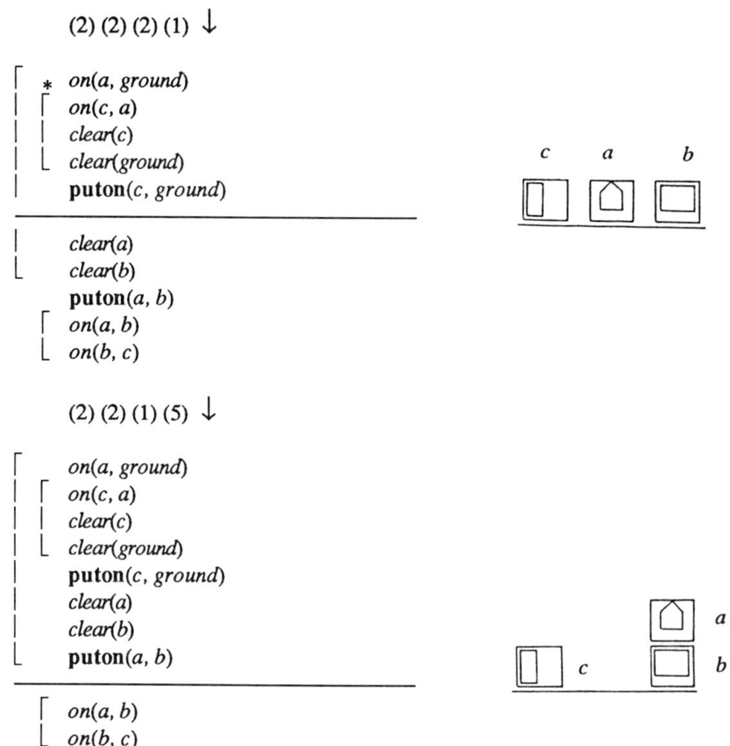

Figure 7.8. (continued).

indicated, and the current world state is shown graphically. In effect, the world state is that which is achieved by the application of the actions above the marker. This occurs when the state in Figure 7.9 is achieved. In order to satisfy the goal, *clear*(*b*), just below the marker it is necessary to violate the protected goal, **on*(*a, b*). In order to avoid this the procedure is to search for the protection violating component in the stack. This is the goal, *on*(*b, c*), at the bottom of the bracket. Because this goal cannot be satisfied without undoing the solution to previous goals, it is now inserted just above the action which precedes the protected goal, the action: **puton**(*a, b*), and the marker is placed just above that.

The contents of the bracket in which the violation occurred are eliminated, except for the protected goal, and the bracket is extended upwards to include the goal that has been moved. The world state is also adjusted to reflect this change. This procedure then produces the stack shown in Figure 7.10. Effectively, the task of satisfying the goal, *on*(*b, c*), has been placed before the action of putting A on B. Further goal 'regression' later on ensures that the goal is accomplished even before A is picked up. The end state is shown in Figure 7.11. The action sequence can be read from the stack.

(2) (4) (3) (2) (4) ↓

```
┌     on(a, ground)
│  ┌  on(c, a)
│  │  clear(c)
│  └  clear(ground)
│     puton(c, ground)
│     clear(a)
└     clear(b)
      puton(a, b)
┌   * on(a, b)
│  ┌* on(b, ground)
─────────────────────────────────────
│  │  clear(b)            ← violates * on(a, b)
│  └  clear(c)
│     puton(b, c)
└     on(b, c)             ← protection violation component
```

Figure 7.9. Detection of a violation.

```
┌   * on(a, ground)
│  ┌  on(c, a)
│  │  clear(c)
│  └  clear(ground)
│     puton(c, ground)
│   * clear(a)
│   * clear(b)
─────────────────────────────────────
└  ┌  on(b, c)
   │  puton(b, c)
   └  on(a, b)
```

Figure 7.10. Change to goal stack in order to rectify violation condition.

Hierarchical Systems

The approach here is to enhance the efficiency of the goal-chaining model of STRIPS by distinguishing between factors which are most important in determining the shape of the plan and those which are less important. In order to do this the planner operates at various levels of abstraction. A high abstraction level is that in which only a few of the attributes of the blocks world are considered. When a plan is formulated considering the most important factors, the system is operating at the highest level of abstraction. When the least consequential factors are being considered it is operating at the lowest level. In effect, the plan worked out at the highest level of abstraction

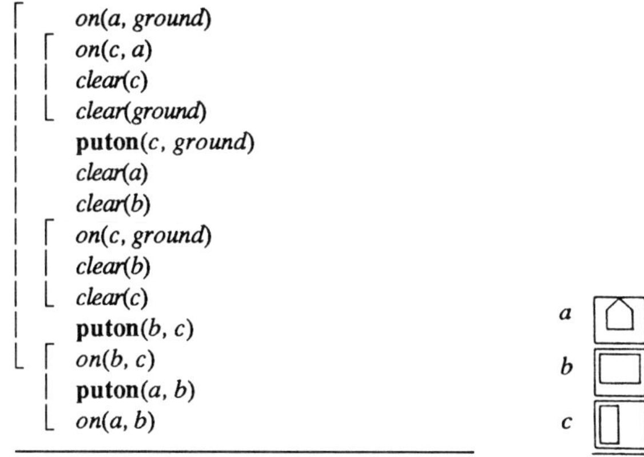

Figure 7.11. The end state incorporating the final ordering of actions.

is a skeletal or partial plan (that is, it is correct, but incomplete) and the details are filled out at the next level down in the hierarchy. Goal conflict is therefore handled by resolving conflicts at a higher level of abstraction before the details of the plan are worked out.

This approach introduces efficiencies by relatively simple means. The difficulty lies in assigning degrees of importance to the preconditions of the actions. These levels are not intrinsic to the problem domain, but must be derived experimentally or intuitively (that, by making a good guess). The hierarchical approach has been developed in the ABSTRIPS planning system by Sacerdoti (1974).

STATE DESCRIPTION. States are basically as for STRIPS except that a fourth component is added (*s.4*) which contains a record of the abstraction level being considered. The end state is achieved when the abstraction level in *s.4* has a value of 1 and the goal stack in *s.2* is empty. As before, the output to the system is the action stack in *s.3*.

CONTEXT. As for STRIPS, the context consists of the actions and their precondition, delete and add lists. Also included is the ordering of precondition facts according to their perceived importance in contributing to an overall plan. Only preconditions need to be ranked in this way. The assignment of facts to a hierarchy of levels is determined heuristically:

level 2. *on*(*X*, *Y*)
level 1. *clear*(*X*)
clear(*Y*)
on(*X*, *Y*)

It will be noted that the levels are accumulative, that is, at level 1 all three preconditions are considered, at level 2 only *on* is considered.

PLANNING OPERATORS. The Planning operators are as for STRIPS with the revision of rule 3 and the addition of rule 4.

3. **if** the top fact in *s.2* is a fact describing the state of the world **and**
   it is not true in *s.1*
   then find an action with that fact in its add list **and**
   add that action to the top of the stack in *s.2* **and**
   add the preconditions of that action appropriate to the level indicated in *s.4*

4. **if** the state *s.2* is empty **and**
   the level in *s.4* is greater than 1
   then transfer the contents of the action stack *s.3* to *s.2* **and**
   subtract 1 from the value of the level in *s.4* **and**
   place the preconditions of each action applicable to the level in *s.4* directly above each action in the goal stack *s.3* **and**
   revert to initial condition in *s.1*

CONTROL. The control mechanism is as for STRIPS. Figure 7.12 shows how states are transformed in order to satisfy the world goals, *on*(*c*, *b*) and *on*(*a*, *c*). The procedure is as for STRIPS, the difference being that only preconditions appropriate to the level of abstraction are added to the goal stack (*s.2*). Rule 4 ensures that, after formulating a plan at one level of abstraction, the plan is reconsidered at the next level down. The states along the path to a solution are shown. Level 2 provides the skeleton of a plan which is filled out at subsequent levels. The plan sequence is: **puton**(*c*, *b*) and **puton**(*a*, *c*). In this simple example, no alteration to the plan is required at level 1. In the event of failure, the system would revert back to the earlier abstraction level where a revised skeletal plan would be generated. This is demonstrated in the next chapter.

Knowledge-Based Control Models

The systems discussed so far have been concerned with the efficient solution of the interacting subgoals problem. The control structure is generally that of search and backtracking, although the more efficient systems incorporate more complex mechanisms. How the knowledge about efficient planning can be made more *explicit* is considered here.

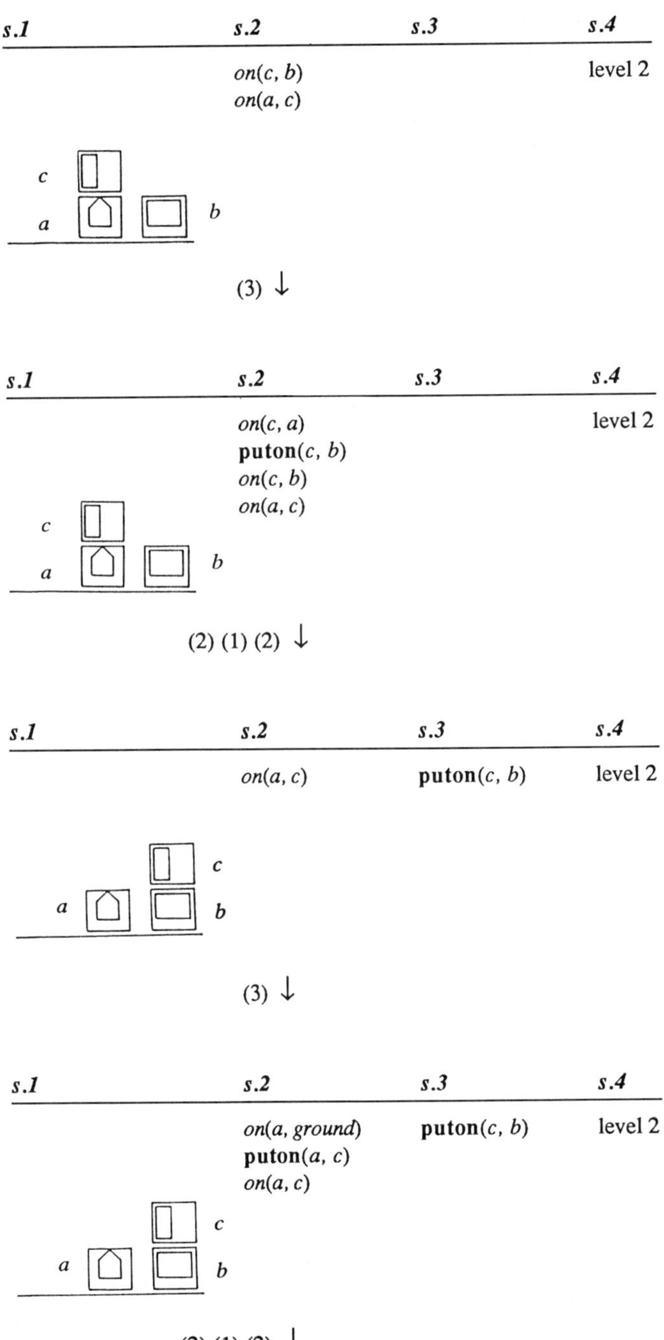

Figure 7.12. Transformation of states in a hierarchical planning system.

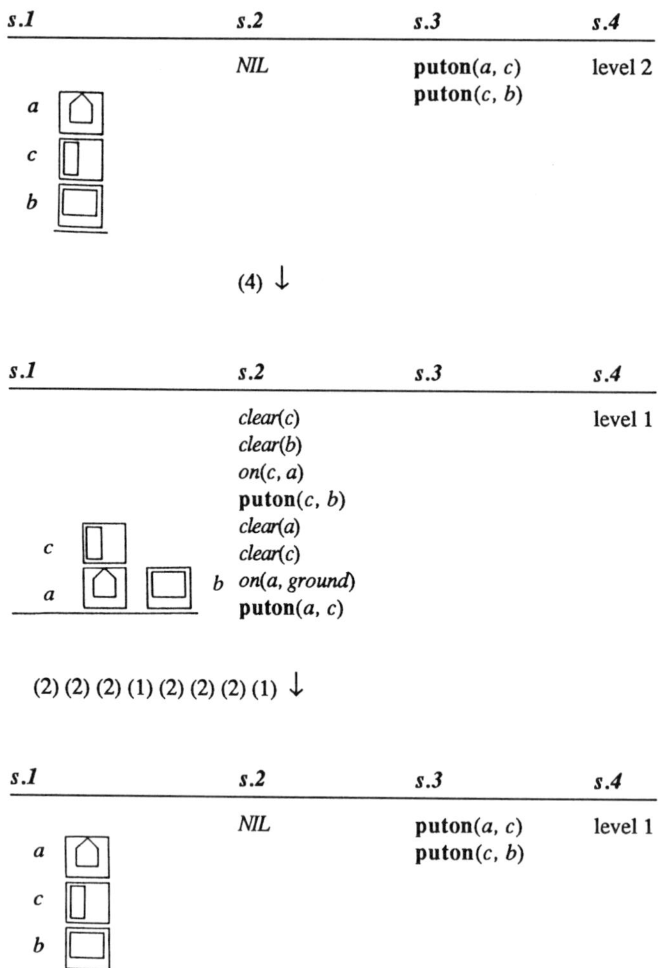

Figure 7.12. (continued).

Hierarchical Refinement of Plan States

In the NOAH planning system (Sacerdoti, 1977) an attempt is made to make the knowledge about efficient planning explicit. Operators called *expansion rules* and *critics* are employed to transform partial plan states. Critics effectively 'observe' what is happening to states and are triggered into action when something occurs that they are designed to respond to (Sussman, 1975; Dietterich and Buchanan, 1981).

In this formulation a planning state contains explicit information about actions and how they are related to one another. Actions can be related serially (that is, they can be laid out in the order in which they are to be executed) or groups of actions may be related in some parallel configuration. It is therefore possible to represent a partial ordering of actions. The *procedural network* is a convenient structure for representing these relationships. The initial state consists of a parallel arrangement of a few, high-level actions, derived from the goals, and the final state consists of a serial arrangement of low-level actions able to be executed by a design system.

States are transformed by means of expansion rules, which substitute low-level actions for high-level actions in the network, and critics are rules which incorporate knowledge about resolving conflicts between actions. Figure 7.13 shows the simple example given by Sacerdoti which illustrates the major principles behind NOAH. A goal is represented by the high-level actions: paint

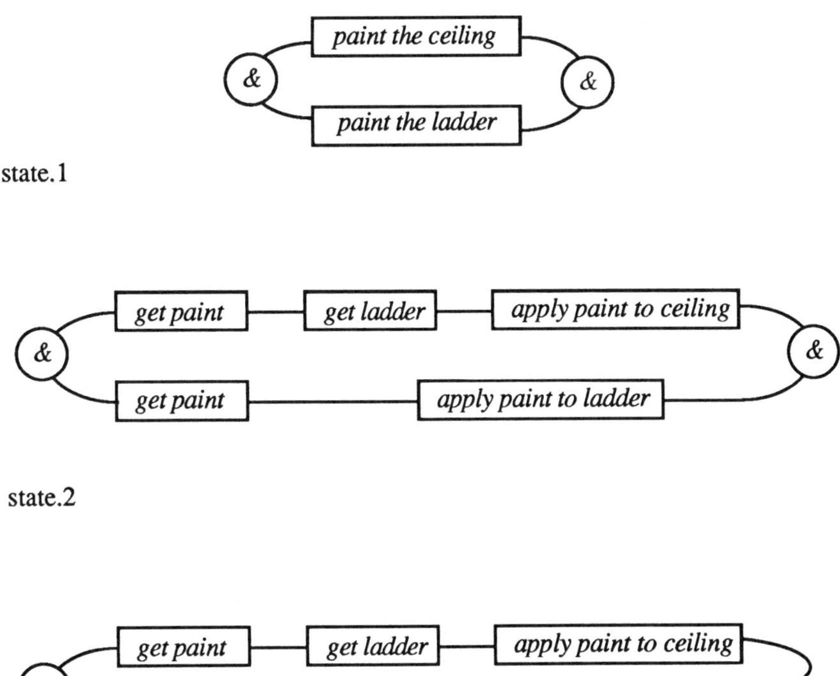

Figure 7.13. States in the development of a procedural network (after Sacerdoti, 1977).

the ladder and paint the ceiling. These are represented in parallel in the network, as there is no commitment to order, as yet. When this network is expanded, it becomes clear that certain actions conflict. (It is not possible to 'get' something that has just been painted.) The ordering of the actions matters, and it becomes necessary to apply one of the critics (the Resolve Conflicts Critic) in order to adjust the network. The network can then be expanded further if necessary, and further conflicts resolved by the critics as they appear.

This approach ensures that partial plans are refined by critics before they become too large. The system therefore proceeds from a less detailed to a more detailed plan, the critics making sure that the actions make some sort of global sense before the network is expanded further. It can also be seen as a hierarchical approach where attempts are made to create simple, correct, high-level plans before they are expanded to greater detail where the costs of rectifying plans are greater. This approach means that backtracking is not necessary. The cost is that knowledge about conflict resolution has to be made explicit.

STATE DESCRIPTION. The initial state is a conjunction of high-level actions depicted as a procedural network and which are to be expanded to form a plan that can be executed. The components of the end state are not specified, but it is achieved when no operators can be applied. The end state would be expected to contain a substantial serial component.

CONTEXT. The context consists of facts about the preconditions and deletions of the various actions. Both the action, **puton**(*X*, *Y*), and the facts, *on*(*X*, *Y*) and *clear*(*X*), are handled in a similar manner in the procedural network. The On and Clear facts can be regarded as 'non-executable actions' which are of assistance in helping to formulate the final plan. Only the delete list of the **Puton** action is of interest in the example presented here:

action	delete list
puton(*X*, *Y*)	*clear*(*Y*)

PLANNING OPERATORS. There are two classes of operators in NOAH (and therefore two types of procedures for transforming states). One is a hierarchical mapping between actions (which are call *expansion rules* here), the other is the *critic*. Expansion rules contain knowledge about how individual actions are achieved. The procedure for handling this type of operator is to substitute the actions on the right of a rule for the action on the left. The critics contain more global knowledge. They are procedural modules of specialized knowledge which enables them to detect certain interactions between actions, and to make changes to procedural networks. Each critic may have a different procedure so it is not always possible to represent the knowledge they contain in a uniform way.

Two expansion rules are shown graphically in Figure 7.14. Three critics which are of use in this domain bear the names:

Resolve Conflicts
Remove Redundant Preconditions
Use Existing Objects

CONTROL. The control system is very simple as the power of this approach lies within the critics. The procedure is to cycle through each expansion rule in turn and, after each expansion, cycle through the critics. There is no need to consider backtracking (although the system, as described by Sacerdoti, retains a record of earlier states to assist in monitoring the execution of robot actions). Figure 7.15 shows how the goals, *on*(*c, b*) and *on*(*a, c*), are achieved. *State.1* can be seen as the conjunction of two high-level actions, *on*(*c, b*) and *on*(*a, c*). This is expanded to *state.2*. The Resolve Conflicts critic detects that the action, **puton**(*a, c*), deletes (or *denies*) the action, *clear*(c). In order to resolve the conflict, the critic adjusts the network so that the sequence of actions of which *clear*(c) is a part occurs before **puton**(*a, c*). This is shown in *state.3*. The Remove Redundant Preconditions critic produces *state.4*, and this is expanded to *state.5*. The critic, Use Existing Objects, instantiates the values of any variables. This critic plus the Remove Redundant Preconditions critic produce *state.6*. The nodes, *clear*(*b*) and *clear*(c), exist in the initial state and so can be ignored. The plan is therefore: **puton**(*c, b*), **puton**(*a, c*).

An alternative way of visualizing states is to regard them as partially formed search graphs indicating subgoal chainings. Critics are therefore designed to construct an end state which has been pruned. The procedural network formulation of states, however, makes it easier to represent partial orderings than branched search trees.

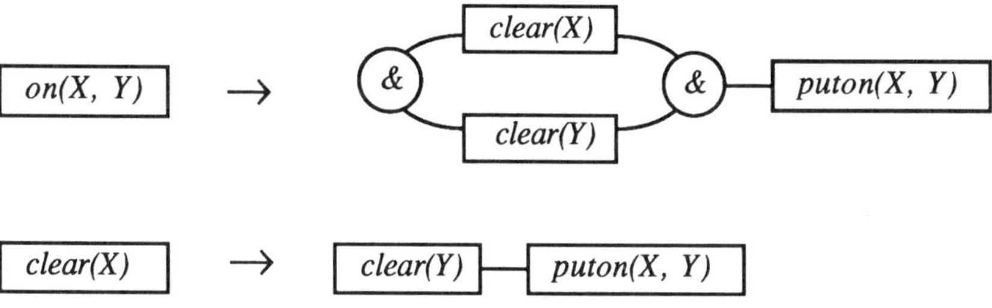

Figure 7.14. Expansion rules for the blocks world.

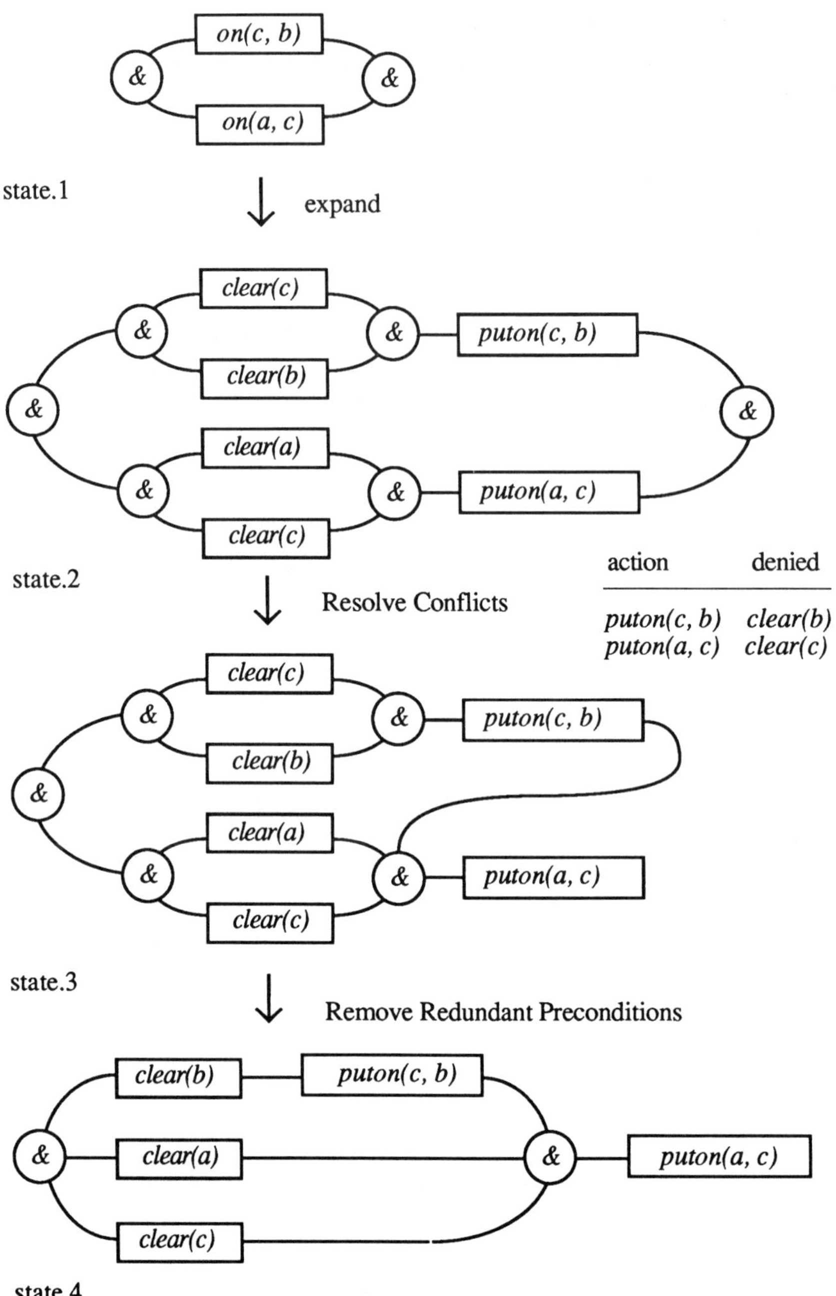

Figure 7.15. States in the transformation of a procedural network for a plan which satisfies the goals: *on*(*c*, *b*) and *on*(*a*, *c*).

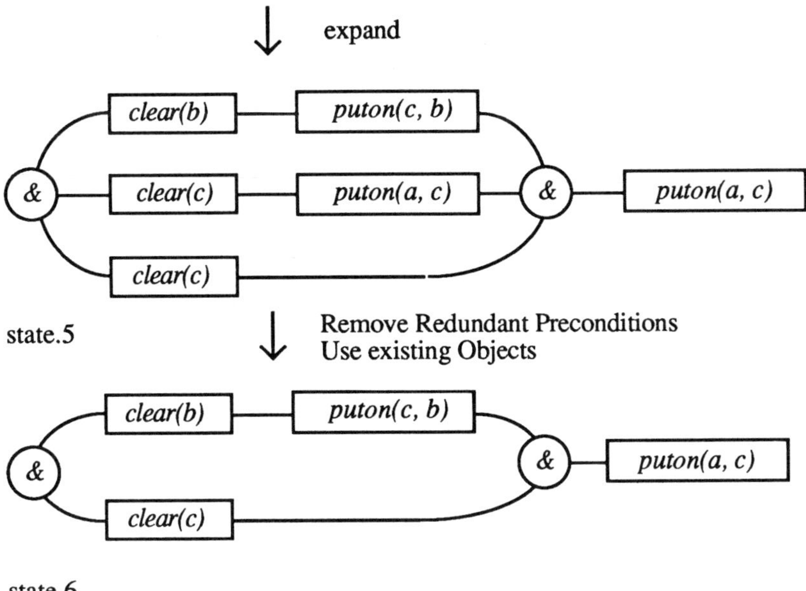

Figure 7.15. (continued).

The expansion rules and critics constitute a production system that is commutative, that is, it always produces the same end state irrespective of the order in which the operators are applied. There are no failed states, and changing the ordering of operators (expansions or critics) only has a bearing on the efficiency with which an end state is achieved. The system also has the major advantage that the intermediate states are 'legible' to a greater degree than the goal stacks of the systems described above. The system therefore lends itself to being understood by human observers while the plan is generated.

Scheduling Planning Knowledge

This approach was developed as a structure for handling complex problems which rely on a rich body of knowledge for their solution, but which are not amenable to the above formulations. (Most design tasks would come under this category.) The essential feature of this approach is that the states and the knowledge (rules) which operate on states are partitioned in such a way as to make explicit various types of knowledge. Some of this knowledge relates to control, that is, determining which rules to apply next. The approach is applicable to problem solving in general, and not just planning. The ideas gained currency with the development of the HEARSAY-II speech understanding project (Erman et al, 1980). This led to the development of a generalized system appropriate to other domains, called HEARSAY-III (Balzer et al, 1980; Erman et al, 1981), and a system called AGE (Nii and Aiello, 1979). These latter two systems can be regarded as computer tools for experimenting with and creating rule-based problem-solvers, and are also described by Hayes-Roth et al (1983). Hayes-Roth and Hayes-Roth (1979) have demonstrated the applicability of this approach to modelling cognitive planning activity.

The structure which records the current state is commonly referred to as a *blackboard*. It may be divided into various parts and subparts. The part concerned with ordering the application of rules (scheduling) typically contains records placed there by actions *competing* to be executed, including an ordered list (*schedule*) of actions to be performed. The part of the blackboard concerned with representing the state of the problem is the *domain blackboard*.

The rules for transforming states are commonly termed *knowledge sources*. They are similar to the critics, described above, in that they may incorporate complex procedures for bringing about changes to the current state, but they differ in the way they are implemented. Knowledge sources are generally represented as production rules, the main feature of which is the way that the matching of preconditions is separated from the actual execution of the consequents. The part of a knowledge source which looks for preconditions in the current state description is termed the *trigger*. When it finds a match it causes two types of records to appear on the scheduling blackboard: the elements of the current state which caused the triggering (considering that a match may be made with more than one element in the current state description for the same knowledge source); and the name of the knowledge source to which the trigger belongs.

In general, more than one trigger will be applicable, that is, more than one knowledge source could be activated given the current state. The scheduling knowledge sources decide which of these to activate based on scheduling heuristics, the information recorded on the scheduling blackboard and the domain blackboard. Hayes-Roth and Lesser (1977) proposed a set of selection criteria for use in the HEARSAY speech understanding system. Examples of such scheduling rules are:

if one of the competing tasks is known to make the others unnecessary
then select that one

if a knowledge source is operating on a part of the blackboard known to contain more reliable information
then select that knowledge source

if a knowledge source is operating on a part of the blackboard known to contain more important information
then give it priority

if a knowledge source is known to be more efficient
then select that one

if a knowledge source is known to be more likely to lead to a final state which matches the goals of the system
then give it priority

A systems of weightings is applied in order to select between competing knowledge sources. The control task consists simply of taking the first element from the ordered list maintained by the scheduler and executing it. Scheduling can be illustrated in the context of the NOAH example described above.

Even though the example is very simple, and can readily be solved without scheduling the operators, there are in fact choices to be made at each state: the expansion operators could be applied to different elements in the network; it may be possible to apply the critics in a different order. An example of two scheduling rules for such a system might be:

if a critic and an expansion rule are competing
then give the critic higher priority

if several critics are competing
then give priority to those which reduce the size of the network

Blackboard systems have formed the basis of the Hayes-Roth and Hayes-Roth (1979) model of human planning activity. This approach makes it possible to reproduce the *opportunistic* way in which (it is maintained) people make plans. Planning is treated as a *multi-directional process*, where the process of formulating plans actually leads people to change and adapt strategies as they think through a problem. Human planning activity operates at different levels of abstraction in both a *top-down* and a *bottom-up* fashion, and it involves both forward search and backward chaining. The blackboard approach provides a loosely structured, knowledge dependent mechanism for simulating such behaviour.

Providing the problem has been formulated such that the operators (knowledge sources) operate as a commutative system, the scheduling approach is reasonably sound, as even an incorrect ordering of actions will lead eventually to the solution. For non-commutative rule sets it is more important that the heuristics which guide the scheduling process are effective in producing a solution.

This approach provides the advantage that knowledge which would otherwise have been part of a control procedure is made explicit in the form of scheduling rules. This provides scope for creating a system in which control knowledge is explicit and legible, although, perhaps at the expense of efficiency.

Meta-Planning

A major objective in the design of planning systems is described here rather than a particular planning system. Some systems have been proposed which contain components called meta-planners, including MOLGEN, a system for planning steps in laboratory experiments (Stefik, 1981b), the Hayes-Roth and Hayes-Roth (1979) model and a general system developed by Wilensky (1981). The term *meta-planning* is generally employed in two different senses (although there is some overlap). First, it is employed in the sense of describing a particular level of control in a planning system (usually the top level). A meta-planner is therefore a control mechanism which contains knowledge about the formulation of plans within a particular domain. In this sense the scheduling knowledge in the example above is meta-planning knowledge.

The second view concentrates on the contents of that knowledge. Meta-planning knowledge is seen as completely independent of any particular problem domain. It concerns universal principles generally adopted in decision-making. Wilensky outlines the sort of *meta-themes* or goals which might guide the planning process. These include:

conserve resources
achieve as many goals as possible
maximize the value of the goals achieved
avoid impossible goals
do not violate desirable states

It can be seen that these are the sorts of principles that have guided the formulation of the various planning systems described above. If the knowledge by which these goals are achieved can be made explicit, as in a scheduling system, then it is possible to devise a completely general problem-solving system responsive to any domain. No system has yet been devise which effectively exploits this idea.

Constraint Posting and the Refinement of Skeletal Plans

Two other developments within planning systems, which have not been discussed so far, include the mechanism of *constraint posting* as exemplified in the MOLGEN system (Stefik, 1981a), and the refinement of stored plans as exemplified in the version of MOLGEN developed by P. Friedland and discussed by Cohen and Feigenbaum (1982). So far in this discussion it has been assumed that the selection of objects (for example: objects *a*, *b* and *c*) in the design actions, can be achieved by simple pattern matching. Constraint posting involves deferring decisions about objects for as long as possible. As the plan is being developed, constraints on the attributes of those objects are set up. Eventually it becomes necessary to select a suitable object. This can be achieved by finding an object which matches all the constraints.

The refinement of stored plans involves the selection of abstract, or *skeletal* plans (from a *repertoire* of plans) appropriate for solving a particular problem. Planning involves selecting skeletal plans and filling in the details appropriate to the specific problem at hand. These approaches have not been developed to the same extent as the systems already discussed.

Summary

A planning system is simply a controller for a production system which selects and orders rules before they are executed, in order to achieve some objective. At a very simple level, planning systems therefore provide a mechanism by which designs can be produced to exhibit some intended performance.

A major issue in satisfying goals is the *interdependence* of goals and subgoals. The general ways in which different systems handle goal interaction have been reviewed.

It should be noted that in the systems discussed, an increase in efficiency is generally accompanied by a decrease in legibility. The more efficient the system, the less explicit, accessible and flexible is the knowledge contained within it.

The NOAH planning system provides the genesis of a model applicable to design which is developed in this thesis. Design appears to be a loosely structured, knowledge-rich activity and as such requires a medium for representation which allows free rein to that knowledge. In the next chapter the applicability of these planning approaches to particular generative grammars of design will be discussed.

Chapter 8

Planning Models and Design

As discussed in the previous chapter control is a key component in the operation of a design grammar, particularly as it concerns the selection and ordering of rules. There are five models of planning considered here in relation to design. One model is that of exhaustive generate and test (or forward search) in an abstraction space. The second model is to start with the goals and work backwards, determining what actions are necessary to accomplish certain goals and subgoals. This regards design knowledge as essentially concerned with how goals are accomplished. The third model is to consider the hierarchical nature of planning decisions.

The fourth model leads towards a more comprehensive view of control in the design process, where it is considered that planning can be viewed as a design task itself. The artifact in this case is an ordered set of design operators, and states are transformed by means of *planning* operators. This leads to a multilevel view of control, which is developed further in Chapters 9 and 10. Each of these models is subsumed by the view that design is a multilevel task with activities occurring at different levels of control.

These models are illustrated with a simple building design grammar. A site context is considered, for which sequential planning can assist in locating a building. This example is 'artificial' but affords a prelude to a spatial layout system discussed in the next chapter. Examples are described as implemented as logic programs in Prolog (in 'Edinburgh syntax'). Search and backtracking is explained in detail. Detailed explanations may be passed over by readers for whom this provides little interest.

Forward Chaining

The knowledge required for generating the simple building structure described in Chapter 6 (Figures 6.10-6.13) is considered here. The rules for generating building forms from wall and column elements are shown in Figure 6.10. The elements form rooms, each of which has a name and an orientation. One of the rules, labelled *rule*(2), is also depicted in program form in Figure 6.12 and graphically in Figure 6.13. These rules can be incorporated into a generative system which exhaustively searches the tree of states depicted in Figure 6.11. Planning involves selecting and ordering an appropriate sequence of rules in order to create an end state with the particular intended attributes, without having to generate all the states of Figure 6.11 in the process.

In the *forward search* and backtracking model an appropriate sequence of rules is derived by searching within a higher level of abstraction than that depicted graphically. The abstraction of *rule*(2) is illustrated here.

Rule(2) can be fired if *room_a* has been located and if there is nothing abutting its right side. The consequent of this rule is that *room_a* is still located, *room_c* is also now located, and *room_c* is clear on its top, right and left sides. (Note that these orientations—top, right and left—are relative to the orientation of the object. The dot marks the *top* of a room.) An example of such a rule abstraction is shown formally below:

```
rule(2)# [located(room_a), clear(room_a, right)]
    >>
    [located(room_a), located(room_c), clear(room_c, top),
    clear(room_c, right), clear(room_c, left)].
```

If each rule is represented in this manner it is possible to search the design space for states which contain those particular attributes. An example is to consider the goal that both *room_a* and *room_d* are to be located. This produces the search space shown in Figure 8.1. It is only necessary to evaluate each state as it is produced to see if it contains the goal attributes and backtrack when dead-end states are reached.

Backward Chaining

Backward chaining, involves knowing what rules must be applied in order to satisfy certain goals. This knowledge is contained in the rules themselves. For example, for the goal: *located*(*room_d*), there are two rules that satisfy this condition, *rule*(*4*) and *rule*(*6*). Selecting the first rule, it is necessary to look at what conditions must be satisfied before that rule can be implemented. These conditions are that *room_b* is located and that the right side of *room_b* is clear, both of which can be satisfied by *rule*(*3*). By chaining back through these conditions the initial state is reached. Backward chaining is a trivial process when there is only one goal to be achieved, but becomes

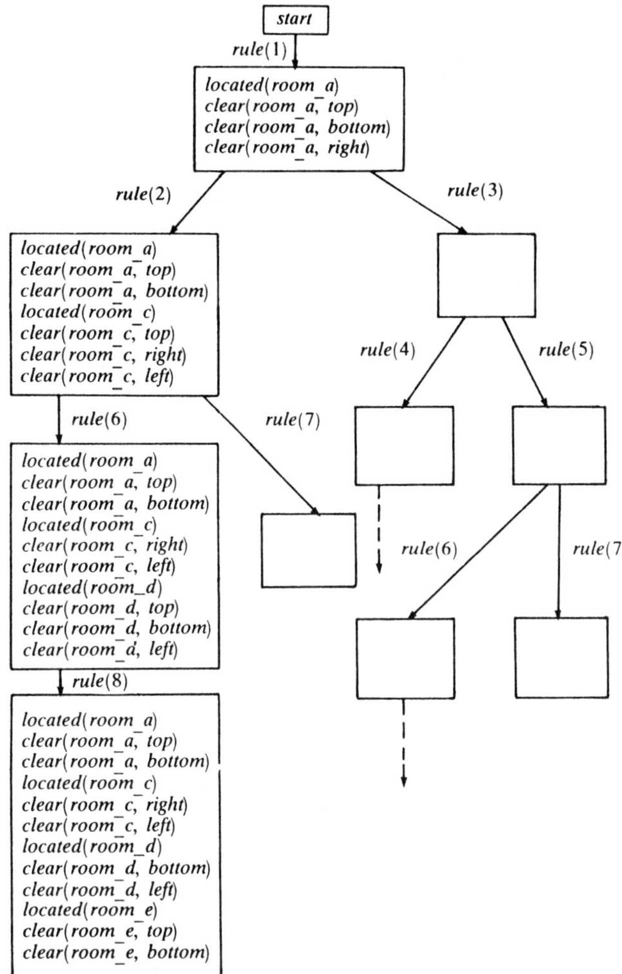

Figure 8.1. An abstraction of part of the search space of Figure 6.11.

difficult when there are more, as satisfaction of one goal can produce a state which precludes the satisfaction of another.

The planning system, STRIPS (Fikes and Nilsson, 1971), has been described in the previous chapter and represents a general paradigm for backward chaining to satisfy multiple goals. A simple STRIPS-like planner is demonstrated here.

In Figure 8.2 the mechanism is illustrated by which the multiple goals, *located(room_d)* and *located(room_b)*, are satisfied. The boxes contain goals and subgoals. A downward arrow points to the subgoals which must be satisfied before a particular goal can be met. Goals are considered one at a

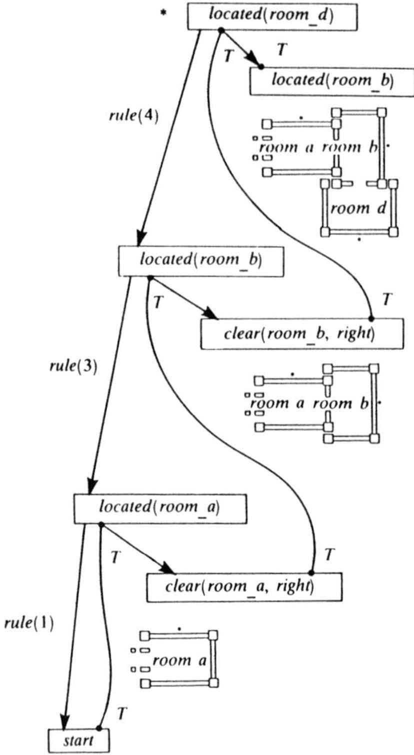

Figure 8.2. Backward search graph to satisfy the goal: *located(room_d)* and *located(room_b)*.

time in a recursive fashion. A goal is satisfied when it matches the current state description or can be achieved by means of some rule. The condition *start* is the first to be satisfied, as this matches the initial condition. Once it has been found that *rule(1)* achieves the subgoal, *located(room_a)*, this rule can be employed to change the current state. The subgoal, *clear(room_a, right)*, matches the current state of the world and is therefore true (indicated by *T*). The sequence of rules, *rule(1)*, *rule(3)* and *rule(4)*, therefore results in a state that satisfies the goal, *located(room_d)*. The second goal, *located(room_b)*, also matches the current state. So both goals are satisfied.

It will be noted that the goal, *located(room_d)*, could have been achieved by another rule, *rule(6)*. It should be possible to generate other plans by forcing backtracking to the last goal that could be achieved by another rule. In all of these figures that goal or subgoal is indicated by the symbol '*'. Figure 8.3 shows an attempt to achieve a second plan. The rule sequence, *rule(1)*, *rule(2)* and *rule(6)*, satisfies the goal, *located(room_d)*. The only rule that can be invoked to satisfy the second goal, *located(room_b)*, is *rule(3)*

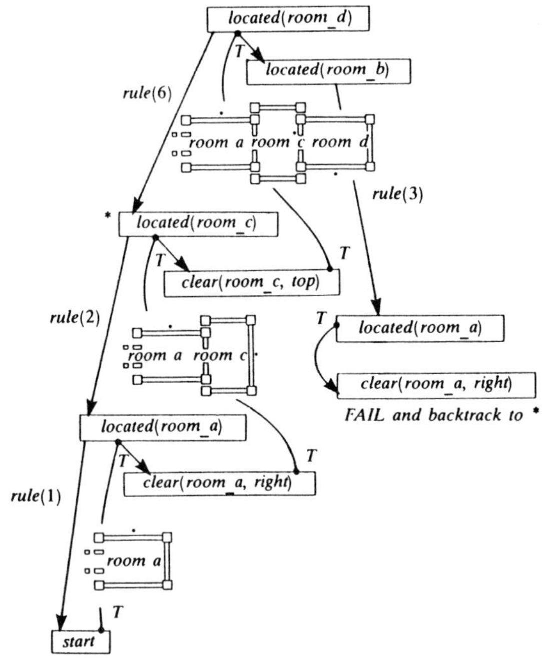

Figure 8.3. Continuation of the search graph in Figure 8.2 to produce a second solution, resulting in failure.

which requires as its precondition that *room_a* is located and that the right side of *room_a* is clear.

As the second of these subgoals cannot be matched against the current state description, and as there is no rule which enables this goal to be satisfied, the plan as formulated so far reaches a dead-end. In logic programming terms the plan has *failed.* A fail causes backtracking to the last goal which presents an alternative proof, that is, the last goal that is able to be achieved by means of another rule. This is the goal indicated (*). Figure 8.4 shows how a new plan is constructed from that goal. In this case both goals, *located*(*room_d*) and *located*(*room_b*), are satisfied.

It should be noted that the representations of states are depicted as full geometrical entities in these diagrams, whereas the state descriptions maintained by the planner are similar to those abstractions shown in Figure 8.1. The diagrammatic representation of states has been presented for ease of comprehension.

This example illustrates the backward chaining model. In most domains it is unlikely that goals will be able to be matched against facts contained within a

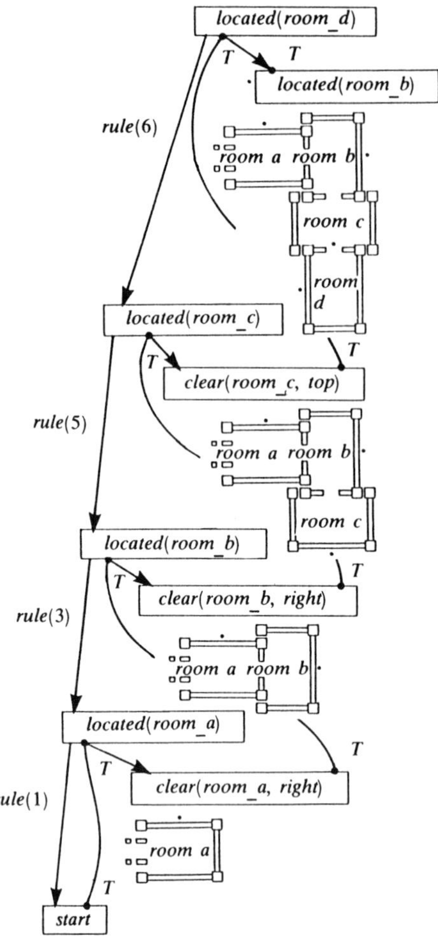

Figure 8.4. Continuation of the search graph in Figure 8.3.

state description, that is, the goals are not always expressed in the same terms as the facts describing states. This model therefore requires some refinement in incorporating mechanisms for mapping goals onto the literals of design rules. This requires knowledge which enables the inferring of facts from state descriptions and rules.

Goal Hierarchies

Rules of inference can be utilized to determine whether a goal state has been achieved. Two approaches to this problem are considered here: (i) the use of knowledge about the design rules; and (ii) the use of knowledge about design states. Both approaches involve augmenting the design knowledge (the design rules themselves) with additional knowledge about the domain.

A simple example of this is where the goal that two rooms are next to each other is to be achieved, for example: *next_to(room_c, room_d)*. The rules themselves contain information which is useful in achieving this goal. This information can be exploited by the inference rule:

if the goal is that two rooms are to be next to each other
then the room in the precondition part of the rule is next to the room in the consequent part of the rule.

When the planning system searches for a match with the goal: *next_to(A, B)*, this rule about rules (or *metarule*) ensures that a *next_to* fact appears on the consequent side of a design rule, by implication. The search tree which produces the first sequence of rules for satisfying this goal is illustrated in Figure 8.5.

The second approach is to employ knowledge about design states in determining whether goals have been achieved. For example, it can be inferred from the abstracted state description that a particular room is located on a corner of the building by noting if two walls from that room are clear and form a corner. This can be expressed in the same form as a design rule:

inference_rule(1) # [*clear(X, A), corner_wall(A, B), clear(X, B)*]
>>
[*corner_room(X)*].

in which *corner-wall(A, B)* is derived by the following knowledge, which states that *A* and *B* are corner walls if they are both found within a fact headed by the predicate *corner*:

corner_wall(A, B) **:-** *corner(A, B) ; corner(B, A)*.

As described in Chapter 3 the *if* (⇐) connective is represented as ':-' in this syntax, and variables are represented with upper case characters. The semicolon (;) indicates an *or* (∨) condition, the comma between predicates on the right side of a rule (,) indicates an *and* (∧), and the period (.) indicates the end of a fact or rule.

Corner is defined with the following facts:

corner(top, right).
corner(top, left).
corner(bottom, right).
corner(bottom, left).

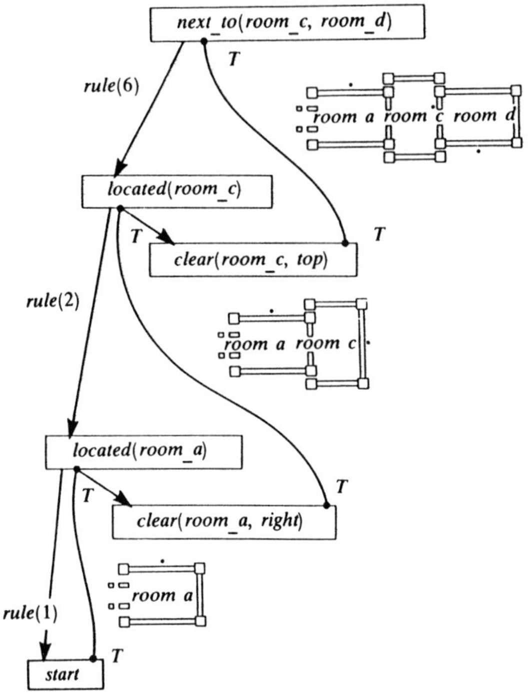

Figure 8.5. Search graph showing the satisfaction of the implicit goal: *next_to(room_c, room_d)*.

Considering the goal: *corner_room(room_d)* and *located(room_e)*, Figure 8.6 shows how the first rule that enables the goal: *corner_room(room_d)*, to be satisfied is *inference_rule(1)*. The preconditions that must be satisfied are the subgoals: *clear(room_d, A)*, *corner_wall(A, B)* and *clear(room_d, B)*. It should be noted that these subgoals contain variables which cannot be instantiated until the subgoals are matched against the current state description. So their values will not be known until a partial sequential plan for achieving these subgoals has been discovered. The rule sequence: *rule(1)*, *rule(3)*, *rule(4)*, produces a design state that satisfies these conditions and instantiates the variable of *A* to *top* and *B* to *left*.

The goal: *corner_room(room_d)*, is satisfied by this rule sequence, but the second part of the goal: *located(room_e)*, fails. Figure 8.7 shows the rule sequence that results from backtracking. The sequence is: *rule(1)*, *rule(2)*, *rule(6)*, *rule(8)*.

Design goals are rarely expressed in these terms, however, and the

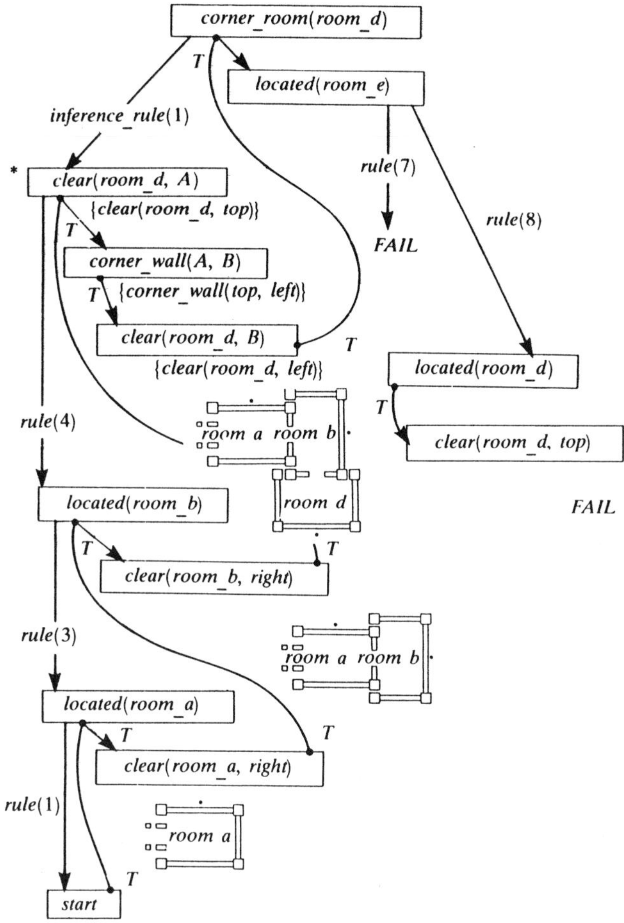

Figure 8.6. Search graph for the satisfaction of the implicit goal: *corner_room(room_d)* and *located(room_e)*, resulting in failure.

aspirations of a designer for the object being created are generally articulated at a higher level. One way to accomplish high level goals is to explicate the knowledge which enables high level goals to be satisfied in terms that can be understood by a mechanistic planning system. Figure 8.8 illustrates this. If the building under consideration is some kind of public building then one of the ways in which the goal, *high public utility*, can be achieved is by providing an attractive restaurant facility. This is achieved if the restaurant has good views and is accessible to the public. In order for the restaurant to enjoy good views it should be on the corner of the building. This last goal is a *system goal*: that

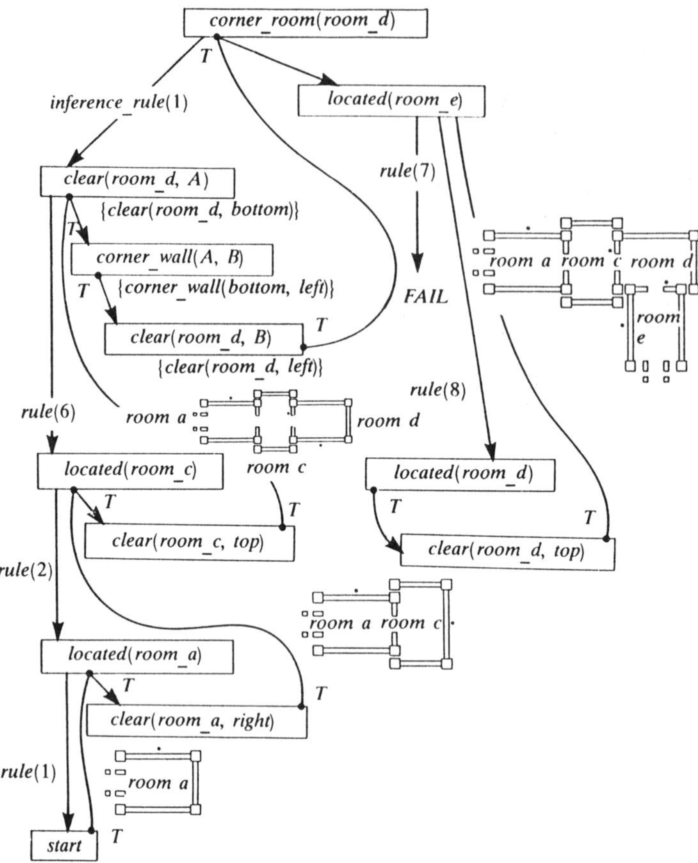

Figure 8.7. Continuation of the graph in Figure 8.6.

is, one that can be understood by the planning system.

The selection of appropriate planning goals may therefore be regarded as an 'abductive' process in the manner discussed in Chapter 4. Here we have considered goals with which there is no conflict. Where there is no conflict between goals it is relatively straightforward to provide rules of deductive inference by which mappings can be made between system goals and high level goals.

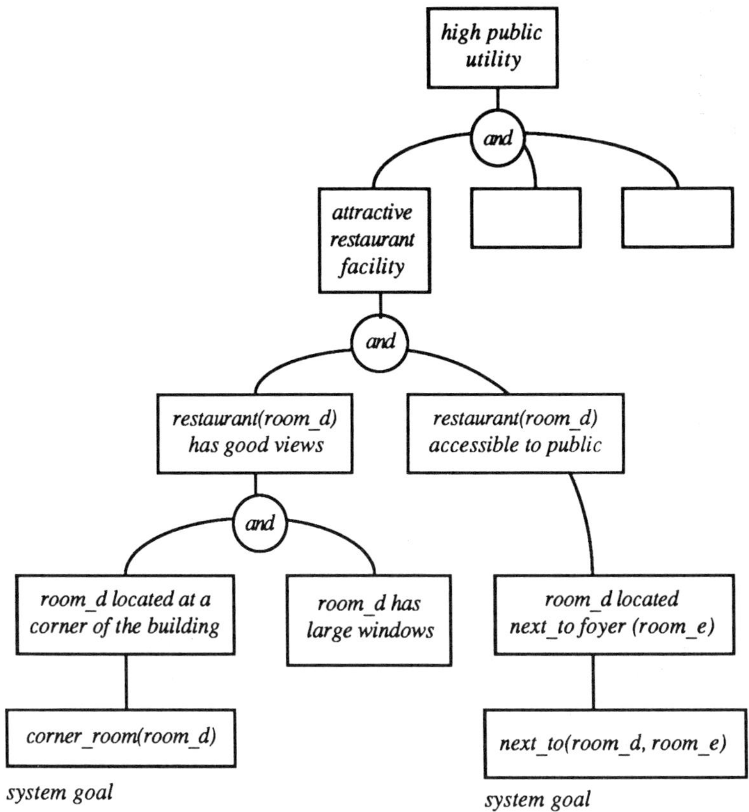

Figure 8.8. Part of an inference network for translating high-level goals to system goals.

Hierarchical Planning

The hierarchical approach to planning has also been discussed in the previous chapter and will be summarized here. Figure 8.9 illustrates the idea of formulating a sequence of design actions (a plan) in a three-level planning system. The three levels constitute subsystems. Level three considers the most important or influential attributes and produces a sequence of rules to satisfy an input goal set. The plan is passed down to the next level and evaluated taking into account the attributes of level 3 plus those considered to be of secondary importance. Provided it passes the approval of this subsystem it is channelled down to level 1 and evaluated to see if it is an appropriate plan when all attributes are taken into account. If at any level the plan fails then the subsystem at the level above must generate another plan. This is one way in which planning at different levels of abstraction can be demonstrated.

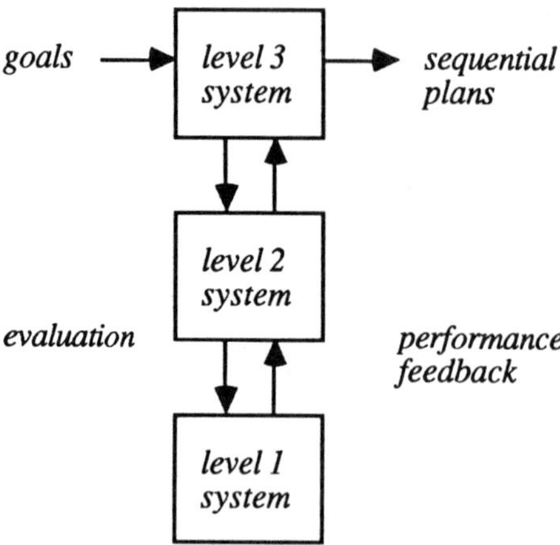

Figure 8.9. A three-level hierarchical planning system.

A more sophisticated model is that in which a partial or imperfect plan is passed down from a higher level and is filled in or corrected at the lower levels. However, it can be shown that even the approach outlined in Figure 8.9 can introduce efficiencies in the planning process, and this approach will be adopted here.

A Site Context

In order to illustrate the hierarchical planning model it is necessary to extend the design domain of the previous example. The extra complication of trying to fit the building form onto a 'site' is considered. The siting requirement is simply that the artifact can assume any spatial characteristics provided it does not extend beyond the boundaries of a spatial envelope. This envelope is shown diagrammatically in Figure 8.10. This information is presented as a fact in Prolog:

```
envelope([[4, 6], [3, 5], [4, 5],[2, 4],
          [3, 4], [4, 4], [5, 4], [2, 3], [3, 3],
          [4, 3], [5, 3], [6, 3], [3, 2], [4, 2], [4, 1]]).
```

The predicate has one argument which is simply a list of cells contained within the envelope, each cell identified by an address giving its x and y grid

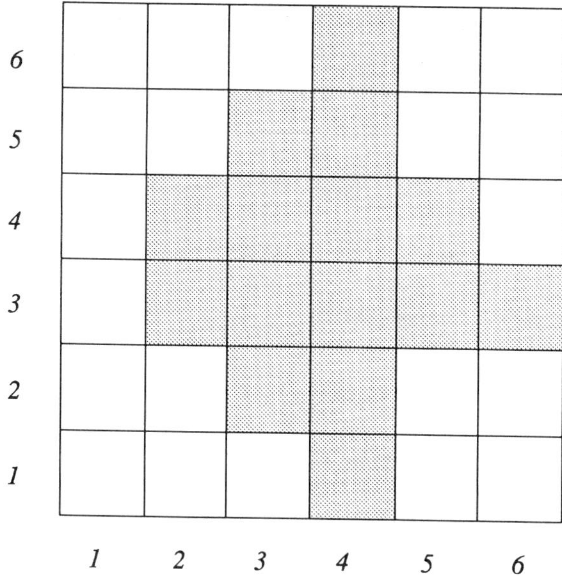

Figure 8.10. Spatial envelope within a gridded world.

coordinates. Coordinate pairs are grouped together in square brackets. The centre of each room in the rules is to coincide with the centre point of a grid cell in the context.

The design rules have been reformulated so that they are sensitive to this context: for example, *rule*(2) can be fired if *room_a* is located and if it is clear on its right side. But in order to fit the context certain conditions about the room's location and orientation must also be satisfied. The cell to the right of *room_a* must be within the envelope: that is, if the cell location of *room_a* is [*X*, *Y*] and the cell to the right of *room_a* is [*X1*, *Y1*] and the envelope is the list *L* then [*X1*, *Y1*] must be a member of the list *L*.

Finding the address of the cell to the right of *room_a* introduces a slight complication as the design space in Figure 6.11 shows that an object can be at almost any orientation. The address of the cell to the right of *room_a* can be deduced from the address and orientation of *room_a*. It is therefore desirable to maintain facts about the orientation of objects in the current state description and to provide knowledge about how to determine the location of the right cell from the position of *room_a* and its orientation.

The knowledge for finding the cell (and its orientation) to the right of a cell oriented to the north is given by the Prolog rule:

right_cell(north, east, [X, Y], [X1, Y]) :- X1 is X+1.

where the first argument of the predicate: *right_cell*, is the orientation of *room_a*, the second argument is the orientation of the object in the neighbouring cell, the third argument is the address of the cell containing

```
rule(1) # [start, envelope(L), member([X, Y], L)]
          >>
          [located(a), clear(a, top), clear(a, bottom), clear(a, right), cell(a, [X, Y]),
          orientation(a, north)].

rule(2) # [located(a), clear(a, right), cell(a, [X, Y]), orientation(a, D1),
          right_cell(D1, D2, [X, Y], [X1, Y1]), envelope(L), member([X1, Y1], L)]
          >>
          [located(a), located(c), clear(c, top), clear(c, right), clear(c, left),
          cell(c, [X1, Y1]), orientation(c, D2)].

rule(3) # [located(a), clear(a, right), cell(a, [X, Y]), orientation(a, D1),
          right_cell(D1, D2, [X, Y], [X1, Y1]), envelope(L), member([X1, Y1], L)]
          >>
          [located(a), located(b), clear(b, top), clear(b, right), clear(b, left),
          cell(b, [X1, Y1]), orientation(b, D2)].

rule(4) # [located(b), clear(b, right), cell(b, [X, Y]), orientation(b, D1),
          right_cell(D1, D2, [X, Y], [X1, Y1]), envelope(L), member([X1, Y1], L)]
          >>
          [located(b), located(d), clear(d, top), clear(d, right), clear(d, left),
          cell(d, [X1, Y1]), orientation(d, D2)].

rule(5) # [located(b), clear(b, right), cell(b, [X, Y]), orientation(b, D1),
          right_cell(D1, D2, [X, Y], [X1, Y1]), envelope(L), member([X1, Y1], L)]
          >>
          [located(b), located(c), clear(c, top), clear(c, right), clear(c, left),
          cell(c, [X1, Y1]), orientation(c, D2)].

rule(6) # [located(c), clear(c, top), cell(c, [X, Y]), orientation(c, D1),
          top_cell(D1, D2, [X, Y], [X1, Y1]), envelope(L), member([X1, Y1], L)]
          >>
          [located(c), located(d), clear(d, top), clear(d, bottom), clear(d, left),
          cell(d, [X1, Y1]), orientation(d, D2)].

rule(7) # [located(c), clear(c, top), cell(c, [X, Y]), orientation(c, D1),
          top_cell(D1, D2, [X, Y], [X1, Y1]), envelope(L), member([X1, Y1], L)]
          >>
          [located(c), located(e), clear(e, top), clear(e, bottom), clear(e, left),
          cell(e, [X1, Y1]), orientation(e, D2)].

rule(8) # [located(d), clear(d, top), cell(d, [X, Y]), orientation(d, D1),
          top_cell(D1, D2, [X, Y], [X1, Y1]), envelope(L), member([X1, Y1], L)]
          >>
          [located(d), located(e), clear(e, top), clear(e, bottom), clear(e, left),
          cell(e, [X1, Y1]), orientation(e, D2)].
```

Figure 8.11. Abstracted design rules of Figure 6.11 sensitive to the spatial context.

room_a, and [*X1*, *Y*] is the address of the neighbouring cell. The *x* coordinate of the neighbouring cell is found by adding 1 to the value of the *x* coordinate of the *room_a* cell. There are similar inference rules for finding neighbouring cells under different conditions.

The preconditions for implementing rule(2), taking account of this context, are therefore given formally by the following list of facts (where the atom, *room_a*, has been abbreviated to *a* for clarity):

> [*located*(*a*),
> *clear*(*a*, *right*),
> *cell*(*a*, [*X*, *Y*]),
> *orientation*(*a*, *D1*),
> *right-cell*(*D1*, *D2*, [*X*, *Y*], [*X1*, *Y1*]),
> *envelope*(*L*),
> *member*([*X1*, *Y1*], *L*)]

The first three facts match directly against the current state description. The last four facts are contextual. In this case the last three are facts about the world which must be inferred from other facts. In this implementation such attributes are unchanged by the transformation rule and they are not stored as part of the current state description. The consequent of this rule is given by the following list of facts. These are asserted as part of the current state description.

> [*located*(*a*),
> *located*(*c*),
> *clear*(*c*, *top*),
> *clear*(*c*, *right*),
> *clear*(*c*, *left*),
> *cell*(*c*, [*X1*, *Y1*]),
> *orientation*(*c*, *D2*)]

The values of the variables in the consequent list are the same as those instantiated in the preconditions list. Figure 8.11 shows the rules of Figure 6.10, such that the antecedents and consequents of the rules refer to facts about the context.

Figure 8.12 shows the appropriate search graph for satisfying the goal: located(d). The goal: *located*(*d*), can be satisfied by chaining backwards through *rule*(*4*), *rule*(*3*) and *rule*(*1*). *Rule*(*1*) requires as its precondition the fact: *start*, and the existence of a cell with the address [*X*, *Y*], which is a member of the envelope list *L*. The first cell to satisfy this condition is the first member of the list, which is [*4*, *6*]. So all the preconditions of rule(1) are satisfied and the values of *X* and *Y* are instantiated to *4* and *6* respectively.

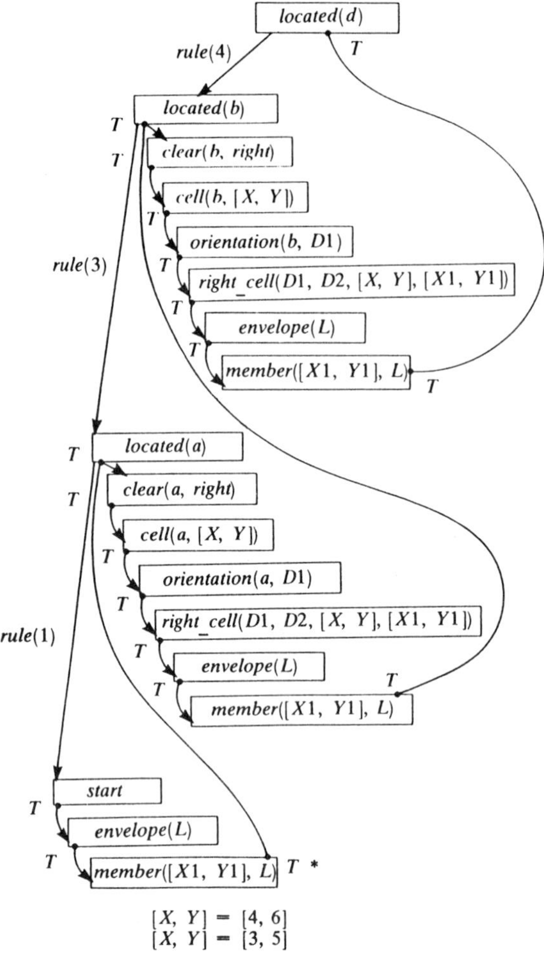

Figure 8.12. Search graph for satisfying the goal: *located(d)*, using the rules of Figure 8.11 and taking account of the spatial context.

These values form part of the current state description along with the consequents produced by *rule(1)*. The other subgoals forming the preconditions to *rule(3)* are evaluated against the current state descriptions as follows:

clear(a, right)	TRUE
cell(a, [4, 6])	TRUE
orientation(a, north)	TRUE
right_cell(north, east, [4, 6], [5, 6])	TRUE

envelope([[*4*, *6*], [*3*, *5*], [*4*, *5*], [*2*, *4*], [*3*, *4*],
[*4*, *4*], [*5*, *4*], [*2*, *3*], [*3*, *3*], [*4*, *3*],
[*5*, *3*], [*6*, *3*], [*3*, *2*], [*4*, *2*], [*4*, *1*]]) TRUE
member([*5*, *6*], [[*4*, *6*], [*3*, *5*], [*4*, *5*], [*2*, *4*],
[*3*, *4*], [*4*, *4*], [*5*, *4*], [*2*, *3*],
[*3*, *3*], [*4*, *3*], [*5*, *3*], [*6*, *3*],
[*3*, *2*], [*4*, *2*], [*4*, *1*]]) FAIL

The fail causes backtracking to the last goal that could be resatisfied in some other way. This happens to be the subgoal indicated with '*' in Figure 8.12. Another member of the list *L* is the second element [*3*, *5*], and so backward chaining occurs again, this time with *X* and *Y* instantiated to *3* and *5* respectively. This time all the preconditions of *rule*(*3*) are satisfied:

clear(*a*, *right*) TRUE
cell(*a*, [*3*, *5*]) TRUE
orientation(*a*, *north*) TRUE
right-cell(*north*, *east*, [*3*, *5*], [*4*, *5*]) TRUE
envelope([[*4*, *6*], [*3*, *5*], [*4*, *5*], [*2*, *4*], [*3*, *4*],
[*4*, *4*], [*5*, *4*], [*2*, *3*], [*3*, *3*], [*4*, *3*],
[*5*, *3*], [*6*, *3*], [*3*, *2*], [*4*, *2*], [*4*, *1*]]) TRUE
member([*4*, *5*], [[*4*, *6*], [*3*, *5*], [*4*, *5*], [*2*, *4*],
[*3*, *4*], [*4*, *4*], [*5*, *4*], [*2*, *3*],
[*3*, *3*], [*4*, *3*], [*5*, *3*], [*6*, *3*],
[*3*, *2*], [*4*, *2*], [*4*, *1*]]) TRUE

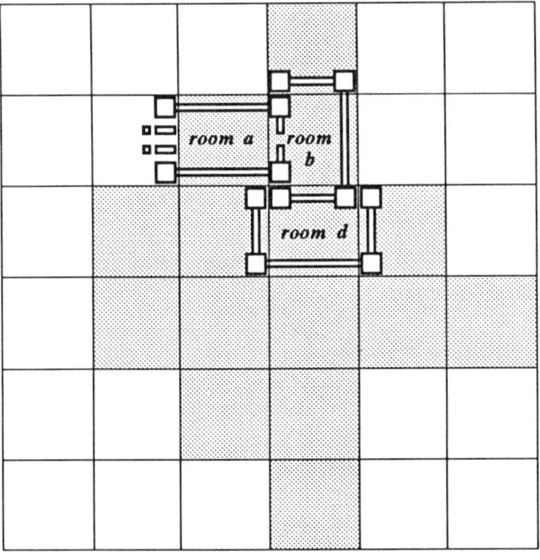

Figure 8.13. The first layout generated by the rule sequence in Figure 8.12.

All the preconditions of *rule(4)* are also satisfied in a similar manner. The final state is represented diagrammatically in Figure 8.13. Further solutions can be generated by subsequent backtracking.

In this example the procedure is similar to that which a designer might adopt. Conceptually, this involves generating a configuration of objects, then moving the configuration about until it fits within the envelope. If that configuration will not fit, then an attempt is made to generate another configuration. Although this mechanism has some intuitive appeal, the search procedure can become extremely inefficient when there is more than one goal to be satisfied at the top of the search tree. This is illustrated in Figures 8.14, 8.15 and 8.16.

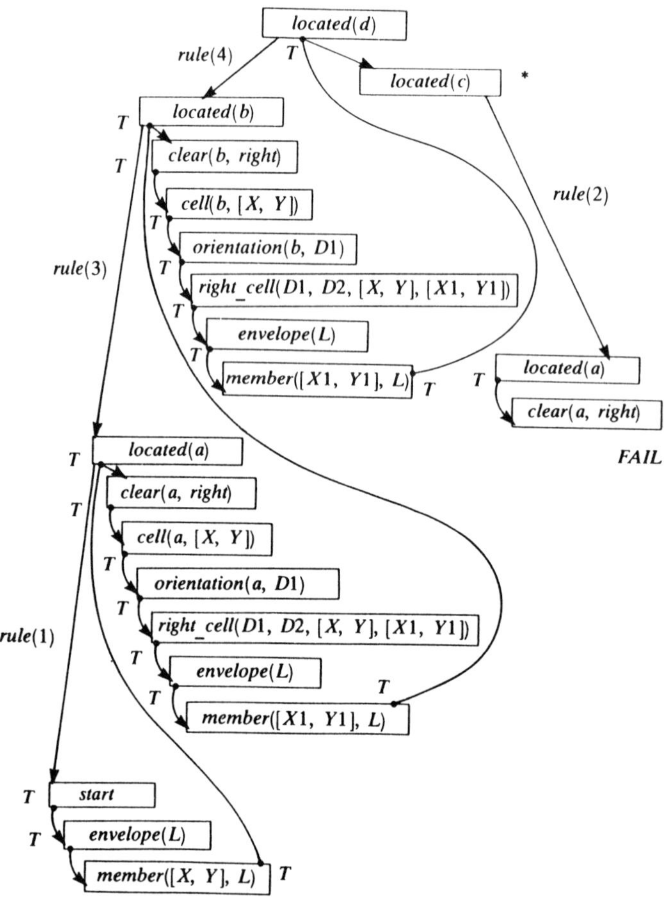

Figure 8.14. Search graph for satisfying the goal: *located(d)* and *located(c)*. The search results in failure at the subgoal: *clear(a, right)*.

The goals are *located(d)* and *located(c)*. *Rule(4)* satisfies the first goal. The first precondition of *rule(4)* is: *located(b)*. This can be satisfied by *rule(3)*, which has as its first precondition: *located(a)*. This can be satisfied by *rule(1)*, which has as its first precondition *start*. As this is the initial condition it is satisfied. The other preconditions of *rule(1)* are also satisfied, with *X* and *Y* instantiated to *4* and *6* respectively. The other preconditions of *rule(3)* are now also tested. The process is the same as that described for Figure 8.12, and involves backtracking until the configuration and positions shown in Figure 8.13 are generated.

A problem arises when an attempt is made to satisfy the second goal: *located(c)*. This can be satisfied by *rule(2)*, provided its preconditions can

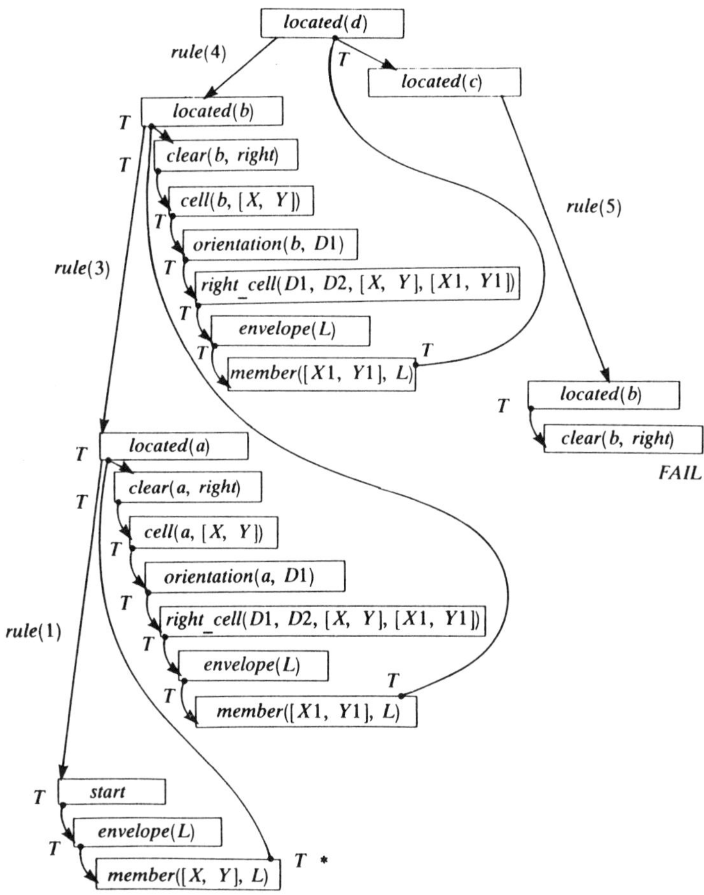

Figure 8.15. Continuation of the search graph in Figure 8.14 resulting in failure at the subgoal: *clear(b, right)*.

be met. The second precondition of *rule*(2) does not match the current state description and so fails. Backtracking proceeds to the last goal or subgoal that could be satisfied in an alternative way. This is the goal indicated with '*'. *Located*(*c*) can also be achieved by *rule*(5), except that it also fails when an attempt is made to match its second precondition against the current state description. Backtracking now proceeds back to the subgoal indicated '*' in Figure 8.15. This subgoal can be resatisfied by the selection of an alternative cell from the envelope list *L*. The procedure will continue as before, again failing inevitably on the subgoal: *clear*(*a*, *right*).

When all of the cells have been investigated, backtracking returns the system to the goal: *located*(*d*), and a new rule sequence is generated, as

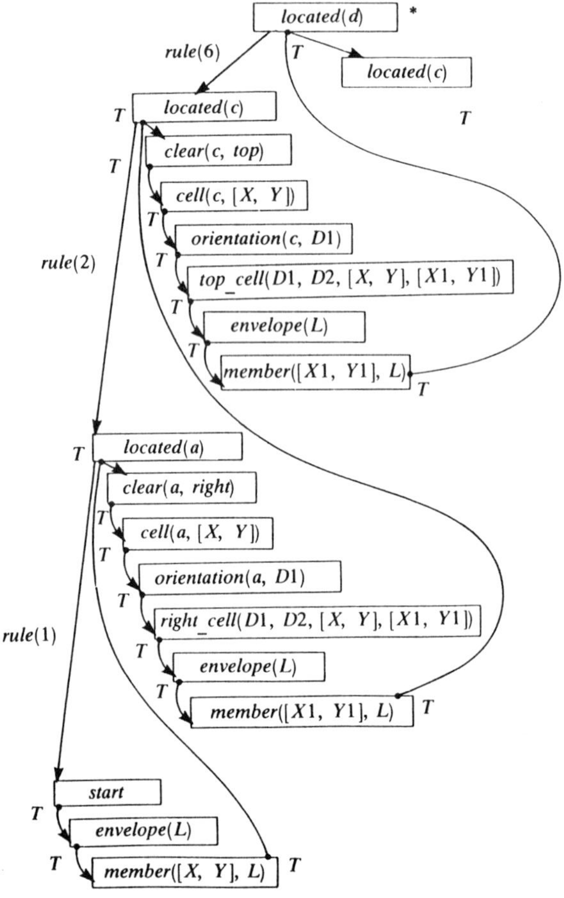

Figure 8.16. Continuation of the search graph in Figure 8.15 resulting in the satisfaction of both goals: *located*(*d*) and *located*(*c*).

shown in Figure 8.15. Again, each cell is considered in turn until the rule sequence is validated. This involves an unnecessary amount of searching. It should not be necessary to investigate every cell in the envelope to try and satisfy the goals. It is not the inappropriate selection of cells which is causing failure, but the rule sequence itself. It would fail irrespective of the context.

This would become an even greater problem with a larger envelope. It would be more efficient, therefore, to first find an appropriate sequence of rules which will generate a configuration of objects, without taking the context into account, then to adjust the position of the configuration to fit the context.

Planning Levels

This requires the addition of some knowledge about the importance of different attributes. In this case it may be decided that facts relating to the configuration of objects are more important than those which relate to context. Furthermore, it may be decided that the fact that an object is located is more important than whether or not it has a clear side.

A plan of actions is therefore formulated taking into account the most important considerations first. This is the highest level of the hierarchy. The plan is then reconsidered also taking into account factors which exhibit the next level of importance. If the plan is satisfactory when those factors are considered, the plan is reconsidered at the next level.

There are two main ways that a plan can prove unsatisfactory at any level. There may be gaps in the plan that require 'patching'. In this case the plan passed down from a higher level to a lower level is a skeletal plan which requires the insertion of certain actions to ensure that factors at the next level of importance receive consideration. A mechanism for patching plans is required to take account of successive levels of detail. The second way that a plan proves unsatisfactory is if the plan proves totally impossible, with or without patching, at the next level down. In this case the plan could be amended or new plans could be produced by backtracking to levels already considered.

The latter approach is perhaps the simplest and only this will be considered here. It is less powerful than patching or amending plans, but still produces significant increases in efficiency compared with a non-hierarchical approach.

A simplification of the approach adopted in the ABSTRIPS problem solver (Sacerdoti, 1974) is applied here. The preconditions of each rule are assigned to criticality levels. The higher the level the more critical the precondition. Preconditions and levels are shown below (with variables labelled anonymously).

level 3 *start, located(_)*
level 2 *clear(_, _)*

level 1 *cell(_, _), orientation(_, _),*
right_cell(_, _, _, _),
top_cell(_, _, _, _), envelope(_),
member(_, _)

Figure 8.17 shows the search graph generated by the two goals: *located(d)* and *located(c)*, taking into account preconditions at criticality level 3. The

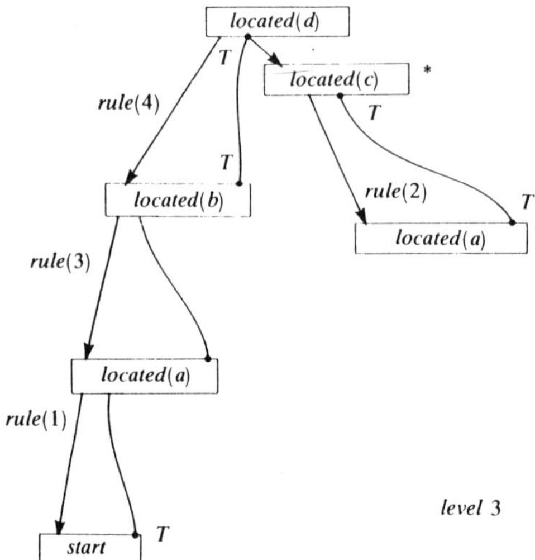

Figure 8.17. Search graph for the goal: located(d) and located(c), considering the preconditions at criticality level 3.

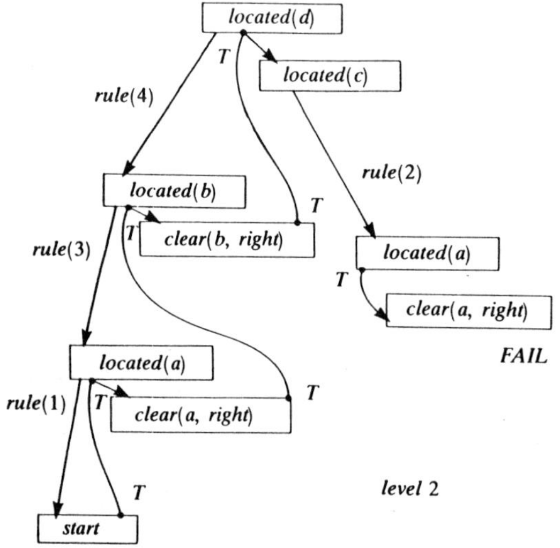

Figure 8.18. Reconsideration of the plan generated in Figure 8.17 by considering preconditions at criticality level 2 as well as level 3.

plan: *rule(1)*, *rule(3)*, *rule(4)*, *rule(2)*, is produced. This plan is then reconsidered taking into account preconditions at criticality 2 (Figure 8.18). The plan proves satisfactory until an attempt is made to satisfy the subgoal: *clear(a, right)*. The plan fails at this level and so the system backtracks to the previous level of abstraction. The last goal at criticality 3 that could be satisfied alternatively is indicated with '*' in Figure 8.17. An attempt to resatisfy this goal results in the rule sequence: *rule(1)*, *rule(3)*, *rule(4)*,

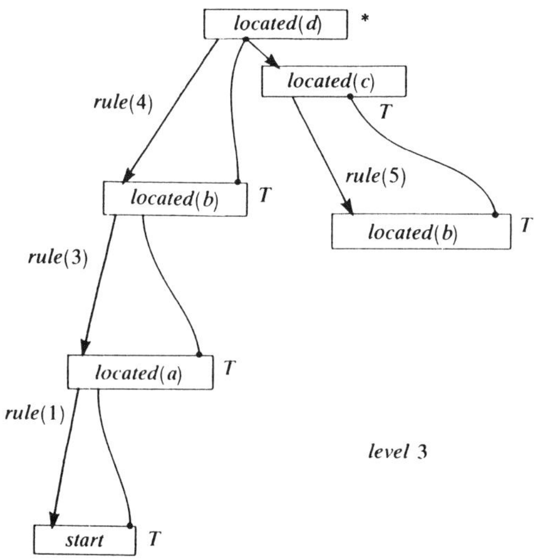

Figure 8.19. Generation of a new plan by backtracking to criticality level 3.

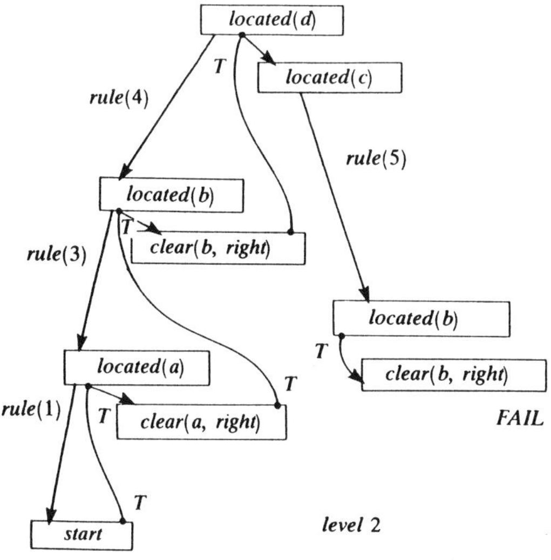

Figure 8.20. Reconsideration of plan generated in Figure 8.19 by considering preconditions at criticality level 2. This results in failure at the subgoal: *clear(b, right)*.

rule(5), as shown in the search graph in Figure 8.19. This rule sequence is again reconsidered at criticality 2, and again fails (Figure 8.20). Backtracking to the goal indicated '*' in Figure 8.19 produces the rule sequence: *rule*(*1*), *rule*(2), *rule*(*6*) (Figure 8.21). This plan also proves satisfactory at criticality 2, as shown in Figure 8.22. The plan is next reconsidered at criticality level 1. The search graph for this level is the same as that shown in Figure 8.16, and it involves a small amount of backtracking to find grid cells

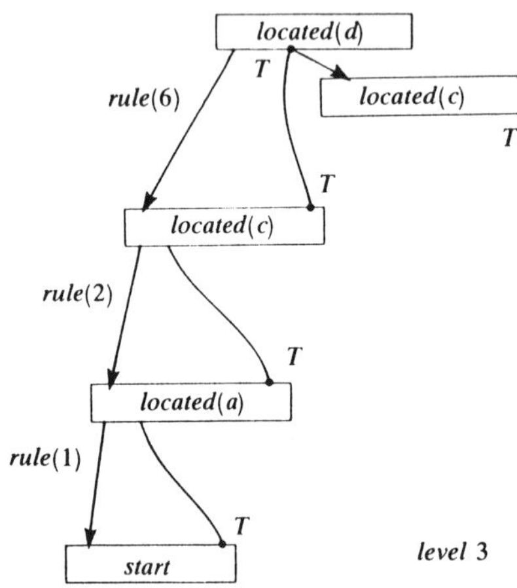

Figure 8.21. Generation of a new plan by backtracking to criticality level 3.

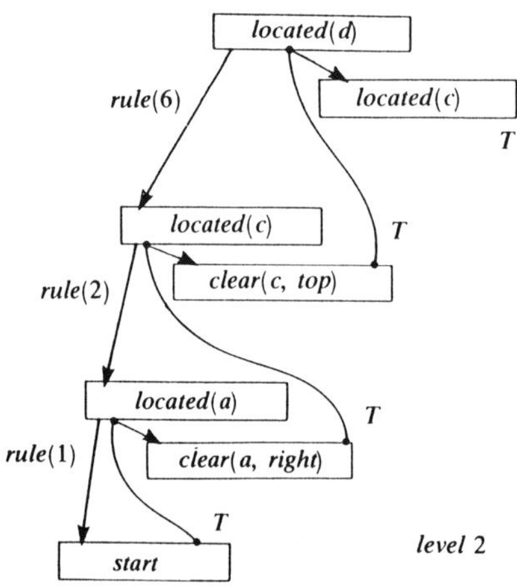

Figure 8.22. Reconsideration of plan generated in Figure 8.21 by considering preconditions at criticality level 2, resulting in the satisfaction of both goals: *located*(*d*) and *located*(*c*) at that level.

which suit the plan and lie within the envelope.

The efficiency of the planning process in this demonstration could have been enhanced had only two levels of abstraction been considered (that concerned with configuration and that which relates to the context) as that would have involved less backtracking. Three levels were selected to demonstrate the mechanism more clearly.

The advantage of the hierarchical approach is that it is not necessary to repeatedly search the entire set of grid cells before a plan is proved unsatisfactory. Unsatisfactory plans are detected much earlier, and the amount of searching reduced. Although the hierarchical approach to planning suits the example given here it has also been shown to be a more efficient mechanism for planning generally (Sacerdoti, 1974).

Reasoning About Context

The set of design rules for generating simple building forms from wall elements, windows and columns described above is extended to include other elements. This grammar is shown in Figure 8.23. Rules 9, 10 and 11 are concerned with the addition of an external terrace area to the building, and rules 12, 13 and 14 the addition of external rooms to the terraces.

Part of the context is represented in Figure 8.24 as a gridded building site. The site is partitioned into areas each of which is homogeneous with respect to some particular attributes. These are labelled: *attribute_1, attribute_2, attribute_3, attribute_4, attribute_5* and *attribute_6*; and could refer to any spatially distributed site attributes such as slope categories, soil types or drainage easements. The distribution of each attribute is shown in Figure 8.25.

It is necessary that this information about the context is interpreted so that it can be employed in determining the building form and location. This is achieved by means of deductive inference, given some knowledge about suitability. It is assumed that different parts of the site are suitable for different uses. The condition is included in the list for each rule that the cell on which the neighbouring object is to be located is suitable for its proposed use. This can be tested by the goal:

suitable([*X*, *Y*], *USE*),

where *X* and *Y* are the coordinates of the cell's address. *USE* is the name of the object to be located on the cell. An example of a transformation rule is therefore:

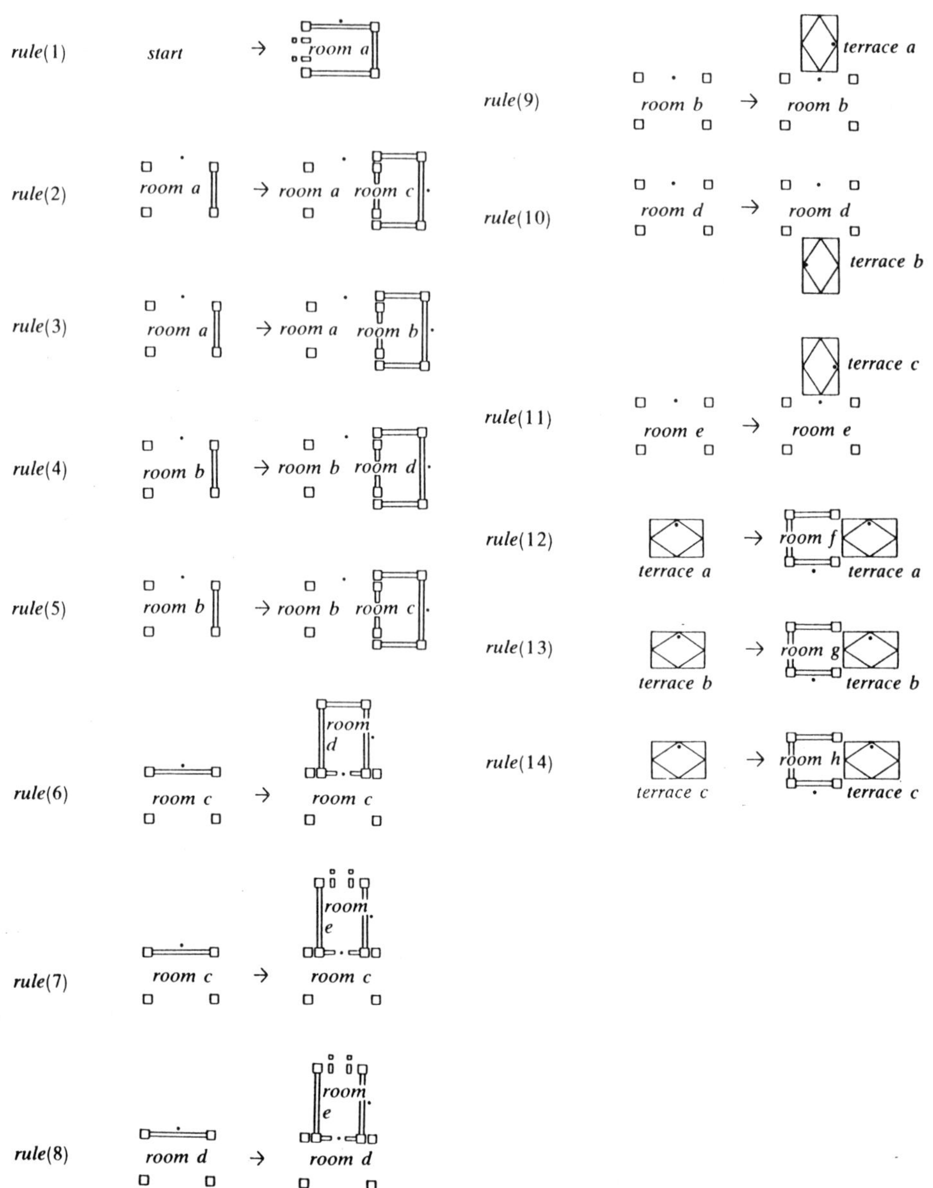

Figure 8.23. Design grammar for a simple building (extending the rules of Figure 6.10).

```
rule(2) # [located(room_a), clear(room_a, right),
        cell(room_a, [X, Y]), orientation(room_a, D1),
        right_cell(D1, D2, [X, Y], [X1, Y1]),
        suitable([X1, Y1], room_c)]
        >>
        [located(room_a), located(room_c),
        clear(room_c, top), clear(room_c, right),
        clear(room_c, left), cell(room_c, [X1, Y1]),
        orientation(room_c, D2)].
```

The knowledge by which it can be inferred that a particular cell is suitable for particular uses can be represented as the Prolog inference rule:

```
suitable([X, Y], USE) :-
        member(USE, [room_a, room_b, room_c, room_d,
        room_e, room_f, room_g, room_h
        terrace_a, terrace_b, terrace_c]),
        site(attribute_1, List_1),
        member([X, Y], List_1),
        site(attribute_3, List_3),
        member([X, Y], List_3).
```

This can be read as: a cell with address [*X*, *Y*] is suitable as a location for a room or a terrace if it has *attribute_1* (that is, it is a member of the list of

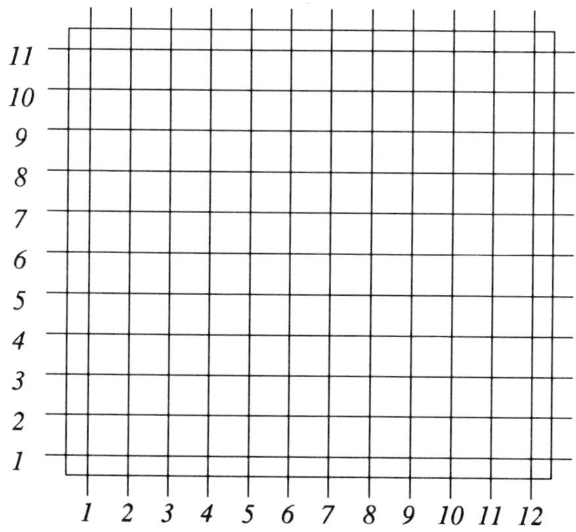

Figure 8.24. A gridded building site as the context.

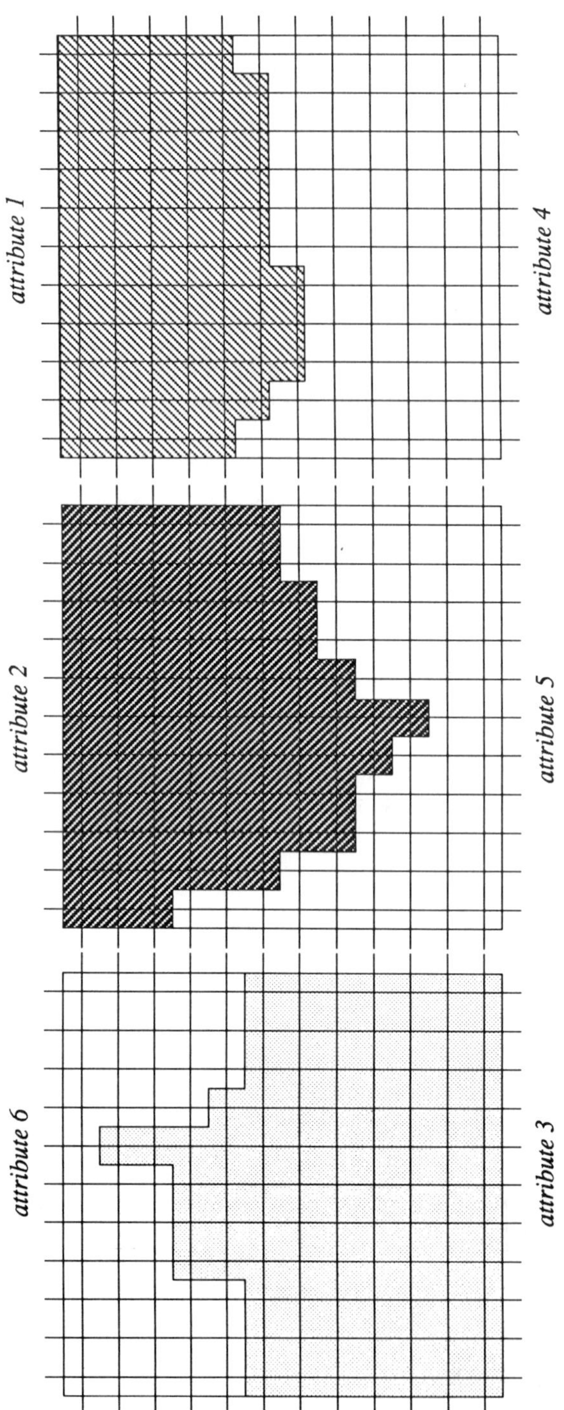

Figure 8.25. Distribution of different attributes across the site.

cells with *attribute_1*) and it has *attribute_3*. This rule requires that facts about cells and suitabilities are stored as:

site(A, B).

where *A* is an attribute and *B* is the list of cell addresses with that attribute. It is, of course, possible to represent quite complex knowledge about site suitability using rules of this form. For simplicity only two rules are represented in tabular form in Figure 8.26.

The task is therefore to generate a building form (or forms) from the design rules, such that the building exhibits a close fit with the site context in terms of suitability. The design problem is considered at two levels by assigning facts to the following criticality levels:

level 2	*start, located(_), clear(_, _)*
level 1	*cell(_, _), orientation(_, _)*
	right_cell(_, _, _, _)
	top_cell(_, _, _, _)
	suitable(_, _, _)

The planning mechanism is the same as that shown in the simpler example above. Only some of the graphic output from such a system is shown in Figures 8.27 to 8.29. The planner therefore produces a sequence of design actions in the form of a list of rules which achieve simple goals. This sequence is then employed by a design generator which implements the rules to produce more complete geometrical descriptions of the artifact.

USE		SITE ATTRIBUTES
room_a,	*room_b,*	*attribute_1*
room_c,	*room_d,*	*attribute_3*
room_e,	*room_f,*	
room_g,	*room_h,*	
terrace_a,	*terrace_b,*	
terrace_c		
room_f,	*room_g,*	*attribute_2,*
room_h,		*attribute_3*
terrace_a,	*terrace_b,*	
terrace_c		

Figure 8.26. Site attributes necessary for two different categories of use.

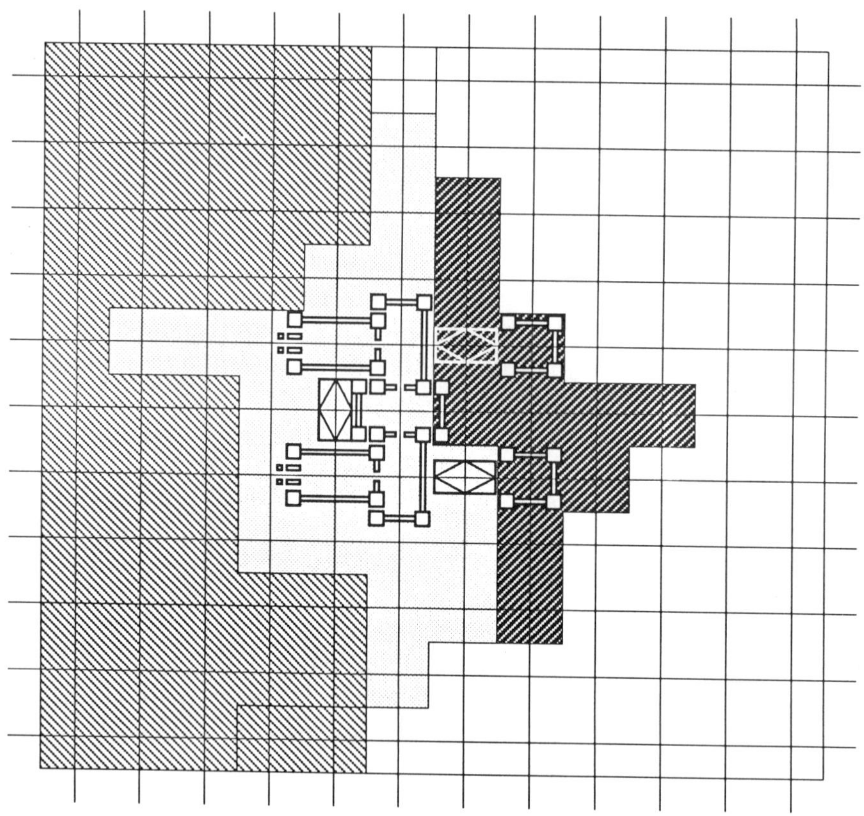

Figure 8.27. One of the layouts achieved by the rule sequence: *rule(1)*, *rule(3)*, *rule(5)*, *rule(6)*, *rule(8)*, *rule(9)*, *rule(12)*, *rule(10)*, *rule(13)*, *rule(11)*.

Constructive Systems

Whereas the approaches to planning described above make use of backtracking in the search for goal states, the *constructive* approach uses operators to successively refine a plan. In order to demonstrate its generality this approach will be discussed using the same design domain as that given above. The ideas discussed here are based substantially on those explored in the NOAH planning system (Sacerdoti, 1975; 1977) discussed in the previous chapter, and which makes use of procedural networks as a method of representing states, employing critics as powerful operators.

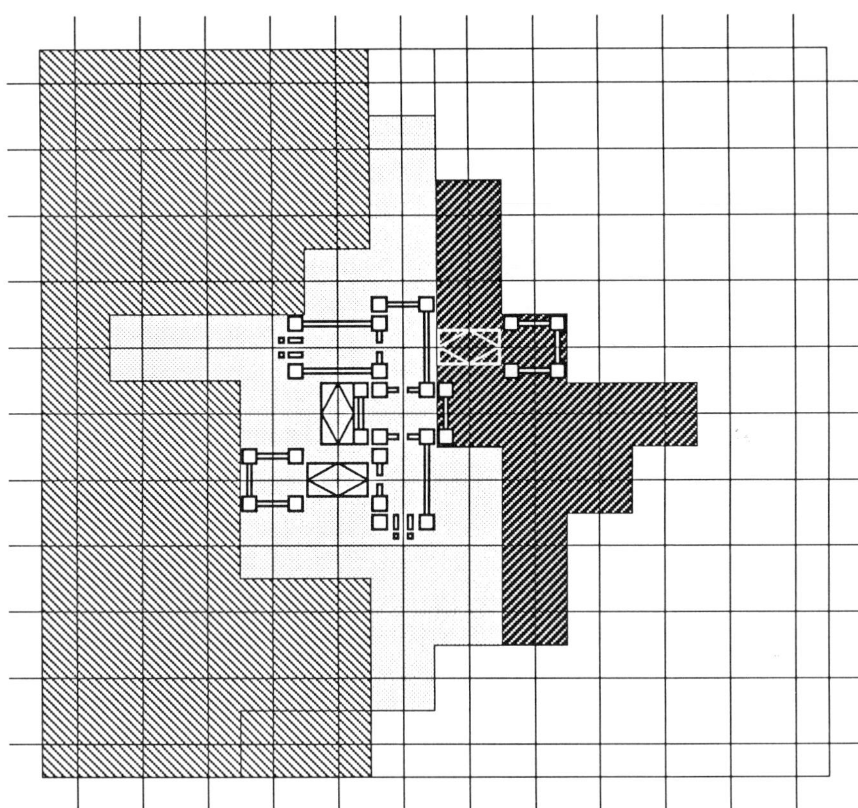

Figure 8.28. One of the layouts achieved by the rule sequence: *rule(1)*, *rule(3)*, *rule(5)*, *rule(7)*, *rule(9)*, *rule(12)*, *rule(11)*, *rule(14)*.

Representing Plan States

The method for representing plan states must be able to represent facts about actions: the names of actions and their attributes, particularly how they are related to one another. Actions can be related *serially*, that is, they can be laid out in order; or groups of actions may be related in some *parallel* configuration, that is, in groups as conjunctions or disjunctions. Procedural networks are simply a way of representing these relationships between actions.

In the example above there are two goals, *located(d)* and *located(b)*. If they are regarded as actions, *locate(d)* and *locate(b)*, then these represent a type of high-level description of the actions necessary in order for a design to be generated. Nothing is known at this stage about the order in which these actions should be executed, nor about how they should be executed. The

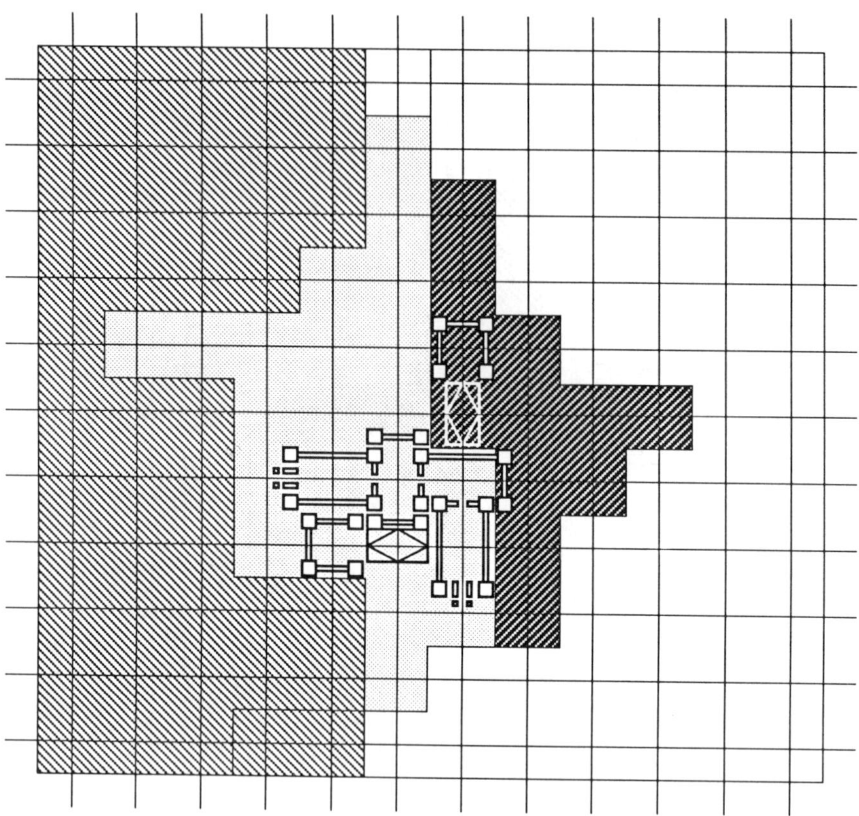

Figure 8.29. One of the layouts achieved by the rule sequence: *rule*(*1*), *rule*(*2*), *rule*(*6*), *rule*(*8*), *rule*(*10*), *rule*(*13*), *rule*(*11*), *rule*(*14*).

procedural network formulation makes it possible to represent this state without any commitment to order, as shown in Figure 8.30. This is the initial state and it constitutes a type of high-level description of the design task.

The end state produced by the planning system needs to have a greater serial component than that illustrated here. The plan should also consist of actions that can actually be executed.

Planning Operators

In the planning systems discussed above a uniform transformation procedure for changing states and a uniform type of knowledge representation were considered. In the planning system considered here two procedures (and hence

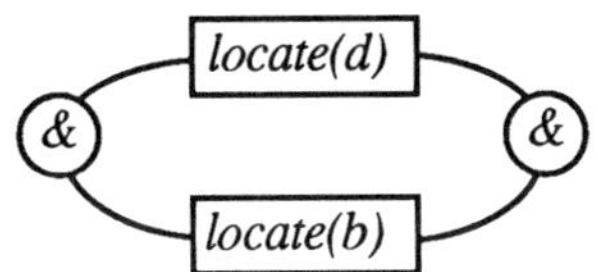

Figure 8.30. Procedural network for the goals: *located*(*d*) and *located*(*b*).

two types of knowledge) are considered for transforming states. The first type of knowledge concerns a mapping between actions and classes of actions. This is a type of semantic/syntactic mapping. It could also be termed an *expansion rule*. An example of such a rule is: in order for task *A* to be achieved, perform task *B*, task *C* and task *D*. The procedure for handling this knowledge is to substitute tasks *B, C* and *D* for task *A* in the procedural network.

The second type of knowledge is the *critic*. Expansion rules concern local knowledge about how individual actions are achieved; here, critics contain a more global type of knowledge. Critics are modules of specialized knowledge about design actions, the relationships between actions, and contextual information. Each critic may have a different procedure so the knowledge cannot always be represented explicitly. Typically, a critic will resolve conflicts between actions resulting from expansions, or otherwise adjust a procedural net in some way. Critics are activated opportunistically, that is, they fire when some condition in a state occurs which they have been designed to recognize and handle.

Only the design rules of Figure 6.10 are considered here. The actions necessary in order to locate an object are represented diagrammatically in the expansion rules of Figure 8.31. The left side of each rule contains an action and the right side of each rule shows the syntactic expression of that action. Three critics are shown diagrammatically in Figure 8.32. They are derived from the general inference rules described on page 39.

Critic 1: Remove Conflicting Disjuncts.
Critic 2: Remove Redundant Disjuncts.
Critic 3: Remove Redundant Conjuncts.

The overall strategy is to expand the initial state by means of expansion rules. This results in the state shown in Figure 8.33. No critics can be applied at this state so the net is expanded to that shown in Figure 8.34. At this state critic 1 (Remove Conflicting Disjuncts) is found to be applicable. It makes use of facts about actions to detect conflicts. These facts are shown in Figure 8.35.

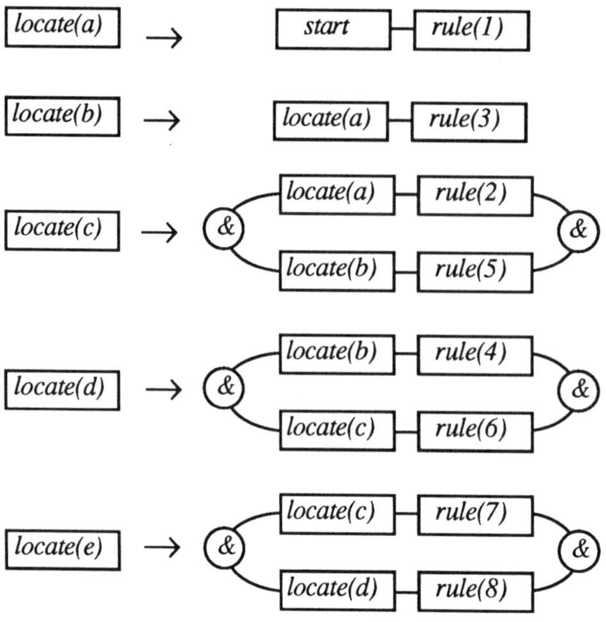

Figure 8.31. Expansion rules derived from the grammar of Figure 6.10.

If a rule has a precondition which is denied by another rule then the two are in conflict. *Rule*(*2*) and *rule*(*3*) are therefore in conflict. It is impossible to formulate a plan where both actions occur in conjunction. The effect of this critic is to produce the state in Figure 8.36. No more critics can be applied so the network is expanded again to produce Figure 8.37. The application of critic 2 (Remove Redundant Disjuncts) produces Figure 8.38.

Already it can be seen that a solution has been produced, namely, the rule sequence: *rule*(*1*), *rule*(*3*) and *rule*(*4*). This net is expanded to that shown in Figure 8.39. After critic 3 (Remove Redundant Conjuncts) the end state in Figure 8.40 is shown. No more expansion rules or critics are applicable so this represents the final plan. It is in fact a disjunction of two alternative plans.

A major advantage of this approach is that states are refined as far as is possible by critics before they become too large. The planner therefore proceeds from a less detailed to a more detailed plan. Critics ensure that the details of a plan make some sort of global sense before the plan is expanded further. This is therefore a hierarchical approach where attempts are made to create simple, correct, high-level plans before they are expanded to greater detail where the costs of rectifying plans are greater.

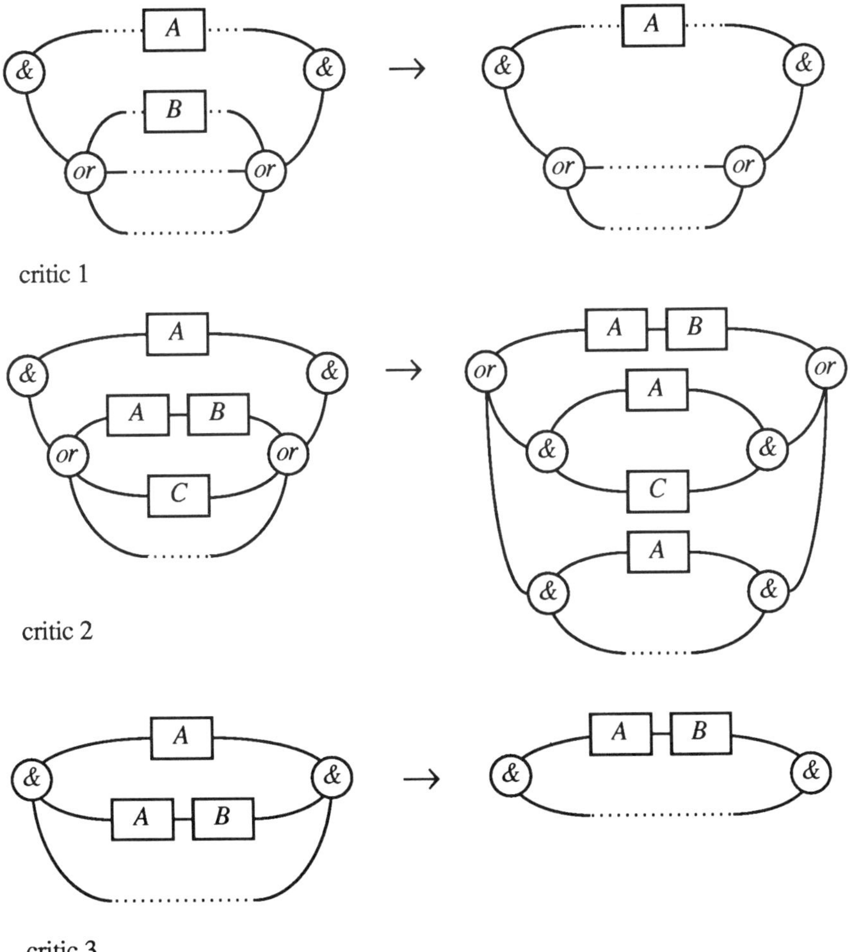

Figure 8.32. Diagrammatic representation of critics—
critic 1: Remove Conflicting Disjuncts
critic 2: Remove Redundant Disjuncts
critic 3: Remove Redundant Conjuncts.

Summary

Design rules (or operators) transform one state into another. Planning as a method of implementing control over the design process has been considered. The first planning model considered was that of forward search and backtracking. This involves selecting and ordering design rules by creating states at a higher level of abstraction than that at which the designs are produced. The second model is backward chaining. This is the process of

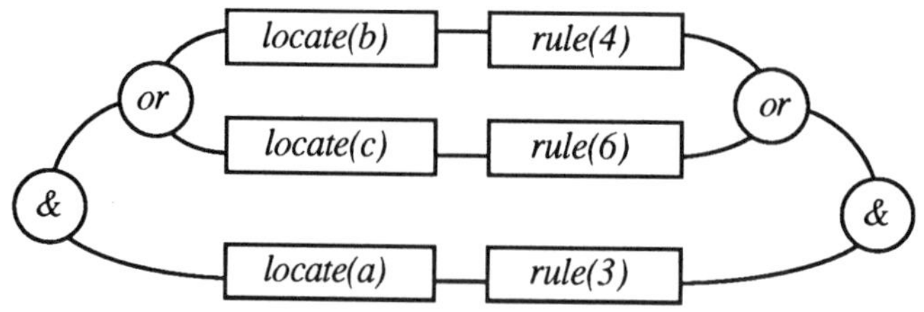

Figure 8.33. Expansion of the initial state shown in Figure 8.30.

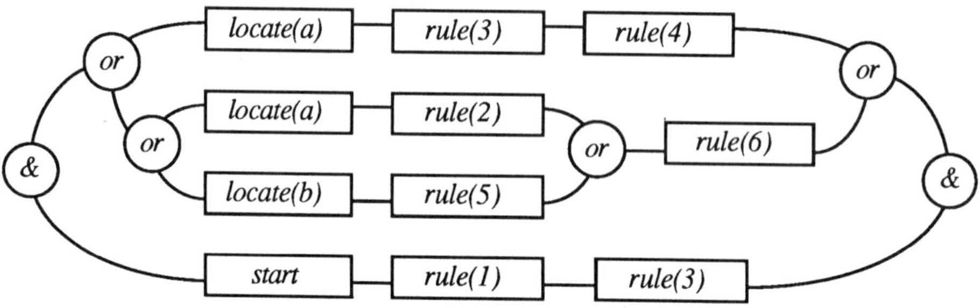

Figure 8.34. Expansion of the procedural network of Figure 8.33.

ACTION	PRECONDITION	DENIED
rule(1)	—	—
rule(2)	*clear(a, right)*	*clear(a, right)*
rule(3)	*clear(a, right)*	*clear(a, right)*
rule(4)	*clear(b, right)*	*clear(b, right)*
rule(5)	*clear(b, right)*	*clear(b, right)*
rule(6)	*clear(c, top)*	*clear(c, top)*
rule(7)	*clear(c, top)*	*clear(c, top)*
rule(8)	*clear(d, top)*	*clear(d, top)*

Figure 8.35. Table for use with critic 1.

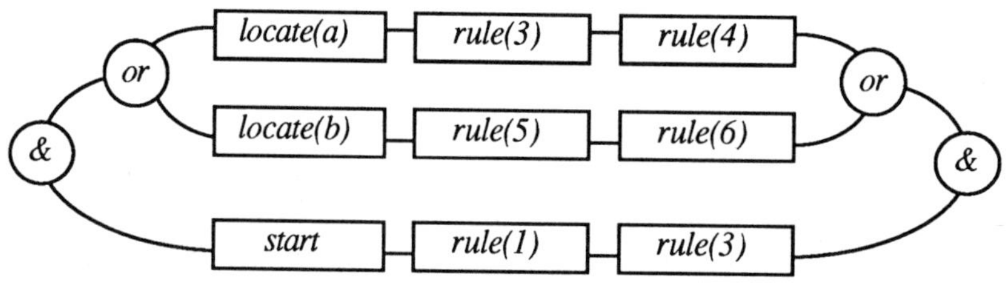

Figure 8.36. Procedural network resulting after the application of critic 1 to Figure 8.34.

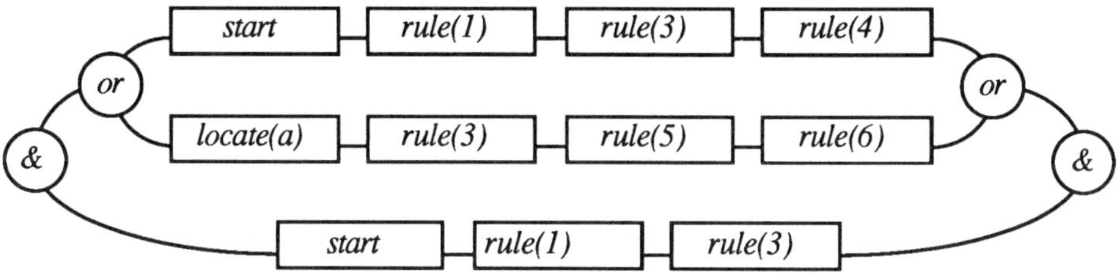

Figure 8.37. Expansion of procedural network in Figure 8.36.

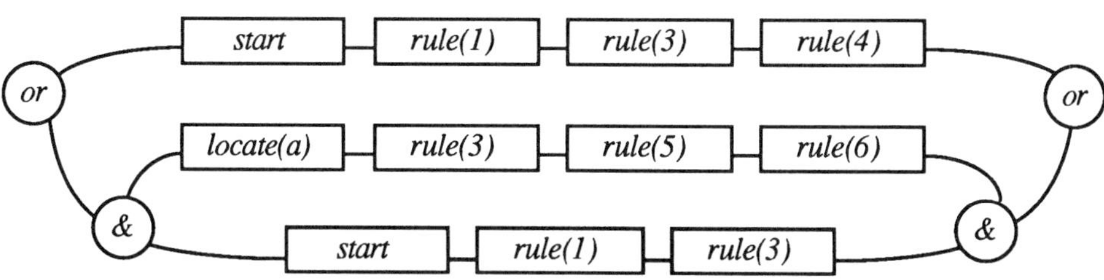

Figure 8.38. The result of applying critic 2.

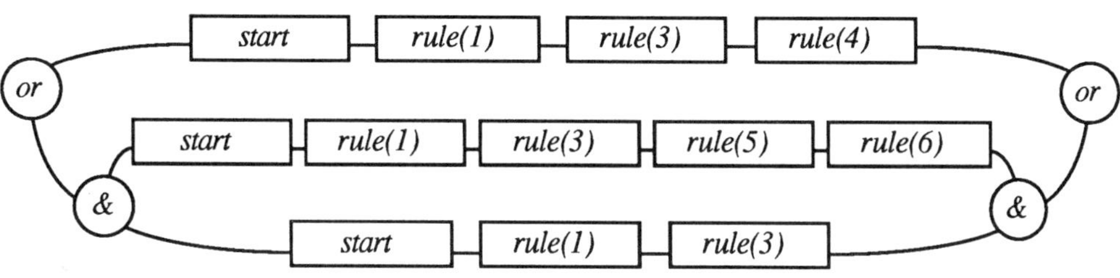

Figure 8.39. Expansion of procedural network in Figure 8.38.

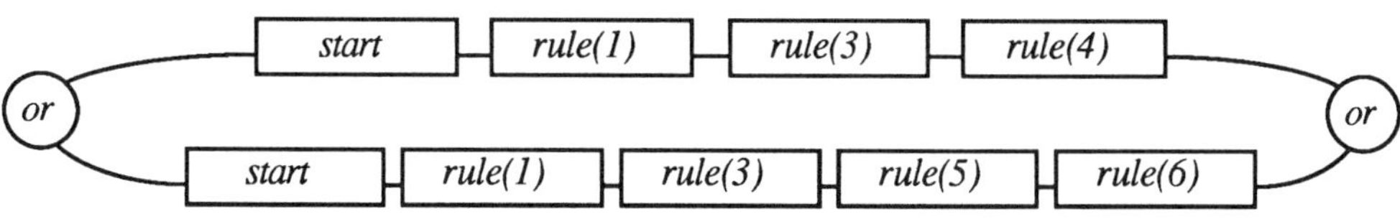

Figure 8.40. Procedural network resulting after the application of critic 3 to Figure 8.39.

chaining backwards from the goal state to the initial state (within an abstracted view of the world). A STRIPS-like planner was demonstrated as a device for producing plans which satisfy goals producing conflicts. In domains involving a large number of possible design states it becomes necessary to approach the planning task utilizing some hierarchical view. This is the third model. An ABSTRIPS-like planner was investigated as a mechanism for hierarchically searching design rule sequences to satisfy goals, where it can be determined *a priori* that some factors are going to be more influential in producing a plan than others. The fourth model affords a constructive view of the planning process. A complete plan is built up from a simple initial description of the task.

The applicability of these models has been demonstrated within a rigidly constrained design example utilizing a simple grammar. The constructive model provides a uniform approach to the representation of design knowledge. Critics and expansion rules are explicit modules of knowledge for manipulating sequences of actions. They constitute a *grammar* within a language of actions. As such they can be modelled as production systems which can also be subject to the methods of control discussed above. This hierarchy of control suggests ways in which knowledge about design can be organized. In the next chapter the principles suggested by the NOAH system will be generalized and tied in with the observations about the properties of grammar systems raised in Chapter 5.

Chapter 9

The Organization of Design Knowledge

The view developed here is that, for certain design domains, the knowledge by which grammar rules are selected can be made explicit. The grammar rules tend to form a 'language' of their own, as argued in Chapter 7. The rules of grammar in design languages are not always anonymous but can be given names, as *actions*. It is possible to model 'languages of actions'.

The argument is developed that design knowledge can be structured such that the advantages of decomposition are exploited. An approach to organizing design knowledge is demonstrated in this chapter by means of a prototype system concerned with spatial synthesis.

Searching Within Design Spaces

A design grammar serves to define a space of designs. As was apparent in Chapter 8, search is a key activity in producing designs that meet particular performance requirements. There is some question as to the applicability of exhaustive search as a model of human reasoning strategies. Experienced designers are generally undaunted by the possibilities presented by large search spaces. Search is generally rendered tractable by reduction (or decomposition).

Experienced designers appear to engage in very restricted search endeavours, to the extent that search may involve the traversal of only one branch of a tree. In this case the design process appears as incremental improvement. Each state of the design is an improvement on the last. It could be argued that the use of extensive search employing backtracking is indicative of the behaviour of a novice rather than of an expert. Search is a strategy reserved by the expert for new and unusual design tasks.

In reduction, tasks are broken into subtasks which are further reduced. The final solution is simply the agglomeration of all sub-solutions. The value of reduction can be demonstrated at a simple level. The design of an object as complex as a hospital can be rendered tractable by considering the design of each of the departments as an independent subtask. These departments may be further decomposed into sub-departments. The task of design is therefore assisted by the mapping between the known hierarchical organization of the overall facility and the spatial configuration. This mapping is not always possible however, and there comes a point at which decomposition ceases to be of assistance. The interactions between components dominates the process. This issue of non-decomposability was pointed out in the context of the spatial organization of cities by Alexander (1972).

But, even where decomposition is not possible at an abstraction level in which spaces are treated as objects, decomposition can be exhibited in various other representational abstractions. This can be exhibited in the way the design *process* is organized as opposed to the way spaces are organized. In the context of urban planning, for example, we may say that even though the spatial form of the city is not decomposable, the processes which bring about that form may exhibit a certain compositional independence. If not the processes, then the *strategies* which order the processes may be decomposable, and so on. That the process can be decomposed even though the artifact cannot is an idea that is often exploited to advantage in design and problem-solving.

Knowledge about design is often represented in the form of prototypical decomposition hierarchies. This is exemplified in documents such as the RIBA Plan of Work. This formally sets out the architect's agenda, from the approach by a client to the closure of the building's maintenance period. It also breaks the design process into manageable chunks, namely sketch design, evaluation, design development and final design. This is a common approach in manuals and guides for all kinds of activities, and conventions exist by which the design process can be further subdivided into component parts. Another example demonstrating the breakdown of the design process for hospital design is provided by Heath (1984).

The role of a fairly detailed strategy based on decomposition can be illustrated with a simple example. The domain is that of the design of a house, the component rooms of which are already known. The decomposition may result in the definition of tasks such as: (1) concentrate on ranking objects in terms of their spatial importance; (2) without locating anything, work out how each object should be placed so that it is adjacent to an object with which it interacts and which is above it on the ranking list; (3) then work out what each object should be adjacent to. There are then further subtasks to be considered. The tasks can be regarded as independent in that the outcome of one task provides information which can be utilized in the next, and the system can be so formulated that backtracking is minimized.

Computer programming makes use of this principle of hierarchical decomposition. Programs are generally structured in such a way that tasks are decomposed into subtasks, in the form of subprograms. When one subtask is completed this provides inputs to another subtask.

Decomposition also has relevance to systems in which knowledge is made explicit as syntactic rules. Each of the above tasks can be seen as the name of an elaborate rewrite rule. If a grammar of such rules is decomposable then it should not be necessary to undo the effects of any rule (that is, backtracking is unnecessary). Each rule firing brings the design closer to a resolution.

As discussed in Chapter 5 a production system is 'well behaved' if it is commutative and decomposable. A production system is decomposable if the description in its global database can be partitioned such that the various components can be operated upon independently. The advantage of such a system is that the order in which rules are considered does not affect the outcome. This means that the control regime can be very simple. We will consider how this can be achieved by considering that design systems can be described in terms of 'languages' operating at several levels of *control.*

Languages of Abstractions

Whether or not linguistic grammars have any basis in psychological reality is a consideration left to others, but it may be supposed that it is not necessary for a speaker to have any concept of a grammar in order to exhibit competence in generating utterances. At the conscious level, being aware of the formalism that a *noun phrase* can be transformed into an *article and a noun* does not generally assist a native speaker. However, designers appear readily able to externalize the idea of rewrite rules (or transformations) in the languages appropriate to their domains. In fact, transformations can carry names, such as *move dining room next to kitchen* and *make living room larger.* These are *actions.*

We can also regard the components (such as actions) of the language system itself as objects upon which the system may operate! There is no stipulation in this linguistic model that the objects of the design system have to relate to form. There are other types of entities on which the system could operate, such as goals, constraints and actions. Design 'actions' can therefore become elements within a designer's 'lexicon'. Just as there are relationships between physical building elements we may suppose that there are relationships between actions. There may be grammars of actions with transformations (meta-grammars) operating on groups of actions.

It is possible to devise a design system in which objects are actions, and vocabulary elements are statements about the relationships between actions. There is therefore knowledge by which we can interpret sequences of actions, and there is syntactic knowledge which defines a language of such actions. This model, in which knowledge about the control of a language system is itself made explicit as a 'meta-language' provides the advantage that certain design knowledge appears to lend itself to this type of representation. Just as there are languages of form there are languages of process. It also provides the advantage that the grammar for generating sequences of actions can exhibit the characteristic of being decomposable. These rules can be made to exhibit properties similar to those of the tasks relating to the design of a house in the previous section.

A linguistic model of design should take account of some such hierarchical view of language. There are many languages which might be brought to bear on a design task including those which control the operations of other languages.

What is the knowledge by which actions can be manipulated? In some cases there appears to be an obvious mapping between the performance of artifacts and the appropriate actions. In some case there is knowledge for mapping action onto particular interpretations of designs:

if the design is to exhibit interpretation X **then** implement action Y.

Following the argument presented in Chapter 4 this would appear to be a kind of abductive rule. The use of this kind of knowledge would also require some knowledge for resolving the conflicts that are bound to arise with competing actions. There is also knowledge by which it is possible to 'configure' actions to obviate conflict. A very simple example is given here:

if action *a* and action *b* are to be performed, and action *a* requires a consequent of action *b* before it can be implemented
then order the actions such that *b* is before *a*.

By undertaking a particular set of actions it may be known that designs with particular attributes will be produced. The links between process (actions) and form have often been made in the context of architectural design. At a simple level, such a mapping is exemplified by the rule: in order to produce a compact building layout start with a square perimeter and attempt to arrange the functions within that; or the rule: the actions of laying out grids and axes tends to produce formal and symmetrical building plans. By making such mappings explicit it may be possible to employ this knowledge in the generation of designs. Further knowledge will be considered in the example presented later on in this chapter.

Structuring Design Knowledge

Knowledge-based systems are computer programs which are intended to make the knowledge about a particular domain explicit and operable (Newell, 1982; Genesereth and Smith, 1983; Robinson, 1983b). In general, this can be achieved if the knowledge is represented and organized to meet certain objectives. These can be summarized as:

1. uniform methods of knowledge representation
2. uniform control mechanisms
3. the knowledge is explicit, and has some meaning in terms of the domain
4. the processes resulting from the application of the knowledge are visible and comprehensible in terms of the domain

It appears that it is possible to meet these objectives, at least in part, with formulations based on production systems, although other methods are actively employed in knowledge-based systems (Quinlan, 1980; Barr and Feigenbaum, 1981). It is desirable that the knowledge contained in the production rules bears some resemblance to the way that human experts understand their knowledge. So the way in which the rules are formulated is also important. The fourth goal suggests that it should be possible to 'see' what is being done with the knowledge, perhaps graphically, and that the intermediate steps during the development of the artifact resemble, in some way, the processes carried out by designers. The formulation of a knowledge-based system which is appropriate to design and which makes use of production systems is considered here as a means of addressing these objectives.

In the linguistic formulation proposed here, knowledge is made explicit primarily in the form of grammars and interpretive rules. Control knowledge is also made explicit in the form of rules. This can be demonstrated by structuring a domain, that concerned with layout planning in buildings, as three layers of knowledge. The layering takes advantage of the properties of 'well behaved' production systems. So, as well as providing a structure for making knowledge explicit, there are implementational advantages as well. The particular layering proposed (and the naming of levels) is pragmatic and is not intended to capture a universally applicable view of design, but is intended merely to illustrate that such layering is possible and advantageous.

Knowledge About Form

The grammar of rectangular dissections presented in Chapter 6 will be considered here. This grammar appears to exhibit the characteristics of the 'poorly behaved' rule set, as the order in which rules are executed clearly determines the outcome, and there can be many end states. The rules concerned with the locations of windows, the locations of openings between rooms, and the deletion of spaces can be considered as 'enhancements' as they do not really affect the location of spaces as determined by the other rule set, nor do they impinge appreciably on one another. These can be regarded as independent subtasks. The rules of Figure 6.14 and Figure 6.16 could operate as a useful set of 'commands' for a design system. (In this discussion the rules of Figure 6.13 only are considered in detail.) The rules contain knowledge about what preconditions are necessary before the consequent can be carried out. They contain no knowledge about whether or not it is desirable that a rule is executed in order to produce a design meeting certain performance requirements. This is the role of the the knowledge about actions.

Knowledge About Actions

The rules of Figure 6.14 can be given names which describe what they achieve. They can be represented in the general form:

put A *Dir* B,
put A Dir_1 B and Dir_2 C,

where *A*, *B* and *C* represent the names of spaces, *Dir*, Dir_1 and Dir_2 are directions (*north_of, south_of, east_of* and *west_of*), *put* is a descriptive predicate indicating that the spaces should be *put* in place, and *and* carries its normal meaning as conjunction. As well as containing a set of conditions which must be matched against a facts base (global database), and a consequent which describes the changes to be made to the database, the rules therefore also carry a descriptive name. Rules *a* and *c* in Figure 6.14 can therefore bear the names:

put A east_of B,
put A east_of B and north_of C,

where *A*, *B* and *C* are variables representing spaces as illustrated in Figure 9.1. The actions:

put bathroom east_of bedroom,
put dining_room east_of kitchen and north_of living_room,

are therefore specific instances of these rules.

Rules which transform states can therefore be regarded as actions and the rules of Figure 6.14 constitute a set of actions. These actions constitute the **vocabulary** of a *grammar of actions.* In this grammar the way in which the actions operate (as rules) can be ignored. So only their names are considered. The relationship between these actions, however, is important. The final state of the system consists of a sequence of actions which provides the control for a system concerned with generating form.

As discussed in Chapter 7, there are two useful relationships between actions which can be considered: *serial* and *parallel* relationships. In serial relationships actions are configured in the order in which they are to be executed. In parallel relationships actions are arranged in groups as conjunctions and disjunctions. It is therefore possible to represent actions with varying degrees of commitment to order. These relationships can be represented in a procedural network which undergoes a series of state transformations according to the actions of critics and expansion rules. Although the use of critics is intended primarily to resolve conflicts between actions the device can be extended to incorporate diverse sorts of knowledge, including heuristics which also help to *avoid* conflicts.

Translating this method into the linguistic paradigm it becomes apparent that, in the same way that a richer understanding of a building is required than than just a knowledge of its basic components, a richer understanding of actions is required. As discussed in Chapter 7, actions bear relationships to each other as exemplified in Figure 7.14. In the context of design the action *put dining_room* ***east_of*** *kitchen* is therefore also a specific instance of the action *put dining_room* ***next_to*** *kitchen* which is a specific instance of *put dining_room* ***near*** *kitchen.* The actions eventually map onto generic actions such as *design_house.*

A grammar system can therefore be described which takes as its initial condition some generic action (or actions), and produces a predominantly serial configuration of executable actions as an end state. Intermediate states consist of actions on different levels arranged with various degrees of commitment to order. The transition is therefore from a high level set of actions to an executable set of actions, and from a set of actions in which there is relatively little commitment to order, to a set of actions with a more complete commitment to order.

The mappings between actions can be employed to transform sets of actions. These mappings can be utilized by a rule called an 'expansion rule', which replaces higher level actions with lower level actions. (An alternative would be to formulate the mappings as rules in themselves, as in Figure 7.14. This approach has not been adopted in order to preserve generality.)

As was illustrated with the example about the conflict in painting a ladder and painting a ceiling (page 153), just substituting executable actions for generic actions is insufficient for producing appropriate sequences. Actions interact with one another. Other rules are required, concerned with *interactions* between actions. In the NOAH system, 'critics' tend to resolve conflicts within a network, but the general idea can be extended to other operations on sets of actions. Such rules are intended to encapsulate more complex knowledge than can be represented by simple mapped pairs. An example of a rule appropriate to the domain of layout planning is one that states:

if the procedural network contains a set of actions concerned with locating spaces and these actions are arranged in parallel (that is, there is no commitment to order)
then order the actions according to the importance of the spaces on which they operate.

This can be interpreted as: if there are several spaces to be located and the desirable interconnections between spaces are known then locate the space with the most interconnections first. Although not entirely general, this is a simple heuristic of the type that a designer might employ in beginning a layout task.

A simple example of states in a domain about actions in the design of a building is illustrated in Figure 9.2. *State.1* contains the single action *design house*. Given that there is a simple mapping between this action and the actions of locating the components of *house*, *state.2* can be produced by an

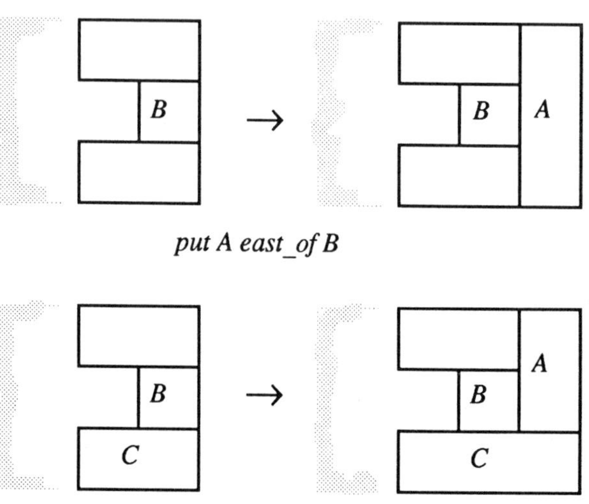

Figure 9.1. Descriptive names associated with rules *a* and *c* in Figure 6.14. *A*, *B* and *C* are variables naming spaces.

expansion rule. *State.3* is produced by applying the rule about locating the most important element first (described above). The application of further rules may expand the network into more specific details and take account of more complex mappings between actions. Further information about building components is required in order to bring about the transformations of Figure 9.2 than is evident from the mappings described. This will be discussed below in connection with *context.*

The 'grammar of actions' therefore captures knowledge about the ordering of actions. As illustrated by the simple example of Figure 9.2 it might be expected that designers readily make use of this sort of knowledge. A further point that can be made about this formulation is that it can be constructed as a 'well behaved' system. In the same way that the system demonstrated in Figure 5.4 has only a single end state it is possible that the continuation of the sequence of states in Figure 9.2 would produce a single end state, and that the order in which the rules are applied only affects the efficiency with which the end state is reached. This is not to say that only a single building layout is produced.

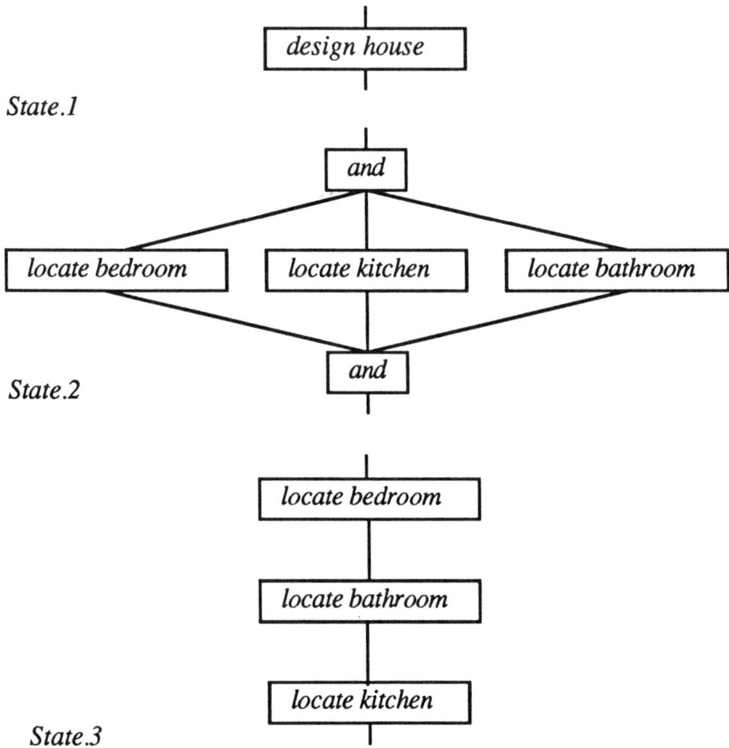

Figure 9.2. States in the transformation of a procedural network in the domain of spatial layout for a house.

The end state may consist of many sequences of actions in disjunction. When executed, the sequence of actions produced by this system constitutes a set of grammatical operations which generate artifacts at the form level. The sequences may result in the generation of many artifacts. The end state of a system employing a grammar of actions is a *plan*. The mechanism that can be employed to control this system in order to produce plans is now considered.

Knowledge About Plans

The type of knowledge which one wishes to encapsulate in order to control knowledge about actions is that which comes under the category of 'meta-planning' knowledge, as suggested by Wilensky (1981; 1983) and Stefik (1981b) (discussed in Chapter 7) or control knowledge as discussed by Davis (1980a; 1980b). The objective is to capture universal principles employed in decision making.

Knowledge about the selection and ordering of actions constitutes the 'grammar of actions' (described above). This knowledge can be represented as a grammar concerned with formulating plans. In the same way that the rules in the 'grammar of form' can be given names which enable them to be treated as vocabulary elements for a 'grammar of actions', it is possible to give the rules of a 'grammar of actions' names and regard them as vocabulary elements in a *grammar of plans*. The 'vocabulary' for this grammar therefore consists of *planning tasks* such as those which were effective in bringing about the state changes in Figure 9.2 such as:

expand actions,
order actions, etc.

Tasks such as these can be organized according to their relationships with one another and they can also be organized as groups which are related to other tasks. One approach is considered here.

Rather than the procedural network schema discussed above it seems convenient to relate these tasks within a simple hierarchical graph. The levels within this graph make explicit certain relationships between the tasks. They can be considered as similar to macro-operators in a structured computer program or, in this context, it is perhaps more meaningful to talk about a *schedule* of tasks. A schedule (unconnected with any domain) is depicted graphically in Figure 9.3. Task *1* can be broken up into the subtasks *1.1* and *1.2*. Task *1.1* can be broken up into the subtasks *1.1.1* and *1.1.2*, etc. There is also an implicit order in that task *1.1* is to be performed before task *1.2*, and task *1.1.1* is to be performed before task *1.1.2*, etc.

The advantage of arranging tasks hierarchically in this fashion is that those which naturally group together can be treated as a block if it becomes necessary to re-arrange the schedule. So, if the order of tasks *1.1* and *1.2* is to be changed then the tasks below these are exchanged by implication as well.

The product of this grammar system is therefore a graph of hierarchically arranged tasks called a 'schedule'. Such a schedule could be built up from some simple initial state, but it is proposed that the initial state of this system is a complete schedule (as in Figure 9.3), modified in some way to make it more responsive to the domain in which the grammar is operating. The grammar for this system should consist of rules that manipulate the schedule. There are two ways in which this could be achieved. The structure could be modified to suit the design context by means of domain specific knowledge. This type of control will *not* be considered here.

The other approach is where there is a choice of tasks to be undertaken, and the ordering has to be decided upon, such as at the branch ends of the graph. Where there are choices the global database (state description) of the grammar of actions can be partitioned in such a way that the effects of each task can be stored temporarily before they are actually executed. The grammar then operates on this information. The procedure is therefore to discover the tasks that apply to the current state of the global database of the 'grammar of form'. This is achieved by *triggering* the tasks, that is, checking that their preconditions exist in the global database and recording what changes each task will make to the database. The 'grammar of plans' therefore requires 'cooperation' from the 'grammar of actions'.

It is possible, therefore, to organize a system such that the subsystem this knowledge is controlling (the 'grammar of actions') tends toward 'well behaved' characteristics and the 'grammar of plans' consists of scheduling rules. An advantage of this formulation is that the importance of domain independent principles becomes apparent. Rules for manipulating tasks could be based on general strategies for problem solving, such as:

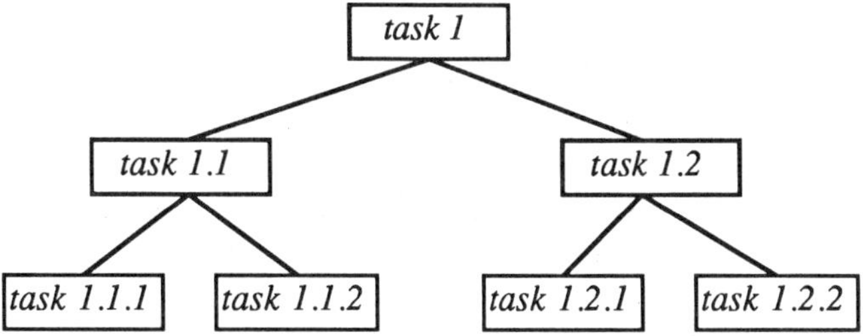

Figure 9.3. A hierarchical schedule of tasks.

1. consolidation
2. diversification
3. convergence
4. divergence

A strategy to consolidate might be expressed as a rule that takes as its precondition the relative sizes of the states produced by each of the planning tasks competing to be executed, and as a consequent selects the task which tends to reduce the size of the database. Alternatively, it may select the task which produces a state with the smallest 'conflict set' (set of competing tasks). A rule about convergence may select the task which operates on the most recently affected database item. This will cause the system to concentrate on particular elements. Rules about convergence may also operate by selecting planning tasks which operate on the most important database items first. It could be maintained that important elements are those which occur earliest on a procedural network, for example.

The control strategy for this system could be one in which only a single scheduling rule is adopted, or there might be an overriding strategy which states, for example:

> attempt to consolidate, and converge attention (whichever is applicable at any given state); if, after a particular period of time, no satisfactory end state is reached then attempt to diversify.

It is possible to conceive of further levels of control operating above knowledge about plans. This will not be developed here however. In the following section attention will focus on the description of a system concerned with representing and manipulating knowledge which develops plans of actions.

Representing Planning Knowledge

Three layers of knowledge appropriate to any domain have been discussed, but here they will be considered specifically in relation to spatial synthesis. The first, knowledge about form ('grammar of form'), takes as its vocabulary elements dimensionless spaces. The knowledge takes the form of a set of rules for manipulating spaces such that the layout 'evolves' as a configuration of rectangles. The rules can also be seen as a set of actions which form the vocabulary elements of a meta-grammar (the grammar of actions). In this grammar, actions are configured on a structure called a 'procedural network'. The outcome of this grammar system is a statement about actions and their ordering. This provides the control for the 'grammar of form', that is, it provides an *a priori* rule list which, when executed, produces descriptions of artifacts.

The knowledge about actions consists of rules which transform procedural networks. These rules can be identified by descriptive names, which constitute a type of planning task. The knowledge about plans ('grammar of plans') takes these tasks as its 'vocabulary' elements arranged within a hierarchical schedule, and selects between competing tasks. These rules operate by deciding between tasks dynamically as choices are demanded by the grammar of actions. So this system operates not by providing an *a priori* list of operations for the system below it, but by operating in consort. It can be seen therefore that the three systems operate differently and they each bear different relationships with one another. These relationships are illustrated schematically in Figure 9.4. The arrows link the syntactic elements of each grammar with the operators of the grammar below it.

Context

Transformational grammar rules can respond, therefore, to control exercised from above (a meta-grammar), to conditions within the global database and also to *context*. Those parts of a problem domain may be regarded as contextual which remain constant throughout the process, but vary from one design task to the next. They therefore contribute to the unique nature of any design. In this formulation it seems appropriate to make this information explicit. Contextual information for the spatial synthesis task may therefore be concerned with factors such as intended spatial relationships, the hierarchical relationship between parts and relative room sizes. The contents of the context could also be seen as a design brief or a set of performance specifications. (The flexible nature of a design brief suggests that a more complete formulation should, of course, allow for knowledge which actually operates on the context.)

A set of facts constituting a design context is represented as terms in predicate calculus notation able to be manipulated in Prolog, and is depicted graphically in Figure 9.5. The first fact is that a particular building (called *building*(*x*)) is composed of seven spaces, six of which are rooms, the last being a *void* (that is, a courtyard or other open space). The desired relationships between the spaces are depicted in an adjacency network. The context constitutes a type of input to the system, but it may itself be a product of another similarly formulated design system. It is not entirely realistic to assume that such relationships will remain static throughout the design process, but they are assumed static for this exercise. In this example the relative sizes of some of the rooms is also considered to be important. This will serve to constrain or, in this example, *guide* the selection of plan actions.

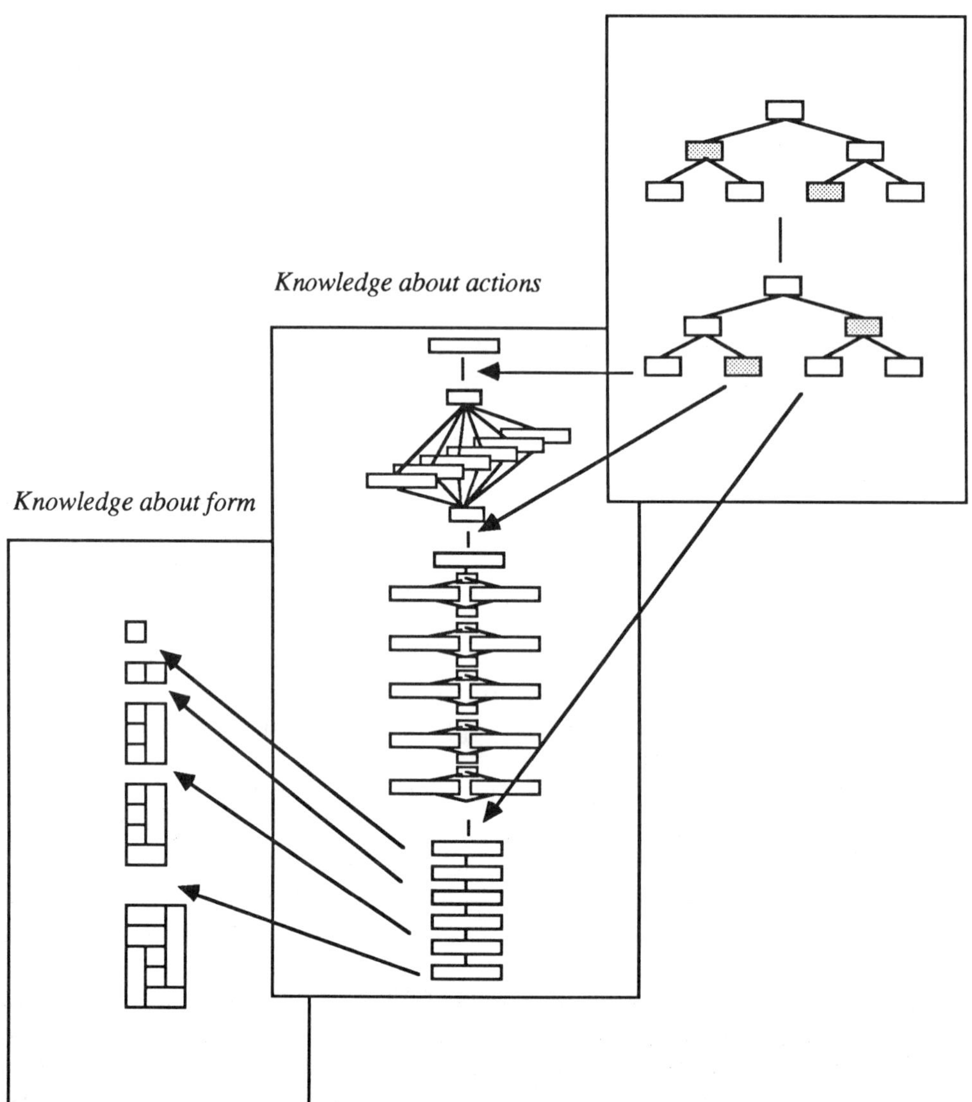

Figure 9.4. Schematic representation of the relationship between grammars in a design language for producing spatial layouts.

The spatial configuration should be such that these relative sizes can be achieved when the rooms are dimensioned, even though the relative size differences are not actually evident from the dimensionless configuration.

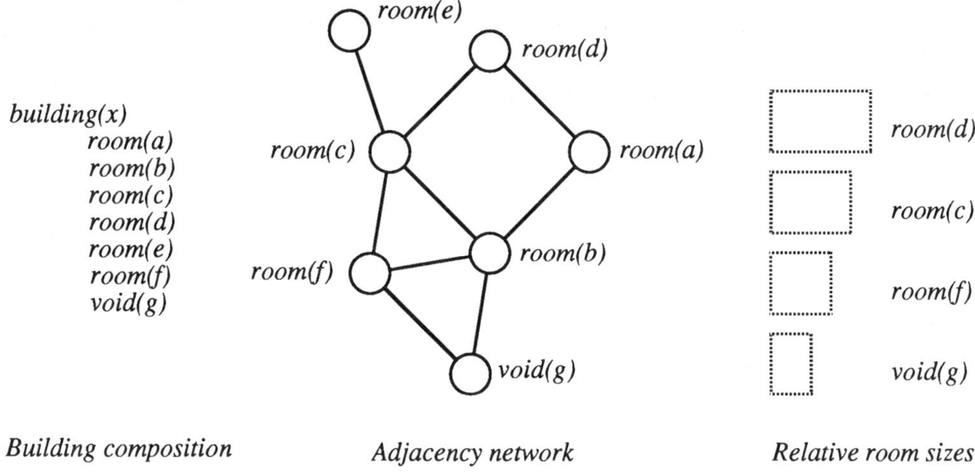

Figure 9.5. Context for a spatial synthesis task.

This set of facts therefore constitutes the desired performance—facts which are to be implicit in the description of the final artifact. Also part of the context is the initial state of the planning process. Here it is the action, *configure(building(x))*, that is, the task is to arrange the components of *building(x)*. This represents a goal, or a generic description of the task at hand, which must be expanded and shaped into a sequence of actions able to be executed. The knowledge for producing a description of an artifact which fits the context therefore 'reads' the other facts in the context as well as the current state of the plan.

A System of Actions for Spatial Layout

Some rules for spatial synthesis are represented schematically in Figure 9.6. (These rules are simplified. They have been represented more precisely than illustrated here in predicate logic and are described more fully in the next chapter.) The expressions in the boxes are Prolog terms where upper case characters are variables. As a rule is executed, its left side is matched against the current state of the global database (that is, the facts representing the state of the plan). The variables are instantiated to corresponding values in the matched facts and the terms on the right side of the rule are substituted in the current state.

Rule *a* is an expansion rule. It means that the action to *configure* an object should be expanded into the conjunction of several actions placing the components of that object. Rule *b* orders a set of such actions according to the valency of the rooms on the adjacency network. This assumes that the placement of rooms with the most interconnections is some how critical and that the placement of these rooms should be accomplished first. Other rules could be devised which order on some other basis, such as size. Rule *c* simply says to anchor the first room on the 'work plane'.

Rule *d* states: if there is a room *B* and, according to the set of adjacency relationships it should be linked to a room *A*, and *A* has already been anchored, then substitute *put*(*B*, *next_to*, *A*) for *put*(*B*). This is equivalent to placing objects adjacent to objects in place and with which they should be linked. Rule *e* arbitrarily locates the second object to the *east* of the first object. This is a simple expedient. It is considered that other configurations can be handled by the rotation and reflection of the entire configuration. Rules *f* and *g* are examples of rules for orientating the rest of the rooms. They take

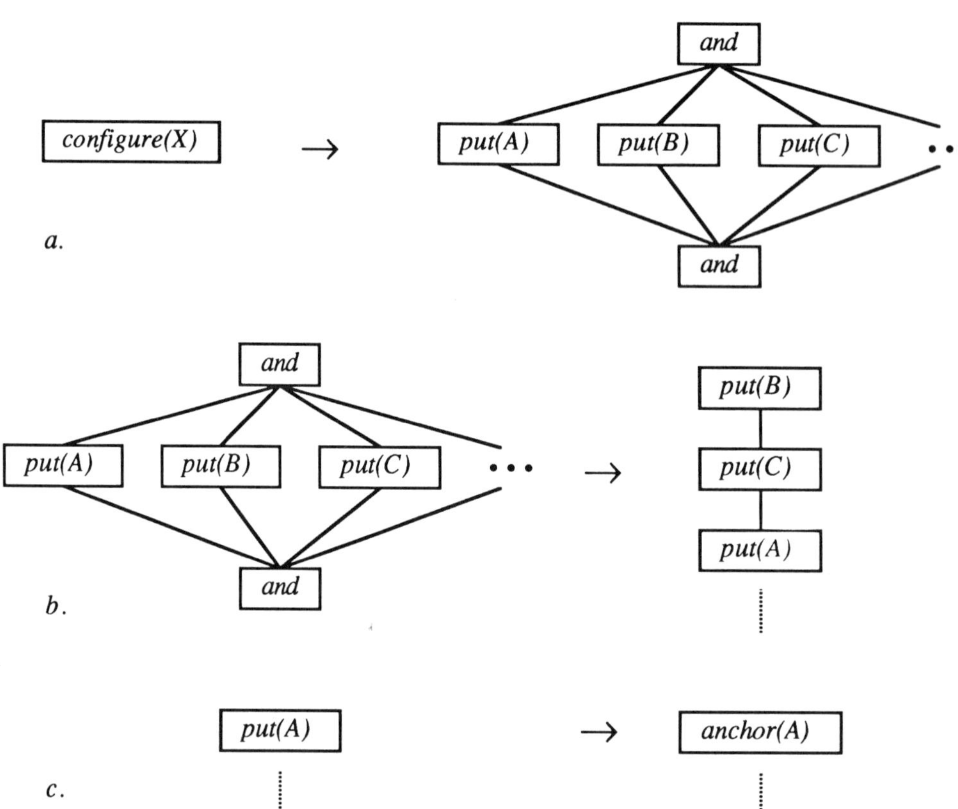

Figure 9.6. A grammar for producing spatial layouts.

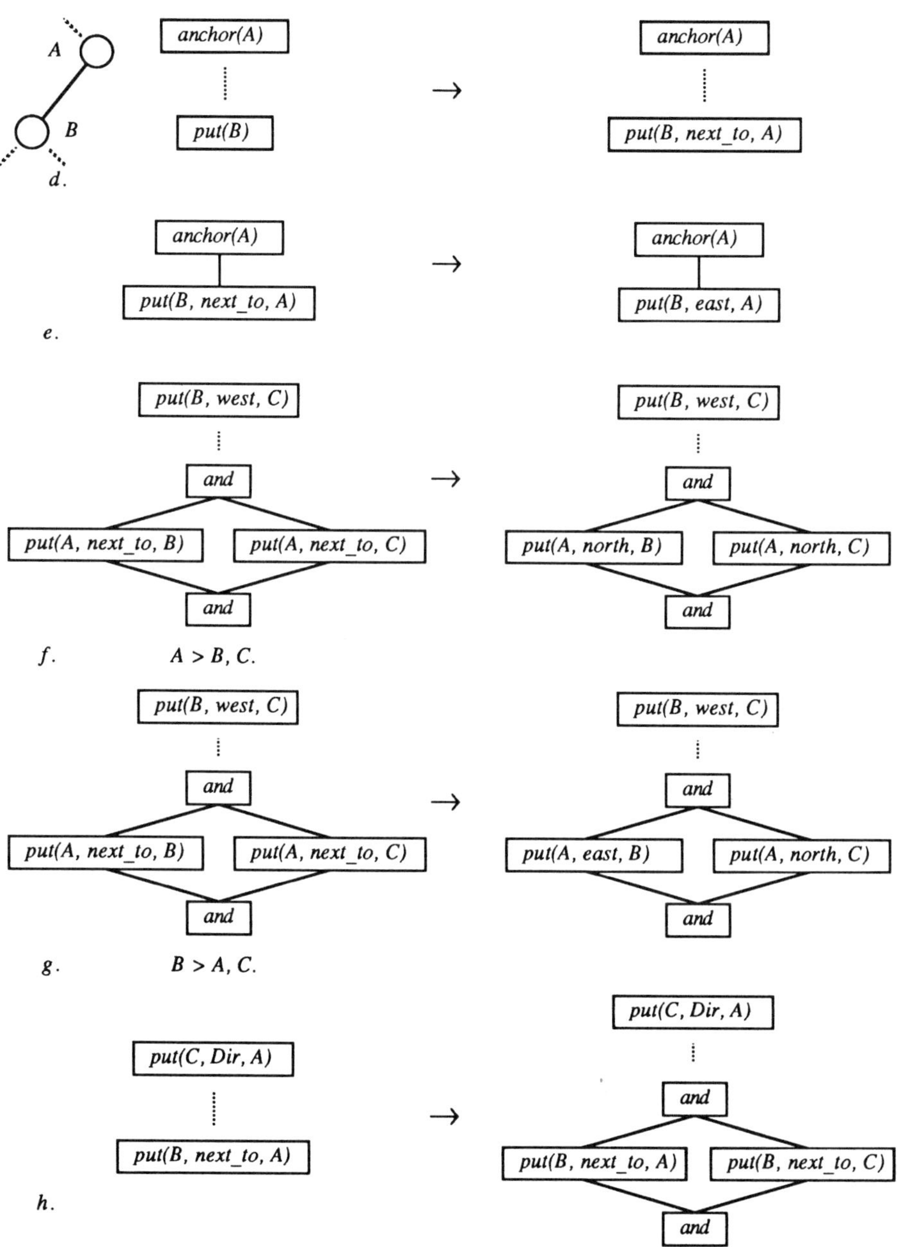

Figure 9.6. (continued).

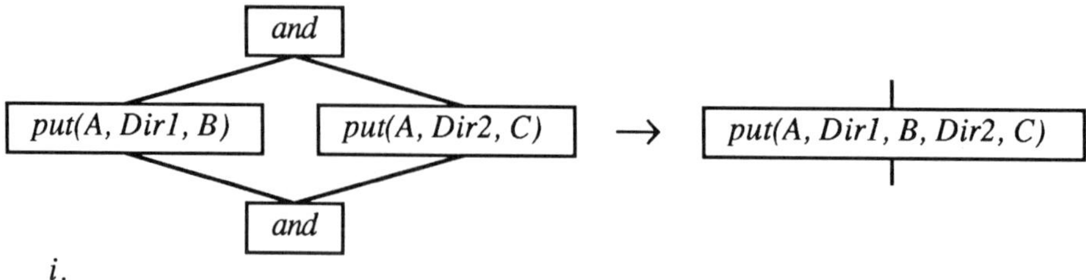

Figure 9.6. (continued).

the *next_to* relationships and refine them into more specific relationships, depending on the relative sizes of the rooms. Rule *f* therefore states that if room *A* is to be *next_to* room *B* and also room *C* and the action for putting *B* west of *C* has already been established, and *A* is to be the larger of the three rooms, then place *A* north of *B* and north of *C* (provided nothing has already been placed there). Rule *g* applies if *B* is to be larger than *A* and *C*. The effects of these alternative rules on the eventual spatial configuration are shown graphically in Figure 9.7. The rules for achieving this and other orientations can be represented in a single rule, but they have been separated here for clarity.

Rule *h* states that if there are no other rules to determine the placement of room *B* the action *put*(*B*, *next_to*, *A*) can be expanded to the conjunction of two actions as shown. *B* is simply located adjacent to *C* and the room next to which *C* is already positioned. Rule *i* replaces the conjunction of two actions with a single action. Implicit in these rules is the general strategy to proceed from less specific to more specific actions (that is, *next_to* relationships to *north, south, east* and *west* directional relationships), and the strategy of using triangulation for fixing objects in place. That is, objects are placed in relation to at least two objects already in place.

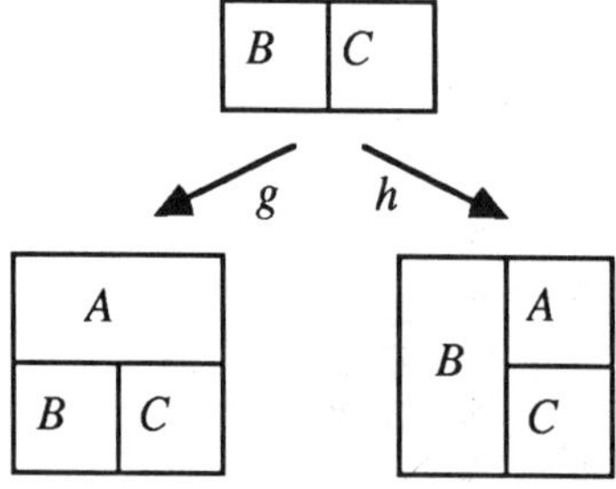

Figure 9.7. Alternative configurations of spaces which result from sequential plans generated by rules *g* and *h* in Figure 9.6.

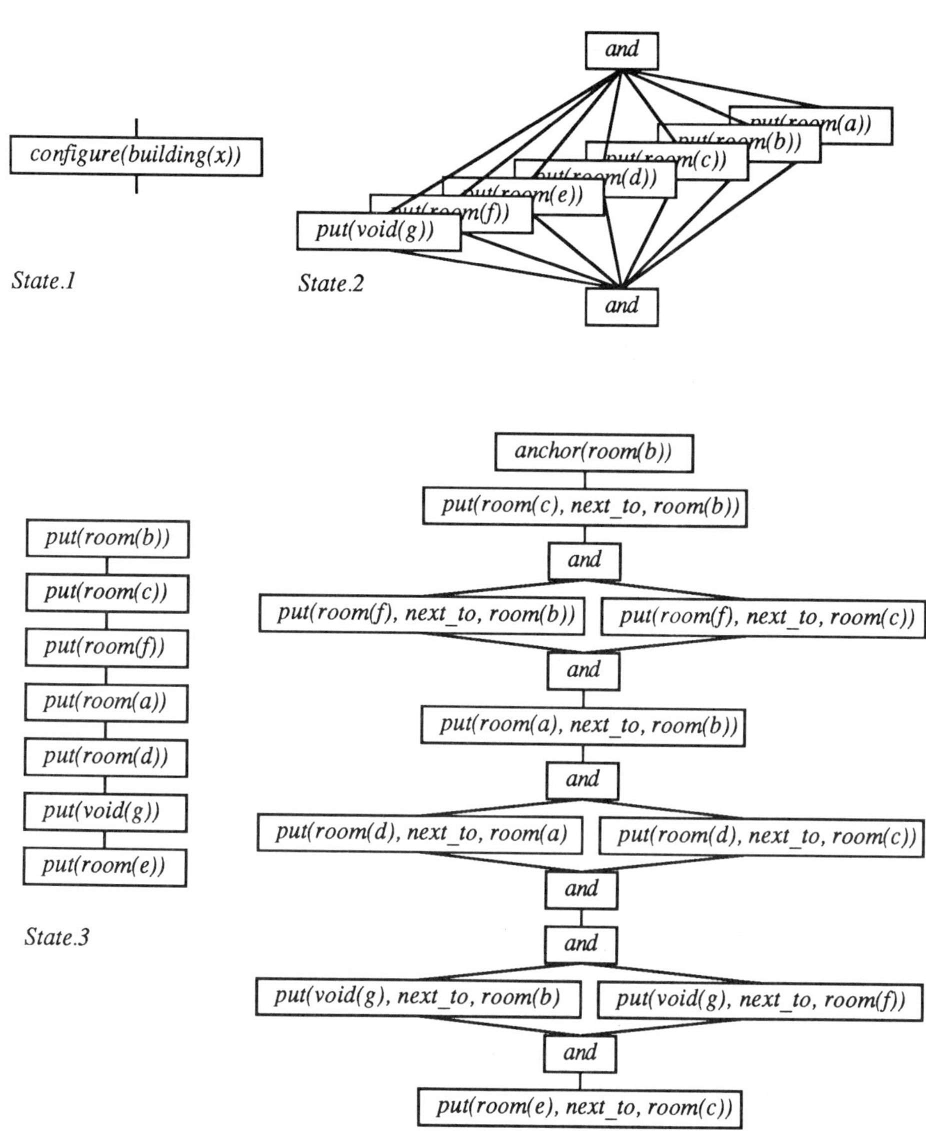

Figure 9.8. States in the development of a plan for the context of Figure 9.5.

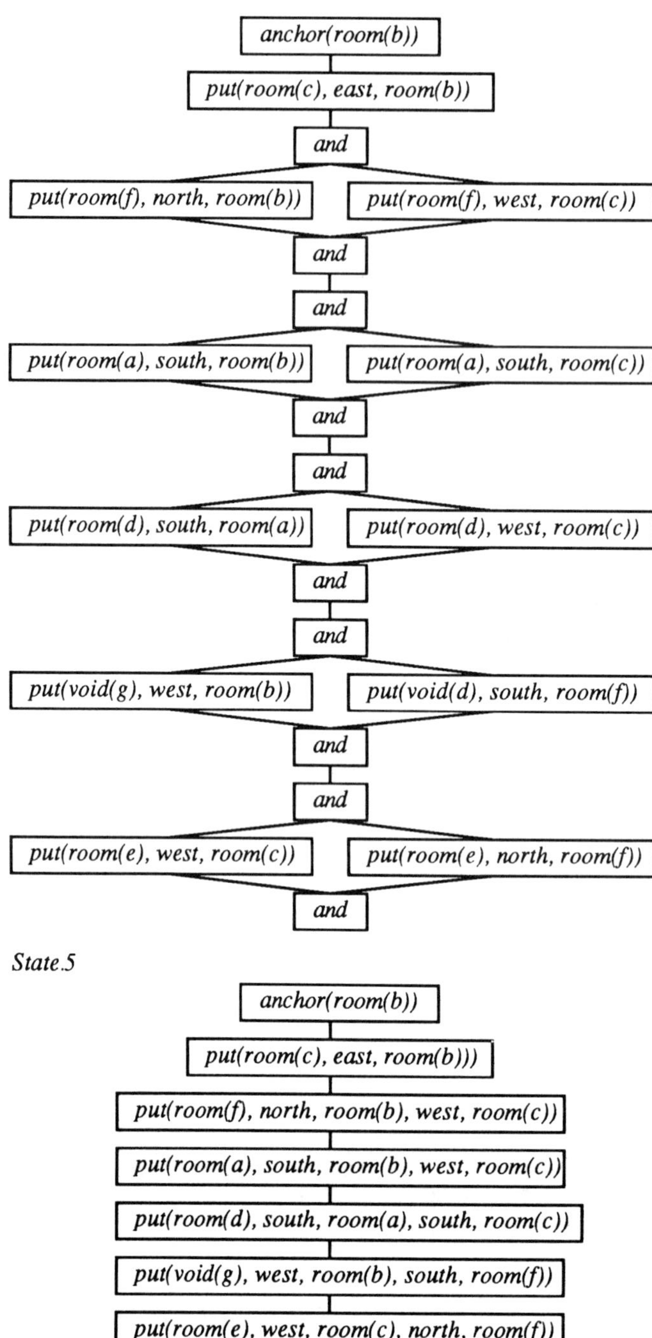

State.6

Figure 9.8. (continued).

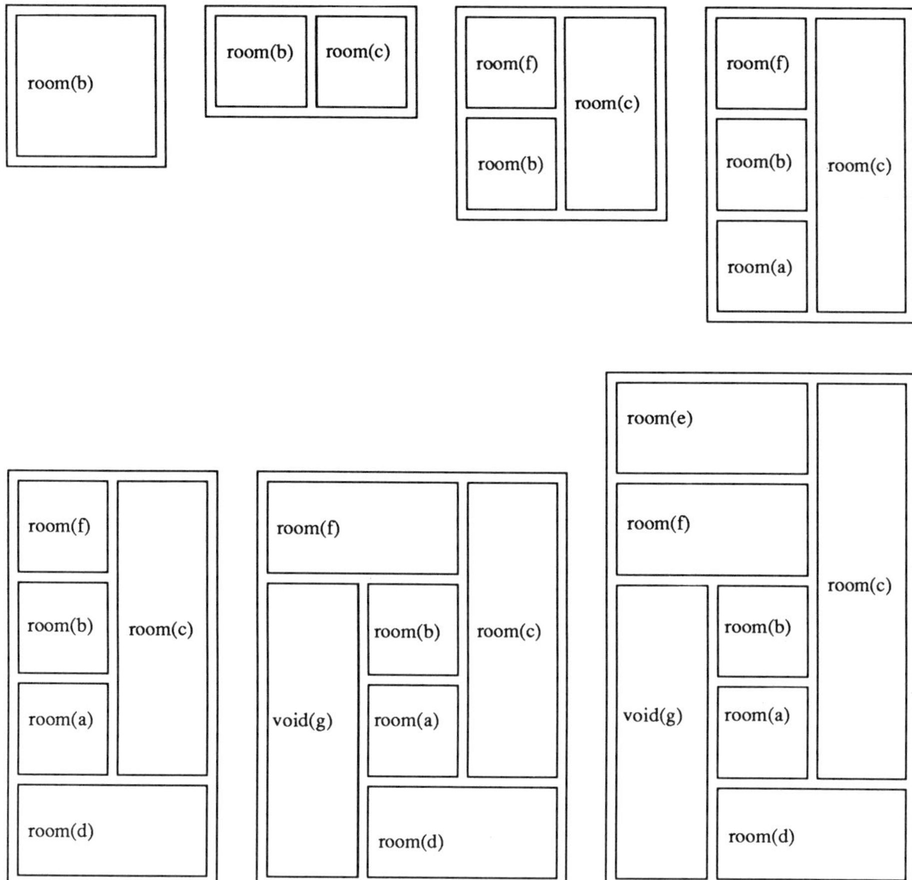

Figure 9.9. States in the development of a floor layout.

These are examples of the types of rules which can be employed in the manipulation of plans of simple design actions. The rules are intended to reduce the likelihood of conflicts between actions by means of simple heuristics. Where conflicts occur these can be handled by means of rules after the fashion of the critics of the NOAH system which might adjust the network by re-ordering actions. Rules which specifically handle conflict resolution have not been illustrated here but these operate in the same way as the other rules. These rules are discussed at greater depth in the following chapter.

Some of the rules are independent of any domain and would appear to be universally applicable; others might be regarded as idiosyncratic and of limited applicability. The programming environment in which this example is implemented is such that the system is not entirely dependent on the appropriateness of the rules. The knowledge base (rules) can be enhanced and developed without detriment to the overall framework. An example of the development of a plan of actions employing the rules of Figure 9.6 is shown in Figure 9.8.

Six states in the development of the plan are shown. *State.1* is the initial state. This is expanded to the conjunction of actions in *state.2* derived from rule *a* of Figure 9.6. *State.3* depicts the ordering produced by rule *b*. It arbitrarily selects one of the two spaces with equivalent highest valencies to be positioned first. *State.4* results from the application of rule *c*, and the repeated application of rules *d* and *e*. *State.4* therefore depicts a sequence of actions starting with the placement of the most important space. Subsequent actions locate rooms next to other rooms already in place and with which they are to be linked. *State.5* is a plan produced by the repeated application of rules *f, g* and *h*. The repeated application of rule *i* produces the end *state.6*.

When this sequence of actions is executed by the system which manipulates form it results in the states depicted in Figure 9.9. The final state is a floor layout. Further rules can be applied to delete voids and to draw openings between spaces which are linked, and to position windows.

Figures 9.10 and 9.11 show a computer graphics environment devised primarily for experimenting with knowledge about spatial synthesis. The computer screen is divided into 'windows' displaying information about context, schedules, plans and the development of the form of the artifact. Figure 9.10 depicts the layout developed in Figure 9.9, and Figure 9.11 shows a different layout generated for another context. This environment can be extended to cover each of the meta-grammars discussed above. The intention is to create a flexible environment in which contextual information, knowledge and system processes are visible and amenable to modification and development.

Summary

Levels of control knowledge have been discussed as a way of formalizing the complex mappings between meaning and artifact in design, such that designs can be generated which exhibit desired attributes. The rules of a grammar which operate on a vocabulary of form are considered as actions. How other knowledge might operate on those actions has been considered. The assumption is made that designers are readily able to articulate such knowledge about design. Some of the relationships between these actions, and between actions and design attributes, may also be exploited. Some attempt has been made to demonstrate how this view can form the foundation of a knowledge-based computer system for spatial synthesis. In the example, three

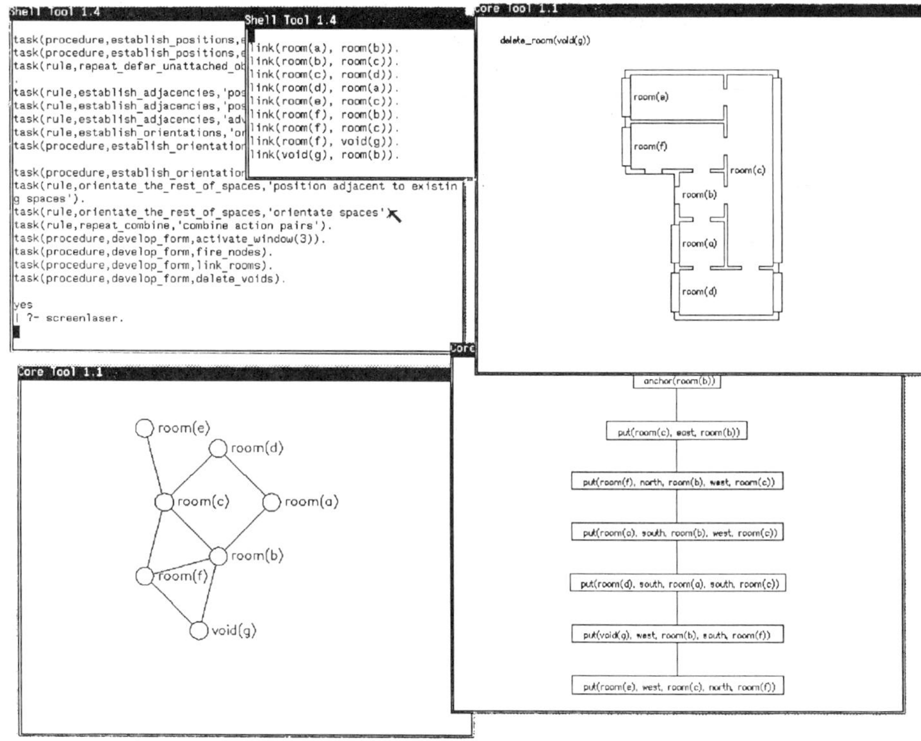

Figure 9.10. Screen display of a planning system.

levels of knowledge were discussed as a way of structuring knowledge: a 'grammar of form', a 'grammar of actions' and a 'grammar of plans', though the knowledge could be defined otherwise.

A basic principle being exercised here is that of exploiting the redundancies inherent in the way designers (or any problem-solvers) view the world. Design systems can therefore operate on multiple abstractions of the world, such as adjacency graphs, procedural representations (at various levels), and formal and geometrical arrangements of spaces.

The implementational advantage of this multi-level view of design is that grammars can be made to resemble what have been termed 'well behaved' systems, that is, systems which require only simple control mechanisms. The ideas put forward here are not dependent on the sophistication of the

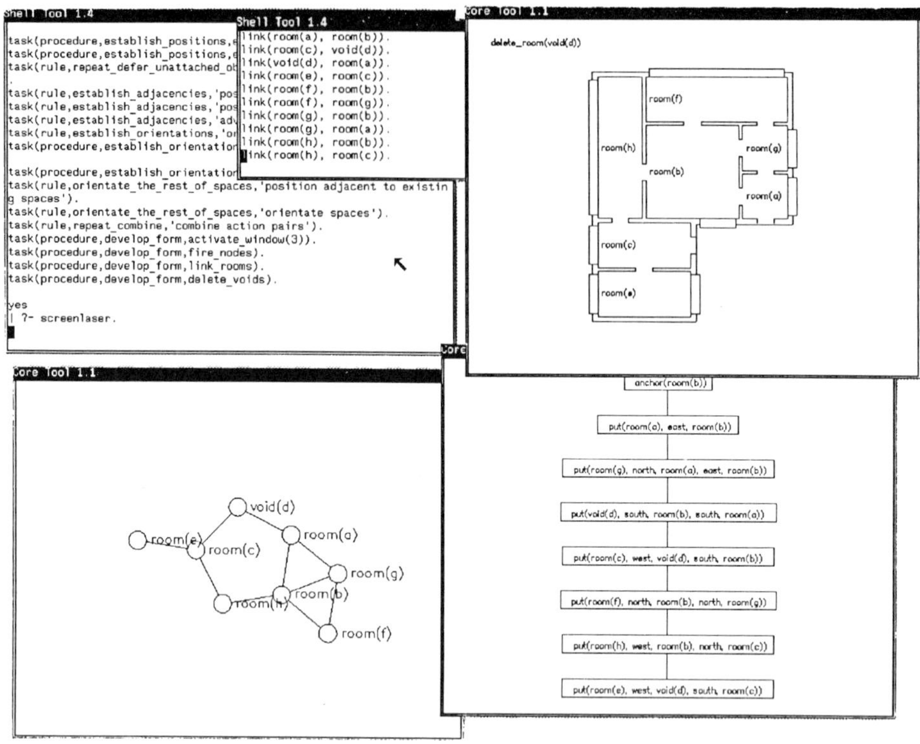

Figure 9.11. Output resulting from a context other than that in Figure 9.10. An extra space, *room*(*h*), has been added.

grammars described, though more complex grammars may be required to demonstrate conclusively the utility of this view. A detailed explanation of a spatial design system utilizing this approach is given in the following chapter.

In this model design processes require grammars which operate upon other grammars not only by the selection of rules but in the creation and modification of rules. Further investigation is required into the dynamics of the design process in order to effectively model the exploratory nature of design.

Chapter 10

A Design System

The intention of this chapter is to demonstration how a hierarchy of control abstractions can be exploited in a prototypical design system implemented in Prolog. A detailed implementation is required in order to bring certain issues to light.

An approach to the organization of knowledge within a design system was demonstrated in the previous chapter. In this chapter the knowledge itself is discussed in detail. Spatial layout is considered as a subtask representative of design tasks in general. A grammar, in the form of production rules for generating plans, is presented along with the knowledge by which the rules can be controlled. There are two parts to this chapter: the implementation of a spatial layout system in Prolog is explained and demonstrated; the second part is a discussion of the implementation and its extensions, and incorporates a critical review of what has been achieved.

Spatial Layout as an Example of a Design Task

Spatial layout is representative of design tasks in general. It is concerned with the satisfactory arrangement of objects in space in order to meet a set of objectives. It is typical of design tasks that these objectives may be either rigidly or informally defined. Generally, they concern the production of various modifications to the environment such that a composition of objects functions as a useful system in some way. In architectural design the objects may be walls or other space-defining elements, or they may be the spaces themselves (such as rooms or groups of rooms). Spatial layout may also involve the determination of dimensions to objects and to the spaces between them.

The objectives may be to satisfy certain adjacency and dimensional constraints such that the configuration operates as a functional system. Of course, spatial layout includes the organization of objects and spaces to meet objectives that are difficult to make explicit, such as certain stylistic and formal properties. The shape grammar approach is an attempt to incorporate such considerations into generative systems. These grammars are comprised of sets of operators for manipulating forms, and incorporate such 'elusive' considerations as style. The grammar for spatial layout introduced in Chapter 6 and demonstrated in the previous chapter is more prosaic than a shape grammar. However, the same principles by which knowledge can be organized are thought to apply equally to the 'poetic' as well as the prosaic.

The spatial layout problem, taken as an exercise in producing layouts to satisfy certain relational constraints, is for design what the blocks world is for sequential planning. It can serve as a medium for exploring models and methods of design. The layout problem can be formulated in such a way that it exhibits the various ill-structured characteristics of the most difficult design task. It also has the property that methods for investigating arrangements involving small numbers of spaces, when applied to larger numbers of spaces are often encumbered by combinatorial problems. For example, there are estimated to be over 400,000 different ways in which a rectangle can be divided into ten component rectangles in a dimensionless configuration (Steadman, 1983) and there are 10! ways of assigning names to each of those rectangles. To employ a naïve search and backtracking algorithm to find a spatial configuration which meets certain requirements for numbers of rooms greater than 10 is practically infeasible. The formulation comes under the category of problems which are said to be NP-complete (Garey and Johnson, 1979; Sedgewick, 1983). The spatial problem is therefore representative of combinatorially difficult design tasks.

Many artifacts (for example, of the kind that architects deal with) manifest themselves as spatial configurations of some sort. It could therefore be regarded as one of the most interesting and relevant architectural and engineering design subtasks.

Spatial layout can be modelled by means of production systems. States consist of configurations or partial configurations of objects or spaces. The rules which transform states are generally of the type described in Chapter 5: 'poorly-behaved' rule sets. The order in which objects are considered, and the order in which rules are implemented has a strong bearing on the outcome; indeed, it has a bearing on whether or not a configuration can be generated which meets the objectives. A spatial layout system is therefore representative of design languages in general.

A substantial amount of research has been undertaken into the automated production of spatial layouts in various disciplines, including VLSI (very large scale integration of electronic microcircuits) (Brown et al, 1983; Dincbas, 1980; Uehara and Kawato, 1983), land use planning (Trainor et al, 1982) and building design (Eastman, 1973).

Approaches to Spatial Layout in Building Design

In building layout there have been two main approaches to automated spatial layout: one is the *quadratic assignment* formulation; and the other is concerned primarily with adjacency graphs.

In the quadratic assignment formulation a set of indivisible facilities (for example, rooms) are to be assigned to a set of candidate locations in such a way that a certain objective, such as the sum of the cost of travel between all rooms, is minimized. This involves assigning costs to movements between spaces so that different configurations of rooms can be compared. The quadratic assignment problem was originally formulated by Koopmans and Beckman (1957), and there are various approaches developed within operations research theory which attempt to solve this problem. Some of the strategies appropriate to building design are summarized by Mitchell (1977) and also by Broadbent (1981). Typically, such a formulation requires a table indicating the importance of communications between facilities, and there also needs to be a schema of spatial organization, such as a modular grid or a corridor system. There is no known procedure, apart from exhaustive enumeration, for guaranteeing that a solution is optimal, but methods have been developed for producing 'good' solutions (Liggett, 1980; Liggett and Mitchell, 1981; Sharpe and Marksjö, 1985).

The adjacency graph formulation is regarded by Mitchell (1977) as a more natural and appropriate formulation for architectural design. The popularity of this approach is largely attributable to the influence of *The Geometry of Environment* (March and Steadman , 1983) which has become a standard reference for the study of architectural geometry, and the observation that adjacency networks bear some similarity with the way designers think about spatial arrangements. The adjacency graph formulation is also adopted here (Figure 10.1).

The spatial layout task in architecture is frequently expressed in terms of adjacency or connectivity requirements. A spatial layout can be seen as a type of network diagram (or graph) with wall junctions as nodes and wall segments as arcs. The objective is to produce a spatial configuration, the dual graph of which is a subgraph of the adjacency requirements graph. (Dual graphs are discussed by March and Steadman [1971].) As there are generally many possible configurations the problem is not a trivial one, particularly when

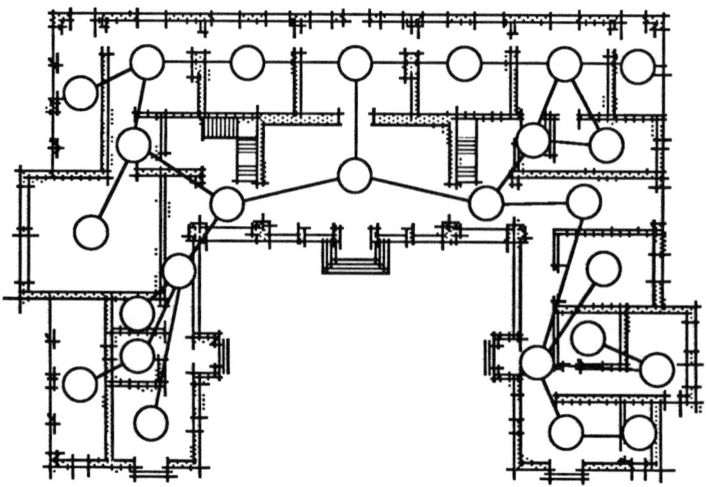

Figure 10.1. Network theory has direct relevance to the analysis of building forms. It also has a bearing on the production of design descriptions. This diagram shows one step in the analysis of the 'morphology' of Aston Hall, Warwickshire.

dimensioning is taken into account. The example in Figure 10.2 shows that it is possible for two layouts to satisfy similar connectivity graphs and yet display different relative room positions and room sizes.

Various approaches for transforming adjacency graphs into spatial layouts are summarized by Steadman (1983). A computer system has been developed by Flemming (1978, 1985) for generating spatial arrangements from adjacency graphs and dimensional constraints. (It is also summarized by Steadman [1971].) The program adds rooms to the spatial configuration one at a time so that: no required adjacency that is satisfied by an earlier addition is disrupted by the addition of a new room; and all adjacencies required between the new room and those already placed are satisfied. The procedure is to search through a tree of alternative sequences until a solution meeting the

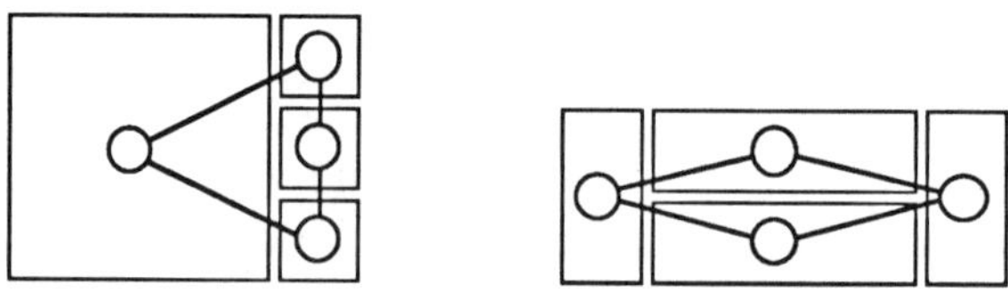

Figue 10.2. Two spatial layouts with similar connectivity (adjacency) graphs.

stated adjacency constraints is produced. Linear programming is then employed to dimension the spaces. This approach of adding rooms incrementally provides the genesis of the system described below, although the rules for the addition of spaces are simpler than those formulated by Flemming, advantage is made of abstraction levels, and the approach is knowledge-based rather than algorithm-based.

Other knowledge-based approaches to spatial layout not considered here include the use of frames (Willey and Toller, 1981; Toller and Willey, 1983). The approach adopted here is based on production systems.

Knowledge About Actions

The operations by which rooms are added to a plan are design actions, and the sequence of such actions is a plan. As discussed in Chapter 8 a major activity in devising plans of actions is the resolution of conflict. In the realm of spatial layout designers seem to adopt strategies: to actively avoid situations where conflicts occur; or to detect conflicts at an early stage when they are relatively easy to rectify. One strategy is to proceed from highly abstract levels of operations to less abstract levels. The use of hierarchical abstraction levels discussed in Chapters 7 and 8 is one formal strategy. Another is to consider that designers frequently regard spatial layouts at two levels of abstraction at least. One is the level of dimensionless 'bubble' diagrams: more formally as nodes on an adjacency network. Plans are then considered as geometrical entities which are only loosely formed. A final level of abstraction may be where dimensional constraints are taken into account.

This approach is evident in the rules devised for spatial layout here. A plan is devised for the reconstruction of the adjacency network (which is an abstraction of the spatial layout) before a plan is developed for the construction of a *geometrical* layout. By anticipating, and therefore avoiding, conflicts at this level of abstraction there is less to cause problems at the geometrical level. For example, it is a fact that certain adjacency constraints are not able to be realized by a planar configuration of rectangular rooms. A simple principle is that no more than three rectangular rooms can each share a common wall segment with one another. This is a situation that can be detected and avoided at the level of the adjacency network.

The rules of the grammar are therefore devised to detect patterns within the context and within partially developed plans, and to transform plans from highly abstract sequences into more specific sequences of actions. Partial plans therefore proceed from actions which state that rooms are to be *put* in place to actions about adjacencies, then to placements in terms of orientation. The final task of assigning dimensions to spaces is not considered here.

The general strategy is therefore to make use of several systems of decomposition. The task of devising a spatial layout can be reduced to a series of subtasks which can be treated independently, each providing information for the next task. The problem can therefore be formulated as a type of 'well-behaved' production system in which it is a relatively simple matter to choose between rules applicable at any given state. The control of such a system is trivial. This is, of course, an idealized approach. There can be flaws in the rules, the constraints can be ill-conceived and may require adjustment, there may be other criteria for evaluating end states which only come to light during the process of design. For the purposes here it is sufficient to observe that there need to be overriding control structures to handle such eventualities. Control will be discussed in a later section of this chapter.

Knowledge Base

Rules for transforming states in a network of actions for spatial layout were introduced in Chapter 9. Here they are described in greater detail. The rule set can be considered as the minimum set required to demonstrate the principles discussed here, and to ensure that a plan is produced for most planar adjacency graphs. Each rule is discussed under numbered section headings.

1 Expand Composition

This rule relies on explicit semantic-syntactic mappings to reduce a task to its component subtasks. The subtasks may be known, or the subcomponents of the artifact may be such that they suggest a task division. It may be known, for example, that the design of a hospital can be accomplished by concentrating on the components of which it is composed, namely the various departments. These can be treated as subtasks. In the simple building example given here, the building called *x* is composed of the components (in this case rooms) *a*, *b*, *c*, *d*, *e*, *f*, *g*, and *h*. So the subtasks are the placement of each of these objects.

The Prolog fact which makes this mapping explicit is contained within the context:

composition(*object*(*x*), [*a*, *b*, *c*, *d*, *e*, *f*, *g*, *h*]).

The initial task of designing object *x* is therefore transformed into the following sequence of actions:

put(*a*) and *put*(*b*) and *put*(*c*) and *put*(*d*) and *put*(*e*) and
put(*f*) and *put*(*g*) and put(*h*)

This representation of actions is a simplification of the procedural network of the previous chapter. These actions are to occur in conjunction and there is no commitment to order as yet. *Put* is an action which states simply that an object is to be located, though it is not known where or in what relationship to other objects.

2 Order According to Valency

This rule orders a sequence of actions such that those spaces which have the most interconnections with other spaces are placed first. This is a simple heuristic. Later rules require that spaces are placed adjacent to spaces already in place. The most likely way of ensuring that these later rules can operate without conflicts occurring appears to be by locating the spaces with the most connections first. The argument is that these are the most problematic spaces and should be dealt with first.

This heuristic favours adjacency networks that tend to have a nucleus, that is, there is a single core of rooms which are heavily interrelated. Circulation spaces generally ensure that this is the case in building layouts, but it is by no means a certainty. Subsequent plans are not dependent on the resultant ordering but this rule enhances the efficiency with which a suitable plan is generated.

Where several spaces have the same valency then the actions which place them are ordered arbitrarily. The plan for the adjacency network in Figure 10.3 which results after the application of this rule is illustrated below as an ordered list of actions. Valencies (number of interconnections with other rooms) are also shown.

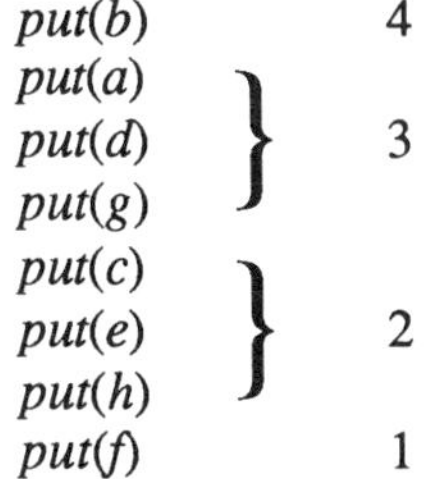

The plan is now that the rooms are to be placed in the order given.

3 Anchor the First Object

This rule assumes that the most connected space is also the one whose geographical location is the most influential. Other spaces can be configured

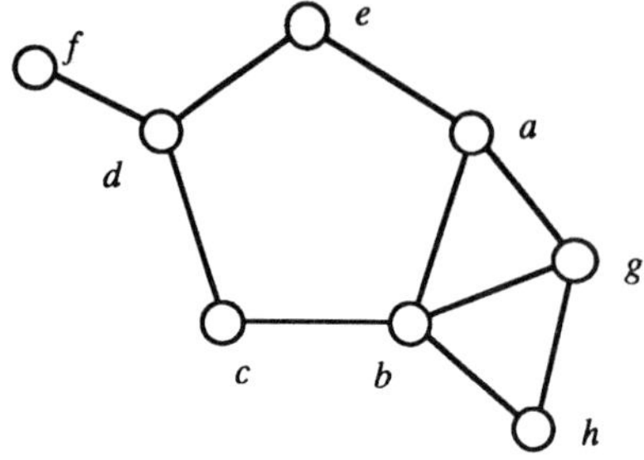

Figure 10.3. An adjacency requirements graph.

around this one. The plan resulting from this change is as follows:

anchor(b)
put(a)
put(d)
put(g)
put(c)
put(e)
put(h)
put(f)

As there is no site context being considered here the first action means simply that the first object is to be 'drawn' and subsequent objects placed in relation to it.

4 Defer Placement of Unattached Objects

This rule ensures that a room can only be placed if there is an object to which it is to be linked already in place according to an earlier action in the plan. If the ordering of placements suggests that an object is 'unattachable' then its placement is deferred to the end of the sequence. This can be illustrated with the above example. The space *d* is unattached. If its placement is deferred until last then it is guaranteed that it will be able to be placed adjacent to at least one other space with which it is to be connected. This may violate the placement of other spaces, such as that of room *f*, in which case the action which places it must also be deferred. By cycling through this rule an appropriate sequence of actions is produced which ensures that rooms are positioned only when there is a space to which they are to be linked already in place.

A more sophisticated rule could be one that defers the placement of objects to immediately after objects with which they are to connect, rather than at the end of the sequence. This approach is analogous to the system of reordering subgoals, as described in Chapter 7. However, instead of problematic actions in the plan being moved to an earlier place, they are moved to a later position.

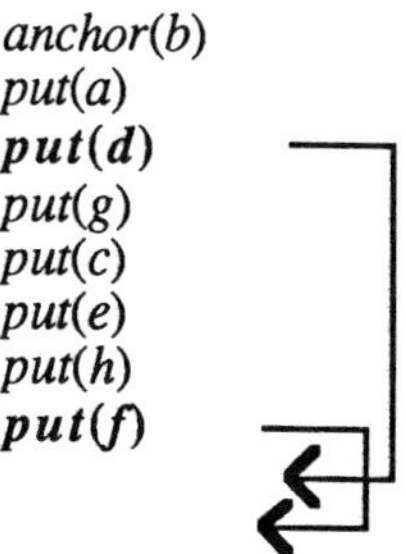

The action which locates *d* is moved to the end of the plan (indicated with arrows). This results in *f* being unattached, so its action is moved to a position after *put(d)* to produce the following plan:

anchor(b)
put(a)
put(g)
put(c)
put(e)
put(h)
put(d)
put(f)

5 Position Adjacent Objects

The task is now to transform the actions in the above sequence such that rooms are placed adjacent to rooms located by an action earlier in the sequence. The repeated application of this rule produces the plan:

anchor(b)			(i)
put(a, next_to, b)			(ii)
put(g, next_to, a)	and	*put(g, next_to, b)*	(iii)
put(c, next_to, b)			(iv)
put(e, next_to, a)			(v)
put(h, next_to, b)	and	*put(h, next_to, g)*	(vi)
put(d, next_to, c)	and	*put(d, next_to, e)*	(vii)
put(f, next_to, d)			(viii)

The plan inevitably contains conjunctions of actions as an object can sometimes be placed adjacent to more than one other object. The actions have here been labelled with Roman numerals, and it can be seen that this action sequence serves to partially reconstruct the network of Figure 10.3. This reconstruction is illustrated in Figure 10.4. The black nodes are those positioned by the current action.

6 Advance Connection

This is the most complicated of the rules. In Figure 10.4 it can be observed that the actions only partially ensure the reconstruction of the network of Figure 10.3. Where an object is to be placed next to two other objects the set of triangular relationships thus formed dictates that there is only a finite number of candidate positions for the new object. (Assuming that the network is to grow outwards, it is usually just one). In the case of *c* being placed next to *b*, and *e* placed next to *a*, there is no such certainty. As *d* must later be placed adjacent to both *c* and *e* this poses a problem, at least in drawing the network by following the steps of Figure 10.4. It is expedient to adopt one of two strategies:

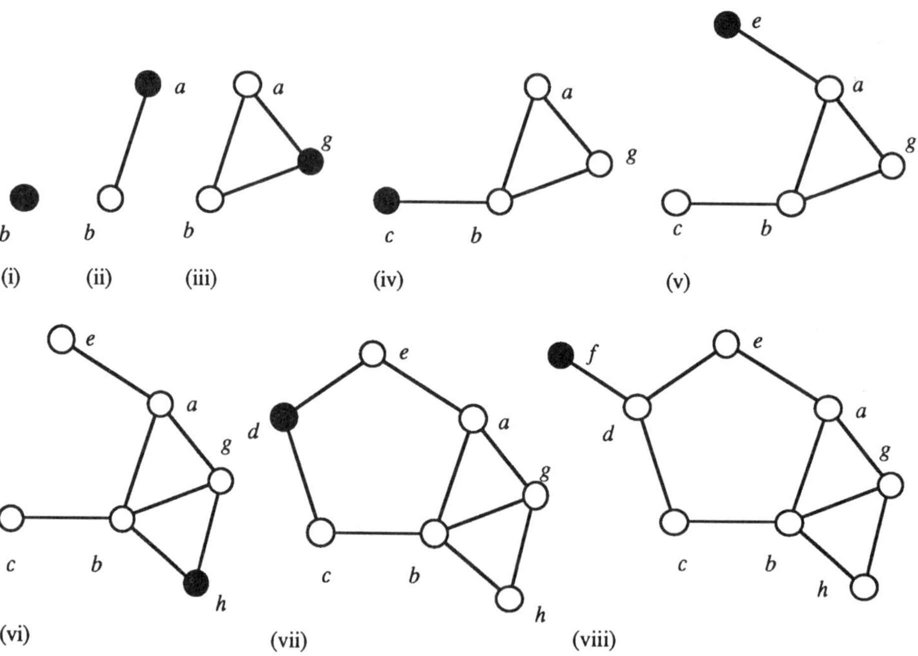

Figure 10.4. Reconstruction of the network of Figure 10.3 according to the plan of rule 5.

(1) if there are actions which suggest that an object (*X*) is to be placed adjacent to two objects, then ensure that these two objects are also placed next to one another, prior to the actions which place *X*
(2) if this is not possible, and the two objects are both adjacent to a third object (*Y*) then ensure that the two objects are placed either side of *Y*

The following state of the action sequence results from applying the first strategy:

anchor(b)			
put(a, next_to, b)			
put(g, next_to, a)	and	*put(g, next_to, b)*	
put(c, next_to, b)			
put(e, next_to, a)	and	***put(e, next_to, c)***	←
put(h, next_to, b)	and	*put(h, next_to, g)*	
*put(d, next_to, **c**)*	and	*put(d, next_to, **e**)*	┘
put(f, next_to, d)			

The arrow indicates the actions which have determined the placement of the new action (in bold type). This modification to the plan requires a further modification as shown below. As *e* must now be adjacent to both *a* and *c* these two objects should be positioned such that they are also adjacent to one another.

anchor(b)				(i)
put(a, next_to, b)				(ii)
put(g, next_to, a)	and	*put(g, next_to, b)*		(iii)
put(c, next_to, b)	and	***put(c, next_to, a)***	←	(iv)
*put(e, next_to, **a**)*	and	*put(e, next_to, **c**)*	┘	(v)
put(h, next_to, b)	and	*put(h, next_to, g)*		(vi)
put(d, next_to, c)	and	*put(d, next_to, e)*		(vii)
put(f, next_to, d)				(viii)

This action sequence now ensures that the network can be reconstructed. The new connections are shown with half-tone lines in Figure 10.5 (i to vii).

There are some cases where: it is not possible to 'advance connections' in this way without violating some adjacency already established; or, if the plan were modified according to strategy (1) above, conflicts would inevitably occur later on in the plan development and execution. Such a problem is illustrated with reference to the adjacency network depicted in Figure 10.6. This network can be reconstructed with the following sequence of actions:

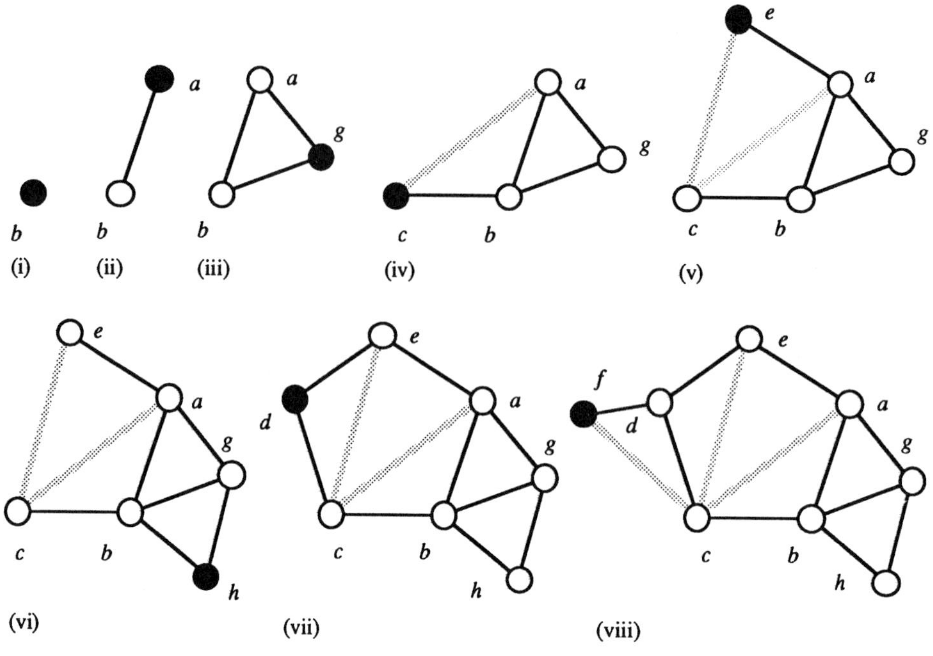

Figure 10.5. Reconstruction of the network in Figure 10.3. The lines in half-tone indicate connections brought about by rule 6 (advance connections).

anchor(b)
put(a, next_to, b)
put(c, next_to, b) and *put(c, next_to a)*
put(e, next_to, b) and *put(e, next_to, a)*
put(d, next_to, c) and *put(d, next_to, e)*

To advance the connection of *e* so that it is adjacent to *c* would result in the following sequence:

anchor(b) (i)
put(a, next_to, b) (ii)
put(c, next_to, b) and *put(c, next_to a)* (iii)
put(e, next_to, b) and *put(e, next_to, a)* and ***put(e, next_to, c)*** ⇐ (iv)
put(d, next_to, ***c****)* and *put(d, next_to,* ***e****)* (v)

When this sequence of actions is employed to reconstruct the network of Figure 10.6 it results in a particular configuration of adjacencies which happens to be impossible in a rectangular dissection: four non-overlapping rectangles cannot be adjacent to one another on a single plane (where adjacency is defined as a configuration where wall segments are shared). The

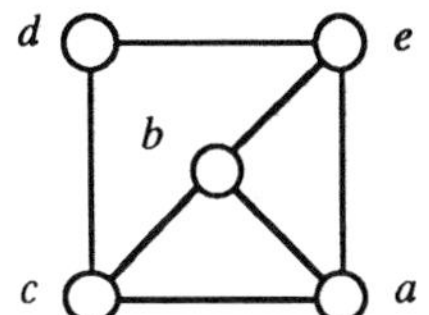

Figure 10.6. An adjacency network for which it is impossible to produce a rectangular dissection with *c* and *e* adjacent to each other.

four cases of adjacency relationships which must be tested for are illustrated in Figure 10.7. It is *impossible* to achieve a rectangular dissection in each of these cases if the black nodes are connected with a single arc. The last graph shown is a generalization of the third. So, there are actually three cases. In case (iv) there exist two nodes from which it is possible to trace independent paths to the two black nodes and a third node to which they are both connected. The paths can each pass through any number of nodes provided the paths do not pass through any of the *same* nodes.

One of the conditions of the first strategy (1) above is therefore that 'advancing' the connection does not create an impossible network configuration.

In the event that the first strategy cannot be applied, the second may be appropriate. In the above example, for *d* to be adjacent to both *c* and *e* it is not necessary that *c* and *e* be adjacent to one another. Provided both rooms have a free edge on the same side of the spatial configuration then *d* can be adjacent to both of them. If *e* and *c* are configured as in Figure 10.8 then *d* can be connected to *e* and *c* as shown in Figure 10.9. For this type of configuration to be possible it is necessary for *e* is to be placed next to *b* but on the *opposite* side to *c*. This action is incorporated into the plan, resulting in the modification shown below.

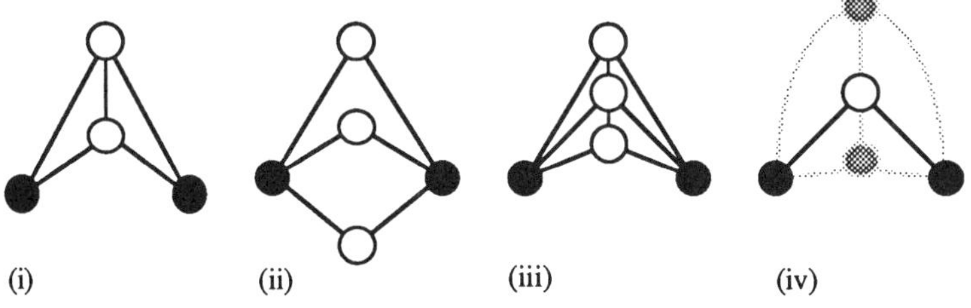

Figure 10.7. Four adjacency networks in which it is impossible for two nodes, indicated black, to be adjacent to one another in a rectangular dissection.

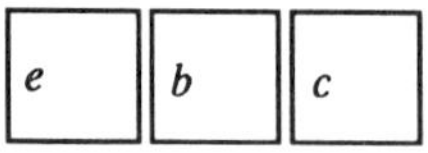

Figure 10.8. A configuration of three spaces such that *c* and *e* can both be adjacent to a fourth space.

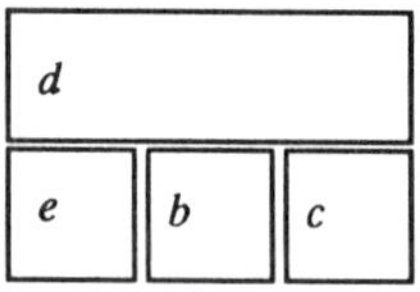

Figure 10.9. A configuration in which *d* is adjacent to both c and e

anchor(*b*) (i)
put(*a*, *next_to*, *b*) (ii)
put(*c*, *next_to*, *b*) and *put*(*c*, *next_to a*) (iii)
***put*(*e*, *next_to*, *b*, *opposite*, *c*)** and *put*(*e*, *next_to*, *a*) (iv)
put(*d*, *next_to*, ***c***) and *put*(*d*, *next_to*, ***e***) (v)

The reconstruction of the network according to these actions is illustrated in Figure 10.10, where the *opposite* link is indicated with a semicircular arc.

7 Arbitrarily Position Adjacent Objects

In the example relating to the adjacency network of Figure 10.3, the above rule produced a sequence of actions where all but the first, second and last room *f* are located adjacent to those rooms already in place and with which they are to be linked. In order to 'fix' the position of *f* this rule introduces an action that ensures that it is positioned adjacent to two rooms. The action states that it is to be adjacent to room *d*. Any room adjacent to this neighbour will suffice (such as *c*). The room *f* is therefore placed next to its neighbour's *neighbour*. This convention favours close packing of rooms. It is otherwise an arbitrary expedient. The resultant plan is therefore as follows:

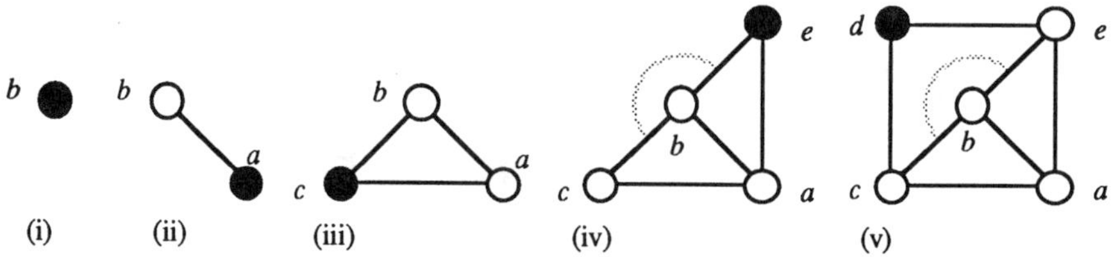

Figure 10.10. Reconstruction of the network of Figure 10.6 according to the plan developed by rule 6 (advance connection).

anchor(b)			(i)
put(a, next_to, b)			(ii)
put(g, next_to, a)	*and*	*put(g, next_to, b)*	(iii)
put(c, next_to, b)	*and*	*put(c, next_to, a)*	(iv)
put(e, next_to, a)	*and*	*put(e, next_to, c)*	(v)
put(h, next_to, b)	*and*	*put(h, next_to, g)*	(vi)
put(**d**, next_to, **c**)	*and*	*put(d, next_to, e)*	(vii)
put(f, next_to, d)	***and***	***put(f, next_to, c)***	(viii)

The full execution of this partial plan is illustrated in Figure 10.5.

8 Orientate First Two Objects

Once a plan is formulated such that an adjacency network can be constructed, further rules are required to replace the *next_to* relation with a more specific action concerning ordinal directions. The first decision to be made in this regard is the relationship between the first two rooms. This can be an arbitrary choice when it is considered that the entire configuration could later be rotated or reflected:

anchor(b)
put(a, east, b)
...

9 Orientate Objects

There are six ways in which a space can be located adjacent to two other spaces which are already adjacent to one another. From the above example *g* is to be located adjacent to *a* and *b*. The ways that this can be realized geometrically are illustrated in Figure 10.11. The second three possibilities are simply mirror images of the first three. In each case one of the rectangles is, of necessity, larger than the other two. Information about the relative sizes of rooms is required in order to determine which configuration to adopt. This rule interprets a fact in the context such as:

size_order([*d, a, b, c*])

This fact contains a list of rooms in order of size, starting from the largest to the smallest. Because the resultant spatial configuration is dimensionless it is only necessary to provide a configuration of rooms which can *accommodate* these relative sizes when dimensioned. Where relative sizes are not specified then the orientations selected are arbitrary. Conflicts can occur, however. The repeated application of this rule results in the following plan:

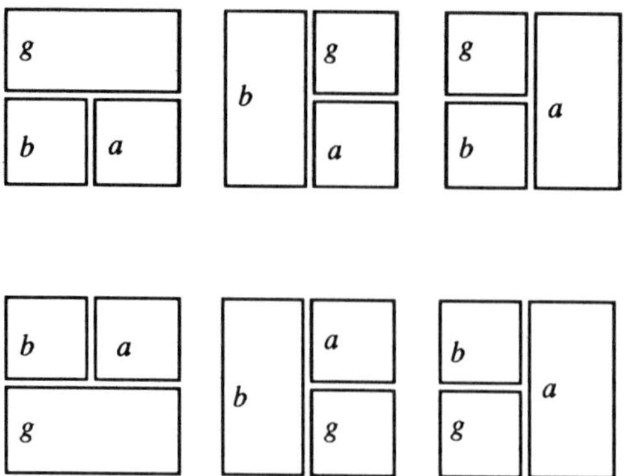

Figure 10.11. Six ways in which *g* can be located adjacent to both *a* and *b*.

anchor(b)		
put(a, east, b)		
put(g, west, a)	and	*put(g, north, b)*
put(c, south, b)	and	*put(c, west, a)*
put(e, west, a)	and	*put(e, south, c)*
put(h, north, b)	and	*put(h, west, g)*
put(d, west, c)	***and***	***put(d, west, e)***
put(f, next_to, d)	and	*put(f, next_to, c)*

If the size order is [*d, a, b, c*], then the actions highlighted in the above sequence, *put(d, west, c)* and *put(d, west, e)*, would cause a conflict with the actions immediately below them in the plan. As shown in Figure 10.12, if *d* is located to the west of both *c* and *e* it will effectively prevent a position being available for anything else to be placed next to *c* (such as *f*), as required by the last action in the plan. This rule therefore requires the condition that a clear side is maintained on any room that is to have a room placed against it by an action later in the plan. Where there is an alternative orientation to that which caused the obstruction this will therefore be selected. An alternative spatial configuration is shown in Figure 10.13. The plan resulting from the repeated application of this rules is therefore:

anchor(b)		
put(a, east, b)		
put(g, west, a)	*and*	*put(g, north, b)*
put(c, south, b)	*and*	*put(c, west, a)*
put(e, west, a)	*and*	*put(e, south, c)*
put(h, north, b)	*and*	*put(h, west, g)*
put(d, south, c)	***and***	***put(d, west, e)***
put(f, north, d)	***and***	***put(f, west, c)***

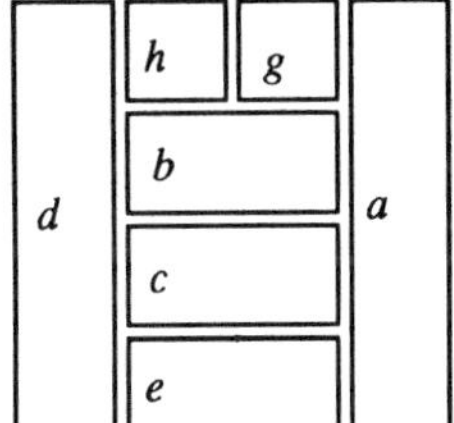

Figure 10.12. Space *c* is 'locked in' by *d*.

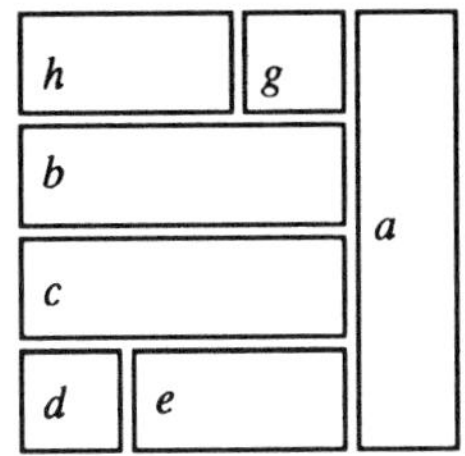

Figure 10.13. An alternative configuration of *c* and *d*.

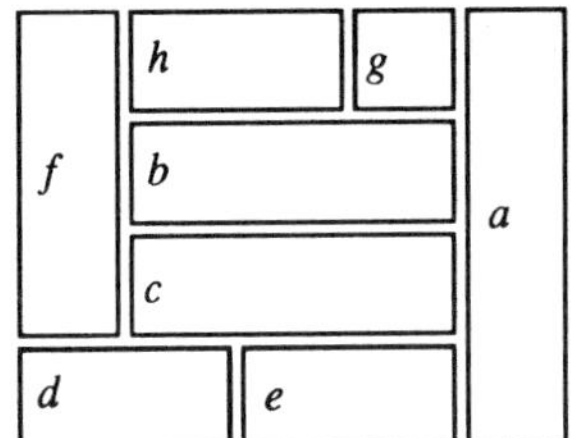

Figure 10.14. Space *f* can now be adjacent to *c*.

10 Orientate Opposites

This rule takes actions which involve placing rooms *opposite* another room and converts them into actions which *orientate* the objects relative to one another. In the example relating to Figure 10.6, therefore, the action: *put(e, next_to, b, opposite, c)*, will be replaced by *put(e, Dir, b)*, where *Dir* is the same direction that *b* is of *c*.

11 Combine Action Pairs

This rule simply takes the conjunctions of actions and combines them into a single action of the general form:
put(A, Dir1, B, Dir2, C)
where *A* is to be placed in the orientation *Dir1* of *B* and *Dir2* of *C*. These actions are of the type that can be interpreted by a system which implements primitive design actions. The resultant plan is therefore:

anchor(b)
put(a, east, b)
put(g, west, a, north, b)
put(c, south, b, west, a)
put(e, west, a, south, c)
put(h, north, b, west, g)
put(d, south, c, west, e)
put(f, north, d, west, c)

This plan, when executed, produces the spatial configuration illustrated in Figure 10.14.

Control

The system of planning rules defined above is controlled by planning knowledge as defined in Chapter 9. The operation of a control mechanism is addressed in detail here.

There are four types of control structure that might be considered for a knowledge base composed of rules such as those described above: to implement the rules in a given order; to allow rules to be implemented opportunistically; to partition the rules in some way; and to combine aspects of each approach. Each of these will be considered in turn.

Ordering Rules

The above knowledge base is so formulated that the layout problem has been partitioned into relatively independent subproblems. The rules can be regarded as ordered subsystems each of which takes as input the output of the preceding system. The ordering of the rules given above appears to provide an appropriate sequence of actions for this to occur in many cases.

A disadvantage of a rule order that is given *a priori* is that when new knowledge is provided (in the form of further rules) the correct relationship to existing rules must be taken into account. The *ordering* of rules therefore constitutes a body of domain dependent knowledge which is itself *not* rule-based. There is also the possibility that the rule order is incorrect, in which case a suitable plan will fail to be generated. This is, however, the most efficient approach from the point of view of implementation as there are no computational overheads associated with rule selection.

Opportunistic Control

The second approach is to allow free rein to the rules such that they fire whenever the opportunity arises. Each rule is therefore a *potential* candidate for implementation at any time. Where several rules are competing to be fired then there needs to be some mechanism for selecting between them. The number of rules applicable at any state can be minimized by ensuring that the antecedents of each rule include preconditions that only permit their implementation if certain other rules have already been fired.

One of the preconditions of the rules 8 to 11, could be that they are only applicable if the action sequence contains *conjunctions* of actions with the *next_to* argument. So these rules are only considered as possible candidates once all the other rules have established the desired adjacencies.

In spite of this provision several rules may still be applicable at certain states. If the rules set is imperfectly 'well-behaved', then the selection of the right rule might mean the difference between achieving and not achieving an end state. Or the selection of the appropriate rule might affect the *efficiency* with which the end state is reached. The third possibility is that which ever rule is selected makes no difference at all, in which case the selection can be arbitrary.

For the above knowledge base it so happens that the rules *advance connection* and *arbitrarily position adjacent objects* are often applicable at the same time. Where this occurs the former should take precedence over the latter, as it is undesirable that arbitrary actions should occur in the place of more certain reasoning. There does *not* appear to be a condition that can be coded into either of these rules that will ensure that an attempt is made to implement all applicable non-arbitrary rules before the arbitrary rules are attempted. Certain control heuristics can be adopted, however.

One approach to rule selection is to provide a control mechanism which *triggers* each competing rule and evaluates the effects of that rule in some way before committing the system to a decision. There are several domain-independent heuristics that are appropriate for selecting between competing rules:

select the rule which produces the least number of actions
select the rule which produces the greatest number of actions
select the most recently fired rule
select the least recently fired rule
select the rule affecting the most recently changed action
select the rule affecting the least recently changed action
select the rule affecting the earliest action in the sequence
select the least arbitrary rule

These heuristics can be formulated as production rules (called *scheduling rules*) which detect patterns in the state of the problem and recommend simple strategies for dealing with them. The last type of scheduling heuristic provides an obvious solution to the problem as described above:

if a rule contains the string *arbitrary* (or a variant of that word) in its name
then consider that rule last.

The first scheduling heuristic in the above list can also be employed. In their implementation it so happens that the planning rule: *arbitrarily position adjacent objects* deletes and creates more facts than the rule: *advance connection*. This subtle difference between the rules is not immediately apparent from their descriptions given above, but it can be exploited in this context. The controller can operate in such a way that, given a choice between rules, the one that produces the smallest state should always be selected.

Partitioning Rule Sets

A further control issue concerns the computational cost of testing the applicability of all rules for each state when it is known that only *some* of the rules are candidates. The third control strategy is therefore to organize the rules into groups such that those which are likely to compete are placed together. The grouping can take the form of a schedule as discussed in Chapter 5. Such a schedule obviates the need to test the preconditions of all rules for each state. This *a priori* grouping ensures that only rules likely to compete, and appropriate to that stage in the development of the plan, are tested. Efficiency is improved, but with the added cost that knowledge about the organization of the rules must be stated explicitly.

By way of summary, the three types of arrangement of the rules into schedules is given in Figure 10.15. The black nodes depict planning rules. The

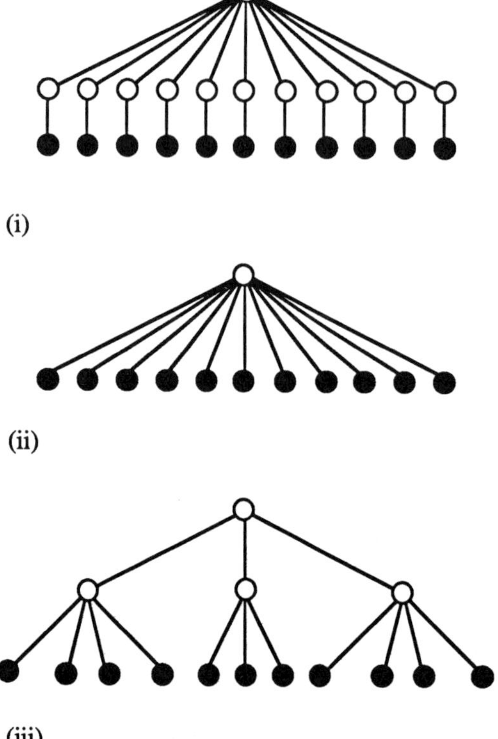

Figure 10.15. Schematic representation of three types of schedule.

white nodes indicate groupings. In schedule type (i) each rule is implemented as many times as it is applicable, in the order given in the schedule leading from left to right. This is the most efficient scheduling device, but it requires that the correct rule order is known *a priori*. In schedule type (ii) any rule can be tested at any time. In this case the ordering of rules in the schedule does not affect the outcome. There must be a control device for selecting between competing rules. In type (iii) there are three groupings of rules. When the system can no longer implement rules from the first group it proceeds to the second—and then the third—group of rules. Only rules that are grouped together compete to be implemented.

A suitable organization of the rules for the spatial layout system based on the third type of schedule (iii) is given in Figure 10.16. The task of generating a plan is therefore divided into subtasks, which can each be subdivided in turn in the manner outlined in Chapter 9. The actions at the branch ends represent

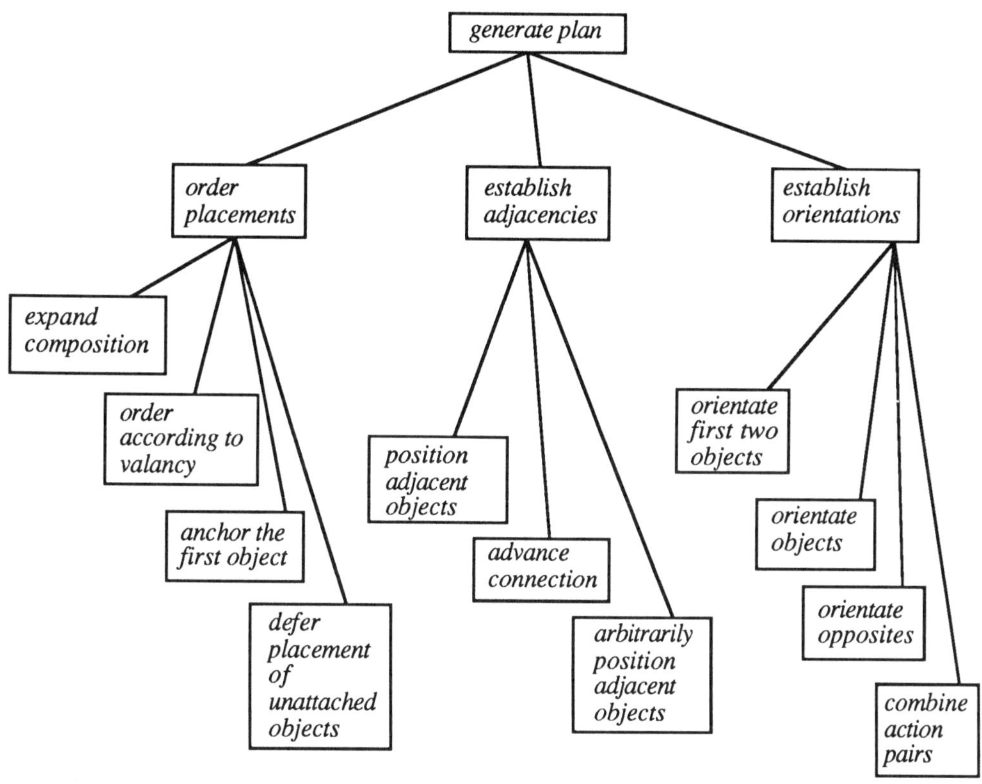

Figure 10.16. The organization of the rules 1 to 11 into a hierarchical schedule. Planning rules are grouped so that no more than three or four rules are tested at any state.

groups of candidate actions. The schedule is followed procedurally in a top-down, left-to-right fashion until a group of candidate actions is encountered. Each rule is tested for its applicability. Where more than one rule is applicable then a selection is made on the basis of heuristics such as those outlined above.

Generation of Alternatives and the Resolution of Plan Failure

In an ideal system alternative plans should be embodied within the final plan as demonstrated in Chapter 8. Plans should contain not only conjunctions of actions but also disjunctions representing alternative courses of actions as illustrated in Figure 8.40. Unfortunately two factors militate against the overt representation of alternative courses of action within plans. One factor is that plans rapidly become very large—the combinatorially explosive nature of the search space becomes overt in the plan. The second factor is that the planning domain is non-deterministic. The application of each planning rule is not a certain one, and decisions (the application of rules) may have to be revoked. The system described above can only cautiously be assumed to exhibit the characteristics of a 'well behaved' system as described in Chapter 5.

The knowledge by which alternative plans are generated can be made explicit by the incorporation of meta-rules which exercise control at some level above the system as described so far—in the form of scheduling rules, or at some level above that. Pending the incorporation of this type of knowledge a default control mechanism can be employed: namely backtracking.

The issue here is with both the generation of alternatives and the appropriate strategies to follow in the event that the system proves unable to generate a suitable end state. There are two control issues to be considered. First, even though the resultant plan may produce layouts which conform to the context, there may be other solutions which conform equally well. It is desirable that these solutions are also able to be generated. Second, as the properties of the above system are not fully known, it is conceivable that plans or partial plans are generated which cannot be executed. Some of the above rules involve arbitrary choices from among various options—for example, the selection of orientations by the rule: *orientate spaces*. In the event of plan failure it may be necessary to investigate these other options.

The control strategy of *backtracking* achieves both of these tasks: generating alternatives; and handling failure. One way in which knowledge about backtracking can be implemented effectively is by the provision of a meta-rule which states that it is possible to revert to earlier states by undoing the last rule implemented. *Undoing* is accomplished by identifying the last rule applied and re-applying it in reverse: that is, matching the *consequents* of the rule and substituting its *antecedents* into the facts base. Records must be kept of which rules have been fired. Records are also required serving as pointers to various options already attempted, so that backtracking and the

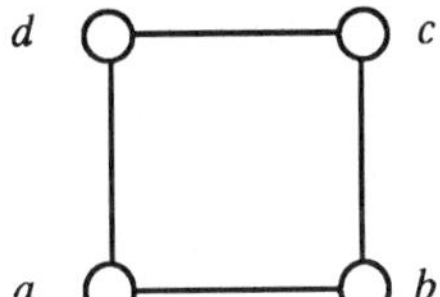

Figure 10.17. An adjacency requirements graph.

subsequent re-application of rules results in the generation of *new* plan states. Examples of some alternative plans generated by means of backtracking for the context of Figure 10.17, where size order is not specified, are illustrated in Figure 10.18.

A further method of generating alternatives is by altering the context in some way. If certain decisions are dependent on the ordering of information

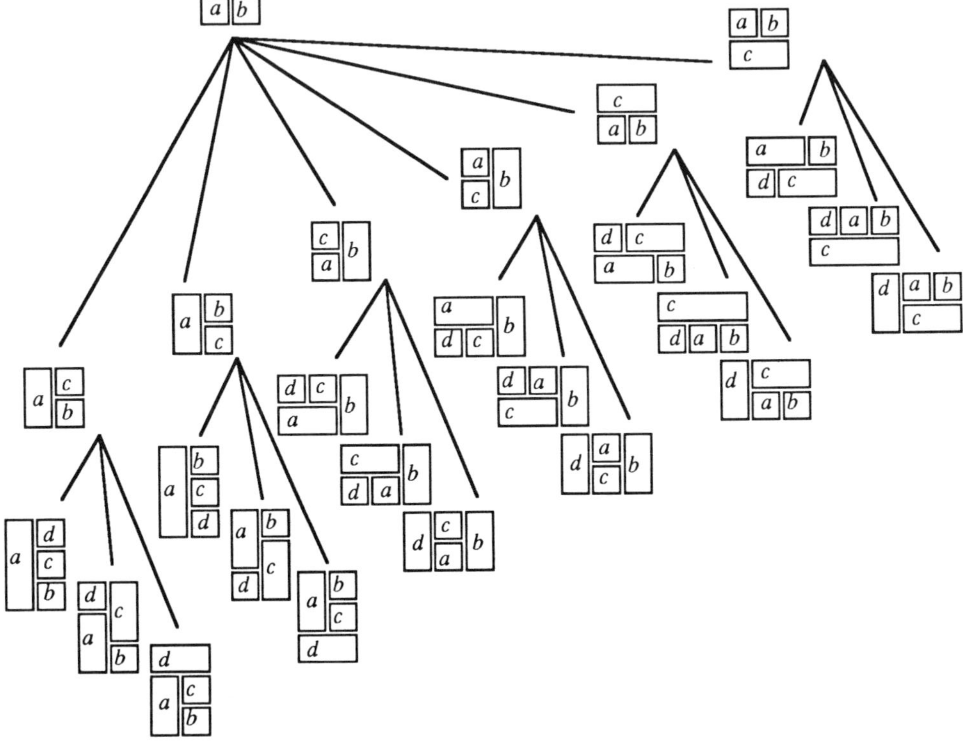

Figure 10.18. Examples of some alternative plans able to be generated from the adjacency network of Figure 10.17.

contained within the context then that information can be reordered. Another approach is to consider the imposition of different rules, or to introduce new rules, for generating alternatives. For example, rule 2 of the planning system could initially order spaces according to increasing size rather than decreasing valency. This may mean that smaller spaces would tend to be located to the centre of the configuration with larger spaces arranged around them. The selection of appropriate strategies for generating alternatives is also a control issue which can be handled by means of simple heuristics.

The selection of appropriate control devices is dependent on the environment in which a knowledge based system is to be exploited. If the system is to perform as an 'intelligent assistant' then a range of control options may need to be available, and selecting from among these can be regarded as an 'expert' task.

Implementation

As discussed in Chapter 3, a logic programming language such as Prolog provides a means for describing the operations of a production system. States can be represented as collections of facts. Production rules can be represented as a particular type of fact, and control devices can be described in terms of Prolog rules. Facts are retracted and asserted into the facts base according to the rules, and as implemented by the control regime. In Chapter 6 a simple language for transforming networks was illustrated, where nodes in the network and their links are represented as facts in predicate calculus notation. As plans can be represented in the form of procedural networks (as discussed in Chapters 8 and 9) it is clearly possible to implement a system of rules which operates on actions, as described above, in logic.

A system which manipulates rules such as those described above has been implemented in Prolog and is described here.

State Descriptions

A set of facts describing the initial state in the development of a procedural network consists of facts such as the following:

node(*start*, [], [*configure*(*x*)]).
node(*configure*(*x*), [*start*], [*end*]).

This represents the position of the single node with the label: *configure*(*x*). As described in Chapter 6, the first argument of the *node* predicate is the name of the action, the second argument contains a list of the parent nodes, that is, the actions which precede it in the network, and the third argument is a list of child nodes—that is, the actions which immediately follow that node. The nodes *start* and *end* indicate the beginning and end of the network. These facts can be interpreted by a graphics system in order to construct a network. The graphic representation of the above facts by such a system is shown in Figure 10.19. In this case it is a single node. The *start* and *end* nodes are not

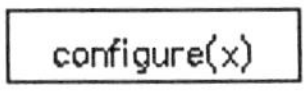

configure(x)

Figure 10.19. The first node in the development of the network.

drawn, as they are implied in the way actions are ordered in the network. The start of the network is at the top. The following facts show an intermediate step in the development of this plan:

node(start, [], [anchor(b)]).
node(put(a, next_to, b), [start], [and(1)]).
node(and(1), [put(a, next_to, b)], [put(c, next_to, b), put(c, next_to, a)]).
node(put(c, next_to, b), [and(1)], [and(2)]).
node(put(c, next_to, a), [and(1)], [and(2)]).
node(and(2), [put(c, next_to, b), put(c, next_to, a)], [and(3)]).
node(and(3), [and(2)], [put(e, next_to, b), put(e, next_to, a)]).
node(put(e, next_to, b), [and(3)], [and(4)]).
node(put(e, next_to, a), [and(3)], [and(4)]).
node(and(4), [put(e, next_to, b), put(e, next_to, a)], [and(5)]).
node(and(5), [and(4)], [put(d, next_to, c), put(d, next_to, e)]).
node(put(d, next_to, c), [and(5)], [and(6)]).
node(put(d, next_to, e), [and(5)], [and(6)]).
node(and(6), [put(d, next_to, c), put(d, next_to, e)], [end]).

The graphical interpretation of these facts is shown in Figure 10.20. Even though the *and* nodes have the same meaning, and they are drawn without arguments, it is necessary that they are identified differently (as by a numbering system) in order for the network to be drawn.

Knowledge Base

It is the purpose of the rules to facilitate: the recognition of patterns in lists of facts such as the above; the testing of various conditions; and the implementation of changes. The general form of a rule is the same as that

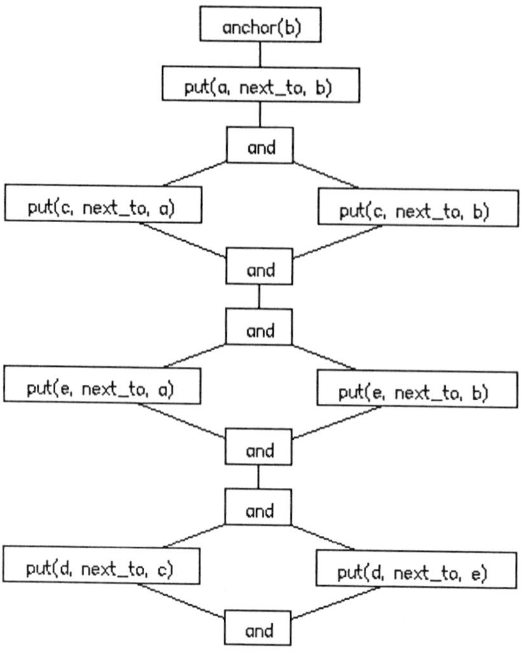

Figure 10.20. Screen output showing the graphical version of the network on page 249.

given in Chapter 6. A more general form is given here:

$$N, A_1, C_1 \rightarrow B_1 \textit{ or } ... \textit{ or } N, A_n, C_n \rightarrow B_n$$

This states that a rule can consist of a series of alternative preconditions and resultants in the form of subrules connected by an *or*. In Prolog the disjunctive syntax is implied by the way terms are listed in the program, so a subrule can be described as a Prolog fact: *rule(Name, Ant, Cond, Cons)* and alternative subrules of the same rule can be expressed as sequentially arranged rules with the same name. In the above rule the predicate *rule* has four arguments represented here as variables. *Name* is the identification of the rule. *Ant* is a list containing those facts which are preconditions to be matched directly in the current state and are to be changed. *Cond* is a list of conditions, some of which have to be inferred, and *Cons* is a list of consequents. A typical subrule is given below:

```
rule('defer unattached object', [
    node(P, Q, [put(A)]),
    node(put(A), [P], [R]),
    node(R, [put(A)], S),

    node(E, F, [end])
    ],
    [
    node(anchor(_), _, _),
    not(S=end),
    unattached(A)
    ],
    [
    node(P, Q, [R]),
    node(R, [P], S),

    node(E, F, [put(A)]),
    node(put(A), [E], [end])  ]).
```

The antecedent and consequent parts of the rule are shown graphically in Figure 10.21. Of the three conditions the first checks that the first action in the plan is to *anchor* something, the second is that the action being tested is *not* the penultimate action, and the third condition is that *A* is unattached. The first condition therefore ensures that this rule can only be implemented after

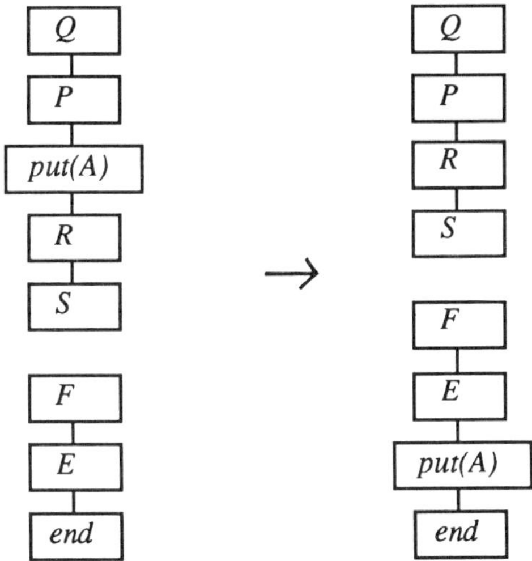

Figure 10.21. Graphical representation of the rule on page 251.

the rule *anchor first object*. The second condition avoids a special case where the rule, as formulated here, would not work. (A separate subrule is provided to handle the case where the action concerning an unattached space is the penultimate action in the plan.) The third condition is checked by means of a Prolog rule which takes information from the context about desirable linkages and 'reads' the network to determine if *A* can be placed adjacent to an object which is placed by an action above *put*(*A*) in the plan. A further subrule to take care of the special case follows this rule in the program.

Control Implementation

The two major operations concerning rules are often referred to as *triggering* and *firing*. Firing was discussed in Chapter 7 in the context of blackboard systems, and also in Chapter 9. When a rule is triggered its antecedents and conditions are tested and the effects of the rule are recorded, but no changes are made to the procedural network representation. If the rule is subsequently fired, the antecedents of the rule are deleted from the facts base and replaced by the consequents. Because each rule may be comprised of several subrules, the antecedents and conditions of each subrule are tested in turn until an appropriate match is made.

The type of controlling strategy that considers rules in some order is relatively simple to represent in Prolog. The rules need to be stored in the order in which they are to be applied. Each rule is then taken and applied as many times as possible until it is no longer applicable. Then the next rule in the list is attempted. This is the first type of scheduling illustrated in Figure 10.22 (i).

In the opportunistic approach records are kept of the *effects* of each rule that can be triggered, such as: the number of new facts asserted; the precedence in the network of the first fact changed by each rule; and the list of facts themselves changed by the rule. Where there is more than one choice the scheduling rule is employed to determine the selection. When a rule is fired these triggering records are deleted, and a record containing the list of rules in firing order is kept up-to-date.

In the approach where rules are grouped as in Figure 10.15 (iii) a separate set of facts expresses this grouping. This *schedule* of tasks serves as a convenient means of ordering the complex control of a Prolog system where the ordering of tasks is partially known and is to be amenable to change. It is only necessary to adjust the schedule to accommodate changes. The schedule for the spatial layout system is listed in Figure 10.22. Each fact *task* has three arguments. The first argument indicates whether the action is a production rule or a procedure. A procedure is defined here as either a node in the schedule which has links with a set of subtasks, or an action which can occur at

```
task(procedure, control, display_context).
task(procedure, control, generate_plan).
task(procedure, control, draw_network).
task(procedure, control, generate_form).

task(procedure, display_context, activate_window(1)).
task(procedure, display_context, partition).
task(procedure, display_context, position_nodes).
task(procedure, display_context, normalize_net).
task(procedure, display_context, draw_adjacency_net).

task(procedure, partition, check_for_pivots).
task(procedure, partition, create_cycles).
task(procedure, partition, check_for_bridges).
task(procedure, partition, create_strings).

task(procedure, generate_plan, activate_window(2)).
task(procedure, generate_plan, order_placements).
task(procedure, generate_plan, establish_adjacencies).
task(procedure, generate_plan, establish_orientations).

task(rule, order_placements, 'expand composition').
task(rule, order_placements, 'order according to valency').
task(rule, order_placements, 'anchor the first object').
task(rule, order_placements, 'defer placement of unattached objects').

task(rule, establish_adjacencies, 'position adjacent objects').
task(rule, establish_adjacencies, 'advance connection').
task(rule, establish_adjacencies, 'arbitrarily position adjacent objects').

task(rule, establish_orientations, 'orientate first two objects').
task(rule, establish_orientations, 'orientate objects').
task(rule, establish_orientations, 'orientate opposites').
task(rule, establish_orientations, 'combine action pairs').

task(procedure, generate_form, activate_window(3)).
task(procedure, generate_form, implement_plan).
task(procedure, generate_form, link_rooms).
task(procedure, generate_form, draw_network_overlay).
```

Figure 10.22. The organization of knowledge for a spatial layout system represented in schedule form in Prolog. The knowledge for displaying the context (display_context) is essentially procedural, and involves the invocation of Prolog clauses that interpret the connections described in the context as graphical primitives. The part of the schedule headed generate_plan is illustrated in Figure 10.16. Part of the schedule, headed generate_form, is concerned with implementing the plan. This is treated here as a purely procedural operation. The procedures labelled activate-window refer to the areas of the display screen in which graphics are to appear.

any time and does not have a set of preconditions to be tested. Rules only occur at branch ends in the schedule tree. Where there is more than one rule at a branch end then these are each triggered. If more than one rule is then applicable a scheduling rule is brought into play to decide between them. An example of an interaction with a system which illustrates the operation of scheduling rules is shown in Figure 10.23.

Backtracking

The built-in backtracking facility of Prolog does not enable facts which have been asserted to be retracted on backtracking. The reverse is also not permitted: facts which have been retracted cannot be re-asserted. This implies that the logic of backtracking for the production system formulation described here must be represented explicitly in the logic program.

There are three issues in backtracking: the mechanism of backtracking; when it should operate; and to what state the system should return on backtracking. The mechanism is fairly straightforward. It is common in backtracking procedures to maintain either a record of states encountered by the system, or a record of the rules employed. In the system described here the latter approach has been adopted. As a rule is fired a counter is decreased by a

```
..
select between rules:
advance connection
position adjacent to existing spaces

rule position adjacent to existing spaces produces 12 new facts
rule advance connection produces 10 new facts
-------------------------------
1: select_rule_with_smallest_record_set
2: select_rule_with_largest_record_set
3: select_most_recently_fired_rule
4: select_least_recently_fired_rule
5: select_rule_affecting_most_recently_changed_data_item
6: select_rule_affecting_least_recently_changed_data_item
7: select_rule_affecting_most_important_ie_earliest_data_item
-------------------------------
select scheduling rule number: 1.
SCHEDULE RULE:
select_rule_with_smallest_record_set
select: advance connection
***********
FIRE(advance connection)
***********
..
```

Figure 10.23. Interaction with a system that allows rules to be selected on the basis of scheduling heuristics. In this example the selection criterion is provided by the computer operator (in bold type). The heuristic can also be set as a default, such that no interaction is required.

value of 1, and a record of the rule and the facts asserted by it (including all instantiations) is stored along with the value of the counter. When backtracking occurs the counter is increased by 1, and records of changes made by rules, whose counter value is less than the current value, are deleted. When each rule is triggered a test is carried out to see that the changes which that rule is to make have not been made already at the current value of the counter. Different states are therefore generated on backtracking.

The advantage of representing this mechanism explicitly in logic programming is that backtracking can be controlled more readily. For example, it is possible to backtrack to specific stages in the development of the plan. It is therefore possible to implement a kind of context-dependent backtracking, which operates selectively rather than exhaustively (Pereira and Porta, 1982).

As well as an *undo* meta-rule, it is possible to define a rule which will *redo* the placement of a particular space. Once a layout is generated, if the location or configuration of a particular space is unsatisfactory, it is possible to undo all of the rules up to and including that space. An alternative orientation for the space can be generated, and the other rules proceed as before. Part of the knowledge for this operation can be represented as:

redo(A) :- *undo_to(A), generate_plan, generate_form.*

undo_to(A) :- *node(put(A, next_to, _), _, _)*, !.
undo_to(A) :- *undo, undo_to(A).*

Given the goal:

?- ***redo(a).***

the program will recursively apply the rule *undo* until a state is reached at which *a* is found in a *put next_to* action. At this juncture the system will stop undoing rules and will re-generate a plan. This enables backtracking to strategic points in the generation procedure and the investigation of alternative configurations of that particular space.

The automation of this process is not considered in detail here. Clearly, it would be advantageous for a controller which makes use of backtracking to exploit knowledge about the context of a conflict, or a request for the regeneration of an alternative plan, to determine to what state backtracking should return.

A Worked Example

In this section a worked example serves to demonstrate some of the control features discussed in the previous sections. It also give some indication of how graphics can be employed to make the operations of the system clear to an operator. Figures 10.24 to 10.51 are of graphical output produced on a SUN 2 graphics workstation. (The overall screen environment is shown in Figures 9.10 and 9.11).

As determined by the schedule of Figure 10.22, the system begins by responding to the command *control*. The first task is to display the context in graphical form. The context of a design task is shown in Figure 10.24. The information provided is a set of Prolog clauses describing the components (rooms) of an object *x* (a type of building), the linkages between these components, and the initial task: to *configure* the components of *x*. The facts about room linkages are processed by a graphics interpreter in order to produce the display shown in Figure 10.25. The interpreter searches for patterns within the set of linkages, such as *rings*, *cycles* and *strings* of nodes, and nodes about which the configuration appears to pivot. The path-finding program described in Chapter 3 serves in the detection of such patterns. Spatial coordinates are assigned to nodes on the basis of groupings and the connections between groupings. The subtasks in the generation of the graphical image are contained in the schedule of Figure 10.22.

Figure 10.26 shows the network of actions resulting from the activity of the group of rules labelled as *order_placements* (Figure 10.16). The network in Figure 10.27 is a partial state resulting from the implementation of the group of rules labelled as *establish_orientations*. Figure 10.28 is the result of the

```
composition(x, [a,b,c,d,e,f,g,h,i]).

link(a, b).
link(c, d).
link(d, a).
link(e, c).
link(f, b).
link(h, b).
link(h, c).
link(h, i).
link(f, i).

size_order([d, c, f]).

node(start, [], [configure(x)]).
node(configure(x), [start], [end]).
```

Figure 10.24. Program listing of a design context.

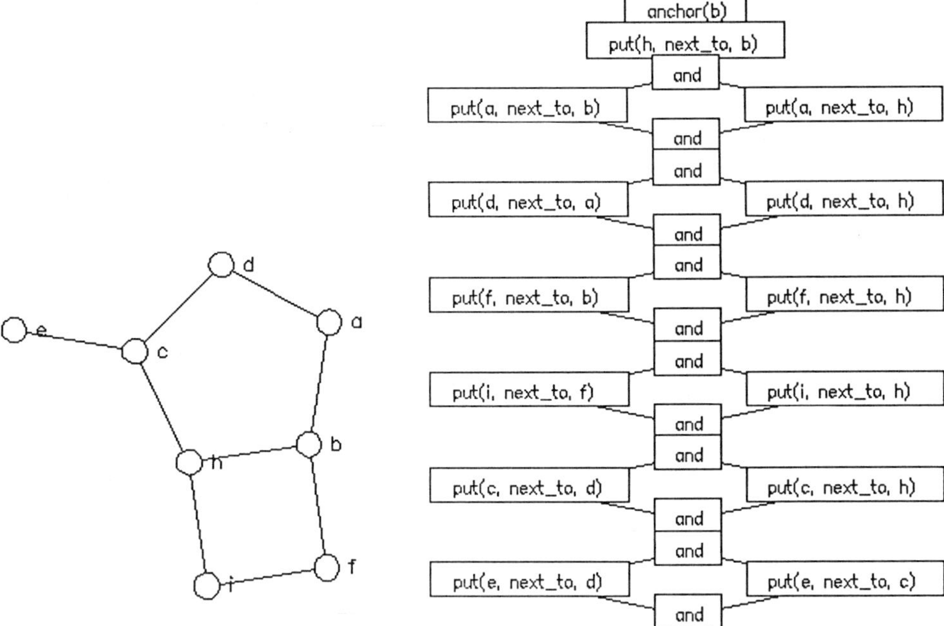

Figure 10.25. Graphical interpretation of the linkages in the context of Figure 10.24.

Figure 10.26. State in the development of the plan to meet the requirements of the context in Figure 10.24.

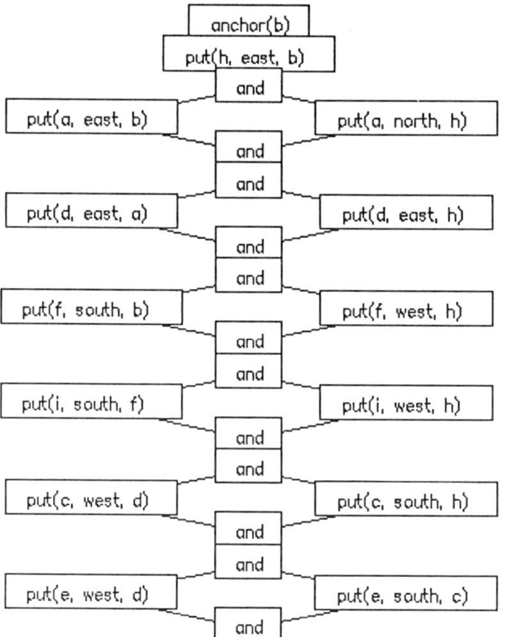

Figure 10.27. Development of the plan of Figure 10.26.

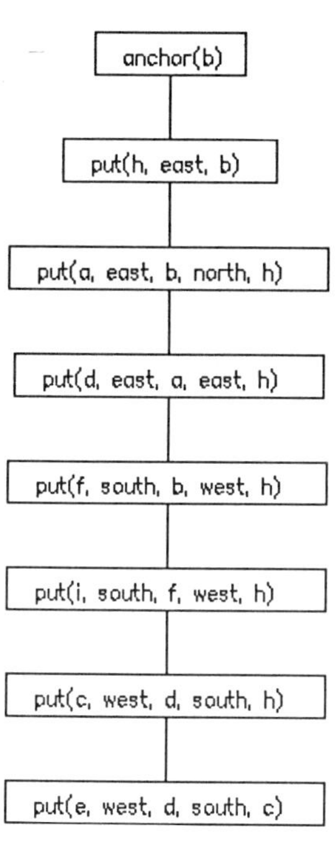

Figure 10.28. Final plan.

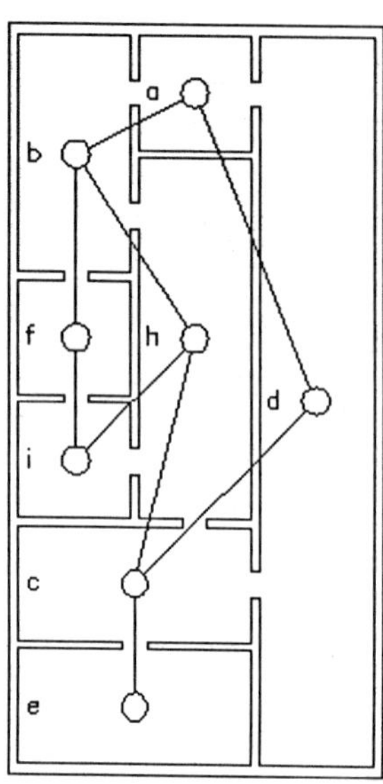

Figure 10.29. Spatial layout resulting from the execution of the plan in Figure 10.28.

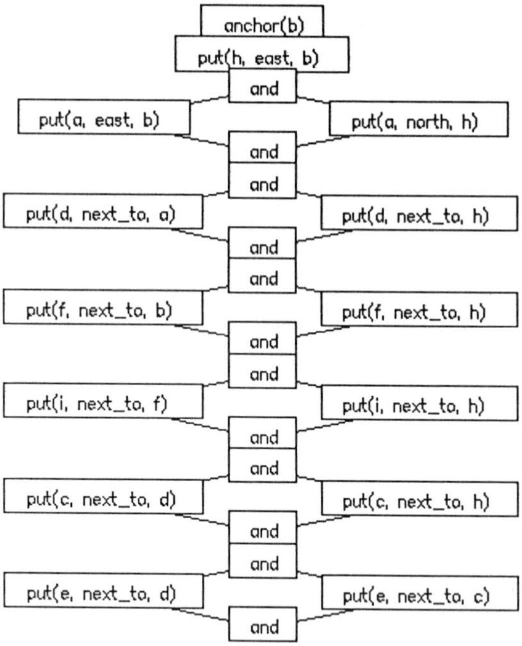

anchor(b)
put(h, east, b)
and
put(a, east, b)
put(a, north, h)
and
and
put(d, next_to, a)
put(d, next_to, h)
and
and
put(f, next_to, b)
put(f, next_to, h)
and
and
put(i, next_to, f)
put(i, next_to, h)
and
and
put(c, next_to, d)
put(c, next_to, h)
and
and
put(e, next_to, d)
put(e, next_to, c)
and

Figure 10.30. Plan produced by backtracking to the placement of room *d.*

repeated application of the rule *combine action pairs*. The schedule task, *generate_form*, takes this sequence of actions and *executes* the plan. When executed, the actions of the plan serve as commands for a graphics system which places objects in relation to one another as specified. (The development of a configuration, in response to such commands, was illustrated in Figure 9.9.) The task *link_rooms* draws in doorways between rooms which must be connected, and *draw_network_overlay* superimposes the network on the layout (Figure 10.29).

As well as achieving the set of desired adjacencies, the layout should also be able to accommodate the required relative sizes as specified in the context. According to the context of Figure 10.24 the relative size order (from largest to smallest) is: *d, c, f.* The influence of these relative sizes can be observed with reference to Figure 10.28. The action *put(d, east, a, east h)* ensures that *d* is the larger of the three rooms mentioned in the action. In the following action, *put(f, south, b, west, h), f* should be positioned such that it is larger than *b* and *h*. It should therefore be *south* of *h*. There is a condition in the *orientate spaces* rule that a room must not be 'closed off' by a space if there is

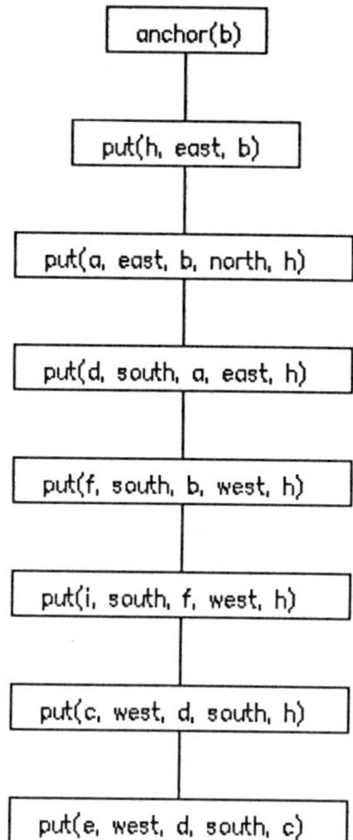

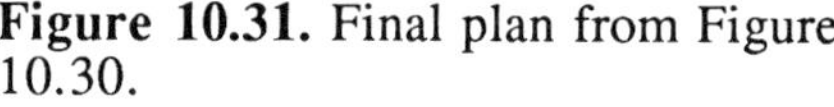

Figure 10.31. Final plan from Figure 10.30.

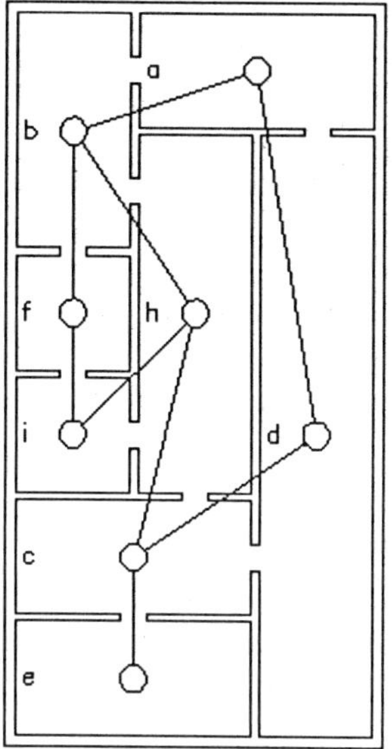

Figure 10.32. Spatial layout resulting from the execution of the plan in Figure 10.31.

a later action that requires another room to be connected to it. (See Rule 9.) The same condition applies to the location of *i* in relation to *f* and *h*. In the case of *put(c, west, d, south, h)*, *d* is to be the larger of the three rooms. In the final action *d* is again the larger of the three rooms. In this example, therefore, one of the rooms, *d*, in the size order appears to dominate over the other three. The system, in fact, exercises relatively little control over size order in this case. However, adjustments can be made to the layout by means of backtracking.

There are generally choices to be made about the relative orientations of rooms. The results of different choices can be explored by means of the Prolog predicate *redo* described above . The goal:

?- ***redo(d).***

causes the system to 'undo' all the rules up to and including the action concerning the placement of room *d*. The state of the network after this operation is illustrated in Figure 10.30, and Figure 10.31 shows the final, revised plan where an alternative orientation for *d* has been found. The resultant layout is illustrated in Figure 10.32. The layout is not markedly different from that produced in Figure 10.29 as no other actions are affected by this decision. However, backtracking to *d*, again, produces the plan in Figure 10.33 and the layout in Figure 10.34. Placing *d* east of *a* and north of *h* appears to affect the positions of the other rooms.

The action *put(f, south, b, south, h)* in Figure 10.33 reflects the dominance of *f* over *b* and *h*, but the following action is unable to accommodate the greater size of *i* over *f* and *h* due to the conflict caused by blocking *h* off from a subsequent connections with *c*. The action *put(c, south, d, east, h)* correctly reflects the relative size orders of the rooms in that action—as does the last action in the plan.

Another way of generating different layouts is to change the size order in the context. The plan resulting from the size order: *h, f, a,* is illustrated in Figure 10.35.

The resultant layout is illustrated in Figure 10.36. In this case *h* dominates over all the other rooms. The result of a different size order (*b, e, h*) is illustrated in Figure 10.37 and Figure 10.38.

The system therefore enables various plans to be generating satisfying

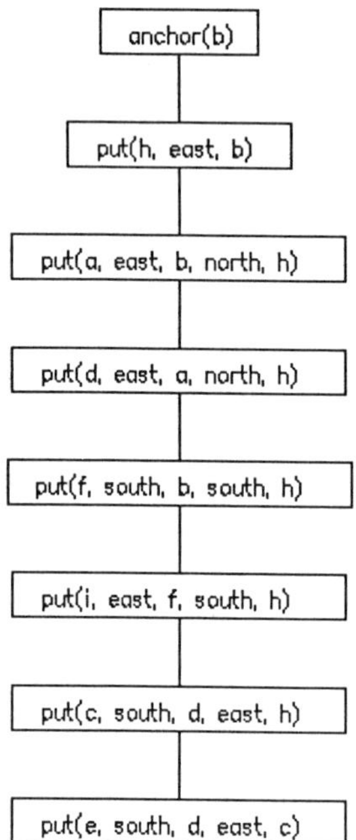

Figure 10.33. New plan generated by 're-doing' the placement of room *d*.

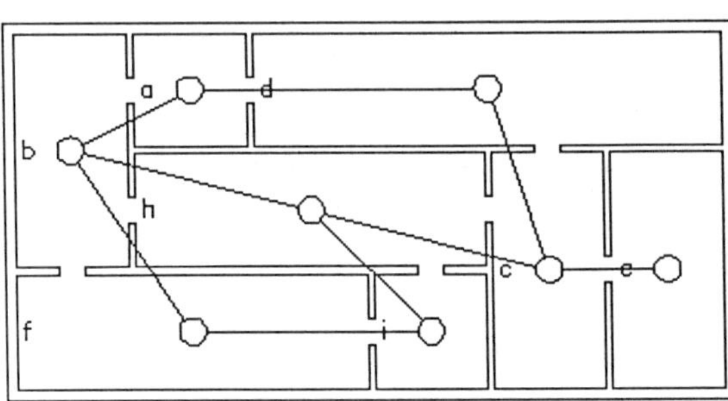

Figure 10.34. Spatial layout resulting from the execution of the plan in Figure 10.33.

similar adjacency constraints. Backtracking can also be employed in handling *conflicts*, as demonstrated in the next section.

Failure Handling

In the case of large adjacency networks the performance of the rules as outlined above becomes less predictable and the certainty of an executable plan less assured. This is demonstrated by means of an example.

The context for a design task in which seventeen rooms are to be located is given in Figure 10.39. The graphic interpreter produces the network configuration shown in Figure 10.40. Two of the states in the development of the plan network are shown in Figure 10.41 and 10.42. Even though the plan is incomplete at the state in Figure 10.42 no further rules are applicable. This is due to an unresolved conflict in locating room *i*.

According to the plan of Figure 10.41, *i* must be next to *h*, and next to *f* on the opposite side to *g*. That this configuration is not able to be achieved can be demonstrated by observing the spatial configuration which would be generated by the plan up to this point (Figure 10.43). There is no rule in the

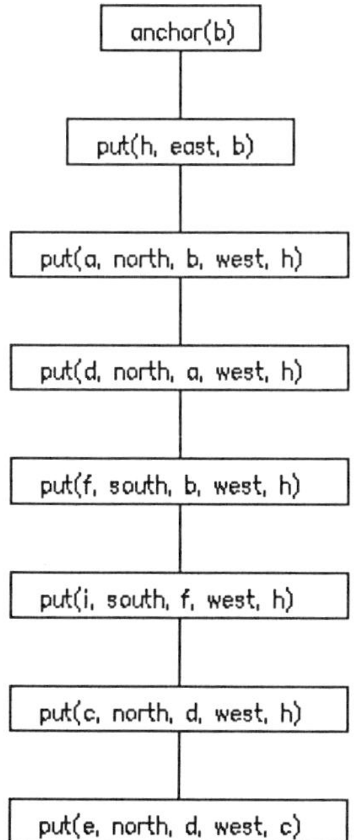

Figure 10.35. Plan for which the relative size order has been changed to: *h, f, a*.

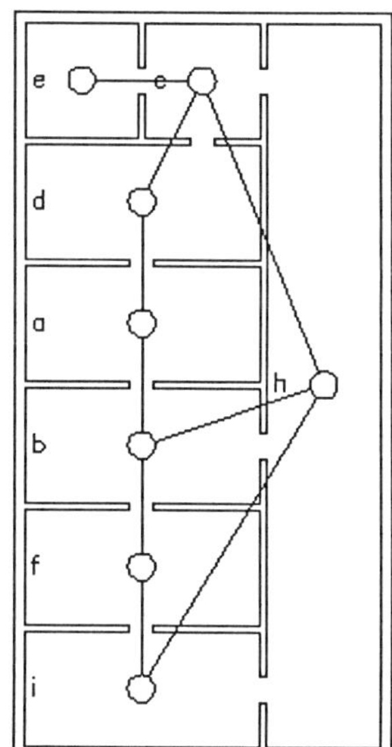

Figure 10.36. Spatial layout resulting from the execution of the plan in Figure 10.35.

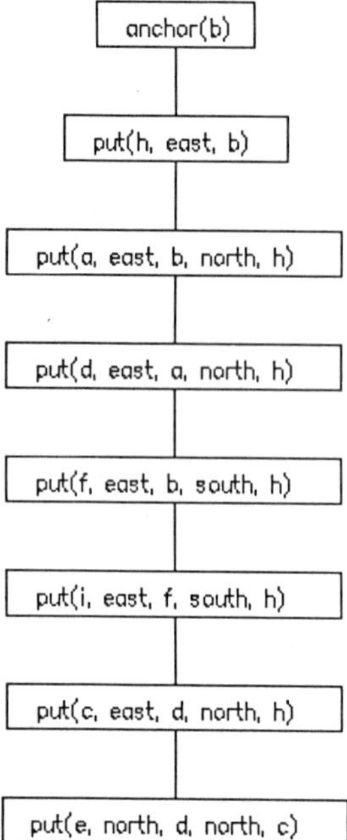

Figure 10.37. Plan resulting from the relative size order: *b, e, h.*

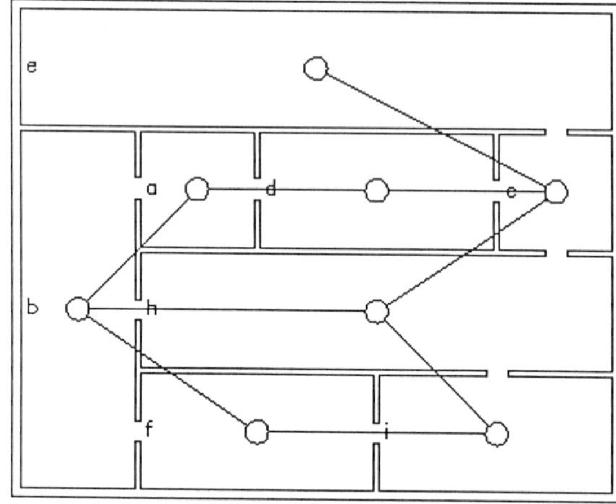

Figure 10.38. Spatial layout from the execution of the plan in Figure 10.37.

```
composition(x, [a,b,c,d,e,
   f,g,h,i,j,k,l,m,n,o,p,q]).

link(a, b).
link(c, d).
link(d, a).
link(e, c).
link(f, b).
link(f, g).
link(g, b).
link(g, a).
link(h, b).
link(h, c).
link(h, i).
link(f, i).
link(j, a).
link(j, g).
link(k, d).
link(l, k).
link(m, f).
link(m, g).
link(n, h).
link(n, i).
link(o, n).
link(p, o).
link(q, p).
link(q, m).
size_order([p, d, c, f, g]).

node(start, [], [configure(x)]).
node(configure(x), [start], [end]).
```

Figure 10.39. Program listing of a design context.

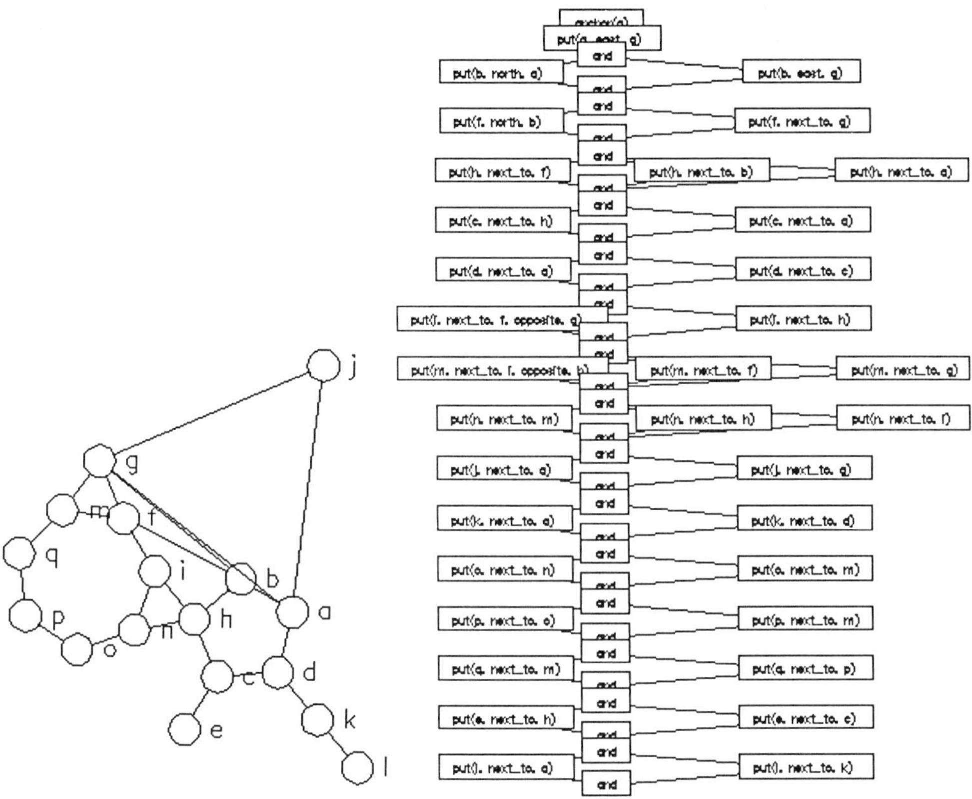

Figure 10.40. Graphical interpretation of the adjacencies in the context of Figure 10.39.

Figure 10.41. Intermediate state in the development of a plan for the context in Figure 10.39.

system to avoid or resolve this type of conflict. One appropriate strategy is to find the room which is most likely to be the cause of the conflict, backtrack to the placement of the room, and generate a new plan. In the example here *f* is selected. Backtracking such that *f* is positioned north of *b* and east of *g* produces the layout shown in Figure 10.44. The complete plan is shown in Figure 10.45 and the final plan in Figure 10.46. Figure 10.47 shows the resultant layout.

The conflict described above would not have arisen had there been a planning rule, or a condition within a rule, which checks that an action which places a space both next to one space and opposite another can, in fact, be accomplished. The backtracking device (or some means of general conflict resolution) is required to make up for shortcomings in the knowledge base.

In this example, backtracking is controlled by a human operator giving the

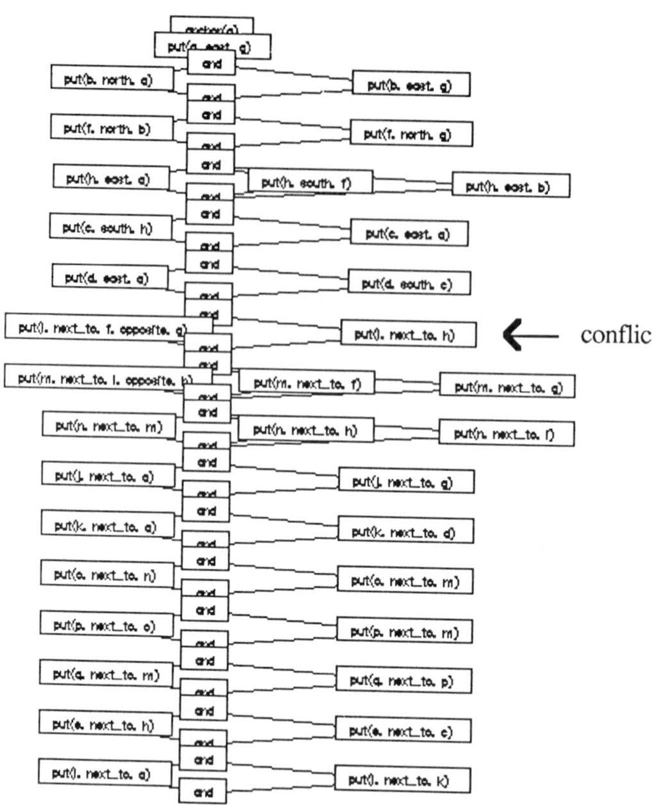

Figure 10.42. A plan in which conflict arises. It is not possible to place *i* next to *f*, opposite to *g* and next to *h*.

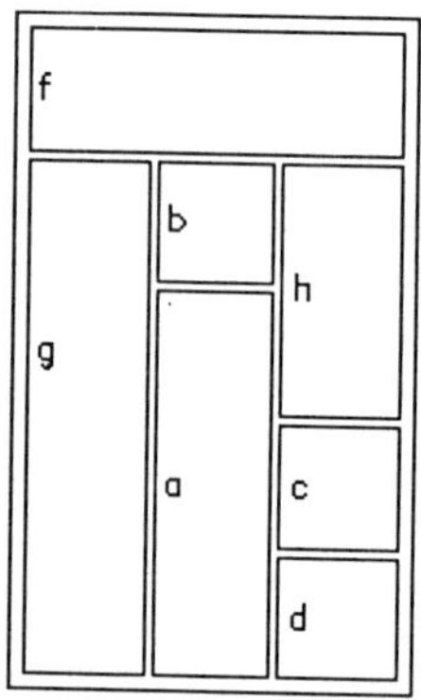

Figure 10.43. Spatial layout resulting from the 'executable' part of the plan of Figure 10.42.

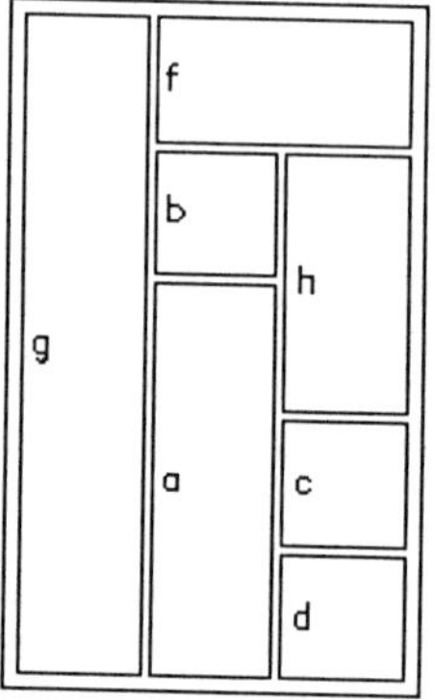

Figure 10.44. Alternative configuration in which the conflict of Figure 10.43 does not occur.

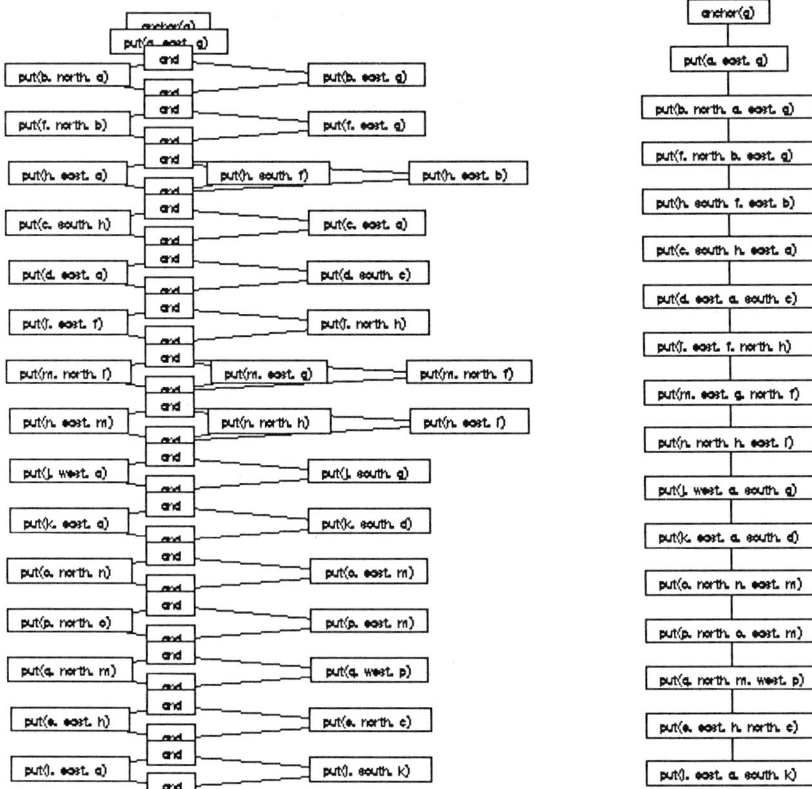

Figure 10.45. New state in the development of the plan subsequent to backtracking to the state in Figure 10.41.

Figure 10.46. Final state of plan following on from state in Figure 10.45.

Prolog program an explicit goal. A richer view of control would be one in which control rules are employed to detect the source of the conflict, and backtracking would proceed to that point under a meta-controller. Such a mechanism has not been fully explored here.

As in the previous example it is also possible to control the generation of alternative configurations by means of backtracking. Figure 10.48 results from 're-doing' the placement of room *b*. The layout is, in fact, an inverted form of the plan in Figure 10.47. By re-doing the placement of room *h* the layout in Figure 10.49 is generated. Figure 10.50 is the result of backtracking to the placement of room *h* and then *c*. Figure 10.51 shows the result of deleting room *m* to form a courtyard, and adding external doors and windows.

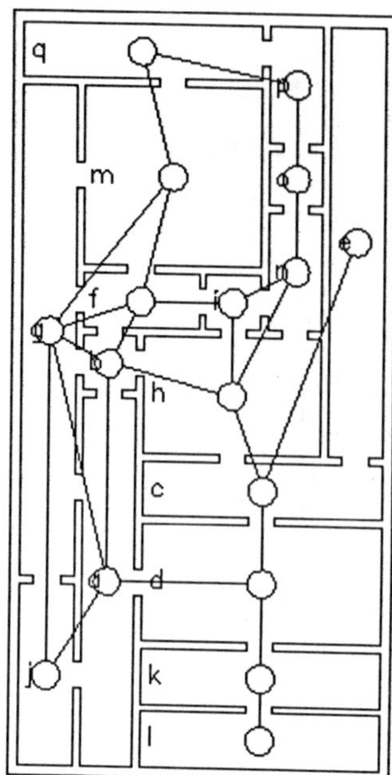

Figure 10.47. Spatial layout resulting from the execution of the plan in Figure 10.46.

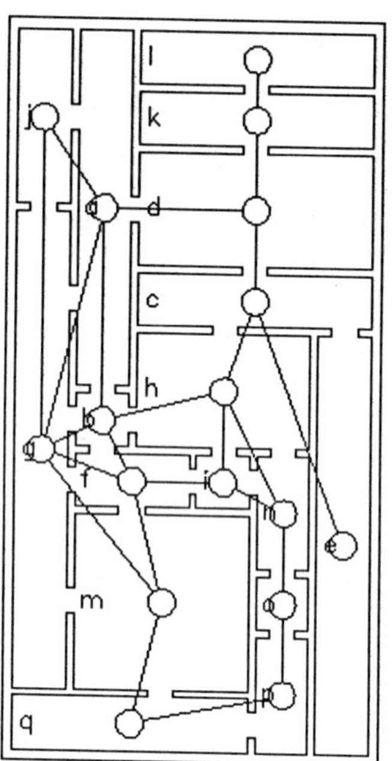

Figure 10.48. Spatial layout resulting from 're-doing' the position of room *b*.

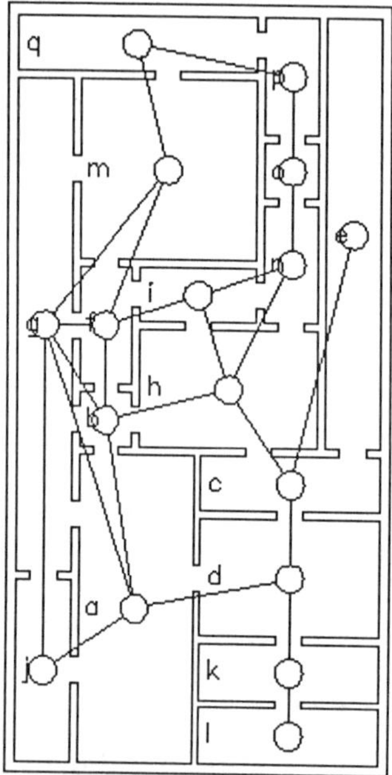

Figure 10.49. Spatial layout resulting from 're-doing' the placement of room *h*.

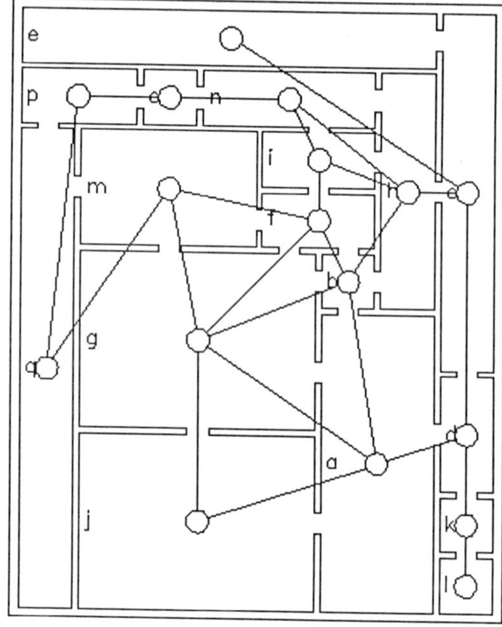

Figure 10.50. Spatial layout which results after 're-doing' *h* then *c*.

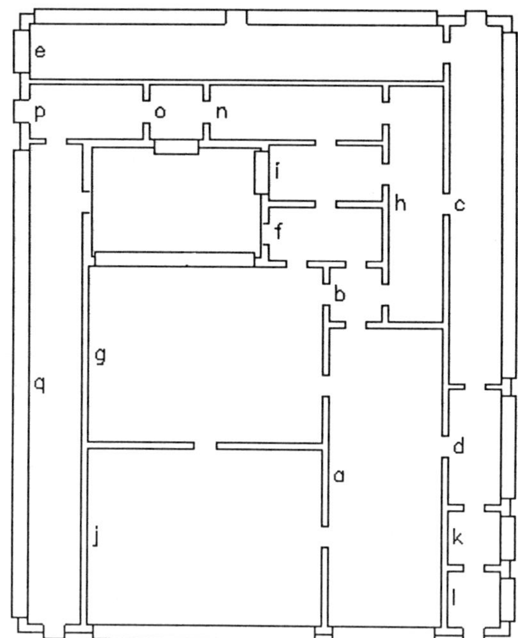

Figure 10.51. 'Enhanced' spatial layout of Figure 10.50.

Discussion

The system described above exemplifies a model of design in which knowledge about certain design processes is made explicit. Both the implementation discussed above and the model in general will be considered in this section. Extensions to the system are considered first, then the generalization of the model, followed by a discussion of how the model might be applied to other design domains. The section includes a discussion of the limitations of both the model and the application, and concludes with a summary of the merits of the model.

Extensions to the Implementation

There are six main areas that can be identified in which the implementation discussed above can be enhanced and extended. A discussion of how the *model* can be extended is left until the following chapter.

(i) Enhanced Control Abstractions

The target in the design of a system based on the model here is to bring it closer to the performance of the idealized system described in Chapter 5: that is, a system that is 'well-behaved' in terms of control. This requires the formulation of levels of control such that the uppermost level is the simplest. Ideally, this means doing away with complex control structures such as backtracking.

There are two means of achieving this. One is to introduce more and better planning knowledge (in the form of rules) so that conflicts such as that detected in the example of the previous section are avoided. The second approach is to impose further levels of control above the system. If backtracking is required then the system is effectively poorly-behaved—planning rules interact. The means by which a planning system formulated as a production system can be 'tamed' is to reformulate it in the manner discussed in Chapter 5. This suggests that there should be a system in which planning rules are the objects to be operated upon by rules of a higher order.

Whereas this formulation is the goal of such a system, how it might be achieved has not been considered here. Rather a scheduling approach has been adopted, which is thought to accommodate the behaviour of systems which conform approximately to the idealized system of Chapter 5.

(ii) Enhanced Scheduling

The scheduler, as proposed here, requires further development. Three modes of operation have been proposed for a scheduler. The decomposition of actions into groups of actions is a task that should be accomplished by explicit scheduling knowledge. This requires the incorporation of knowledge about categorizing actions.

(iii) Operations on Adjacency Networks

That which constitutes the context for the spatial layout task could also be the product of a system which is concerned with generating adjacency networks. Such a system might take as its context certain intended attributes, and from these produce a network of adjacencies. This network then forms the context of the system discussed above.

Planning rules may also operate on adjacency networks by the detection and remedy of nonplanar or otherwise impossible networks. They may reduce complex interconnections to simpler networks: for example, by introducing circulation spaces to simplify connections, or by decomposing networks into simpler units which can be treated independently and them merged.

(iv) Operations on the Geometrical Layout

Where the performance of a system is poorly understood certain properties of the final product (for example, a spatial layout) cannot be anticipated. The knowledge by which such predictions can be made may be poorly understood or the quantity of knowledge required makes prediction prohibitive. Certain properties of artifacts cannot be known until the description of the artifact is sufficiently developed in order for these properties to be determined. This is reflected in the role in design of sketching to externalize ideas and to make certain properties of objects overt. This suggests that there is a place for rules which operate on formal compositions in response to certain interpreted properties of geometrical descriptions.

Such rules might constitute critics which modify or enhance geometrical configuration in some way, such as by exchanging the positions of spaces, or making other adjustments. Such a system might work on the basis of generating a layout then modifying, or fine tuning, the layout. This is an expression of a type of decomposition where the generation of the form and its refinement are seen as two independent subtasks.

(v) Extended Design Attributes

The contextual information discussed above has been concerned primarily with connectivity. Other functional relationships should also be considered, such as the intended orientations of spaces, the avoidance of undesirable connections and adjacencies, visual connections, privacy considerations, and functional groupings for purposes of servicing. Site considerations (as suggested in Chapter 8) could also constitute the context of a design task. These and other properties of spatial layouts can constitute the goals of a design system.

These issues can be handled by fine tuning in the manner suggested above or, where the knowledge is available, as conditions which contribute to the operations of the planning rules.

(vi) General Issues in Knowledge-Based Systems

Other issues about knowledge based systems are *not* within the ambit of the theoretical development proposed here. These concern the problems associated with multiple knowledge sources, the distinctions to be made between domain dependent and domain independent knowledge, and the manner in which a designer might interact with such a design system. These issues need to be considered if the system described here is to be incorporated into a working design system.

Generalization of the Model

The implementation discussed above serves to exemplify an operational model of design. Two major principles have been demonstrated within this model. These are subsumed by a third principle.

(i) *Uniformity Between Operations on Form and Process*

It has been demonstrated that it is possible to establish a kind of uniformity between the operations on form and process. Just as there are rules or grammars for operating on form there are rules which treat those rules as objects and operate upon them. Just as grammars of design can be readily articulated there are grammars of actions. This kind of knowledge is available in design and can be brought to bear on design tasks.

(ii) Exploiting Decomposition

This also provides the advantage that, whereas design grammars operating at the object level (about configuring spaces) involve complex interactions and are not therefore decomposable, the organization of rules which operate on actions can be relatively simple to control. They can exhibit 'well-behaved' properties which make their control relatively simple to manage. The system can be organized such that the order in which planning rules are fired is less critical to the outcome of the system. These rules can be organized into relatively independent groups of actions in a decomposition hierarchy.

(iii) Exploiting Multiple Abstractions

The principle behind each of these maxims is that of exploiting multiple abstractions in task domains. In the above example procedures for establishing abstract descriptions of plans progress to more concrete descriptions. A design task is considered both in terms of formal abstraction and in terms of the procedures by which forms are brought about. This provides the advantage that *knowledge* which is pertinent to particular abstractions can be brought to bear on the design task.

Other Applications

Although the application above is concerned primarily with spatial layout the model is applicable to any design or expert task domain. Certain design decision-making can be modelled by deductive inference systems, as discussed in Chapter 4. Spatial layout is representative of difficult design tasks as it involves complex interactions between operators. The principle by which operations are carried out on sequential plans of operators, rather than on formal objects, can be applied to any such task. It would appear that a design task can be readily modelled in the manner depicted above if the following conditions apply.

(i) The design of an artifact can be described in 'linguistic' terms. There are components constituting a vocabulary, and there are operators (grammars) which operate on those components and which can be made explicit.

(ii) There are rules (or algorithms) of deductive inference by which the implicit attributes of the artifact can be derived. Mappings between descriptions of artifacts can be made explicit in the form of interpretive knowledge.

(iii) The grammar which operates on vocabularies can also be expressed in terms of actions, and the actions can be described as constituting part of a language: that is, the actions constitute a vocabulary, and actions map onto one another to provide hierarchies of actions.

(iv) The relationships between actions in time can be represented, such that certain actions should precede other actions and there can be conjunctions and disjunctions of actions. When executed, plans of actions will produce descriptions of designs.

(v) The intended performance of the task can be made explicit: that is, a set of intended attributes can be identified.

(vi) There is a grammar which operates on actions. This grammar is sensitive to the context and can be made explicit.

(vii) There is some kind of control advantage, in terms of decomposition and commutativity, in devising this formulation of the design task.

To demonstrate the suitability of a particular design domain to the model an example of an architectural design subtask will be considered in terms of the above criteria. The example is that of architectural detailing. In detailing subtasks there is generally a vocabulary of components, such as beams, rafters, fascias, roofing materials and fixing devices. There is a set of operators (constituting a grammar) by which these components can be manipulated. The grammar is able to transform certain configurations of components into other configurations (Radford, 1985; Mitchell and Radford, 1986) (Figure 10.52).

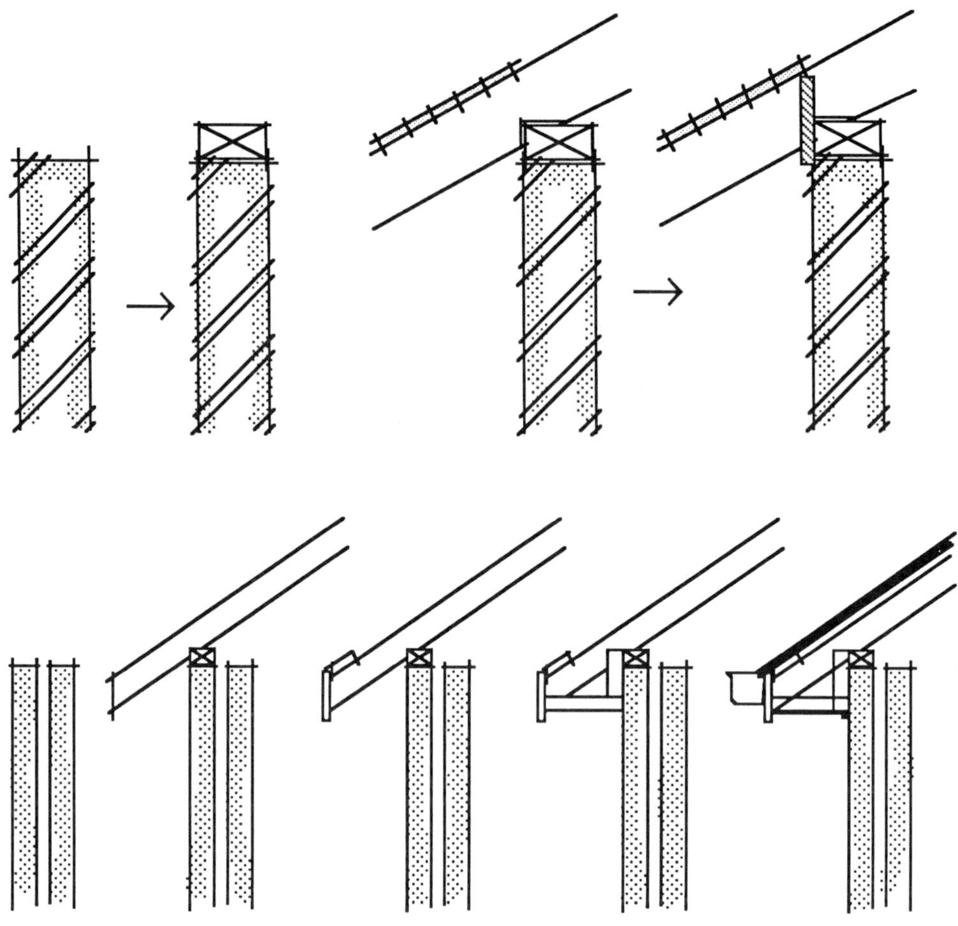

Figure 10.52. Two of the grammar rules for manipulating building components in producing eaves details (roof and wall junctions) in the manner outlined by Mitchell and Radford (1986). States in the development of a detail are also shown.

There are also levels of representation by which components and configurations can be described. There is a body of knowledge by which interpretations can be made of descriptions to produce other descriptions.

The grammar by which the components can be manipulated can also be depicted as a set of actions. In the building layout example the actions by which design components were manipulated mapped simply onto the relationships between the spaces. In the case of detailing the relationships between the components are more complex, therefore the actions will be more complex.

There are generally mappings between the actions by which components are configured on a drawing. These are actions about placing components *next_to* other components, leading to more specific relationships such as placing components *to_the_right_of*, *to_the_left_of*, *above* and *below* one another on a sectional drawing. There are also three-dimensional abstractions of which the relationships on a drawing are but a representation. For example, two objects may be *adjacent* on a drawing, but in three dimensions they may be on different planes. A decision needs to be made as to whether the artifact description is to depict relationships on a drawing or in three dimensions. If the latter approach is taken then actions can also depict functional relationships between components, such as fixings. An action to *put fascia next_to rafter* may constitute a generic abstraction of several other actions, such as to *support fascia on rafter,* and *abut fascia to rafter*. The *support_on* action may find syntactic expression in the actions: *hang fascia from rafter* or *prop fascia on rafter*. A further abstraction may be to *fix fascia* and there may be several appropriate types of fixing action, such as *nail fascia*, and *glue fascia.*

Plans of actions can be formulated such that it is possible to talk of fixing objects together in a particular order and, when executed, the plan produces the representation of an artifact which depicts a spatial configuration of components. A plan might proceed from the action: *detail eaves* to a sequence of actions *support rafter on top plate, nail fascia, strap gutter to fascia*, etc. The plan provides a sequence of actions by which formal representations can be generated (for example, graphical images), but also provides part of the specification by which the artifact can be manufactured.

In this example of detailing there is also a context in terms of intended relationships between components. In the case of detailing it is most likely that the context will be expressed in terms of structural and other performances, and in terms of a partial set of connections. For example, the objective may be that the roof abuts the wall. This represents an intended connection of two building components, but one which must be expanded in terms of the connections between the subcomponents of the roof and wall. It will probably be necessary to introduce other components, such as fixing devices, in order to make this possible. In the case of performances, it may be necessary for these to be translated into a specific set of components and their relationships. Once the relationships are established then the context may resemble the connectivity relationships in the building layout example. Functional relationships may include those of support, material compatibility, and functional relationships in terms of cooperation between components in keeping out moisture.

Intuitively, therefore, it can be seen that the first five requirements testing the applicability of the operational model to architectural detailing are satisfied.

It may also be assumed that there is a grammar which can operate on sequences of actions. The manipulations of adjacency and orientation discussed in the building layout example may also be extended to planning rules which consider support and fixing.

There may also be some advantage in terms of decomposition. The grammar which transforms actions may be such that its operations can be partitioned into relatively independent clusters of tasks in the manner described in the building layout example. This is something that would have to be tested by applying the model in a more rigorous manner than the discussion here allows.

Limitations of the Model

The limitations of logic as a medium for modelling design behaviour have already been outlined in Chapter 3. Here the limitations of the model presented in this chapter are considered in terms of its reference to the terminology of linguistics, knowledge-based systems and in terms of the model itself.

(i) Problems in Linguistics

The assumption has been made that design can be readily modelled in terms of language. Design models based on linguistics inherit the problems of linguistics, and there are problems in relating language to design.

Chomsky's models of grammar (from which linguistic models of design are developed) do not effectively account for the concept of semantics. (This is an observation which Chomsky freely acknowledges.) Clearly there are other devices at work in natural language than phrase structure grammars. There are other models of language, for example those based on generative semantics, semantic networks and conceptual dependency graphs (Winograd, 1983; Sowa, 1984), but there is, as yet, no uniform theory. An attempt is made in this thesis to account for the mapping between syntax and semantics by means of meta-grammars. This constitutes a hypothesis within a field for which there is no accepted paradigm.

Language is employed here primarily as an operational model. The points of dissimilarity between design and natural language must be considered however. It could be argued that the concerns of design are not well-served by a discipline which takes *communication* as its primary interest.

An example of the problems of attempting to match the mechanisms of design with those of language is the place of *style* in design. In the shape grammar literature style is embodied within grammar. The origin of style in natural language appears not to be so clear. The style of an author is certainly not captured in the rules of grammar (of the phrase structure type) which are common to all native speakers of the language, although it may be embodied in meta-grammars.

Another objection rests on the fundamental differences in the way natural language and design manifest themselves. Under most circumstances speech is spontaneous. Design is characterized by its exploratory component. On the face of it, both the processes and the products of speech and design generation appear to have very little in common. These observations therefore sound a warning against an over-enthusiastic translation between design and the concerns of linguistics.

(ii) Problems in Knowledge-Based Systems

The knowledge representation scheme here has been essentially that of production systems modelled in logic. There are other representation mechanisms which have not been considered, such as frames (Minsky, 1975; Fikes and Kehler, 1985; Willey and Toller, 1981), semantic networks (Baykan and Eastman, 1982) and procedural representations.

The emphasis in knowledge-based systems is on the primacy of knowledge. The mechanisms by which it is controlled are regarded as relatively minor—hence the aphorism: 'in the knowledge lies the power' (Davis, 1982). This knowledge-based approach is in contrast to an algorithmic approach in which domain knowledge is bound to a set of procedures.

It should be noted, however, that there are both good and bad examples of knowledge represented explicitly and algorithmically. *Good* algorithms are procedural modules which are concise and efficient. As well as being modular and 'legible' good declarative knowledge bases are also marked by simplicity, effectiveness and reliability. An elegant algorithm may be better than a poorly constructed set of production rules.

Knowledge based systems are generally considered necessary for tasks where there is poor theoretical understanding, that is, for tasks considered the 'sole' domain of the human expert. The tendency within knowledge-based systems is therefore to compensate for lack of theoretical understanding by the provision of vast quantities of knowledge representing a poor understanding of the problem. Quantity tends to compensate for quality. This is both a strength and a weakness of knowledge-based systems. For tasks where there appears to be no substantial theoretical foundation, knowledge-based systems tend to provide tools which render heuristics (or rules of thumb) safe and manageable. Heuristics are too readily lost within algorithmic programs, and their influence cannot be checked.

There are other approaches to the spatial layout task described in Chapters 9 and 10. Perhaps all that is required is an elegant algorithm for providing the mapping between an adjacency diagram, its dual graph and a set of dimensional constraints. This could be modelled on some sort of analogy, such as the analogy between room dimensions and electrical resistance in a circuit, described by March and Steadman (1971).

The spatial layout task is employed as a vehicle for exploring the utility of the proposed model. The model's true value would be shown by its application to tasks for which algorithmic methods prove inadequate. This suggests prospects for future research.

(iii) Non-Uniform Control

Further objections rest on the specific model developed in this thesis. Exercising control over a grammar system by means of meta-grammars raises several questions. Where do the levels of control stop? Is there a theoretical limit on the number of grammars that can be 'stacked' in this way?

Operations within grammars tend to be recursive, but the operations of a meta-grammar on an object grammar are not the same as the operations of the object grammar. Rules of an object grammar do not constitute vocabulary elements in the same way as the vocabulary of an object grammar. Is it therefore meaningful to talk of grammars as if there was some sort of uniformity between them? The defence against these arguments is that the linguistic model is intended merely to provide a terminological framework within which these mechanisms can be explored.

Objections to the model at a more fundamental level are addressed in the following chapter. These relate to the intractable nature of design and to the elusive nature of the knowledge required to tackle realistic design tasks.

Advantages of a Logic Model of Design

Notwithstanding the criticisms raised in the previous section an operational model of design based on logical reasoning provides a good model. Logic helps to explain what design is, and it provides a formalism for describing design processes.

That logic provides a useful framework with which to describe design reasoning is illustrated in Chapter 2, where Peirce's models of the roles of deduction, induction and abduction in reasoning are discussed. Logic provides the basis for describing reasoning in general, including reasoning in science, language and design. It appears that design involves the process of *abduction* which is a poorly-understood mode of reasoning.

As a language, logic provides a useful formalism for describing designs. Descriptions of designs constitute sets of beliefs in the form of premises or statements about some object or configuration of objects. Redundancies of representation are permitted, but in a logic system these beliefs must be consistent with one another. An advantage of an explicit knowledge representation is that contradictions can be rendered obvious.

It is generally not practical (or even possible) to make explicit all that is known, or all that is knowable about a design. (In fact it is sometimes desirable to describe designs in a canonical form, that is, by means of the smallest and most complete set of premises possible from which all other attributes can be derived.) Logic provides a means not only of representation but of *interpretation*. That which is unknown can be inferred from what is known by means of statements or axioms *about* the interpretation of design descriptions. An advantage of logic is that there is a uniformity in the representation of beliefs about designs and beliefs about interpretation.

Given a set of premises and axioms further beliefs can be compared with what is known to see if they are consistent. Such inferred statements are generally regarded as theorems or, in the terminology of design, performances. In the terminology of linguistics the inferred properties of a design description constitute its *meaning*. It is also possible to infer what is *unknown* from what is known. Given a canonical body of knowledge new knowledge can be inferred.

The operational task in logical deduction is one of testing the consistency of sets of beliefs. If there is a set of specific instances under which the logical theorems are true then they may constitute the inferred properties of the design. Consistency provides the impetus of logic. It also provides a good model of reasoning about designs. 'With what set of beliefs is this known set of beliefs consistent?' is the same as asking: 'What does this representation of an artifact mean?'

In *abduction* the theorems are known, but the premises from which these are derivable are not. The axioms may also be unknown, although in the model that is developed here it is assumed that they are known. In the terminology of design, the performances are available, but the design description from which these performances are derivable is not known. In the terminology of linguistics this amounts to knowing the *meaning* of an unseen artifact.

The approach of producing designs by *generation* has been explored. A design is seen to pass through a series of description states according to a set of generative rules. These rules embody knowledge about how one state can be transformed into another. Knowledge about the generation of designs constitutes a higher order of complexity than that involved in deduction. It is necessary to make knowledge about *how* designs are generated explicit, and the consistency of the statements about a design depend on the states to which they apply.

Statements can be made involving beliefs about consistencies between states. *Beliefs about beliefs* therefore constitute a type of design knowledge. The representation of design knowledge appears to require this higher order of complexity. Knowledge *about* designs is insufficient on its own to generate designs. Knowledge about design *processes* is required, as is knowledge about how those processes are controlled.

Design knowledge can therefore be made explicit as statements in logic, and this is accomplished by appealing to higher orders of reasoning in which axioms about design processes are made explicit.

In this discussion no consideration has been given as to how theorems might be derived from premises and axioms, nor about how proof procedures might operate. It is the strength of logic as a medium for representing knowledge about design processes that the consistency of a set of logical statements is independent of computational mechanisms. Knowledge about design is extricated from knowledge about proof procedures. Logic therefore provides a good basis on which to build theories of design unconstrained by certain computational considerations.

Conclusion

A design system based on a certain operational model of design has been developed and applied to spatial layout in buildings. The model constitutes a language which has a grammar consisting of transformation rules for locating spaces adjacent to one another in particular configurations. These rules can also be depicted as actions. There is also a meta-grammar for manipulating sequences of actions. These are the planning rules described in detail in this chapter. The various methods by which this grammar can be controlled have been discussed. Control knowledge is able to be made explicit by means of various types of schedules and by means of scheduling rules. Controlled backtracking was demonstrated as a means of accommodating shortfalls in the knowledge-base, and as a simple expedient for generating alternatives. In an ideal system which is 'well-behaved', backtracking should not be necessary. A system which displays these characteristics could probably be achieved by the introduction of further, specialized rules.

In the implementation of the spatial layout system described here, backtracking is accomplished by the intervention of a human operator who gives the system a Prolog goal directing the process. The system environment is such that suggestions for conflict resolution and the generation of alternatives could be accomplished by means of graphical interaction—such as *pointing* to elements within a plan or within a spatial configuration. However, this possibility was not explored here.

No consideration has been given to the dimensioning of layouts. Presumably this operation could highlight further conflicts which need to be resolved. This may require rules which make adjustments to the spatial configuration in some way, or it may require mechanisms for backtracking to earlier states in the development of the sequential plan. The intention of the system described in this chapter has been to demonstrate the utility of the model developed in the preceding chapters.

Extensions to the system have been considered in the discussion following the description of the implementation. The applicability of the model to another design task has also been considered. This was in the domain of architectural detailing.

The principle of exploiting multiple abstractions has been restated as one of the major advantages provided by the model. Limitations of the model in terms of its appeal to linguistics and theories of knowledge-based systems have been addressed. Extensions to the model are considered in the next chapter.

This chapter demonstrates that a model of design based on the logical manipulation of grammars and meta-grammars provides a rich basis on which to formulate a design system. It is contended that a logic model of design provides a good basis on which to construct design theories.

Chapter 11

The Intractability of Design

In this chapter the argument is presented that the various characteristics of design, which are considered to distinguish it from other problem solving activities, can be modelled in logic. This chapter therefore focuses on the issues of ill-definedness, the role of learning and the mechanism of exploration, each of which may be said to contribute to the intractable nature of design tasks. In this chapter an attempt is made to extend some of the concepts developed in previous chapters to demonstrate their general applicability. This chapter is intended to be speculative and discursive—suggesting avenues for further research. As an introduction some assumptions about the place of logic are reinforced.

The Ubiquity of Logic in Design

An assumption underlying this book is that, irrespective of the processes by which humans make decisions, important aspects of design can be *modelled* as logical processes. (This idea is also argued elsewhere [Coyne and Gero, 1986; Coyne et al, 1987; Coyne et al, 1988; Gero and Coyne, 1985]). One of the major lessons from expert systems is that judgements often considered intuitive, idiosyncratic and even capricious can be simulated mechanistically. There are rules of common sense, judgement and even style (Simon, 1975); and these rules can constitute the axioms of a logical system. In logic there is no stipulation that the axioms have to reflect reality. A system may even give the appearance of denying the canons of common sense. This is because logic can constitute a meta-language by which other 'logics' are defined. One example is 'non-monotonic logics', but it is even possible to devise 'nonsense logics' such as one which abrogates the *modus ponens* rule:

$$(X \wedge (X \rightarrow Y)) \rightarrow \sim Y$$

Informally, this system would allow a statement such as: if it is raining and rain implies that you should carry an umbrella, then do *not* carry an umbrella. All kinds of apparently irrational behaviour is 'logical' in a system which has as an axiom to do the opposite to what you *should* do.

The consistency between theorems and axioms is often obscured until the system is observed at the right meta-level. In this example it is necessary to look for consistency at the level of the resolution rules (or metarules) as given in Chapter 3.

Even if behaviour which is often regarded as outside logic can be simulated by logical systems, what of the acquisition of that knowledge? Popper (1972) intimates that the acquisition of knowledge stands, somehow, outside the processes of logic.

In his paper entitled 'Does scientific discovery have a logic?' Simon (1973b) refutes Popper's reference to the 'irrational element' and 'creative intuition' by which the process of scientific discovery is said to proceed. Simon contends that it is possible to construct a normative theory or logic of discovery processes. This theory is less well developed than that of problem solving and hypothesis testing, but there have been sufficient practical developments, in the form of computer programs which appear to engage in discovery and learning, to hint of theoretical developments.

Popper's comments about the inadequacy of *deduction* as a model of *induction* is a question of levels. Just as 'raw' logical *deduction* is an inadequate model of design, it can, however, be employed to *describe* generative processes. Logic is a meta-language with which a generative system can be defined. The assumption is therefore that a body of knowledge can be brought to bear by which new knowledge is discovered from observation, and that this can be modelled in logic.

Some of the limitations of logic as a modelling medium for design were discussed in Chapter 3. One of the important assumptions of logic is that of monotonicity. This mode of reasoning appears to differ considerably from that represented in logic systems and as discussed in this book. It should be noted, however, that attempts to model 'enhanced logics' occur within a computing environment involving normative forms of mathematics and logic (Doyle, 1981b).

Ill-Definedness in Design

That characteristic of design which has received the greatest attention in this book (and within the theory of problem solving in general) is the control issue. Design shares with many domains the combinatorial and search problems. The number of intermediate states along the path to a solution becomes too large to explore with reasonable time and computational resources. Further knowledge has to be introduced into the process to control search. This issue has been considered in the previous chapters.

There are other considerations, however, some of which are common to most real-world tasks, but which are considered to define the character of design. These were introduced in Chapter 2 and include the notion of ill-definedness.

The distinction is often made between design processes and those which are employed in such tasks as game playing. Designing a house is an ill-structured task and playing a game of noughts and crosses is well-structured. This distinction has been taken by some theorists to imply that it is therefore inappropriate to apply problem solving methods to design, and that the resulting theory even leads to a simplistic view of design which is socially reprehensible (Rittel and Webber, 1974).

Ill-definedness refers to the uncertainty with which a problem is formulated. Once a design system is adequately structured (as a production system, for example) it only remains to activate the system. In a linguistic model of design the definition of the system involves establishing a vocabulary set, defining the grammar, establishing what the artifact is to mean, and devising methods for guiding the generative process. This has a bearing on representation, interpretation, grammar and goals, in particular. So these will each be discussed below.

There are three distinctions that can be made regarding the ill-definedness of the components of a design system: that which cannot be known; that which is simply unknown; and the multifaceted nature of the knowledge. Design may be the kind of task which is the sole prerogative of the human by virtue of the fact that design knowledge of any consequence cannot be externalized. In this view design is an act of the will and therefore beyond the scope of deterministic processes. The assumption outlined in the previous section above (and which is well-supported by a substantial number of design theorists) runs counter to this view. The second issue is that the formulation of any particular design system is made difficult by the fact that design is an information-rich and a knowledge-rich activity, and not everything that is relevant to a task is generally known. The vast banks of knowledge required for design have yet to be filled. This is an acquisition problem. (It is becoming less of a storage problem.) Finally, the formulation of the problem changes from one design task to the next and, more significantly, during the same task, to reflect the multiplicity of roles assumed by the components of a partial design. These issues affect the components of a design system in various ways, and they will also be considered below.

Modes of Representation and Interpretation

Here we consider how the problem of ill-definedness impinges on the nature of design vocabularies, and the nature of artifacts. It is also a semantic problem. The vocabulary and its interpretation may be unknown or subject to change for different purposes. One manifestation of this is in the different descriptive understanding assumed by various players in the design process. For example, a brick wall may be regarded by some as a homogeneous medium for withstanding certain forces. For another purpose it may be part of a continuous enclosure and have no meaning if considered in isolation. For another purpose it may be a symbol of solidity, or merely an object to be measured and costed. This difference of purpose implies the need for temporary descriptive structures that can be assembled and reassembled for different purposes. The multiplicity of roles assumed by components are partially addressed by frame-based systems.

The issue of the wholeness and discreteness of parts in transient design descriptions for CAD systems is considered by Bijl (1985a), and the representation of knowledge in frame-based systems is motivated partly by a recognition of such issues (Minsky, 1975; Manago and Gero, 1986).

Grammars

The problem of poor definition in the case of grammars is even less well understood. A grammar may be unknown or changing. This is where differences between natural language and design are most pronounced. The grammars underlying natural language (at least as modelled by phrase structure grammars) appear to be finite, reasonably stable and accepted by large numbers of natural language speakers. In contrast there appear to be many grammars of design which, as demonstrated by the vagaries of style, are subject to change and modification for different purposes.

An important part of the design task is therefore selecting or *designing* a grammar, and the constraints on this process are often dependent on the context in which the design task is formulated. The derivation of grammars is a complex issue, though it has been addressed, to some extent by research into language acquisition which will be considered briefly in a later section.

Goals

Whereas there can be many rules in a design grammar, a relatively small number will generally suffice to generate a rich and substantial (often infinite) universe of possibilities. A more vexing issue is that of the ill-definedness of design goals. This issue appears to fuel the most common criticisms levelled at mechanistic models of design.

Goals can assume different roles depending on the context of a design task. In some cases goals appear unnecessary, but are implicit in a grammar formulation. Certain grammars might be so constrained that they produce only variations of a particular theme, and any variation will do. An extreme example might be the production of wallpaper patterns, where it is sufficient that a certain design is different from the rest while conforming to a certain geometrical grammar. The final design is one of many artifacts that could have been produced. Computer art can also be seen in such a way as an exploratory medium (Leavitt, 1976; Cohen et al, 1985; Lansdown, 1985).

Goals are ubiquitous to most design endeavours, however. Goals which exist at the outset of a design task may be of the type which are implicit and difficult to articulate. Even for a sculptural work there is generally an intention by the sculptor (designer) which can be made overt. An example of a goal might be: to create something sharp and aggressive out of steel that fits into the context of an urban plaza. Another example of an ill-defined goal is that a design must be 'interesting'. The measure of 'interestingness' by which a solution can be evaluated is difficult to externalize, and it varies from person to person. This is partly a perceptual problem (Rapoport, 1982).

Apart from the issue of the *form* goals can take (also discussed in Chapter 7) there is the problem that the objectives of a design task are often not known at the outset of the design process. This does not mean that any 'solution' will suffice, but that the derivation of the goals appears to proceed as the design which meets those objectives is developed. A common case is where the qualities to be expected in the final design are unknown until it is known what is *possible*. This highlights the exploratory nature of design. Certain discoveries during the design process direct the process towards a final design. The role of exploration will be reviewed below in a later section.

The Role of Learning

Vast amounts of knowledge are required to carry out even simple design tasks. The derivation of rules, such as those discussed in the previous chapter, is a tedious task, and the formulation of large numbers of rules which are widely applicable poses a serious conceptual barrier for knowledge-based systems. Whereas there are whole books presenting rules for designers, the formalization of those rules so that they would be amenable to automation is a formidable task. Attention in artificial intelligence research is therefore focusing on the automation of knowledge acquisition, otherwise known as *induction* (Quinlan, 1979; 1982b).

Knowledge acquisition and exploration go hand in hand. In the process of discovery new things are being learned by which the exploration can continue further. Random movement through a maze is *not* exploration as nothing is learned from dead-ends and repeated cycles. Search and backtracking is a limited model of exploration. If a path is unsuccessful then it is known that that path should not be attempted again. However, when the same process is repeated from the beginning the same mistakes will be made.

Induction was introduced in Chapter 2. In science it can be defined as the derivation of theories from the observation of phenomena and the testing of predictions. In natural language it is generally referred to as language *acquisition* (Lyons, 1981) and is the derivation of knowledge by which interpretations can be made and by which utterances can be generated. More generally it can be seen as *learning*.

Learning changes the state of an organism or system to improve its performance in some way. It is important that it is the *structure* that is affected and not just the states within the system. In the case of a design system learning therefore implies creating or changing the vocabulary, grammar, interpretive knowledge and control of the system.

There are various approaches to *machine learning*. These can be characterized under headings such as: learning by examples; learning by being told; learning by introspection; and learning from experience (Langley and Carbonell, 1984). A different classification will be considered here.

The distinction between hypothesis-driven and data-driven learning is discussed by Mackenzie and Gero (1986). The most commonly understood form of learning is that in which a structure (or model) which accounts for observed phenomena is proposed, and the model is evaluated for its ability to account for observations. The hypothesis is then revised in the light of observation. In the case of data-driven learning the structure is suggested by the data. An attempt is made to induce a structure where none is imposed.

Simple learning processes based on the hypothesis-driven approach can be modelled by production systems. A description of the system which is to be modified according to what is learned constitutes the global database. The operators constitute inductive knowledge (a 'learning grammar'). Induction can also be discussed in relation to the components of a production system which are affected by the learning system.

Learning Rules for Interpretation

Descriptions of designs can be interpreted by means of inference rules. The induction of such rules has been the subject of considerable attention in machine learning.

One influential approach is that developed by Winston (1970, 1975) for inducing inference rules from examples. This can also be seen as the task of learning class descriptions from samples. The example devised by Winston is of learning the features of a simple construction, such as an arch, from positive and negative instances. The operators of the system are *generalizing* and *specializing* rules. The objective is to produce a general description, in the form of a hypothesis, that is able to account for the various ways in which a set of blocks can be arranged to form an arch, and which is specific enough to exclude 'non-arches'.

For complex descriptions this process is one of search. Hypotheses are formulated which include different combinations of descriptors and which describe all positive instances and which preclude all negative instances as they are encountered. The hypothesis so formulated constitutes the set of antecedents for a rule by which a configuration of elements is interpreted as an arch.

The problem with such a system (and learning systems in general) is that acquired knowledge cannot be completely validated (Michalski, 1983). The number of examples and counter examples with which the hypothesis can be tested is endless, and the point at which the hypothesis is considered to have sufficient utility is somewhat arbitrary.

The question of learning how to *design* an arch is a variation of the problem of learning how to interpret a description. If an arch can be recognized then presumably the normal planning methods can be applied to produce a series of actions which results in a configuration of blocks resembling an arch (Dechter and Michie, 1985). But learning the *operators* by which an arch, or any other configuration of blocks, can be produced requires the induction of a design grammar.

Learning New Grammars

The problem considered here is the induction of generative rules. The system described above attempts to address the classification issue: how to detect the characteristics by which objects can be grouped together. There are several approaches which might be adopted in order to induce generative rules.

Statistical methods have been developed for detecting common patterns amongst objects and clustering objects together, and these have some application to learning. However, statistical analysis is limited as it tends not to reveal underlying structure (Simon, 1973b).

Generative rules could be acquired by the observation of another design system, such as a human designer. While observing many state transformations the question is asked: what is the general rule being applied of which this particular rule is an instance? This involves taking transformations one at a time and observing how the system responds to different situations. This appears not to be a fruitful means of inducing grammars as human design operations are rarely divisible and observable in this way.

A more promising approach is by observing the start and end states of many different design tasks: that is, observing the contexts of design tasks and the resultant artifacts. There are two sets of unknowns in this process: the set of operators; and the path followed from one operator to another in the investigation of states. The process is somewhat simpler when the grammar is based on classification, as in natural language. The following model of learning natural language grammar is discussed by Charniak and McDermott (1985).

Phrase structure grammars are one of several formal methods of parsing which bear some resemblance to cognitive activity. A sentence has to be parsed in order to be understood. This means exploring the ways in which a string of words can be divided into categories. One of the ways in which it is thought that humans learn language serves as an example. The abbreviated sentence:

little girl drop red block

can be parsed according to the associative network of Figure 11.1. The process of acquiring a grammar is made relatively simple when an infant is given simple sentences to start with. Nouns are presented as objects, and verbs are action words. The pattern of *relation*, *agent* and *object* are categories generalized from simple sentences. The process is similar to that discussed in relation to the formation of hypotheses about rules of interpretation. More complex sentences are introduced gradually so that further categories can be assimilated.

An example of a further refinement of categories is with the phrase: *the red block*. A child soon discovers that this phrase is grammatically acceptable, whereas *red the block* is unacceptable. This suggests that *the* and *red* belong to different classes. How such a hypothesis might be formed is discussed by Berwick (1980). In human language acquisition this process takes place over a long period of time and involves trial and error. There are powerful feedback and correction mechanisms from the environment. If the

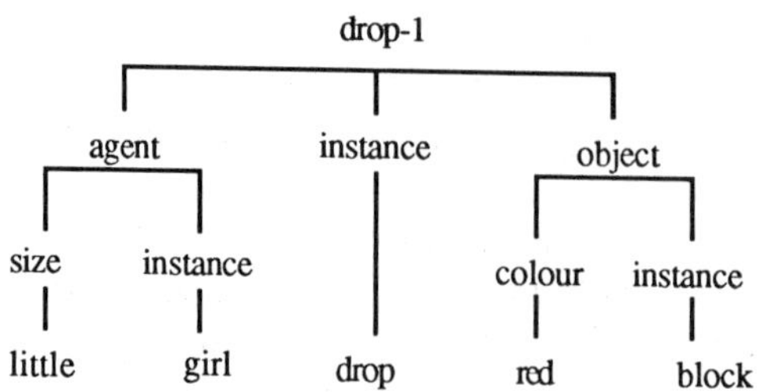

Figure 11.1. An associative network (as a parse tree) by which a simple sentence is broken down into phrase structure rules.

child makes an utterance from its own mistaken grammar it will either be corrected, or the failure in understanding will imply that that particular grammatical pattern (hypothesis) has failed and another one is required. The theoretical basis of these processes is explored by Anderson (1977).

It is possible that these processes can be applied to the acquisition of design grammars. For example, several house designs which belong to the same language can be analyzed to discover commonly occurring attributes such as spatial groupings of components. This could effectively produce parsing rules which constitute hypotheses. An example might be a set of common spatial subdivisions which can be formalized as a grammar:

food-area	→	kitchen, dining
entertaining	→	living, dining
sleeping	→	hall, bedrooms, bathroom
visitor-area	→	hall, entry, living
service	→	kitchen, laundry, back-door
semi-private	→	visitors, entertaining
private	→	sleeping, food, service
house	→	semi-private, private

In order to design a house, therefore, the term *house* is expanded according to the grouping of its components. The rules embodying geometry would be more subtle and complex, and there would be greater difficulty in forming hypotheses about them, however.

One useful approach is demonstrated by a system for learning a grammar appropriate to generating floor plans. The system is developed by Mackenzie (1987). The system induces a *grammar* for generating simple floor plans from a set of existing plans. Several assumptions underlie the operation of the system. The first assumption is that a design can be described in terms of geometrically orthogonal relationships. Second, the system assumes that it is *not* concerned with dimensions of spaces in describing designs. Third, there is the assumption that designs can be generated through actions that split spaces in a north-south or east-west direction. These spaces can be further split in a recursive fashion. Finally, there is the assumption that this system of actions can be employed to account for the commonalities between plans. It can effectively form the basis for a set of actions that defines a space of designs.

The system developed by Mackenzie is given a set of pre-existing designs. The strategy embedded in the system is to first find an appropriate *parse tree* for each design. There may be many possible trees that could be produced, that is, there may be many ways that the design could be successively split. So the system uses certain heuristics to find the 'best' tree. One heuristic is to favour generative procedures that combine simple shapes in simple ways. Several trees may be generated for each design. The task is then to generalize on parse trees—that is, refine the sequences and partial sequences of actions to a more succinct but general set of actions. Where no useful generalizations can be made then alternative parse trees are generated. The generalizing mechanism is based on the methods of Fu and Booth (1975) for inducing relational 'tree grammars'.

Mackenzie has applied the method to the induction of a grammar for defining a 'language' of Palladian villa plans, and also floor plans for standard project homes. An entire grammar constitutes a hypothesis, the testing of which is accomplished by attempting to employ it in re-generating known designs. The hypothesis could then be subject to further testing and refinement. Formulating and refining grammatical hypotheses presumably requires domain dependent knowledge that embodies assumptions about what to look for in example designs: such as spatial organization, perimeter configurations, common adjacencies, common connections, fenestration, and room proportions. The representation of this kind of design knowledge is an important research area that poses considerable challenge.

Improving Control

Just as common properties of forms can be detected to induce categories of attributes of artifacts, so patterns can be detected in different *control instances*. Learning from commonalities between successful sequences of rule firings in production systems can result in the better organization of rules. The schedule illustrated in Figure 10.15, for example, could be the product of induction over several cases where it was discovered that there were recurrent patterns of rule firing. This could bring about the refinement of a schedule after repeated use, resulting in more efficient control.

Another manifestation of control improvement would be in learning from failure. An ideal system would be one in which a system was able to learn from its experiences of backtracking on failure, such that a planning rule could be induced by which recurring conflicts are resolved. Substantial developments in theories of learning are required in order to tackle such tasks. Other approaches to enhancing control by means of learning are described by Langley and Carbonell (1984).

Exploration

Where goals are not fully specified the search for criteria by which a design can be evaluated is just as important as the search for a suitable design.

Searching for Goals

The search for design goals is a common activity that is often made explicit in design practice. A search space of possible designs is often explored prior to the investment of resources on detailed design work. Several schematic designs may be produced from a provisional specification. Representative schemes are evaluated, and the desirable characteristics of the best solutions are effectively classified so as to provide a detailed brief for subsequent designs. This process occurs both formally (for example, in an 'ideas competition') and at the detailed level of design. It is not until a designer has explored different schemes that interesting possibilities present themselves as useful goals to aim for.

This is a common activity of human intelligence and has parallels in scientific research. A system called AM (Lenat, 1978; 1982), and a later variant called EURISKO, is intended to engage in discovering interesting new concepts in elementary mathematics. The system is open-ended: a theorem *proposer* rather than a theorem *prover*. The initial goal is therefore ill-defined: to maximize the 'interestingness' value of what is being worked on at the moment. The process is guided by relatively general rules of thumb which direct the system to define and study the most useful thing next. One of the rules for defining 'interestingness' is described informally as follows (Lenat , 1982):

if two apparently disparate parts of the work are suddenly recognized as being very closely related
then that increases the interestingness of both parts and of the whole work as well.

This is an example of a search principle that appears to have universal applicability. The justification for this particular heuristic is given by Lenat (1982, p. 1096):

> This explains the eternal popularity of the 'recurrent theme' in all genres of literature and cinema. It explains the impact of having a single melody recur frequently but with slight differences each time (the concept of 'musical variations'). Dickens' success is due in no small measure to his mastery of this heuristic (ie, 'coincidence'): the reader is always astonished and pleased when two separate characters are discovered to be one and the same person.

Other guides can also be employed for design exploration, such as approximation to certain patterns of spatial organization, rules about unity and variety (Stiny and Gips, 1978), or conformity to principles such as those of Appleton (1975): that a favourable environment is one that appears to meet the primeval needs of prospect and refuge.

As well as learning from their successes, designers also appear to learn from failure. Mostow (1984, p. 25) has pointed out that a simple search algorithm merely learns not to repeat an unsuccessful path, but a more intelligent algorithm would use what it learned from one failure to avoid a larger class of similar failures. It appears that designers learn a great deal about a problem from their first unsuccessful attempts to solve it, and they use this knowledge to focus rapidly on a solution. In order to exploit this type of knowledge it is necessary to find out what is learned by failure and how it is learned. This aspect of exploration is, as yet, largely unexplored—although a method of search known as *context dependent backtracking* hints at what can be done (Doyle, 1981a).

Exploration and Meta-Grammars

Learning is basically the task of discovering commonalities between instances and forming generalizations from these observations. Instances can be of any repeated event or classifiable group of objects, such as: descriptions of artifacts; states in the development of descriptions; sequential plans; and schedules. A knowledge-based approach in which control levels are made explicit can facilitate the learning of such patterns. One of the ways in which the exploratory nature of design could be demonstrated with relation to the system explained in the previous two chapters is presented here.

An ill-defined goal set might be one in which only some of the desired connections between spaces are defined. The system then generates various alternative spatial layouts satisfying these constraints. It is then necessary for the system to look for patterns within the spatial configurations (a learning set) which suggest, or come close to, certain preferred models of spatial organization, such as grid patterns, corridor systems and axial systems. Heuristics are employed to select the most interesting or otherwise appropriate system of organization observed in the learning set. The constraints imposed by this method of organization constitute a revised specification (context) for which further designs are generated.

This can be a recursive process where the generation of plans suggest further refinements of the context. The tendency in this example, is therefore to emphasize and build upon those attributes of a plan which are considered to lead towards good patterns of organization, and to negate tendencies towards disorder.

Similar activities could also be pursued at the control level. This could involve a search for the 'interestingness' or organizational advantage of certain sequential plans. Just as certain procedures in the making of a clay vase are known to produce 'interesting' results, so certain strategies in design can have a strong bearing on the outcome: for example, the selection of the medium in which the design process is to be externalized; or the order in which certain actions are considered. A simple case is where it is considered that actions which locate spaces with similar functions should be performed within close succession to one another. If a sequential plan appears to exhibit this property then it should be investigated before a plan in which this grouping of actions does not occur. In a richer system than that described here, therefore, there should be some provision for the exploration of design possibilities occurring at various levels of abstraction.

Future Directions

The discussion above suggests several areas of research by which the proposed model can be enhanced. Attention needs to be focussed on the discovery aspect of design activity, that is, the tentative exploration which leads to the definition of goals. Design goals are as much the product of a determination of what is possible as they are a statement of intent. In linguistic terms this exploration amounts to a concurrent search for meaning as well as a search for the artifact which conveys that meaning.

It is also necessary to further investigate the intuitively appealing notion that some advantage is provided by the articulation of generative grammars into abstractions which operate on both form and process as proposed by the model described in this book.

So far in this chapter we have considered the acquisition of knowledge as *rules*. Other models of how knowledge can be stored and rendered operable in design systems constitute important research topics. There is a strong argument for dispensing with the idea of *knowledge as rules* altogether. In extracting knowledge (as rules) from examples (and then discarding the examples) certain information is lost. An alternative approach is to store representations of existing designs and reason with them 'analogically'. This means finding similarities between the current design problem and a store of existing designs. Put simply, the idea is to make decisions by looking for patterns in data, a process considered to closely match human cognitive processes (Dreyfus and Dreyfus, 1986). The important points about this process are (i) the recognition of computer models that are more soundly based on what we understand of human cognition, and (ii) the ability of a system to 'learn' and reason by memorizing past 'design episodes'.

Two major approaches to *analogical reasoning* can be identified. The first is where we reason from design 'episodes' and attempt to find a match with the current problem. This is accomplished with the aid of a 'black box' metric (Stanfill and Waltz, 1986). The second approach is to reason from stored explanations of certain decisions made in previous design tasks (Schank, 1982, 1986; Mitchell et al, 1986, Dejong and Mooney, 1986). A direct application of the idea to design has been developed by Navinchandra and Sriram (Navinchandra, 1987; Navinchandra and Sriram, 1987) in the development of the CYCLOPS design system. A similar approach is developed in EDISON, an engineering design 'invention' system (Dyer et al, 1986). In this system generic designs (prototypes) are organized and indexed in an 'episodic memory'. The system selects designs from memory and attempts to create novel devices by altering them. Some of these generic designs may end up being used quite differently from their intended purpose, such as using an umbrella as the basis of a new kind of door. At a particular level of abstraction we can describe a door as functioning to block the passage of physical objects. An umbrella can also be so described. EDISON makes use of a system of indexing where these levels of abstract description are accessed easily to form links between problems and prototypes.

Similar ideas are developed by Maher and Zhao (1987) for the design of building structures 'from experience' and Murthy and Addanki (1987) have developed a system (PROMPT) for selecting prototypes (standard cross sections for structural members) and modifying them to create 'novel' profiles. Discovering the right analogies to draw and modifying prototypes is a very sophisticated form of reasoning. These ideas are at an early stage of development and their realization represents an important step in the development of knowledge-based design systems.

Certain kinds of analogical reasoning represent attempts to closely model neural processes. Although these applications of 'analogical reasoning' are computationally expensive, they are becoming more feasible as computer power increases. These approaches also lend themselves to new kinds of computer architecture, such as those based on parallelism (McClelland and Rumelhart, 1986).

Summary

In order to demonstrate the utility of a logic-based view of design the discussion has touched on those areas of design considered to be most characteristic and most difficult, namely: that design tasks are ill-defined; and that design is exploratory in nature. Apparent ill-definedness can be made explicit and this explicit representation can be modelled in logic, particularly when the same principles that are applied to the generation of a design are applied to the creation of the components of a design system. These processes include: those by which interpretive rules and grammars are induced; and those by which exploration leads to the specification of a design task.

The proposed model affords an environment in which some of these features of design can be investigated. Just as there are grammars which manipulate form, and meta-grammars which operate on object grammars, it may also be possible to define grammars which change the structure of other grammars. By extending the notion of generative grammars in design, in the manner proposed, possibilities are opened up for modelling complex design processes.

References

Aida, H., Tanaka, H. and Moto-Oka, T. (1983). A Prolog extension for handling negative knowledge, *New Generation Computing*, Vol.1, No.1, pp.87-91.

Akin, O. (1978). How do architects design? *Artificial Intelligence and Pattern Recognition in Computer Aided Design*, ed. J-C. Latombe, Proceedings of IFIP Working Conference, Grenoble, France, North-Holland, Amsterdam, pp.65-119.

Akin, O. (1979). *Models of Architectural Knowledge: An Information Processing View of Architectural Design*, PhD Thesis, Carnegie-Mellon University, Pittsburgh.

Akin, O. (1984). Psychology of Architectural Design, Unpublished manuscript, Department of Architecture, Carnegie-Mellon University, Pittsburgh.

Akiner, T. (1985a). *TOPOLOGY1: A System That Reasons About Objects and Spaces in Buildings*, PhD Thesis, Sydney University, Sydney.

Akiner, T. (1985b). Topology-1: a reasoning system for object and space modeling via knowledge engineering, *Proceedings of ASME Design Engineering Division Conference*, The American Society of Mechanical Engineers, New York, pp.1-5.

Alexander, C. (1964). *Notes on the Synthesis of Form*, Harvard University Press, Cambridge, Massachusetts.

Alexander, C. (1972). The city is not a tree, *Human Identity in the Urban Environment*, eds G. Bell, and J. Tyrwhitt, Pelican, Harmondsworth, Middlesex, pp.401-428.

Alexander, C. (1977). *A Pattern Language*, Oxford University Press, London.

Alexander, C., Ishikawa, S. and Silverstein, M. (1968). *A Pattern Language that Generates Multi-Service Centres*, Center for Environmental Structure, Berkeley, California.

Alexander, C. and Poyner, B. (1970). The atoms of environmental structure, *Emerging Methods in Environmental Design and Planning*, ed. G.T. Moore, MIT Press, Cambridge, Massachusetts, pp.308-321.

Allwood, R.J. and Stewart, D.J. (1984). *Interim Report on Expert System Shells Evaluation for Construction Industry Applications*, Loughborough University, Loughborough.

Amble, T. (1987). *Logic Programming and Knowledge Engineering*, Addison Wesley, Wokingham, England.

Anderson, J.R. (1977). Induction of augmented transition networks, *Cognitive Science*, Vol.1, No.2, pp.125-157.

Appleton, J. (1975). *The Experience of Landscape*, Wiley, London.

Arbab, F. and Wing, J.M. (1985). Geometric reasoning: a new paradigm for processing geometric reasoning, *IFIP WG5.2 Working Conference on Design Theory in CAD*, ed. H. Yoshikawa, Tokyo University, Tokyo, pp.107-121.

Archer, B.L. (1969). The structure of the design process, *Design Methods in Architecture,* eds. G. Broadbent, and A.Ward, Lund Humphries, London.

Archer, B.L. (1970). An overview of the structure of the design process, *Emerging Methods in Environmental Design and Planning*, ed. G.T. Moore, MIT Press, Cambridge, Massachusetts, pp.285-307.

Balachandran, M. (1988). *A Model for Knowledge-Based Design Optimization*, PhD Thesis, Department of Architectural Science, University of Sydney, Sydney.

Balachandran, M. and Gero, J.S. (1986). Dimensioning of architectural floor plans under conflicting objectives, *Working Paper*, Architectural Computing Unit, University of Sydney, Sydney.

Ballard, D. and Brown, C. (1982). *Computer Vision* (selected chapters), Prentice Hall, New Jersey.

Balzer, R., Erman, L.D., London, P.E. and Williams, C. (1980). HEARSAY-III: A domain-independent framework for expert systems, *Proceedings of the First Annual National Conference on AI (AAAI)*, Stanford University, Stanford, California, pp.108-110.

Barr, A. and Feigenbaum, E.A. (1981). *The Handbook of Artificial Intelligence Vol.I*, Pitman Books, London.

Berger, S.R. (1980). Artificial intelligence and its impact on computer-aided design, *Design Studies*, Vol.1, No.3, pp.166-171.

Berwick, R.C. (1980). Computational analogues of constraints on grammars: a model of syntactic acquisition, *Proceedings of 18th Conference of the Association for Computational Linguistics*, Association for Computational Linguistics, pp.49-53.

Bijl, A. (1984). Non-prescriptive computing technology for designers, *Design Policy Conference Proceedings*, Vol.6, Design Council, London, pp.62-66.

Bijl, A. (1985a). An approach to design theory, *IFIP WG5.2 Working Conference on Design Theory in CAD*, ed. H. Yoshikawa, Tokyo University, Tokyo, pp.1-23.

Bijl, A. (1985b). A CAD logic modelling environment, *Architectural Science Review*, Vol.28, No.4, pp.104-114.

Bloch, C.J. (1979). Catalogue of small rectangular plans, *Environment and Planning B*, Vol.6, pp.155-190.

Bobrow, D.G. and Collins, A. (1975). *Representation and Understanding*, Academic Press, New York.

Bramer, M.A. (1979). A survey and critical review of expert systems research, *Expert Systems in the Micro-Electronic Age*, Edinburgh University Press, Edinburgh, pp.3-29.

Bratko, I.B. (1986). *Prolog Programming for Artificial Intelligence*, Addison Wesley, Wokingham, England.

Broadbent, G. (1969). Meaning into architecture, *Meaning in Architecture*, eds C. Jencks and G. Baird, Braziller, New York, pp.51-75.

Broadbent, G. (1977). A plain man's guide to the theory of signs in architecture, *Architectural Design*, July/August, pp.474-482.

Broadbent, G. (1979). Design and theory building, *Design Methods and Theories*, Vol.13, No.3/4, pp.103-107.

Broadbent, G. (1981). *Design in Architecture*, Wiley, London.

Bronowski, J. (1966). The logic of the mind, *American Scientist*, Vol.54, No.1, pp.1-14.

Brown, H., Tong, C. and Foyster, G. (1983). Palladio: an exploratory environment for circuit design, *Research Paper*, Department of Computer Science, Stanford University, Stanford, California.

Buchanan, B.G. (1982). New research on expert systems, *Machine Intelligence 10*, eds J.E. Hayes and D. Michie, Wiley, London, pp.269-299.

Buchanan, B.G. and Shortliffe, E.H. (eds) (1984). *Rule-Based Expert Systems*, Addison-Wesley, Reading, Massachusetts.

Charniak, E. and McDermott, D. (1985). *Introduction to Artificial Intelligence*, Addison-Wesley, Reading, Massachusetts.

Chomsky, N. (1957). *Syntactic Structures*, The Hague, Mouton.

Chomsky, N. (1963). Formal properties of grammars, *Handbook of Mathematical Psychology*, Vol.2, eds R. Luce, D. Bush and E. Galanter, Wiley, New York, pp.323-418.

Chomsky, N. (1971). Deep structure, surface structure and semantic interpretation, *Semantics*, eds D. Steinberg and L. Jakobovits, Cambridge University Press, Cambridge, pp.183-216.

Chomsky, N. (1975). *The Logical Structure of Linguistic Theory*, Plenum Press, New York.

Christiansen, A.D. (1985). The history of planning methodology: an annotated bibliography, *SIGART Newsletter*, October, No.94, pp.44-46.

Church, A. (1936). An unsolvable problem of elementary number theory, *American Journal of Mathematics*, Vol.58, pp.345-363.

Churchman, C.W. (1967). Wicked problems, *Management Science*, Vol.4, No.14, December, pp.B-141 and B-142.

Churchman, C.W. (1971). *The Design of Inquiring Systems*, Basic Books, New York.

Clark, K.L. (1978). Negation as failure, *Logic and Databases*, eds H. Gallaire and J. Minker, Plenum Press, New York, pp.293-322.

Clark, K.L. and McCabe, F.G. (1982). PROLOG: A language for implementing expert systems, *Machine Intelligence 10*, eds J.E. Hayes, D. Michie, Y-H. Pao, Wiley, London.

Clark, K.L. and McCabe, F.G. (1984). *Micro-PROLOG: Programming in Logic*, Prentice-Hall, New Jersey.

Clocksin, W.F. and Mellish, C.S. (1981) *Programming in Prolog*, Springer-Verlag, Berlin.

Cluster Titles Committee, (1979). *Model Cluster Code*, Department of Local Government, Melbourne.

Coelho, H., Cotta, J.C. and Pereira, L.M. (1980). *How to Solve it with Prolog*, Laboratorio Nacional de Engenharia Civil, Lisbon.

Cohen, H., Cohen, B. and Nii, P. (1985). *The First Artificial Intelligence Coloring Book*, Kaufmann, Oxford, p.11.

Cohen, P.R. and Feigenbaum, E.A. (1982). *The Handbook of Artificial Intelligence Vol.III,* Pitman, London.

Colmerauer, A., Kanovi, H., Pasero, R. and Roussel, P. (1973). *Un systeme de communication homme-machine en Francais*, Groupe Intelligence Artificielle, Universite d'Aix Marseille, Marseille.

Cowan, H.J. (1973). *Dictionary of Architectural Science*, Applied Science, Barking, Essex.

Coyne, R.D. and Gero, J.S. (1986). Semantics and the organization of knowledge in design, *Design Computing*, Vol.1, No.1, pp.68-89.

Coyne, R.D., Rosenman, M.A., Radford, A.D. and Gero, J.S. (1987). Innovation and creativity in knowledge-based CAD, *Expert Systems in Computer-Aided Design*, Gero, J.S. (ed.) North-Holland, Amsterdam, pp.435-465.

Coyne, R.D., Rosenman, M.A., Radford, A.D., Balachandran, M. and Gero, J.S. (1988). *Knowledge-Based Design Systems*, Addison Wesley, Reading Massachusetts (forthcoming).

Cross, N. (1985). Styles of learning, designing and computing, *Design Studies*, Vol.6, No.3, pp.157-162.

Cross, N., Naughton, J. and Walkers, D. (1981). Design method and scientific method, *Design:Science:Method*, eds R. Jacques and J.A. Powell, Westbury, Guildford, pp.18-29.

Darke, J. (1979). The primary generator and the design process, *Design Studies*, Vol.1, No.1, pp.36-44.

Davis, R. (1980a). Meta-rules: reasoning about control, *Artificial Intelligence*, Vol.15, pp.179-222.

Davis, R. (1980b). Content reference: reasoning about rules, *Artificial Intelligence*, Vol.15, pp.223-239.

Davis, R. (1982). Expert systems: where are we? and where do we go from here? *The AI Magazine*, Spring, 1982, pp.3-22.

Davis, R. (1977). Generalised procedure calling of content-directed invocation, *SIGPLAN Notices*, Vol.12, No.8, pp.45-54.

Davis, R. and King, J. (1977). An overview of production systems, *Machine Intelligence 8*, eds Elcock and Michie, Ellis Horwood, Chichester, pp.300-332.

Dechter, R. and Michie, D. (1985). Induction of plans, *Research Paper*, The Turing Institute, Glasgow.

de Kleer, J. (1986). An assumption-based truth maintenance system, *Artificial Intelligence*, Vol.28, pp.127-162

Dejong, G. and Mooney, R. (1986). Explanation-based learning: an alternative view, *Machine Learning I*, Vol.1, No.2, pp.70-73.

DeLong, H. (1971). Unsolved problems in arithmetic, *Scientific American*, Vol.224, No.3, pp.50-60.

Dietterich, T.G. and Buchanan, B.G. (1981). The role of the critic in learning systems, *Research Paper*, Stanford University, Stanford, California.

Dietterich, T.G, and Ullman, D.G. (1987). FORLOG: a logic-based architecture for design, in J.S. Gero (ed.) *Expert Systems in Computer-Aided Design*, North-Holland, Amsterdam, pp.1-17.

Dincbas, M. (1980). A knowledge-based expert system for automatic analysis and synthesis in CAD, *Information Processing 80*, ed. S.H. Lavington, North-Holland, Amsterdam, pp.705-710.

Doyle, J. (1981a). A truth maintenance system, *Readings in Artificial Intelligence*, eds B.L. Webber and N.J. Nilsson, Tioga, Palo Alto, California, pp.496-516.

Doyle, J. (1981b). Three short essays on decisions, reasons and logics, *Research Paper*, Department of Computer Science, Stanford University, Stanford, California.

Dreyfus, H. and Dreyfus, S. (1984). Mindless machines, *The Sciences*, November/December, pp.18-22.

Dreyfus, H. and Dreyfus, S. (1986). Why computers may never think like people?, *Technology Review*, January, pp.41-61.

Duda, R.O., Hart, P.E. and Nilsson, N.J. (1976). Subjective Bayesian methods for rule-based inference systems, *AFIPS Conference Proceedings*, Vol.45, Artificial Intelligence Center, Technical Note 124, pp.1075-1082.

Dyer, M.G., Flowers, M. and Hodges, J. (1986). EDISON: an engineering design invention system operating naively, *Artificial Intelligence in Engineering*, Vol.1, No.1, pp.36-44.

Earl, C.F. (1977). A note on the generation of rectangular dissections, *Environment and Planning B*, Vol.4, pp.241-246.

Earl, C.F. (1985). Creating design worlds, *Research Paper*, Centre for Configurational Studies, Open University, Milton Keynes, Buckinghamshire.

Earl, C.F. (1987). Shape grammars and the generation of designs, in Rooney, J. and Steadman, P. (eds) *Principles of Computer-Aided Design*, Pitman, London, pp.297-315

Eastman, C.M. (1973). Automated space planning, *Artificial Intelligence*, Vol.4, pp.41-64.

Eco, U. (1984). *Semiotics and the Philosophy of Language*, Macmillan, London.

Erman, L.D., Hayes-Roth, F., Lesser, V.R. and Reddy, D.R. (1980). The Hearsay-II speech understanding system: integrating knowledge to resolve uncertainty, *Computing Surveys*, Vol.12, No.2.

Erman, L.D., London, P.E., Fickas, S.F. (1981). The design and an example use of HEARSAY-III, *Proceedings of IJCAI 7*, pp.409-415.

Feibleman, J. (1970). *An Introduction to the Philosophy of Charles S. Pierce*, MIT Press, Cambridge, Massachusetts.

Feigenbaum, E.A. (1979). Themes and case studies of knowledge engineering, *Expert Systems in the Microelectronic Age*, ed. D. Michie, Edinburgh University Press, Edinburgh, pp.3-25.

Fikes, R. and Kehler, T. (1985). The role of frame-based representation in reasoning, *Communication of the ACM*, Vol.28, No.9, pp.904-920.

Fikes, R.E. and Nilsson, N.J. (1971). STRIPS: A new approach to the application of theorem proving to problem solving, *Artificial Intelligence*, Vol.2, No.3/4, pp. 189-208.

Flemming, U. (1978). Wall representations of rectangular dissections and their use in automated space allocations, *Environment and Planning B*, Vol.5, pp.215-232.

Flemming, U. (1985). A generative expert system for the design of building layouts, *Research Paper*, Department of Architecture, Carnegie-Mellon University, Pittsburgh.

Fu, K.S. and Booth, K.L. (1975). Grammatical inference: introduction and survey, Parts 1 and 2, *IEEE Trans Sys. Man. Cybern,* SMC-5, Part 1: pp.95-111, Part 2: pp.409-423.

Fuchi, K. (1983). The direction the FGCS Project will take, *New Generation Computing*, Vol.1, pp.3-9.

Garey, M.R. and Johnson, D.S. (1979). *Computers and Intractability: A Guide to the Theory of NP-Completeness*, Freeman, San Francisco.

Garvey, T.D., Lowrance, J.D. and Fischler, M.A. (1981). An inference technique for integrating knowledge from disparate sources, *Proceedings of IJCAI 7*, pp.319-325.

Gaschnig, J. (1982). Application of the PROSPECTOR system to geological exploration problems, *Machine Intelligence 10*, eds J.E. Hayes, D. Michie and Y-H. Pao, Wiley, London, pp.301-323.

Genesereth, M.R. and Ginsberg, M.L. (1985). Logic programming, *Communication of the ACM*, Vol.28, No.9, pp.933-941.

Genesereth, M.R. and Smith, D.E. (1983). An overview of meta-level architecture, *Research Paper*, Department of Computer Science, Stanford University, Stanford, California.

Gero, J.S. and Coyne, R.D. (1984). The place of expert systems in architecture, *CAD84*, Butterworths, Guildford, pp.529-546.

Gips, J. and Stiny, G. (1980). Production systems and grammars: a uniform characterisation, *Environment and Planning B*, Vol.7, pp.399-408.

Gödel, K. (1931). Uber formal unentscheidbare satze der *Principia Mathematica* und verwandter systeme, I. *Monatshefte fur Mathematik und Physik*, Vol.38, pp.173-198.

Gödel, K. (1962). *On Formally Unprovable Propositions*, Basic Books, New York.

Green, C. (1969). Application of theorem proving to problem solving, *Proceedings of IJCAI 1*, pp.219-239.

Hammond, P. (1982). *Logic Programming for Expert Systems*, Technical Report: DOC 82/4, Imperial College of Science and Technology, London.

Hammond, P. and Sergot, M. (1983). *A PROLOG Shell for Logic Based Expert Systems*, Imperial College of Science and Technology, London.

Hawkes, T. (1977). *Structuralism and Semiotics*, Methuen, London.

Hayes-Roth, F., Waterman, D.A. and Lenat, D.B. (eds) (1983). *Building Expert Systems*, Addison-Wesley, Reading, Massachusetts.

Hayes-Roth, F. (1984). The knowledge-based expert system: a tutorial, *Computer*, September, pp.11-28.

Hayes-Roth, F. and Lesser, V.R. (1977). Focus of attention in the Hearsay-II System, *Proceedings of IJCAI 5*, pp.27-35.

Hayes-Roth, B. and Hayes-Roth, B. (1979). A cognitive model of planning, *Cognitive Science*, Vol.3, No.4, pp.275-309.

Hayes-Roth, B. (1985). A blackboard architecture for control, *Artificial Intelligence*, Vol.26, pp.251-321.

Heath, T. (1984). *Method in Architecture*, Wiley, Chichester.

Hillier, B., Musgrove, J. and O'Sullivan, O. (1972). Knowledge and design, *Environmental Design: Research and Practice*, ed. W.J. Mitchell, University of California, Los Angeles, California, pp.29.3.1-29.3.14.

Hofstadter, D.R. (1982). *Gödel, Escher, Bach: An Eternal Golden Braid*, Penguin, Harmondsworth, Middlesex.

Hogger, C.J. (1982). Concurrent logic programming, *Logic Programming*, eds K.L. Clark and S-A. Tarnlund, Academic Press, London, pp.199-212.

Hogger, C.J. (1984). *Introduction to Logic Programming*, Academic Press, London.

Hutchinson, P. (1985). *An Expert System for the Selection of Earth Retaining Structures*, MBdgSc Thesis, Department of Architectural Science, University of Sydney, Sydney.

Jencks, C. (1969). Semiology and architecture, *Meaning in Architecture*, eds C. Jencks and G. Baird, Braziller, New York, pp. 11-25.

Jencks, C. (1981). *The Language of Post-Modern Architecture*, Academy Editions, London.

Kalay, Y.E. (1985). Redefining the role of computers in architecture: from drafting (modelling tools to knowledge-based design assistants), *Computer-Aided Design*, Vol.17, No.7, pp.319-328.

Koning, H. and Eizenberg, J. (1981). The language of the prairie: Frank Lloyd Wright's prairie houses, *Environment and Planning B*, Vol.8, pp.295-323.

Konolige, K. (1982). An information-theoretic approach to subjective Bayesian inference in rule-based systems, *Research paper,* SRI International, Menlo Park, California.

Koopmans, T.C. and Beckman, N. (1957). Assignment problems and the location of economic activities, *Econometrica*, Vol.25, No.1, pp.53-76.

Kowalski, R.A. (1979). *Logic for Problem Solving*, North Holland, Amsterdam.

Kowalski, R.A. (1981a). Prolog as a logic programming language, *Research Report No: Doc 81/26*, July, Imperial College, London.

Kowalski, R.A. (1981b). Logic as a database language, *Research Report 82/25*, Imperial College, London.

Krishnamurti, R. (1980). The arithmetic of shapes, *Environment and Planning B*, Vol.7, pp.463-484.

Krishnamurti, R. (1981). The construction of shapes, *Environment and Planning B*, Vol.8, pp.5-40.

Krishnamurti, R. (1985). Representing design knowledge, *Research Paper*, EdCAAD, University of Edinburgh, Edinburgh.

Krishnamurti, R. and Giraud, C. (1984). Towards a shape editor, *Research Paper*, EdCAAD, University of Edinburgh, Edinburgh.

Kuhn, T.S. (1970). *The Structure of Scientific Revolutions*, University of Chicago Press, Chicago.

Kurokawa, T. (1982). Logic programming - what does it bring to the software engineer, *Proceedings 1st International Logic Programming Conference*, Faculte des Sciences de Luminy, Marseille, pp.134-138.

Langley, P. and Carbonell, J.G. (1984). Approaches to machine learning, *Journal of the American Society for Information Science*, Vol.35, No.5, pp.306-316.

Lansdown, J. (1982). *Expert Systems: Their Impact on the Construction Industry*, RIBA, London.

Lansdown, J. (1983). Dealing with uncertainty of imprecision, *PARC83*, Online, Pinner, Middlesex, pp.233-241.

Lansdown, J. (1985). Computing in the creative professions, *Research Paper,* Department of Design Research, Royal College of Art, London.

Lansdown, J. and Maver, T. (1984). CAD in architecture and building, *Computer-Aided Design*, Vol.16, No.3, pp.148-154.

Latombe, J-C. (1983). Survey of advanced general-purpose software for robot manipulators, *Computers in Industry Vol. 4*, pp.227-242.

Leavitt, R. (ed.) (1976). *Artist and Computer*, Harmony Books, New York.

Lenat, D.B. (1978). The ubiquity of discovery, *AFIPS Conference Proceedings*, eds S.P. Ghosh and L.Y. Liu, American Federation for Information Processing, Montvale, Vol.47, pp.241-257.

Lenat, D.B. (1982). The nature of heuristics, *Artificial Intelligence*, Vol.19, pp.189-249.

Liggett, R.S. (1980). A partitioning approach to large floor plan layout problems, *CAD80*, IPC Science and Technology Press, Guildford, Surrey, pp.705-714.

Liggett, R.S. and Mitchell, W.J. (1981). Optimal space planning in practice, *Computer-Aided Design*, Vol.13, No.5, pp.277-288.

Lloyd, J.W. (1983). An introduction to deductive database systems, *The Australian Computer Journal*, Vol.15, No.2, pp.52-57.

Lloyd, J.W. (1984). *Foundations of Logic Programming*, Springer-Verlag, Berlin.

Lyons, J. (1970). *Chomsky*, Fontana, London.

Lyons, J. (1981). *Language and Linguistics*, Cambridge University Press, London.

MacIntyre, A. (1968). Noam Chomsky's view of language, *The Listener*, Vol.79, No.2044, pp.686-691.

Mackenzie, C. (1987). Inducing relational grammars from design interpretations, AI' 87, *Australian Joint Artificial Intelligence Conference,* Sydney, Australia, pp.207-222.

Mackenzie, C.A. and Gero, J.S. (1986). Learning from Designs, *Working Paper*, Department of Architectural Science, University of Sydney, Sydney.

McHarg, I.L. (1969). *Design with Nature*, Doubleday-Natural History Press, Garden City, New York.

Maher, M.L. and Zhao, F. (1987). Using experience to plan the synthesis of new designs, *Expert Systems in Computer-Aided Design*, ed. J.S. Gero, North-Holland, Amsterdam, pp.349-369.

Manago, C. and Gero, J.S. (1986). Construction of frame-based semantic model for rule-based expert systems, *Working Paper*, Department of Architectural Science, University of Sydney, Sydney.

March, L. (1976). The logic of design and the question of value, *The Architecture of Form*, ed. L. March, Cambridge University Press, Cambridge, pp.1-40.

March, L. (1983). Design in a universe of chance, *Environment and Planning B*, Vol.10, pp.471-484.

March, L.J. and Steadman, J.P. (1971). *The Geometry of Environment*, RIBA Publications, London.

March, L. and Stiny, G. (1985). Spatial systems in architecture and design: some history and logic, *Environment and Planning B*, Vol.12, pp.31-53.

Markusz, Z. (1982). Design in Logic, *Computer-Aided Design*, Vol.14, No.6, pp.335-343.

Maver, T.W. (1970). Appraisal in the building design process, ed. G.T. Moore, *Emerging Methods in Environmental Design and Planning*, MIT Press, Cambridge, Massachusetts.

McClelland, J.L. and Rumelhart, D.E. (eds) (1986). *Parallel Distributed Processing: Explorations in the Microstructure of Cognition,* MIT Press, Cambridge, Massachusetts.

Medawar, P.B. (1967). *The Art of the Soluble*, Methuen, London.

Michalski, R.S. (1983). A theory and methodology of inductive learning, *Artificial Intelligence*, Vol.20, pp.111-161.

Michie, D. (1982). *Machine Intelligence and Related Topics*, Gordon and Breach, New York.

Minsky, M. (1975). A framework for representing knowledge, *The Psychology of Computer Vision*, ed. P.H. Winston, McGraw-Hill, New York, pp.211-277.

Mitchell, J.R. and Radford, A.D. (1986). Adding knowledge to computer-aided detailing, *AUSGRAPH 86*, pp.31-35.

Mitchell, W.J. (1975). The theoretical foundation of computer-aided architectural design, *Environment and Planning B*, Vol.2, pp.127-150.

Mitchell, W.J. (1977). *Computer-Aided Architectural Design*, Van Nostrand Reinhold, New York.

Mitchell, W.J. (1979). Synthesis with style, *PArC79*, AMK, Berlin, pp.119-134.

Mitchell, W.J. (1983). *The Logic of Architecture*, Unpublished manuscript.

Mitchell, W.S., Liggett, R.S. and Kvan, T. (1987). *The Art of Computer Graphics Programming*, Van Nostrand Reinhold, New York.

Mitchell, W.J., Steadman, J.P. and Liggett, R.S. (1976). Synthesis and optimization of small rectangular floor plans, *Environment and Planning B*, Vol.3, pp.37-70.

Mitchell, T.M., Keller, R. and Kedar-Cabelli, S. (1986). Explanations based generalisations: A unifying view, *Machine Learning,* Vol.1, No.1, pp.47-80.

Mittal, S., Dym, C.L. and Morjaria, M. (1986). PRIDE: An expert system for the design of paper handling systems, in C.L. Dym (ed.), *Proc. Winter Annual Meeting of ASME*, ASME, ASME Press, Florida.

Mizoguchi, F. (1983). Prolog based expert system, *New Generation Computing*, Vol.1, No.1, pp.99-104.

Moneo, R. (1978). On topology, *Oppositions,* Vol.13, pp.23-45.

Moore, R.C. (1985). Semantical considerations on nonmonotonic logic, *Artificial Intelligence*, Vol.25, pp.75-94.

Mostow, J. (1984). Rutgers workshop on knowledge-based design, *SIGART Newsletter*, October, No.90, pp.19-32.

Murthy, S.S. and Addanki, S. (1987). PROMPT: An innovative design tool, *Expert Systems in Computer-Aided Design*, ed. J.S. Gero, North-Holland, Amsterdam, pp.323-341.

Nau, D.S. (1983). Expert computer systems, *Computer*, pp.63-85.

Navinchandra, D. (1987). Exploring Innovative Designs by Relaxing Criteria and Reasoning from Precedent Knowledge, PhD Thesis, Department of Civil Engineering, MIT, Cambridge, Massachusetts.

Navinchandra, D. and Sriram, D. (1987). Analogy-based engineering problem solving: an overview, *Artificial Intelligence in Engineering: Tools and Techniques,* in D. Sriram and R.A. Adey (eds), Computational Mechanics, Southampton, pp.273-285.

Newell, A. (1982). The knowledge level, *Artificial Intelligence*, Vol.18, pp.87-127.

Newell, A. and Simon, H.A. (1972). *Human Problem Solving*, Prentice-Hall, Englewood Cliffs, New Jersey.

Newton-Smith, W.H. (1985). *Logic: an Introductory Course*, Routledge and Kegan Paul, London.

Nii, H.P. and Aiello, N. (1979). AGE (Attempt to Generalise): A knowledge-based program for building knowledge-based programs, *Proceedings of IJCAI 6*, pp.645-655.

Nilsson, N.J. (1982). *Principles of Artificial Intelligence*, Springer-Verlag, Berlin.

Ogden, C.K. and Richards, I.A. (1923). *The Meaning of Meaning*, Kegan Paul, London.

Oguntade, O.O. and Gero, J.S. (1981). Evaluation of architectural design profiles using fuzzy sets, *Fuzzy Sets and Systems*, Vol.5, No.3, pp. 221-234.

Pednault, E.P.D., Zucker, S.W. and Muresan, L.V. (1981). On the independence assumption underlying subjective Bayesian updating, *Artificial Intelligence*, Vol.16, pp.213-222.

Pereira, F. (1982). Seelog—A prolog graphics interface, *Research Paper*, EdCAAD, University of Edinburgh, Edinburgh.

Pereira, L.M. (1982). Logic control with logic, *Proceedings of the First International Logic Programming Conference*, Marseille, pp.9-18.

Popper, K. (1972). *Conjectures and Refutations, the Growth of Scientific Knowledge*, Routledge and Kegan Paul, London.

Post, E. (1943). Formal reductions of the general combinatorial decision problems, *American Journal of Mathematics*, Vol.65, pp.197-268.

Quine, W.V. and Ullian, J.S. (1970). *The Web of Belief*, Random House, New York.

Quinlan, J.R. (1979). Discovering rules by induction from large collections of examples, ed. D. Michie, *Expert Systems in the Micro-Electronic Age*, University of Edinburgh Press, Edinburgh, pp.168-201.

Quinlan, J.R. (1980). An introduction to knowledge-based expert systems, *The Australian Computer Journal*, Vol.12, No.2, pp.56-62.

Quinlan, J.R. (1982a). *Consistency and Plausible Inference*, Rand Corporation, Santa Monica, California.

Quinlan, J.R. (1982b). Semi-autonomous acquisition of pattern-based knowledge, *Machine Intelligence 10*, eds J.E. Hayes, D. Michie and J-H. Pao, pp.159-172.

Quinlan, J.R. (1983). Inferno: a cautious approach to uncertain inference, *The Computer Journal*, Vol.26, No.3, pp.255-269.

Radford, A.D. (1985). Approaches to knowledge-based architectural detailing, *Architectural Science Review*, Vol.28, No.4, pp.88-94.

Rapoport, A. (1982). *The Meaning of the Built Environment*, Sage, Beverly Hills, California.

Reiter, R. (1978). On closed world databases, *Logic and Databases*, eds H. Gallaire and J. Minker, Plenum, New York, pp.55-76.

Rich, E. (1984). Natural-language interfaces, *Computer*, IEEE, September, pp.39-47.

Rittel, H.W.J. and Webber, M.M. (1974). Wicked problems, *Man-Made Futures*, eds N. Cross, D. Elliott and R. Roy, Hutchinson, London, pp.272-280.

Robinson, J.A. (1965). A machine-orientated logic based on the resolution principle, *Journal of the Association for Computing Machinery*, Vol.12, pp.23-41.

Robinson, J.A. (1983a). Logic programming - past, present and future, *New Generation Computing*, Vol.1, pp.107-124.

Robinson, J.A. (1983b). Logical reasoning in machines, *Intelligent Systems*, eds J.E. Hayes and D. Michie, Ellis Horwood, Chichester, pp.19-36.

Rosenman, M.A., Coyne, R.D. and Gero, J.S. (1987). Expert systems for design applications, in J.R. Quinlan (ed.) *Applications of Experts Systems*, Addison-Wesley, Wokingham, pp.66-84.

Rosenman, M.A. and Gero, J.S. (1985). Design codes as expert systems, *Computer-Aided Design*, Vol.17, No.9, pp.399-409.

Sacerdoti, E.D. (1974). Planning in a hierarchy of abstraction spaces, *Artificial Intelligence*, Vol.5, pp.115-135.

Sacerdoti, E.D. (1975). The non-linear nature of plans, *Proceedings of IJCAI 4*, pp.206-214.

Sacerdoti, E.D. (1977). *A Structure for Plans and Behavior*, Elsevier, New York.

Sammut, C.A. and Sammut, R.A. (1983). The implementation of UNSW-PROLOG, *The Australian Computer Journal*, Vol.15, No.2, pp.58-64.

Saussure, F.de (1916). *Cours de Linguistique Générale*, Payot, Paris.

Shank, R.C. (1982). *Dynamic Memory: A Theory of Reminding and Learning in Computers and People*,Cambridge University Press, New York.

Sharpe, R. and Marksjo, B.S. (1985). Facility layout optimization using the Metropolis algorithm, *Environment and Planning B*, Vol.12, pp.443-453.

Shortliffe, E.H. and Buchanan, B.G. (1975). A model of inexact reasoning in medicine, *Mathematical Biosciences*, Vol.23, pp.351-379.

Simon, H.A. (1970). *The Sciences of the Artificial*, MIT Press, London.

Simon, H.A. (1973a). The structure of ill-structured problems, *Artificial Intelligence*, Vol.4, pp.181-201.

Simon, H.A. (1973b). Does scientific discovery have a logic? *Philosophy of Science*, Vol.40, pp.471-480.

Simon, H.A. (1975). Style in design, *Spatial Synthesis in Computer-Aided Building Design*, ed. C.M. Eastman, Wiley, New York.

Simon, H.A. (1983). Search and reasoning in problem solving, *Artificial Intelligence*, Vol.21, pp.7-29.

Sowa, J.F. (1984). *Conceptual Structures*, Addison-Wesley, Reading, Massachusetts.

Sriram, D. (1985). A survey of AI tools in industry, *Working Paper*, Department of Civil Engineering, *Research Paper*, Carnegie-Mellon, Pittsburgh.

Stanfill, C. and Waltz, D. (1986). Toward memory-based reasoning, *Communications of the ACM*, Vol.29, No.12, pp.1213-1228.

Steadman, J.P. (1983). *Architectural Morphology*, Pion, London.

Steel, S.W.D. and Szalapaj, P.J. (1983). Pictures without numbers: graphical realisation of logical models, *PARC83*, Online, Pinner, Middlesex, pp.217-232.

Stefik, M. (1981a). Planning with constraints (MOLGEN: Part 1), *Artificial Intelligence*, Vol.16, pp.111-140.

Stefik, M. (1981b). Planning and meta-planning (MOLGEN: Part 2), *Artificial Intelligence*, Vol.16, pp.141-169.

Sterling, L. and Shapiro, E. (1986). *The Art of Prolog*, MIT Press, Cambridge, Massachusetts.

Stiny, G. (1975). *Pictorial and Formal Aspects of Shape and Shape Grammars*, Birkhauser Verlag, Basel.

Stiny, G. (1980a). Introduction to shape and shape grammars, *Environment and Planning B*, Vol.7, pp.343-351.

Stiny, G. (1980b). Kindergarten grammars: designing with Froebel's building gifts, *Environment and Planning B*, Vol.7, pp.409-462.

Stiny, G. (1982). Shapes are individuals, *Environment and Planning B*, Vol.9, pp.359-367.

Stiny, G. and Gips, J., (1978). *Algorithmic Aesthetics*, University of California Press, California.

Stiny, G. and March, L. (1981). Design machines, *Environment and Planning B*, Vol.8, pp.245-255.

Stiny, G. and Mitchell, W.J. (1978). The Palladian grammar, *Environment and Planning B*, Vol.5, pp.5-18.

Stiny, G. and Mitchell, W.J. (1980). The grammar of paradise: on the generation of Mughul gardens, *Environment and Planning B*, Vol.7, pp.209-226.

Sussman, G.J. (1975). *A Computer Model of Skill Acquisition*, Elsevier, New York.

Swinson, P.S.G. (1982). Logic programming: a computer tool for the architect of the future, *Computer-Aided Design*, Vol.14, No.2, pp.97-243.

Swinson, P.S.G. (1983). Prolog: a prelude to a new generation of CAAD, *Research Paper*, EdCAAD, University of Edinburgh, Edinburgh.

Swinson, P.S.G., Pereira, F.C.N. and Bijl, A. (1983). A fact dependency system for the logic programmer, *Research Paper*, EdCAAD Studies, University of Edinburgh.

Szalapaj, P.J. and Bijl, A. (1985). Knowing where to draw the line, *Knowledge Engineering in Computer-Aided Design*, ed. J.S. Gero, North-Holland, Amsterdam, pp.147-164.

Tarski, A. (1969). Truth and proof, *Scientific American*, Vol.220, No.6, pp.63-77.

Tate, A. (1975). Interacting goals and their use, *Proceedings of IJCAI 4*, pp.215-218.

Tate, A. (1985). A review of knowledge-based planning techniques, *The Knowledge Engineering Review*, pp.4-27.

Toller, D.R. and Willey, D.S. (1983). Framed bathrooms, bargains and architectural designing, *Computer-Aided Design*, Vol.15, No.1, pp.7-13.

Trainor, K.M., Brown, A.L. and McDonald, G.T. (1982). Interdependence in optimizing land use plans, *Land Use Modelling Quarterly*, Vol.4, No.2, pp.33-47.

Uehara, T. and Kawato, N. (1983). Logic circuit synthesis using Prolog, *New Generation Computing*, Vol.1, pp.187-193.

Waldinger, R. (1977). Achieving several goals simultaneously, *Machine Intelligence 8*, eds E.W. Elcock and D. Michie, Halstead/Wiley, New York.

Warren, D.H.D. (1974). WARPLAN: A system for generating plans, *Memo 76*, Department of Computational Logic, University of Edinburgh, School of Artificial Intelligence, June.

Weissman Knight, T. (1986). Transformation of the meander motif on Greek geometric pottery, *Design Computing*, Vol.1, No.1, pp.29-67.

Weizenbaum, J. (1976). *Computer Power and Human Reason*, Freeman, San Francisco, California.

Whitehead A.N. and Russell, B. (1910). *Principia Mathematica*, Cambridge, England.

Wilensky, R. (1981). Meta-planning: representing and using knowledge about planning in problem solving and natural language understanding, *Cognitive Sciences*, Vol.5, pp.197-233.

Wilensky, R. (1983). *Planning and Understanding*, Addison-Wesley, Reading, Massachusetts.

Willey, D.S. (1976). Approaches to computer-aided architectural sketch design, *Computer-Aided Design*, Vol.8, No.3, p.181.

Willey, D.S. and Toller, D.R. (1981). SPA: automating bathroom design, *Computer-Aided Design*, Vol.13, No.3, pp.137-144.

Winograd, T. (1983). *Language as a Cognitive Process*, Addison-Wesley, Reading, Massachusetts.

Winston, P.H. (1970). *Learning Structural Descriptions from Examples*, PhD Thesis, MIT, Cambridge, Massachusetts.

Winston, P.H. (1975). Learning structural descriptions from examples, *The Psychology of Computer Vision*, ed. P.H. Winston, McGraw-Hill, New York.

Zadeh, L.A. (1965). Fuzzy sets, *Information and Control*, Vol.8, pp.338-353.

Index